Razzle Dazzle 'Em

To

Ty Baldwin
Deborah Treisman
Paul Davis
&
Nigel Farrow

Who helped make this book possible

RAZZLE DAZZLE 'EM

New Yorker Profiles of Show-Biz Legends

JOHN LAHR

LUND HUMPHRIES

First published in 2025 by Lund Humphries
Lund Humphries
Second Home Spitalfields
68-80 Hanbury Street
London
E1 5JL
UK
info@lundhumphries.com
www.lundhumphries.com

Razzle Dazzle 'Em: New Yorker Profiles of Show-Biz Legends © John Lahr, 2025
All rights reserved

The articles reproduced in this volume were all originally published in
The New Yorker magazine on the year indicated in the contents list.

ISBN: 978-1-84822-733-0

A Cataloguing-in-Publication record for this book is available from
the British Library

All rights reserved. No part of this publication may be reproduced,
stored in a retrieval system or transmitted in any form or by any means,
electrical, mechanical or otherwise, without first seeking the permission of
the copyright owners and publishers. Every effort has been made to seek
permission to reproduce the images in this book. Any omissions are entirely
unintentional, and details should be addressed to the publishers.

John Lahr has asserted his right under the Copyright, Designs and Patents Act, 1988,
to be identified as the Author of this Work.

Designed by Crow Books
Cover design by Paul Davis
Set in Adobe Caslon Pro and Academy Engraved
Printed in Bosnia and Herzegovina

Lund Humphries' EU GPSR Authorised Representative is LOGOS EUROPE,
9 rue Nicolas Poussin, 17000, La Rochelle, France, contact@logoseurope.eu

Contents

Introduction	7
Helen Mirren (2006)	15
Ethan Hawke (2020)	39
Viola Davis (2006)	63
Sean Penn (2006)	83
Julianne Moore (2015)	115
Todd Haynes (2019)	141
Cate Blanchett (2007)	169
Sam Mendes (2018)	193
Claire Danes (2013)	221
Judi Dench (2002)	247
Mike Nichols (2000)	275
Emma Thompson (2022)	321
Al Pacino (2014)	353
Epilogue: Petrified (2006)	385

Introduction

Shakespeare got it right: actors are 'the abstract brief chronicles of their time'. They are metaphors: technicians of spirit who enliven their era and help to define it. They exist to be seen and to be interpreted. We call them 'show people'; they are really entrepreneurs of equipoise whose job description is to make a proper spectacle of individuality. In the characters they inhabit, actors incarnate the longings, the loss, the confusions with which the culture contends and which it often can't name. The charisma of their performing is so powerful, so compelling that it often becomes emblematic. The articulate energy of these show-biz legends corrupts an audience with pleasure. We dream them, quote them, imitate their sound, ape their style, live our little lives within the saga of their often well-broadcast larger ones.

But who are these performing work horses outside the fiction of their roles and their public image? What led these outstanding players to bet their life on their imagination? What is the emotional price of talent? Underneath the practiced public story of these grandees what is it in them that seeks *ex*-pression? The ambition of these *New Yorker* pen portraits is to winkle out of the subjects a sense of their metabolism, to bring the reader closer to their pulse and their process and to dramatize how these supremos navigated the swift water of the entertainment industry to find their eloquence.

The luck of talent is as much a mystery to the performer who serves it as to the public who applauds it. Talent is an unexplainable – sometimes bedevilling – destiny. Some great performers don't want their mystery probed. ('I love what you do, John, I just don't want you doing it to me,' Mel Brooks growled over the phone.) Others in this volume like Ethan Hawke, Emma Thompson, Al Pacino and Mike Nichols, a great comedian turned great director, are fascinated to see themselves and their work reflected back. For all their publicity, these grandees rarely allow themselves to be seen; so curiosity cuts both ways. Their trust and their willingness to collaborate come in large part from the imprimatur of *The New Yorker*, from their knowledge of my work, and from the developing relationship over the course of the extended conversation, which is based on an enthusiasm which can't be faked. 'Where were you when I was growing up', Woody Allen wrote after his profile; and when Mike Nichols professed to having enjoyed the long investigative process, I remember saying, 'I do well with the inconsolable'. Nichols shut his eyes, and looked up. 'We get a lot done,' he said. The privilege of a *New Yorker* profile is to ask the forbidden question.

A profile nowadays is a sort of mini-biography of up to ten thousand words which takes three or more months to report and to write. At the end of it, I have a dossier of about a thousand transcribed pages from which I mine only a handful. Any of the performers who accept the challenge have to agree to the magazine's unusual journalistic terms: a minimum of six hours of interviews, meet-ups in at least three different settings, and some psychological scrutiny. A profile works on the principle of good tailoring: the more sittings the better the fit. The profile pitch comes with one cast-iron guarantee: 'There is no tabloid intention in it.'

There are many ways up the show-biz mountain. The legends in this collection came to acting and directing for a variety of reasons and from a variety of routes. Their histories demonstrate, each in their own idiosyncratic way, how they put themselves in a position to get lucky. Viola Davis grew up mired in the humiliation of poverty – 'You're not even there. You don't exist. It seeps into your brain.' Role-playing was her way to win proper attention from the world and to release the anguish of deprivation she'd grown up trying to hide. 'You're afraid of the shame. I just wanted to get out, to be somebody. I was always so hungry and ashamed. I couldn't get at the business of being me,' she said. Emma Thompson, on the other hand, came from a family of performers; she never took an acting lesson. She puts her protean prowess down to being 'a gibbering empath'. Acting, for her, is 'a holiday from yourself', 'a big fat magic trick. The hat you're pulling the rabbit out of is your own psyche.' For Ethan Hawke shape-shifting was a habit of dissimulation he'd learned at the knee of Leslie Hawke, his intellectually ambitious, progressive Texas mother. 'I was pretending to be from Texas and she was pretending that she wasn't,' Hawke wrote, whose careers as actor, director, and writer answered his mother's call for growth. In a way, Hawke was dreamed up by his mother who, she said, 'expected him to be better than most people, to accomplish more.' Claire Danes, a goofball who's known among her peers as 'the emotional champ', understood from childhood the magic of play's psychic jiu-jitsu by turning her dark insides out. 'You could be a good person and host lavishly violent acts in your imagination,' she said, adding, 'I was so happy.'

In the case of directors included here, their mastery as storytellers answered deep-seated emotional needs. For Todd Haynes, movie making recapitulated the innocence of his original erotic surrender – 'the imaginative rapture' he called it – of seeing *Mary Poppins* at the age of three. Haynes didn't want to rewatch the film; he wanted obsessively to inhabit every aspect of it. He became some kind of prodigy of playfulness: drawing, painting, writing, designing, costuming. At the age of 7, on TV, Art Linklater asked him what he wanted to be. 'An actor or an artist,' Haynes said. By contrast, Sam Mendes didn't come to directing until university. However his skills as a caretaker and his vigilance of emotional detail which distinguish his directing were developed over a lifetime of contending with the wild mood swings of his fragile single-parent mother and her frequent breakdowns. Directing, when he found it, was a milieu where Mendes could be always in control and in mind. The safe room he created for actors was some kind of triumph over the unsafe one of childhood where he was, by his own admission, 'a troubled fantasist'. 'I had a literary bent, but there was something about creating an alternate universe and then populating it,' he said about the instant pleasure of directing. 'I had no family and here is this family.'

Likewise, Mike Nichols's vertiginous theatrical success owes its extraordinary output to his parlous beginnings. In 1938, travelling alone with his younger brother across the Atlantic, he arrived at the age of six on American shores as Igor Peschkowsky, a Russian émigrée whose family was fleeing Hitler. He knew only two sentences: 'I do not speak English' and 'Please do not kiss me.' Nichols found himself traumatized in the New World: without language, without friends, and, thanks to defective whooping cough vaccine, without hair. He felt, he said, 'landlocked'. 'I was a zero. In every way that mattered I was powerless,' he said. Nichols's posture of aplomb – a mandarin confection of erudition, alertness and wit – was an exercise in dissimulation, developed at first to keep people engaged and at arm's length. His superciliousness served also as a great pesticide for the persecuting eyes of others. In time, when he teamed up with Elaine May to create their formidable improvisational comedy act, his practiced hauteur became the sugar to swat the fly of public acclaim. Improvisation showed off Nichols's swift intelligence; it also gave him a sure sense of comedy structure and a singular understanding of the audience. This authority allowed Nichols to transition from famous comedian to directing powerhouse. 'I had a sense of enormous relief and joy that I had found a process that both gave me my father back' – his father died when Nichols was eleven – 'and allowed me to be my father and the group's father' he told me about directing Neil Simon's *Barefoot in the Park* which marked the beginning of their twenty-year partnership, and chalked up the first of about a dozen Broadway hits in a row.

At the age of twenty-one, beginning a six-year project that would be my first book, *Notes on a Cowardly Lion: the Biography of Bert Lahr*, I was struck at how little of a lifetime's press cuttings contained a sense of my father's personality or of the history of show business whose various forms he'd cavorted in for nearly sixty years. I wanted deeper portraits of popular entertainers and set myself the challenge of writing them. With its lavishness of editorial talent and column inches plus the bonanza of over a million readers a week, *The New Yorker* has given me a perfect platform to continue my theatrical inquiry, 'the keys to the dressing room door', as *The Spectator* once put it. From the beginning, the job has been my rear guard action to keep theatricals in the public discussion, to celebrate their achievement and to leave a testament to their talent and their times.

With the exception of the portraits of Mike Nichols and Judi Dench, the profiles included in *Razzle Dazzle 'Em* have never been published in book form. To my mind, every profile is a message in the bottle. Some of the messages *not* included in this volume have done more work in the world than I could ever have imagined. The profile of Bill Hicks ('The Goat Boy Rises') broke out the self-exiled comedian in America months before he died of pancreatic cancer at the age of thirty-two. 'It's almost as though I've been lifted out of a ten-year rut and placed in a position where the offers match my long held and deeply cherished creative aspirations,' Hicks wrote me. The exposée of the machinations of Tennessee Williams's *soi-disant* literary executor Lady Maria St. Just ('The Lady and Tennessee') led to the liberation of Lyle Leverich's *Tom: The Unknown Tennessee Williams*, a projected authorized two-volume study the first volume of which had been blocked from publication for four years by St. Just's caprice. Leverich's death led to me taking over the second volume in my own stand-alone twelve-year study *Tennessee Williams: Mad Pilgrimage of the Flesh*. My first ever *New Yorker* profile about the Australian comedian Barry Humphries and his great comic creation Dame Edna Everage ('Playing Possum', 1991) had been written expressly to introduce the vivacious virago and her Dadaist origins to American audiences before Humphries' planned tour of America. It took Dame Edna longer to get to Broadway than Humphries expected. By the time the Dame finally arrived on the Rialto in 1999 with 'The Royal Tour', the twenty-two-thousand-word profile formed a substantial part of *Dame Edna Everage and the Rise of Western Civilization: Backstage with Barry Humphries.*

By then I was *The New Yorker*'s Senior Drama Critic, and on the aisle when Dame Edna proclaimed from the stage she was 'born again'. In her pink diamante harlequin glasses and her big 'wisteria-hued' hair, Dame Edna sang in her piercing falsetto:

> Spin doctors have spun me
> Dominic's Dunne me
> I'm even a book by John Lahr.
> Call me old fashioned
> I'm a born again Broadway star...

A great clown takes the paying customers to the frontiers of the marvellous. In Humphries' case, his nod to me was an exquisite astonishment beyond hilarity, a never-to-be-forgotten salute across the footlights. One way or another, the journalistic endeavour of a *New Yorker* profile had made it from the page to the Broadway stage. Razzle dazzle, indeed.

John Lahr
17 May 2024

Command Performance

The reign of Helen Mirren

If you go east on Sunset Boulevard and take a left onto one of those burned-out stretches of arterial road which cut across the main drag like stitches on a baseball, you pass laundromats, motels, gas stations, pawnshops, and burger stands, until the road abruptly dead-ends at the base of the foothills beside Runyon Canyon. Towering bamboo plants block any glimpse of what lies up above. To the side are the gates of a private road, a terrace hidden behind palm fronds and hibiscus. This vertiginous landscape is one of the places that the actress Helen Mirren calls home. To enter her driveway is like going from black-and-white to Technicolor.

Since she decamped from Britain to Los Angeles, in 1984, Mirren has spent much of her time living on these fecund six acres with her husband, the director Taylor Hackford (*An Officer and a Gentleman*, *Dolores Claiborne*, *Ray*). (They also have homes in London, Provence, and New York.) Mirren claims to have got Hackford interested in horticulture, but it's forestry, more like. She gardens; he plants trees. Their driveway switchbacks up a steep incline – past Mexican palms, Italian cypresses, birds-of-paradise, jacaranda, oleander, carob, coral, eucalyptus, and Chinese lantern trees – to a clearing in front of a cream-colored Monterey Spanish-style house with faded green shutters, a shake roof, and wrought-iron balconies overhanging a veranda, which looks down onto a long aquamarine pool. Built in 1929 by the silent-screen star Dustin Farnum, the house exudes the patrician restraint of Old Hollywood – a regal indifference to the city, which can't be seen or heard, just a few hundred yards below. The isolation of the place satisfies what the sixty-one-year-old Mirren calls her 'appetite for solitude'; its scenic grandeur suggests her public stature. Much of what dazzles the eye has come into full bloom in the last fifteen years. So has Mirren's career.

Until the first season of the ground-breaking television series *Prime Suspect* aired, in 1991, Mirren, even in her best films – *The Long Good Friday*, *Cal*, *The Mosquito Coast*, *The Cook, the Thief, His Wife & Her Lover* – was always to be found on the edges of the story. 'I used to feel like a racehorse pulling a cart in some of those roles,' she said. Since the success of *Prime Suspect* – 'the most sustained example of great acting in the history of television,' *Esquire* called it – she has driven the narratives. In the last eight years, on the main stages of London and New York, Mirren, who was made Dame Helen in 2003, has played the long-suffering Lady Torrance in Tennessee Williams's *Orpheus Descending*, the trapped Alice in Strindberg's *Dance of Death*, the villainous Christine in Eugene O'Neill's *Mourning Becomes Electra*, and, for the third time in her career, the rapacious Cleopatra in Shakespeare's *Antony and Cleopatra*. This fall, two more virtuoso exhibitions of her work will reach the public. On PBS, in the seventh and final season of *Prime Suspect*, Mirren's steely and vulnerable Detective Chief

Inspector Jane Tennison will fight one last battle against the London police force's patriarchal attitudes, against criminals, and against her own flawed nature. And Mirren's depiction of Queen Elizabeth II, in Stephen Frears's *The Queen*, a deft exploration of the politics of sovereignty and the Royal Family's reaction to the death of Princess Diana, will open the New York Film Festival this week.

Although there is nothing remotely grand about Mirren in person – she is lively and low-key – she is clearly comfortable with herself, and that strength of character translates easily to performances of the formidable. 'Probably no other actress can let you know as fast and economically as she can that she's playing a distinguished and important woman,' Pauline Kael wrote of Mirren, in an otherwise unenthusiastic review of *White Nights* (1985). 'Even as a teenager, she had a thing about regality,' the actor Kenneth Cranham, whom Mirren calls her 'first proper boyfriend,' said. 'She's always had that hauteur. It was that thing of being apart and having poise and taking it all in.' 'I don't mind if I don't have any lines as long as I get to wear a crown,' Mirren once quipped. Her début with the National Youth Theatre, at the age of nineteen, was as the Queen of Egypt in *Antony and Cleopatra*. Over the years since then, her royals have gone from the ridiculous – in the unwatchable soft-porn *Caligula* (1979), a film that won her no glory but provided a down payment on her first home – to the remarkable, her Queen Charlotte in *The Madness of King George* (1994), for instance, a performance for which she earned an Academy Award nomination. Last year, she gave a thrilling, Emmy-winning performance as the title character in the British television miniseries *Elizabeth I*. In *The Queen*, she undergoes an even more extraordinary transformation. 'It may well be that this was the part she was waiting for in some unspoken way,' Frears said. 'She's bright. She's confident. She's open and honest. So she is in herself challenging,' he added. 'It seemed essential to cast somebody who made you nervous.'

As the current monarch, Mirren delivers an inspired study of royal restraint, which rescues the Queen from both satire and sentimentality. 'I cried when I did my costume fitting,' Mirren said. 'I saw the shoes lined up and the tweed skirts and the sweaters. I said, 'I can't do this.' But I grew to love it.' Mirren, who argues that 'you have to allow yourself to grow older in front of the camera – you have to not fight it,' continued, 'Her complete lack of vanity was a comfortable place to be as a woman. You're not striving to look pretty or beautiful or slim. You're "I'm me. This is me." It's a mark of a huge ego.' As she was speaking about the role, she suddenly stopped and held her hands up in front of her face. 'I went like this before I did a take,' she said, pulling her palms slowly toward the back of her head, then suddenly swivelling her wrists and thrusting her hands forward, like beams of light, beside her eyes. 'She's way back inside herself,' she explained. 'Her personality, her intelligence, everything is way back. Then she's steadily looking out, as if through a porthole, with this incredibly nonjudgmental, confident gaze. I loved being her. There was an incredible sort of objectivity . . . a sort of deep knowledge of being a monarch.' She added, 'I thought I had a lot in common with her.'

Mirren also identified with the Queen's punctilio as someone who was 'performing the role of symbol.' 'I admire her as an actress,' Mirren said. 'There's one piece of film I watched over and over again. She was about twelve. She's getting out of one of those big black cars. She's got gloves on. She is very young. She's all alone. It's the way she gets out of the car. She puts her hand forward. She's just doing everything absolutely correctly – that was long before she had any idea that she was going to be queen. She does it with such a sense of dignity and seriousness and discipline.' Mirren went on, 'I think there are elements of that little girl in me. The sense of wanting to do the right thing, not wanting conflict.'

Mirren grew up with the legend of a lost patrician world. Christened Helen Lydia Mironoff, and called Ilyena at home, she was the second of three children born to a handsome, well-educated Russian émigré, Vasily Petrov Mironoff, in 1945. Her mother, Kathleen Rogers, was the thirteenth of fourteen children, a butcher's daughter whose grandfather had been the butcher to Queen Victoria. Until his death, Vasily's father, Pyotr, lived with the family in a two-story house in the suburban working-class backwater of Leigh-on-Sea, in Essex. Pyotr's mother had been a countess whose distinguished military family is mentioned in Tolstoy's *War and Peace*. Pyotr himself was a tsarist colonel and military attaché, who was stranded in London while making an arms deal at the time of the Russian Revolution, which he always referred to as a 'peasant revolt.' At a stroke, he lost his homeland, his pedigree, and his estate, Kuryanov – fifteen hundred acres near the town of Gzhatsk (now Gagarin) – which was, in his day, about twenty-four hours by horse from Moscow. Pyotr, who was, according to Mirren, 'extremely proud, and identified with his Russian roots,' considered Britain 'a gray nation, largely ruled by gray people.' He remained in a state of perpetual Chekhovian nostalgia for the motherland; he kept pre-revolutionary rubles in his dresser and etchings of the Tsar and Tsarina on his bedroom walls. 'I remember sitting in my grandfather's room and him drawing a map of his Russian lands – where the stables were and where the servants lived,' Mirren said. (Vasily, who called himself Basil, waited until his father died, in the early fifties, to change the family name to Mirren.)

If the Mironoffs had been dispossessed of their wealth and their social status, the newly minted Mirrens were, nonetheless, able to generate a sense of their own exclusivity. There was 'a slightly us-and-them feeling,' Mirren said. 'We were quite isolated as a family. We didn't really have friends. Neighbors weren't invited in. We were a little unit unto ourselves. We were trendier than anyone else. We ate yogurt long before anyone else. We were like the first people in our town to wear colored stockings. We were kind of bohemian.' Before the Second World War, Basil had had Communist sympathies; afterward, according to Mirren, he remained 'extreme left wing.' Hatred of the British class system was one of the bonds between him and his wife. His critique was ideological; hers was personal. Kathleen left school at fourteen, and was raised, for the most part, by her sisters. In a sense, she, too, was a displaced person. 'She was resentful and angry,' Mirren said. 'She was anti the class system because it excluded her.' Kathleen always remembered an occasion on which she was turned away by a doorman at the Army and Navy store. Later, ambitious for her own children's mobility, she was strict about proper speech; she scraped together money to buy her daughters – Mirren has an older sister, Kate – elocution lessons. Both parents were anti-monarchist and atheist. (When Kathleen died, at the age of eighty-seven, she requested that no funeral be held, and she donated her body to science.)

The family was not well off, and, with no television, no music, no cinema, and with only occasional exposure to radio, they were almost untouched by popular culture. At St Bernard's High School, a convent school, where Mirren and her sister were taught by nuns, the list of prohibitions included no jewelry, no short skirts, no sex education, no boys. Until the age of sixteen, when the girls were allowed out on dates, their only freedom was intellectual. 'Our stimulation was discussion,' Mirren recalled. 'Over the dinner table, we would have these serious talks about life and art and the soul.' In this straitened atmosphere, she said, there was always a sense 'that this isn't where we finish up. You take your opportunity, you get educated, you make yourself economically independent. And that's still with me.' Mirren's unabashed and un-English ambition was fuelled to some degree by the unspoken disappointment around her. 'There was absolutely a sense of non-realized potential, especially in my father,' she said. By the accounts of both sisters, Basil was gentle, affectionate, attentive, solitary, and, according to Mirren, 'very artistic.' Before the war, he had played the viola with the London Philharmonic; afterward, he drove a taxi. Eventually, he became a driving-test examiner, and drove his cab on weekends.

Mirren, who, according to the director Trevor Nunn, was known as Little Mother Russia during her early days at the Royal Shakespeare Company, identified strongly with her father and the frustrated trajectory of his life. 'I wanted to be a great performer,' she said. 'I mean *great*.' Her sense of drama and of glamour, however, came from her tempestuous mother. 'I don't think my mother was a natural mother,' Mirren said of Kathleen, who once held her out of the window and said, 'If you don't stop crying, I'm going to drop you.' Over the years, according to Kate, the two sisters and their younger brother, Peter, 'all learned to be very protective of our egos, because we would have been completely destroyed. She could be truly horrible.' 'When she was saying stuff I didn't want to hear,' Mirren said, 'I developed this trick of appearing to hear – 'Yes, yes,' 'Right, I'll try that' – but having no idea what she'd said.' Nonetheless, Mirren's own strength was defined by contending with her mother's volatile intensity. 'She was very imaginative, very passionate,' she said. Once, Mirren came home from school to find the house in chaos and her mother stumbling around blindfolded. 'She'd been like that for five hours,' she said. 'She'd read something about a blind person and had been very affected by it. She felt that she had to experience what it was like to be blind.'

Mirren also had an active imagination. Within the family, she was known as Popper or Pop, 'because she would pop off into dreams,' her sister said. She slept with an image of Goya's face under her pillow. 'I thought that somehow I'd been caught in the wrong time zone, and really I was supposed to be Goya's mistress or wife,' Mirren said. At thirteen, she was captivated by an amateur production of *Hamlet* at the local theatre. 'Sword fights and girls going mad, evil kings and queens taking poison – what a fantastic world!' she said. 'So exciting in comparison to walking to the launderette for the washing.' She began to read Shakespeare, and for a school production – grovelling on the ground and growling – she took on Caliban, a part that none of her classmates had wanted to tackle. 'I just got into it,' she said, recalling the exhilaration 'of living in this wonderful exotic world, of a creature locked in this awful physical prison but with a dim sense that there was something else out there.'

Although she has described her younger self as 'totally and ridiculously inhibited,' Mirren found that she could be bolder in role-playing than she was in life. 'All I knew was that I really loved it,' she said. 'It was something I was good at without having to work too hard – or, at least, it was work I wanted to do.' 'I want to be the Sarah Bernhardt of my generation,' she confided to her sister. Her parents weren't pleased. 'Don't be ridiculous,' her mother said. 'People like us aren't actors.' There was no money for drama school, and Mirren grudgingly followed her sister on a scholarship to a teachers' training college in London. Nonetheless, without telling her parents – 'I didn't want to fail publicly,' she said – she successfully auditioned for the National Youth Theatre. Mirren was eighteen; by twenty, she was selling out the Old Vic.

Last July, I joined Mirren and Hackford for their annual trip to Del Mar, in San Diego, for some horse racing: the sport of kings – and, apparently, of sometime queens. The track is two hours by train from downtown Los Angeles. On the way to the station, Hackford stopped to buy the *Daily Racing Form* at a newsstand on Hollywood Boulevard. When he got back in the car, he was pointing to the vender, a woman in sunglasses and a straw fedora behind a wall of magazines. 'A classic Hollywood look,' he said to Mirren, who sat in the back seat with her cap of white hair still damp from the morning's shower. 'Did you see the lady with the nails? She's got these long nails; every one is a different color.' Hackford is tall and thin, with a distinguished white beard and the rumpled nonchalance of a teacher. By nature, he is a doer and an explainer, a take-charge guy who answers to the nickname Jefe and whose knowledge is imparted with brio and the occasional sizzle of impatience. His curiosity has led him over the years from the Peace Corps to television investigative journalism and documentary filmmaking and, finally, to feature films. (He won an Oscar in 1979 for *Teenage Father*, a short; he was nominated again in 2005, for *Ray*.) Although he shares with Mirren a working-class background, he does not share her metabolism. Hackford churns up the water around him; Mirren considers herself 'a slug.' 'I always wanted to be Pierre Bonnard's wife,' she said. 'Lie around, have baths, be painted constantly as a young person surrounded by beautiful flowers and satin gowns.' At the train terminal, Hackford headed off at a trot. 'O.K., babe, we're gonna have to hoof it,' he said.

Mirren met Hackford in 1984, when she went to audition for *White Nights*, which he directed. He was twenty minutes late. 'I was very angry,' she said. 'I was sort of rude.' Hackford told the London *Times*, 'I apologized but there was a cold disdain from her. I tried to make small talk and she said, "Are we going to read?" She was smoking, man! Then she asked if there was anything else, and *boom*, she was out of there.' Mirren and Hackford moved into their Los Angeles aerie in 1986, and were married in 1997 – she for the first time, at the age of fifty-two, he for the third, at fifty-three. (Hackford has two children from his previous marriages; Mirren has none.) 'He wasn't like anyone I'd ever been with,' Mirren said, once we were safely on the train and Hackford had been dispatched to the rear of the top deck to study the nags. 'Much more edgy but also much more exciting, more driven. He still surprises me after however many years. He's incredibly free as a person and he lets me be free. The other thing I've always loved is that he treats women with equality, without even thinking about it. He just looks women in the eye and takes their human value. That's so un-Hollywood.' She added, 'He can be very, very difficult.'

A leader onstage, at home Mirren seems happy to be led. 'Let's face it,' she told Barney Reisz, one of the producers of *Elizabeth*

I, while discussing possible actors for one of the leads. 'Every woman likes a man who makes a decision, doesn't she?' 'She's always been wifely in all her relationships,' Kate told me. 'She's much more "Well, if that's what you want, darling, we'll do it."' To me, Mirren explained, 'I have to say, without sounding like a total tosser, that everything I've learned in life, and that has taken me out of my natural interior life, has been with men. They exposed me to things that I wasn't aware of. I learned from all the guys.' The main relationships to which Mirren was referring were with the actors Kenneth Cranham, Bruce Myers, and Liam Neeson, the photographer James Wedge, and Prince George Galitzine. Onstage and off, Mirren has been defined by her intelligence; however, she still professes to 'feeling rather stupid,' a sense of deficit that, incidentally, makes her a good audience. She listens, she adds to the thought, and she also wants to be told. She glanced out the window of the train. 'There is that awful moment when you realize that you're falling in love,' she said. 'That should be the most joyful moment, and actually it's not. It's always a moment that's full of fear because you know, as night follows day, the joy is going to rapidly be followed by some pain or other. All the angst of a relationship. You go, "Oh, no. Please, no." You go, "Yes, I'm in love. No, I'm in love."'

She settled back in her seat, as the train sped past a beachfront amusement park. 'I've always had that slight attraction to the fairground, the circus, the tattooed,' she said. As a teenager, Mirren worked as a shill for rides at a local Southend amusement park. 'The boys who did the Dodge 'Ems, with their dirty T-shirts and their leather jackets. I never liked the clean guys. I liked the slightly dirty kinds.' From the outset of her career, Mirren made a legend of her daring, which included a certain sexual brazenness. 'She was like a Rubens in bluejeans,' Cranham said. In 1968, as Cressida in the Royal Shakespeare Company's *Troilus and Cressida*, she spun almost naked across the stage, and was soon dubbed by the British broadsheets 'the Sex Queen of Stratford.' 'I never wriggled out of that,' Mirren said. Over the years, she has both condemned and parlayed the idea of herself as a sex symbol. 'I have traded on it,' she told the *Independent* in 2001. 'I do the tousled thing from time to time. I can do the dirty thing. But at some point you decide enough of that, I had better move on.' To me, she explained, 'I think for a long time it was very hard for people to see past my physical outward appearance. I was a blond girl with big tits. I hated that image. It was so uncomfortable for me, and distasteful.' Nonetheless, when Mirren auditioned for the R.S.C., in 1967, Trevor Nunn, then a director with the company, recalled, 'A girl came out who appeared to be wearing a garment constructed of black string. It had more spaces between it than it covered. Conversation stopped completely. Jaws dropped. We saw from her C.V. that she'd had no professional experience. She was passionate about doing classical work. I make no bones about it – I think the red blood cells and testosterone were up a considerable level. I don't think anybody contemplated for a moment that she should be told to go away and get experience somewhere else.' Nunn added, 'We were looking at a major leading player after she'd been with the company a couple of years.'

In 1972, Mirren interrupted her R.S.C. career to join the director Peter Brook's experimental theatre company on a yearlong international tour, which included three months in African villages – what she called 'a voyage into the unknown.'

In *Conference of the Birds: The Story of Peter Brook in Africa*, the critic John Heilpern describes Mirren – the last actor to join the troupe – this way: 'Helen Mirren, twenty-six, a star perhaps, outspoken, generous, bright, luscious, lost.' He continues, 'Part of her dilemma might be that she couldn't decide whether to be a classical actress or a Hollywood movie star. You can't have both apparently. The Brook experiment was entangled with her search for an answer.' According to Mirren, her goal in joining Brook was 'to liberate myself.' Although nudity was not difficult for her – she has bared all in several films, from her first, *Age of Consent* (1969), to *Calendar Girls* (2003), and, at fifty, she posed naked for the cover of Britain's *Radio Times* – she felt weighted down by a sense of physical embarrassment. 'I've always been battling against my sense of dignity and refinement,' she said. 'I was embarrassed by any bodily functions when I was younger. I could never even blow my nose. When I went out on dates as a girl, I could never say, "Excuse me, I want to go to the ladies".' That's why I got a reputation for refusing to kiss anyone at the gate. By the time I got to the gate, I was always dying to go to the loo.'

This conflict between inhibition and exhibition has had a bearing on all aspects of Mirren's performing. 'I think a lot of my life, and especially my work life, has been spent learning how to be brave,' she said. Her sex appeal seems to reside not in her cleavage but in her emotional availability, her complicated combination of hauteur, courage, and empathy. 'Helen doesn't say, "Please love me. Look, I'll smile nicely, and you'll love me,"' Frears told me. 'She's not inviting you in the way other actresses often are. She just says, "This is what it's like," and that's what you love about her. She confronts something, and she doesn't sentimentalize it.' 'She goes for life,' Jeremy Irons, who co-starred with Mirren in *Elizabeth I*, said. 'That's why she's alluring to men. She is the complete antithesis of the vapid.'

Mirren's reputation for wildness owes much to the vividness of her early performances. In the mid-seventies, she followed a sinister and seductive Lady Macbeth ('I really do regret that Shakespeare never knew Miss Mirren,' Harold Hobson wrote in the London *Sunday Times*) with a breakout appearance as the drunk and disorderly rock singer Maggie Frisby in David Hare's 1975 *Teeth 'n' Smiles*, the first and best British play about the barbarity of sex, drugs, and rock and roll. 'It was such a great role,' she said. 'Your first entrance is being carried across the stage over someone's shoulder, completely drunk. Everyone's been talking about you for the last twenty minutes, anyway. It was fabulous.' Mirren, who had to belt out a number of songs, couldn't carry a note. 'I am profoundly unmusical,' she said. 'But I learned this amazing thing. If you've got the chutzpah, you can persuade the audience of anything.'

The same year, at the first read-through for Lindsay Anderson's revival of *The Seagull*, in which Mirren gave an acclaimed performance as Nina, opposite Joan Plowright's Arkadina, the cast was sitting around after deconstructing the first act, when Mirren said, 'I wonder if Nina and Trigorin ever have an affair.' 'Joan looked at me,' she said. "Helen?" – her little brown eyes beadily looking at me. "Have you read the play?" I realized I'd made the most appalling gaffe. I'd just heard that it was a great role. Joan was in it. Lindsay was directing. Of course I said yes. But I'm terribly lazy. I find it very hard to read plays. I find it hard to understand who's who and where they're supposed to be. I get utterly confused.'

Mirren's legend of her own laziness (one that is easily belied by a quick glance at her résumé, with its forty-five films and thirty stage roles) is not, it seems, a pretension but a sort of psychological self defense – a way of protecting the impulsive, childlike part of herself and her imagination. Describing 'Composition VII' by Wassily Kandinsky, her favorite painter, she said, 'Color, form, the appearance of improvisation: in fact, it's intensely, beautifully worked out.' She could easily have been talking about her own acting. Of all her theatrical influences, Mirren claims the painter Francis Bacon as her 'great guru.' Citing the book Interviews with *Francis Bacon*, she said, 'You have to learn technique. He describes how painful the process is. How you feel paralyzed, restricted, frustrated by it. You feel like you lost your early instinctive inspiration. You have to learn it to forget it.' She went on, 'Sometimes you just can't get there. Other times, you're there without thinking.' In Adrian Noble's 1982 Stratford production of *Antony and Cleopatra*, in which she starred opposite Michael Gambon, Mirren felt that she'd reached the pinnacle of 'making it live anew almost every night.' When she didn't win the Laurence Olivier Award for her performance, she left the country. 'I thought, Fuck it, that's it, they obviously don't want me,' she said, in Ivan Waterman's 2003 book *Helen Mirren: The Biography*. 'They don't like me. They hate what I do. I'll go somewhere else. I wasn't being asked to do any work in England. Suddenly, Hollywood was a way of saying, "Fuck you, England."'

Mirren wasn't immediately happy in California. 'I felt like a fish out of water,' she said. 'I was invisible, and really lost my identity as a British theatre actress.' In film, she claims to have felt for a long time like 'a rabbit in the headlights.' Her technical breakthrough came on Peter Weir's *The Mosquito Coast*, in 1986. 'I was working with a lot of children and I thought, I'm just gonna use this experience to make myself feel free,' she said. 'I'm not gonna worry where the camera is. Of course, it drove Peter Weir around the twist, because I was always wandering out of shot. My desire was to learn not to care about the camera.' Mirren added, 'That's where your technique, as Francis Bacon says, supports you. You don't even think about it anymore. You recognize the good accident. You allow the accident to happen.' For one scene in Nicholas Hytner's *The Madness of King George*, Mirren – as the loving consort to the King (Nigel Hawthorne), Queen Charlotte – was sitting on the edge of George's bed, laughing about the events of the day. 'In the middle of the take, Helen suddenly ducked down and bit his belly,' Hytner recalled. 'The cameraman was there, and it's in the film. She just went for it. He loved it. You know – if you're the director – that that's going to pay dividends right through the film: a moment that just says how necessary they are for each other. So that, when you rip them apart, it's heartbreaking.' Hytner added, 'Helen immediately identified that woman's unconditional love for her husband, her physical ease with him. Of the actors I know, she is the one for whom the emotion love is most easily coupled with physical desire. That was a kind of revelation. It became the heart of the film.'

We were well past San Clemente before anybody on the train took notice of Mirren. Then the conductor – a short bleached-blond woman named Marcie, with a nose ring and a tattoo on her wrist – asked if it was O.K. to take a photograph. 'That'd be fine,' Mirren said. Marcie handed me her camera phone and slid in beside Mirren, who promptly took off Marcie's blue Amtrak cap and put it on her own head. They leaned in close. I snapped the picture and held the viewfinder up for Mirren's inspection.

'It's not very good,' she said. 'Make sure we're in the center.' The second shot worked. 'I love your hat,' Mirren said. 'It's done a few miles, hasn't it?'

At the track, Hackford explained his system for betting – a complicated equation of running times, track conditions, jockeys, trainers' and owners' rankings, horses' earnings, and claiming prices. He favored the quinella – a wager that required picking the first and second-place horses, which had a bonanza payout if you hit it. 'It's almost impossible to win,' he said, 'but, when you do, you feel like a god.'

'Taylor and I live a very parsimonious life,' said Mirren, who, according to her sister, could 'use a tea bag twice.' In L.A., she rents an economy car; except for the occasional gourmet birthday treat, she said, 'I go for cheap.' As she stood at the betting window for the first race, her tightfistedness was apparent. 'I'm a two-dollar bettor, so there's no gain, but also no pain,' she said. She put her money on Lockitup. The horse promptly romped first around the six furlongs and earned her almost seven dollars, paying for her next bet. By the third race, all her lessons forgotten, Mirren was flying blind. 'I bet what the guy in front bet,' she said. The fourth race featured a six-to-one shot called Royal Cheer, which she resisted. By the seventh race, a certain wistfulness had crept into her excitement. 'Oh, God, here we go,' she said to Hackford, as the horses were being eased into their gates. 'I arrived with such optimism. Can I borrow your glasses?' Hackford, already bent over his calculations for the next race, handed her his binoculars without looking up. The race began. Mirren stood with the field glasses trained in the direction of her horse, a ten-to-one shot. 'Take off the end, baby,' Hackford said. Mirren glanced quizzically at him, then at the binoculars; the lens caps were still on. Mirren's horse finished third. 'I won nine dollars on the last bet, Tay,' she said, when she returned from the betting window. 'Because I'm doing it across the board.' 'Good luck, baby,' Hackford, who was not having much success, said. 'Really, really good luck.' In the ninth race, Hackford finally won the quinella.

On the way back from the track, Mirren sat by herself as the train sped along the Pacific shoreline, past bonfires, waving children, surfers bobbing like seals on the glistening swells. The sun dipped below the horizon and cast a tangerine glow against the sky. 'Incredible sunset,' she said. 'Glorious.' After a while, she added, 'The ease of American life. The blessing.'

Mirren's London home is a former customs house, near Tower Bridge, on the cobbled backstreets of East London. Her front door looks out over a communal garden – the southeast corner is allotted to her peonies – that is the only garden on the Thames; in the days of sailing ships, it was a loch that led to an inland cove. All that remains from that era are a few black steel pylons along the edge of the greensward, where the big ships used to tie up. Mirren loves this garden and the sense of community with her fellow gardeners. The gardening of her private space, however, sometimes requires some prompting. There is a large note fixed to her kitchen window: 'Don't Forget to Water Me! I'm outside this window!'

On a glistening early-August morning, in a blue-and-white striped boatneck jersey, bluejeans, and espadrilles, she headed off to a small basement dubbing studio on Wardour Street, in Soho, for a looping session, one of her last days of work as *Prime Suspect*'s Detective Chief Inspector Jane Tennison. 'You can't go on,' Mirren said, explaining her decision to end the series. 'I think I've gone on probably too long anyway.'

Prime Suspect was the first British police procedural to put a woman's professional and psychological life squarely center stage. Over the years, Mirren had often complained publicly of the paucity of great female roles. 'There isn't a *King Lear* for women, or a *Henry V* or a *Richard III*,' she said. *Prime Suspect* was a far cry from Shakespeare; nonetheless, her translation of the part into something iconic had to do with her Shakespearean expertise – her ability to transform herself into people who, as Hytner pointed out, 'are larger than life, speak better than life, feel more deeply than life.' He added, 'She can take someone like Jane Tennison and speak for a whole generation.' *Prime Suspect* introduced Mirren to a wider American public; in England, where it attracted more than fourteen million viewers, the show also reintroduced her to the British public, from whom she'd been absent during her California years. ('Helen is the Queen in exile,' Adrian Noble said.) Before *Prime Suspect*, female detective shows (*Dempsey and Makepeace* in the U.K.; *Cagney & Lacey* in the U.S.) had aped the male action formulas. *Prime Suspect*'s creator, Lynda La Plante, looked scrupulously at psychology and criminology and took her story into new areas of sexual politics as well as of crime detection. In the series, many professional women found a metaphor for their frustration. 'They had put up with it for twenty years and none of them had been able to complain publicly about anything because it would have been the death of their careers,' Mirren told the press. 'Suddenly, there on the screen was a woman who was saying, 'Screw you.' A yell went up from all the women in all the professions, saying, 'Yes, that's exactly what it's like.' 'So far, *Prime Suspect* has won twenty-seven awards, including three Emmys for best miniseries and one, in 1996, for its star.

Mirren was the only actress to whom the producers of the series offered the part, back in 1991. Aspects of her emotional profile made her a natural fit for Tennison. Both were smart, independent, and ambitious; both were feminists who liked the company of men; both were Bolshie victims and survivors of the era's sexual politics. 'Women are taught to smile, to be pleasant, to be charming, to be attractive. To say things like "You're a darling – thank you so much." They get their way like that,' Mirren told reporters. 'Tennison doesn't do that. She is driven, obsessive, vulnerable, unpleasantly egotistical, and confused. But she is damn good at what she does and is totally dedicated.' To me, Mirren explained, 'Jane's really weird for me, because I never think about her, not for one second. Of all the characters I've ever played, Jane is the one I've most allowed just to be. I walk out on the set and let it happen.'

Looping is a cleaning-up exercise for already taped footage – fixing sound glitches, misspoken or mistimed words, and adding a fine filigree of vocal nuance. It's painstaking, tedious work, a sort of aural equivalent of needlepoint. When it was time to start, Mirren positioned herself on a stool with the pages to be corrected on a music stand in front of her, about two feet from the screen. The sound engineer watched through a window to her left, lobbing in comments over a microphone; behind her, on a sofa, sat the season's director, Philip Martin. 'There's a kind of visceral, let's-just-do-it-and-think-about-it-later quality to Tennison and to Helen,' he said. 'She likes to work quickly.' And so it proved.

Donning red-framed eyeglasses, Mirren set to work picking through the dialogue and rerecording it – sometimes adding a word, sometimes a mumble, sometimes improvising half sentences or exclamations so that the lines landed better in the scene. She was meticulous and exacting. After each fix, she folded the script page and put it to the side of the podium. With her little nips and tucks, Tennison and the plot became more vivid. At one point, when Tennison came to a door and flashed her I.D., she said, 'Mrs. Philips, I'm Detective Jane Tennison.' Mirren spoke the line, then turned to us. 'Probably the last time I'll ever say that,' she said.

Later, Mirren had to rerecord the lyrics to 'Be My Baby,' which Tennison sang and danced to in a scene set in her childhood home, where she returned on an errand while her father was dying in the hospital. (The song was changed in the final version of the episode.) In the dubbing studio, with her headphones on, Mirren swayed and sang. 'She comes in very strong and hard and sometimes provocative,' Martin said afterward of Mirren's dramatic attack; the dancing scene was a transfixing example. On the screen, Tennison bopped by herself with all the joy of a sixteen-year-old experiencing the song for the first time, then by degrees collapsed into a drunken, exhausted sleep on her childhood bed. With those few seconds of unexpected delight, which only compounded the scene's sadness, Mirren transformed the sentimental into something poetic. 'When she hits the bull's-eye,' Hytner told me, 'it takes on a mythic resonance.'

Earlier in the morning, one of *Prime Suspect*'s executive producers, Andy Harries, had made an official call on Mirren in the dubbing studio. 'That's a fabulous line you've got: "Don't call me 'Ma'am,' I'm not the bloody Queen!"' he said, of one of Tennison's speeches. 'We're gonna put that in the trailer.' The line resonated nicely, of course, with Mirren's career; however, it was her delivery of another bit of dialogue that seemed to carry the most haunting personal weight. Asked, by a teenager, what had made her become a police detective, Tennison replied, 'It was the power. The freedom. And the stupid thought you could do some good.'

★

Mirren's achievements have come at the price of a certain world-weariness. At our first meeting in California, we trudged up the cantilevered steps behind her house, following a sort of nature trail past an olive grove and lemon trees, until we arrived at a plateau high above the house, where, beneath an arbor of ancient cedars, two weathered green chairs were positioned with all of Los Angeles spread out below them. 'I'm in a slightly weird place just now,' Mirren said. 'Of not being sure I ever want to work again. I want to refind the desire to pretend to be somebody.' In what she calls her 'Russian moments,' when she feels 'that somehow there's something between you and life, you don't know how to get out there and participate,' acting has always been what pulls her back into experience. 'It feeds the other side of my Russianness, which is emotional and passionate,' she said. Gazing out over the brilliant horizon, Mirren got to thinking about the many changes in her life – changes of fortune and of family. Among the biggest, she told me, was the change in her attitude toward acting. 'I've lost my idealism,' she said. 'I lost my sense of vocation – that you were fulfilling a serious and necessary function in your culture. It just very slowly slipped away.' Mirren went on, 'It was a fabulous liberation just to be venal and practical and not fucking holy about it. It's a bit of work and a bit of dosh. It was all so angst-ridden. I think I'm a better actor for it. I'm not saying I don't take it seriously; I do. But pomposity has gone out of the enterprise.'

She glanced out toward the Pacific, where sailboats speckled the skyline, then she looked back at me. 'I didn't want to sublimate my ego, my vanity,' she said. 'You know that kind of ensemble feeling – "We're all in this together." No, actually, we're not all in this together. I am the queen. I am the star, and, you know, suck it up.' Just as soon as the words were out of her mouth, she was modifying them. 'Except, I don't behave like that at work,' she said. 'I'm no Ethel Merman.'

The Shape-Shifter

The protean career of Ethan Hawke

On a chilly November morning last year, the sunlight a ribbon of gold on the rolling Virginia hills, Ethan Hawke, who would turn forty-nine the next day, ambled into a replica of Harpers Ferry in 1859. An armory and four short streets had been constructed on the grounds of State Farm, a prison property outside Richmond. Hawke, already in full makeup and sporting a long, shaggy beard, was playing the flinty abolitionist John Brown, in *The Good Lord Bird*, a seven-part Showtime series adapted from James McBride's 2013 National Book Award-winning novel. (The show is the first project that Hawke has produced, co-created, with Mark Richard, and starred in.) For his next scene, he was preparing to re-enact Brown's famous raid on the United States arsenal. Brown was hanged for this botched act of terrorism – an attempt to arm slaves and start a revolt – but it proved to be a tipping point, eighteen months later, for the start of the Civil War.

Hawke was at the end of a six-month shoot on the show, but his connection with Brown's story had begun a few years earlier, in 2015, as he drove to the set of Antoine Fuqua's remake of *The Magnificent Seven*, near Baton Rouge. In that film, Hawke played a Confederate soldier who didn't want to fight anymore. In the scene he was shooting that day, a U.S. marshal (played by Denzel Washington) would say, 'The war is over,' and Hawke's character would reply, 'It's never over. It just keeps going on and on.' As Hawke ran through the scene in his mind, his car radio broadcast news of a legislative battle in South Carolina over the right to fly the Confederate flag in front of the statehouse. It struck him that the Civil War was, indeed, not over, an insight that coincided with one of the directors of photography asking him if he'd read the novel *The Good Lord Bird*. Studying Hawke, with his piercing blue eyes, angular chin, and slicked-back brindle hair, the D.P. added, 'Read the book – you'd make a great John Brown.'

Hawke read the novel on set and couldn't stop laughing. The picaresque saga, which is told more in the style of Redd Foxx than of Toni Morrison, addresses the barbarism of slavery through the faux-naïf eyes of Little Onion, a formerly enslaved boy disguised as a girl, who becomes witness to Brown's rebellion. McBride's impish tone is as incendiary as his subject, precisely because the humor highlights the surreal horror of slavery and the courage needed to survive it. Here is a Black American novelist writing about the nation's greatest wound in an irreverent way that is 'very dangerous in the current atmosphere,' Hawke said. On the other hand, he went on, 'if you're trying to teach people, or yell at them, you rarely change their mind. Humor can really effect change – it's the greatest illuminator.'

Hawke, in his book *Rules for a Knight* (2015) – written for the instruction of his children – styles himself as a medieval knight searching for the holy grail of higher being. 'A knight does not stop at each victory,' he advises. 'He pushes on to risk a more significant failure.' John Brown similarly saw himself as a warrior for moral justice, and his righteous ideals make him a profoundly fascinating character for Hawke. 'There is a mistaken idea that he was trying to save Black folks,' Hawke told me. 'He was trying to save *us*. Seen through the eyes of a serious Christian, Black people didn't need saving. The affluent white communities were the ones living in sin. Harpers Ferry was the great American trumpet sound.' He went on, 'If people said, "Don't you feel bad you got your own sons killed?," he'd say, "Someday, this country will be ashamed of slavery, and I'll never be ashamed of my boys." I just loved that. I found it very inspiring. I don't know how to wrestle with the violence of it, because I'm not a violent person. But I admire his ethics and his ferocity.' He added, 'John Brown's a lightning rod. He forces the question of violence versus non-violence, like Malcolm X. That's why we avoid talking about him. He fans the flames of white guilt.'

On the set in Virginia, Hawke ran through his lines, sitting on a barrel by the gates of the re-created Harpers Ferry engine house, where Brown's ragtag army of eighteen held off about two hundred and forty militiamen and U.S. marines for thirty-six hours. Because McBride's novel is narrated entirely by Onion, Hawke had to invent his own voice for Brown. Channelling the stentorian delivery of his Texan grandfather, a nabob of local politics who spoke in paragraphs, Hawke found both a sound and a subtext for Brown, who, he decided, was always in dialogue with his Maker. That morning, Hawke was working up a prayer that he planned to improvise on camera, as a way of circumventing studio interference – a technique he learned from watching Denzel Washington, when they co-starred in the 2001 film *Training Day*.

'If they see the words in the script, they get scared and note you to death,' Hawke told me. 'If you just improvise it, they think they are brilliant for hiring you.' As he rehearsed, he could see his breath. 'Might we, Lord, as your humble servants, grab the beams of this engine house and pull slavery down on top of us? If so, Lord, grant me the strength of Samson,' he intoned.

By the time he had the speech formed, a hundred or so extras had filed onto the set with guns and horses. It was time to go to work. He thought about the fact that he was the first person to put John Brown's full story on film. As he told me later, 'I couldn't believe that this moment of American history had been relatively untouched in cinema and that my heroes hadn't already played this part. Jason Robards? Chris Plummer? Orson Welles? How did Paul Newman not get this part? I felt like the luckiest actor in America.'

Hawke's mother's family in Abilene, Texas – he was born in Austin – were Yellow Dog Democrats. His maternal grandfather, Howard Green, co-owned and managed the Abilene Blue Sox, a farm club for the Brooklyn Dodgers, and was one of the men who wanted to have Jackie Robinson on the team. Hawke's mother, Leslie, whom he calls 'a wannabe Eleanor Roosevelt,' juggled her work with social action, teaching at an inner-city school, joining the Peace Corps at forty-eight, and founding the Alex Fund, a charity that helps provide education for poor children in Romania. As a teenager, Hawke himself volunteered, under the auspices of the Episcopal Church, in Haiti, during the early days of the AIDS epidemic, and in Appalachia. When he was in high school, in Princeton, New Jersey, his mother took in two Ethiopian students; one of them, who went on to study computer science, was picked up by police for walking in Hawke's suburban neighborhood. 'That was a huge wake-up call for me,' Hawke said. 'He got stopped by the cops constantly. I never did. I could have had a bag of marijuana in my pocket. All he ever had in his pocket was a calculator.'

While shooting *Training Day*, Hawke spent four months riding around Watts, listening to Washington talk about race in America and about Malcolm X (whom Washington had played in Spike Lee's 1992 bio-pic); for Hawke, it was 'a powerful education.' When he and his wife, Ryan Shawhughes, met with McBride, in January, 2016, to discuss turning *The Good Lord Bird* into a limited series, McBride could tell that Hawke knew the territory. 'There's dynamics of this whole race question that we could burn a lot of ink talking about,' McBride told me. 'Ultimately, that would have been a waste of time. Ethan really understood what John Brown represented.' Hawke told McBride, 'I'm not Brad Pitt. I can't afford to option this novel for the money that it deserves.' But they made a handshake deal that allowed Hawke a year to come up with an adaptation. If McBride liked the script, they'd look for someone to buy it. 'Basically, he gave me permission to write it for free,' Hawke said. One afternoon in May, 2017, Hawke rode his bicycle from his town house in Boerum Hill, Brooklyn, to New Brown Memorial Baptist Church, near the Red Hook housing projects, where McBride oversees the children's music program. He was going to pick up McBride's notes on a rough draft of his script. Hawke wandered into the vestibule of the church. 'Are you the guy who's come to fix the air-conditioning?' the church treasurer asked. At that moment, McBride appeared and identified Hawke. 'Last time a white guy was here was to fix the A.C.,' the treasurer said.

'Ethan looked like a white guy who just happens to be looking for a Coors beer,' McBride said. But he also saw a lot of John Brown in him. In the decades since Hawke made his name as a shy, baby-faced teenager in *Dead Poets Society* (1989), his face has become craggy, and he has achieved a fullblown, happy maturity as a rough-edged, raucous actor. 'Brown had a gleam in his eye,' McBride said. 'Part of him was just completely untamed. When he sat down with people, he was almost harnessing this madness within him. You get a little of that with Ethan. His antennae are always out, grabbing, catching every little bit of information. He's an outsider. It's not like he's attempting to do it. It's just that he's at a different radio station. He's operating on his own frequency.'

Throughout his career, Hawke has consistently challenged himself to grow. He has appeared in more than eighty movies, predominantly independent films interspersed with Hollywood money-makers. He has directed four films, written three novels, and cofounded a theatre company. In the process, Hawke has been nominated for four Academy Awards (including two for Best Adapted Screenplay) and a Tony, for his performance, in Tom Stoppard's trilogy *The Coast of Utopia*, as Mikhail Bakunin, the revolutionary Russian anarchist, whose bowwow personality resurfaces in the fulminations of Hawke's John Brown. The range of Hawke's roles – a romantic charmer (in the *Before* trilogy), a drug-addled Chet Baker (in *Born to Be Blue*), a guilt-ridden suicidal priest (in *First Reformed*), to name just a few – is also a reflection of his expansive empathy. 'Acting, at its best, is like music,' he said. 'You have to get inside your character's song.'

Hawke's shape-shifting has its origins in his powerful desire to engage his first audience: his parents. Leslie was eighteen when he was born; his father, Jim, was twenty. They'd met in high school in Texas and moved east after college. Hawke was four when they divorced, a breakup that sent Jim back to Texas, while Leslie and Ethan made their way to Vermont and, later, to Princeton. Alternating between parents, Hawke also alternated between personalities. For his mother, who put 'a super-high value on intellectual pursuits,' he said, he 'played up the artistic, literary, conscientious political thinker.' During his reunions with his much missed father, who became an insurance actuary and was a humble, conservative, deeply religious man, Hawke 'affected a Southern accent,' minded his manners, talked football, and was 'a lot more religious.' 'I loved him so much,' Hawke said. 'I wanted him to like me. I was aware that I was performing for him. I hated myself for it.' After a visit when he was sixteen, Hawke, arriving back at Newark Airport, stripped off his shirt and exited the plane bare-chested. 'I can't find myself,' he told his mother. 'I can't find me.' Recalling the incident, he added, 'As I grew older, I realized that both personalities were just aspects of myself. I became very aware of the ability to shape your personality and do it honestly.' 'Ethan was so extraordinarily accommodating,' Leslie said. 'He never asked for anything except your undivided attention.' Hawke's protean energy was a kind of antidote to the anxiety of abandonment. Dissimulation was a family practice. 'My mother and I were always pretending,' he wrote in an autobiographical novel, *The Hottest State*. 'I was pretending to be a Texan, and she was pretending she wasn't.' Hawke dubbed Leslie 'the Lost Princess of Abilene'. 'She didn't seem to fit in anywhere,' he said. He, by contrast, became expert at fitting in: 'Football team, church youth group, Black kids, white kids, graphic-novel-reading geeks, theatre nerds, punk-rock girls, Deadheads – I was a good bullshit artist. I also didn't judge anybody.'

The skills that acting requires – empathy, imagination, charm, surrender – were habits that Hawke developed from being with Leslie, for whom he was both son and companion. In a very real sense, he was dreamed up by his mother. As she shuttled him up and down the East Coast, bouncing between jobs – from department-store buyer to waitress to, finally, college-textbook editor – she threw herself into the task of making sure that his life was exceptional. 'Patti Smith stole my life,' Leslie joked to Hawke when he was a boy; she projected her own creative aspirations onto him. 'I expected him to be better than most people, to accomplish more,' she said. She chose his name, she told him, 'because it would look good on a book jacket.' Leslie supplied her son with music to listen to and books to read (including James Baldwin's essays, Allen Ginsberg's *Howl*, and Thomas Merton's *New Seeds of Contemplation*). When Hawke was four, she took him to see Ingmar Bergman's subtitled *Scenes from a Marriage*. (He couldn't yet read.) The film *One Flew Over the Cuckoo's Nest* was his fifth-birthday treat. Leslie read Pauline Kael's reviews in *The New Yorker* to him after such outings.

When Hawke was twelve, Leslie enrolled him in an after-school acting program at Princeton's Paul Robeson Center for the Arts. He was immediately cast in a production of George Bernard Shaw's *Saint Joan*, at the nearby McCarter Theatre, as Dunois's page. The serious adult conversations, the costumes, and the standing ovations captivated him. By the time the show had closed and he'd pocketed his thirty-six-dollar salary, Hawke was 'all in on being an actor.' He started going to casting calls, and within half a year, having beaten out, he was told, more than three thousand other actors, he was starring, with River Phoenix, in Joe Dante's *Explorers*, a sci-fi film about two boys who build a spacecraft. 'I thought God had found me,' he said. He first learned that he was likely to get the part by overhearing his mother and his stepfather, Patrick Powers, arguing about the logistics. 'She couldn't leave her job,' Hawke said. 'She couldn't let me go to L.A. What were we going to do as a family?' Despite her ambivalence, Leslie accompanied Hawke to L.A. for his final screen test. As their flight took off, she told him, 'Remember, Ethan, this is just a lark! Nothing more, nothing less.'

Hawke's initiation into filmmaking was exhilarating. Phoenix was charismatic, poetic, and serious about his work. The two stole their first pack of cigarettes together, found cocaine in a crew van, chased girls, and crashed Phoenix's father's motorcycle – slowing down the production until Hawke's broken leg had healed. 'We were sure we were going to be movie stars,' he said. 'In my mind, I was Jack Nicholson.' After the New York première, at the Ziegfeld Theatre, Hawke and Phoenix huddled unrecognized in the men's room, listening to the comments. 'They were talking about what a piece of shit the movie was,' Hawke said. 'It didn't play more than a couple weeks.' His confidence shattered, he blamed himself for the movie's failure. (He recalled hearing that a studio executive had said, 'America has cast its vote, and Ethan Hawke is not a star.') To add to his humiliation, Phoenix was becoming famous; his next movie was *Stand by Me*. 'The envy was intense,' said Hawke, who stopped going to auditions.

But a few years later, as a senior at the Hun School, in Princeton, playing Tom Wingfield in Tennessee Williams's *The Glass Menagerie*, he rediscovered the thrill of acting. Hawke, who is a second cousin of Williams, rode the elegiac rhythms of the play's gorgeous lament. 'I was aware of the full weight of Tennessee's play behind me,' he said. 'I had the sensation of completely disappearing – as if I was consumed by the wind and became wind. I could feel the whole room breathing in unison. It was like a drug and that was the first time I'd used.'

Hawke headed to Carnegie Mellon's School of Drama. 'I wanted to get into college for my mom,' he said. 'When I got there, I realized I couldn't live for her. I was super anxious to start living my life.' In his second week, he hitchhiked to New York to see the Grateful Dead. In his fifth week, a teacher pulled him out of class. 'Are you high?' she asked. Hawke admitted that he was. 'Then why are you here?' she said. It was the last theatre class he ever took. He'd heard that there were auditions in New York for a Peter Weir film called *Dead Poets Society*. He decided that if he didn't get a part he'd become a merchant marine. The sun was not yet up when he got to the Pittsburgh bus station. 'The only thing I remember is my mom on the phone crying,' he said. 'Then – I don't know if I've ever done this since – I got on my knees and prayed that I was making the right decision.'

Hawke was cast in *Dead Poets Society* as Todd Anderson, the reserved teen who, in the heart-wrenching final scene, stands on his prep-school desk to salute his inspirational English teacher (played by Robin Williams). Very soon, he was besieged with offers, among them *White Fang*, *Waterland*, and *Reality Bites*, which eventually made him a poster boy for Generation X. At eighteen, Hawke, nervous about Hollywood's bum's rush, moved to New York, where, a few years later, in 1991, he cofounded the Malaparte Theatre Company, an Off Broadway group that he helped support with his film work. In those days, Hawke's Greenwich Village pad was piled high with scripts. 'They were movie offers. I hadn't seen anything like it. No one I knew had seen anything like it,' the playwright Jonathan Marc Sherman, Hawke's close friend and a cofounder of Malaparte, said. Hawke may have hated Hollywood's urge to 'put a dollar sign next to everything,' but fame was a live wire, and he found it hard to let go. 'I don't want to be a movie star and I don't want not to be a movie star,' he wrote in his journal around that time.

Between acting projects, he wrote his first novel, *The Hottest State*. 'Well, you're not Chekhov,' Hawke recalled his mother saying after reading a draft, though she still encouraged him to publish it. 'Get yourself reviewed, get criticized, live through it. And, when you get bad reviews, only the meek fail after that.' He said, 'I got roasted for it. I remember my favorite review, in some underground paper, said, "Ethan Hawke achieves the impossible." I thought, Oh, I want to read this review. And it said, "He sucks his own cock."' (Hawke's subsequent novel, *Ash Wednesday*, from 2002, was reviewed favorably by the *Times*; a new novel, *A Bright Ray of Darkness*, will be published next year.) In a way, Hawke, who was an indifferent student, got his education in public. 'He's always going, "O.K., what does this person have to teach me?",' Sherman said. On the wall behind his office desk, Hawke keeps framed photographs of the knights of his artistic realm, including James Baldwin, Dennis Hopper, Woody Guthrie, John Cassavetes, Paul Robeson, Neal Cassady, and Sam Shepard, at the grave of Jack Kerouac. 'I saw Ethan as a guy who'd stepped out of a Kerouac novel,' the director Richard Linklater said of their first meeting, in 1993, after a production of one of Sherman's plays. 'He's the extroverted Cassady, the mad-to-live crazy guy. He's also the guy writing it down and taking it in.'

Over the next two decades, Hawke's acting evolved the most in his collaborations with Linklater; Hawke has starred in six of his films. (He will also appear, as Ralph Waldo Emerson, in Linklater's planned movie about the American transcendentalist movement.) When he met Hawke, Linklater was looking for 'creative partners,' he said, 'people I could sit in a room with' to rewrite the screenplay he was working on. The film had no plot and relied exclusively on the immediacy of the actors' dialogue and their chemistry. The challenge for the actors was 'to be brutally honest with themselves, with each other, and with the process,' Linklater told me. 'Ethan was willing to walk that artistic tightrope.'

When he got Hawke and the French actress Julie Delpy into a rehearsal room for the first time, Linklater watched their interaction – 'she had this I'm-the-worldly-European vibe; he's the American puppy dog' – and thought, 'Boom! I have my movie.' The script became *Before Sunrise*, the first part of Linklater's intimate, boundary-pushing *Before* trilogy (which was made between 1995 and 2013). Together, the films chart the swings and reversals of a relationship, from chance meeting to bittersweet reunion to fraught marriage. Although they appear improvised, the movies were actually scrupulously written. Hawke and Delpy revised Linklater's dialogue in the first screenplay (written with Kim Krizan) and co-wrote the second and third films, *Before Sunset* and *Before Midnight*.

Linklater's storytelling method in *Before Sunrise* put new demands on Hawke's acting. At the beginning of the first shoot, Linklater interrupted a scene. 'You seemed like you were really moved by what you said,' he told Hawke. 'Why?' Hawke said he'd been doing his 'classic Elia Kazan thinking about acting' and using a private secret to fuel the scene. Linklater responded, 'It's good acting, but, in this movie, if I see you acting then I'm going to notice there's no plot. And if I notice there's no plot I'm going to get bored. We have to do something different. It's a Zen exercise in letting real life be present. What I want is not your artificial secret. I want *your* secret.' To Hawke, this was a crucial lesson: 'You are enough. Trust your beating heart.'

At first, Hawke was uncomfortable with the process and with how much of his personal life was seeping into the movie. But, gradually, he said, he learned 'how to be present in front of the camera.' He emerged from the experience a more supple actor, with greater access to himself. 'I never looked back after *Before Sunrise*,' he said. 'I could stop imitating other actors. I guess it's about breaking the mask we wear for the world and letting as much truth seep out of the cracks as possible.' Hawke's darker truth is palpable in the trilogy's final installment, *Before Midnight*. Hawke had gone through a difficult divorce from his first wife, the actress Uma Thurman, and elements of the crisis found their way into the film. In the penultimate scene, the couple argue in a hotel room. She calls out his infidelity, and he calls her the 'mayor of Crazy Town.' The characters struggle onscreen with questions that Hawke has said he was also facing in life: 'How do you keep your innocence alive? How do you keep your sense of romance alive, your sense of joy?'

Linklater's *Boyhood* (2014), which follows the coming of age of a son of divorced parents, was filmed over a period of twelve years, so that the passage of time became the plot. In the script, Linklater excavated his own past, as well as Hawke's. (Hawke plays the boy's father.) The two had a lot in common: both were Texan and raised in single-parent families; both had fathers who worked for insurance companies; both loved sports. 'I was a child of divorce and I'm a parent of divorce. And it's been a giant roaring dragon of my psyche,' Hawke told the *Guardian*. 'You have to mine your own life. It's just the only way you're gonna stumble on anything real.' In *Boyhood*, he stumbled onto his father's emotional truth. 'Previously, I was looking at divorce through the eyes of a child, the victim – "How come you weren't there for me?"' he told me. 'Then you see it from the dad's point of view: "It's hard to go pick you up at your mom's house with the new boyfriend. Every time I see you and drop you off, it's like picking a wound."' A lot of the film's father-son scenes were 'ripped right out of my life,' Hawke said, adding, 'My dad's pain, my pain, our pain.'

I got levelled in my early thirties,' Hawke told the *Guardian*, about his divorce from Thurman, in 2005. The pair had met while starring in the sci-fi bio-punk fantasy *Gattaca* (1997), and married when Hawke was twenty-seven, at a time when his world 'felt out of control.' 'I wanted to stop it spinning so fast,' he said. Joining forces with another rising star, however, didn't slow the momentum; it sped it up. The couple, who eventually had two children, Maya and Levon, struggled to balance the duties of acting and family. 'One person works, the other person doesn't,' Hawke explained to ABC News. 'Well, then somebody's always out of town. I'm living in a hotel room taking care of the kids while you're off on a film set six hours a day doing what you love. Do that for nine months and see what a good mood you're in.' For a time, he stewed in his own sourness. His screen roles seemed to embody his self-loathing: a pill-head police sergeant, in *Assault*

on Precinct 13 (2005); a feckless son who robs his parents' jewelry store, in *Before the Devil Knows You're Dead* (2007).

Hawke retreated to the theatre, and immersed himself in plays by Shakespeare (*Henry IV*, *Macbeth*, *The Winter's Tale*), Chekhov (*The Cherry Orchard*), Tom Stoppard (the *Coast of Utopia* trilogy), and David Rabe (*Hurlyburly*). 'I dove into the discipline of training myself as an actor,' he said. 'It's hard to suck in a movie. There are so many people to help you – the editor, the cinematographer, the music, the sound engineers. But when you're on-stage they can hear the quiver in your voice, feel your concentration slip. The stage lacerates you. It exposes you.'

In 2001, while performing in Sam Shepard's *The Late Henry Moss*, Hawke was gripped for the first time by stagefright, which he likened to 'accepting a date with the Devil.' The feeling stayed with him and got worse after his divorce. Each time he stepped out of the wings, 'it felt like walking into a moving propeller.' Part of what helped Hawke overcome the paralysis was making a documentary, *Seymour: An Introduction* (2015), about the concert pianist and fellow-sufferer Seymour Bernstein, who taught him how to take pride in the stage-fright rather than pretend it wasn't happening. Now, although the fear still looms 'in the darkness of my mind,' Hawke said, he considers it 'a friend,' albeit one 'with a wicked, abusive temper.' 'If you focus on the task at hand – the play, the words, the tone, the mood, the music of language – it ceases to be about *you*. You're doing it for others,' he said, adding, 'There is a tremendous confidence that comes from surviving it.'

In creative endeavors, Hawke believes, 'the struggle is everything, the struggle makes everything.' Once, in 2013, after a performance of *Macbeth* at Lincoln Center, he was in the shower, and his daughter Maya, who was then fifteen, sat knitting in a corner of his dressing room, when the play's director, Jack O'Brien, barged in. 'How do you think it went tonight?' O'Brien asked Hawke over the edge of the shower stall. 'Pretty good,' Hawke said. O'Brien responded, 'It's not good, Ethan. If you do the speech in Act III like you did the one in Act II, why the fuck am I sitting here? I already saw that speech. Where was the work we did?' He moved on to the issue of Hawke's mumbling delivery. 'Is it "If it were done when 'tis done," or is it "*If* it were done when 'tis done"? Because if the word is "*if*" then I know we're talking about choice. Human choice. It's a big fucking idea.' O'Brien started out the door. 'You're not there yet,' he said as he left. Hawke and his startled daughter looked at each other. 'You're so lucky,' Maya said.

In 2008, Hawke married Ryan Shawhughes, a month before their first daughter, Clementine, was born. Shawhughes, who had worked briefly as a nanny for him and Thurman while she was a student at Columbia University, 'turned his life around,' according to O'Brien. As well as managing Hawke's finances, she has collaborated with him artistically, co-producing *First Reformed*, *Seymour*, a film version of his novel *The Hottest State*, and *Blaze*, a 2018 biopic about the country singer Blaze Foley, which was Hawke's first major outing as a director. In 2011, Hawke called his mother to tell her that Shawhughes was pregnant with their second child, Indiana. As he remembers it, Leslie said, 'Ethan, you're gonna go broke. You have so many children. You're crazy.' She hung up and then called right back. 'I take that back,' she said. 'The best thing that could happen to you and your children is you go broke. You need to keep your hunger alive. Have more children. Just don't stop making good art.'

I met up with Hawke in early March for lunch at Rucola, a crepuscular Italian eatery in Boerum Hill. 'A career is different than a job in that your inner life is connected to your work,' he said. He admitted that his own freewheeling career had been a chart of his restlessness and his recklessness. 'If you want to live in the arts,' he said, 'you've got to dig in. I would look at Warren Beatty and how carefully he constructed his career and just laugh. Beatty would make, like, one movie every six years and sit around and go to parties and develop material. That kind of preciousness of trying to get everything perfect before you act is not my style.'

Whether writing, directing, acting, or producing, Hawke spends most of his waking hours thinking about story-telling. His productivity is unique among his acting peers. After lunch, we walked around the corner to his office, where he was preparing to direct a film adaptation (written with Shelby Gaines) of Tennessee Williams's lyrical political fantasia *Camino Real*. Set in a barbarous Spanish-speaking backwater, the play is a paean to nonconformity, told, as Williams put it, 'in the spirit of the American comic strip.' Trapped within the town's ancient walls, various literary figures – Casanova, Lord Byron, Don Quixote, Madame Gautier – and Kilroy, a former boxing champ and eternal Punchinello, contend with illusion and desperation. In 1999, Hawke played Kilroy in a memorable production, directed by Nicholas Martin, at the Williamstown Theatre Festival, and the experience stayed with him. 'It's like sticking your finger in an electric socket and having it shoot through the audience,' he said. 'The way Williams deals with iconography and sexuality and self-hatred and self-love – it's just the most incredible bit of performance I've ever had. I've been chasing that feeling and wanting to give it to an audience.'

A big blue Xtracycle bike with seats for Hawke's younger daughters was stashed beside the front door, and his two dogs were sprawled like black and gold throw rugs in front of the gray sofa, where we sat and browsed through a bound collection of a hundred and thirty-eight collages that Hawke and his art director, Beth Blofson, had worked up for *Camino Real*. A 'sizzle book' is the usual term for such guides, which translate the director's vision for the production staff. But Hawke thought of it 'more as a spirit guide,' he said. 'I call it Tennessee Williams's *Book of the Dead*.' He paged through the collages, in which tawdry burlesque houses, caged showgirls with feathers, and nudes suspended in translucent bubbles were juxtaposed with images of slapstick savagery. 'It's got to be decadent,' he said.

In 2014, he organized a reading of the play with Vanessa Redgrave, John Leguizamo, and others, at the Box, a downtown New York night club with a raunchy, offbeat vibe. When he talked about wanting to direct a film version of the play and recalled Elia Kazan's dissatisfaction with his own direction of the Broadway première, Redgrave challenged him. 'Kazan was brilliant. He didn't figure it out. What are you going to do?' Hawke remembered her saying. To anchor the work's surreal playfulness, he restructured the script in a way that allows for a collision of extremes, a fluid, subversive undertow that the cumbersome Broadway sets prevented. 'You can't make it one thing,' he told me. 'Is it a dream? Yes. Is it Purgatory? Yes. No, it's not Purgatory. It's a fantasy. It's life and it's not life. The problem with film is it's literal. But it can be done.'

Almost on cue, at the mention of Purgatory, Michael Daves, a mandolin player, and Dan Iead, a guitarist, appeared at Hawke's front door for his next adventure, a run-through of songs for *Satan*

Is Real, a bio-pic about the country-and-Western icons the Louvin Brothers – another Hawke project long in the making and now financed. Hawke had cast himself as the hell-raising, mandolin-smashing Ira Louvin, and his friend the actor Alessandro Nivola as the God-fearing, guitar-playing Charlie Louvin, in a story that chronicles the abrasions of the brothers' final tour.

Hawke sat cross-legged on a table and, tipping his green-and-white Black Crowes baseball cap back on his head, began to warm up the lower register of his voice. The musicians filled in as he sang the Louvins' dystopian anthem 'Great Atomic Power':

Are you ready for that great atomic power?
Will you rise and meet your Savior in the end?

'When you're singing the verse, you're singing in your character,' Iead told Hawke afterward. 'There are two different vocal sounds, two different people singing.'

For a while, they discussed the Louvin Brothers' different styles of performance. 'I think it'd be good for you to practice singing the part, making the facial expressions and the body language just neutral,' Davies said. 'Focus on what's going on in the throat.' Hawke took out his cell phone and watched himself as he sang. Eventually, he looked at his watch. 'I want to do this forever, you guys, but I made a three-fifteen appointment.'

After the musicians left, Hawke told me that the appointment was a call with the children of Joanne Woodward and Paul Newman, who had asked him to direct a documentary about their parents. On the phone, he swung into director mode, suggesting as a model the dual narrative of Doris Kearns Goodwin's biography of Franklin and Eleanor Roosevelt – 'another couple, that very rare group of people, who used their success to great ends,' he said. As he pitched his concept, he paced the room, emoting into the handset. After some discussion about story and budget, he got down to the details. 'I don't want to invest a year of my life in this and not have it be some kind of expression of what I want it do artistically,' he said. 'My gut is we all want the same thing. You're not scared of darkness. I believe if you ignore the darkness the light doesn't matter, and if you ignore the light the darkness doesn't matter.' At the end of the call, with both parties agreeing to send in the lawyers, Hawke spoke about the benefits of straightforwardness. 'Good things happen to people who talk about scenarios,' he said.

The following day, at The Players club, a landmark nineteenth-century town house on Gramercy Park, Hawke convened a group of eleven actors and Jack O'Brien, the director, to do a reading for another project he was developing, *Texas Red*, an adaptation of *The Cherry Orchard* (with a screenplay by Jonathan Marc Sherman). Hawke arrived early and strolled around the ornate rooms in a short-brimmed cowboy hat – he planned to play a Western version of the bumbling wastrel Gayev – inspecting the portraits of David Garrick, Helen Hayes, and other fabled theatricals that cluttered the walls. The eighty-one-year-old O'Brien was the first of Hawke's recruits to appear, trudging up the carpeted circular staircase.

Hawke and O'Brien huddled together to strategize. 'I think our job today is to hear what it wants to be and what it sounds like out of these voices,' Hawke said.

'Once people are totally in their skins, they'll say those things differently,' O'Brien said. 'More colloquial, much more resolute in terms of the extraordinary canvas Chekhov's given us.' Laura

Linney and Bobby Cannavale – who would read the updated Ranevskaya and Lopakhin roles – appeared in the doorway.

'These losers,' Hawke said, with a roll of his eyes. 'Who do I hug first?' Linney asked. 'We're all touching, right? 'Cause we're artists,' Cannavale said. ('Social distancing' was still a couple of weeks away from entering the lingua franca of lockdown.)

When all the actors had assembled around a table, Hawke gave a brief preamble, recalling the 1992 Broadway production of Chekhov's *The Seagull*, in which he and Linney had starred. 'The worst reviews a human being could get,' he said. 'The review in *New York* was an argument about who was worse – me, Laura, Tyne Daly, or Jon Voight. We were all pretty goddam bad.' O'Brien asked who was responsible for the failure. 'Well, it wasn't Chekhov,' Hawke said, and rode the laugh into an explanation of the genesis of the current screenplay, which involved a 2009 production of *The Cherry Orchard*, directed by Sam Mendes, in which he'd played Trofimov. 'The audience wasn't getting it,' Hawke said. 'I felt like, God, if they really understood how much he's talking about race, poverty, class.' The night after Barack Obama was re-elected, in 2012, Hawke and Sherman discussed the idea of transposing the play to Texas, as a way of making the politics come alive for a contemporary American audience.

When the reading was over, O'Brien stood watching Hawke as he thanked the actors for their work. 'Who else of his generation is doing this?' O'Brien said. 'He's not wasting his time.'

★

One day in April, Hawke piled his family into the car and set off from their house in Connecticut to visit John Brown's birthplace, in Torrington, a few miles away. 'There was something hard about the pandemic happening right after I completed this role,' he said. 'I couldn't move on. The more I learned about John Brown, the more I enjoyed talking to him in my head.' The uprisings across the country in the wake of George Floyd's death made it easy for Hawke to keep talking to Brown. 'I can hear him cheering those protesters on,' he said. 'He would not have been as gentle as they have been.'

When he was starting to work on *The Good Lord Bird*, Hawke visited Brown's grave site, near Lake Placid, New York, to 'pick up the scent' and 'invite him in.' The visit to Brown's birthplace brought the process full circle. 'It was a farewell salute,' he said, adding, 'You want every project to have deep meaning to you, but they don't. This one was magical to me. It's somehow connected to the spine of my life.' The site of Brown's family house – which burned down a hundred years ago – was in the woods, up a somnolent arterial road named for Brown. The day was overcast, the ground wet. A creek ran through the property, which was bounded by a tracery of collapsed stone walls. A rough-hewn granite slab, engraved with Brown's name, stood on the spot where the house had been. 'You feel your spirit get very quiet in these places,' Hawke said. In that emollient stillness, he said his thank-you.

By mid-June, the enforced isolation of lockdown had taken a toll on Hawke. He was, he admitted, struggling. 'The hard part of getting out of character is you have to ask the difficult question "Who am I?"' he said, staring at me over Skype. 'If I say, "Who is John Brown?," I point to all these facts. If I say, "Who is Chet Baker?," I can start to study that person. These characters flow through you. It's very easy to let them in, but if you invite them out you're left with these darker questions.' As a performer, Hawke is a purveyor of presence; what he was experiencing was the confounding sense of not being seen. 'If I'm not trying to please my mother, and I'm not trying to please my father, and I'm not trying to please an audience, I'm pleasing myself,' he said. 'It brings me to a very adult question: Who is this person I've been calling Ethan?' He added later, by e-mail, 'I spent a couple weeks with a cruel case of the blues (the state of the nation not helping) and decided to come out of it with the only answer I could grab: I am my choices.'

Act of Grace

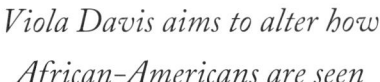

*Viola Davis aims to alter how
African-Americans are seen*

On January 25, 2009, a jubilant Meryl Streep stood before a gala crowd at the Screen Actors Guild Awards, in Los Angeles, having just won an award for her role in *Doubt*, the film adaptation of John Patrick Shanley's Pulitzer Prize-winning play about sexual abuse, race, and the Catholic Church. Clutching her statuette, Streep gave a shout-out to the rest of the cast. When she got to Viola Davis – who had earned her first Academy Award nomination for her performance as the mother of an African-American boy a priest is accused of abusing – Streep saluted her colleague as 'gigantically gifted,' then threw up her hands. 'My God!' she said. 'Somebody give her a movie!'

The industry seems to have listened. Davis – 'a newcomer at forty-five,' as Streep later joked – has made twenty-one films since then. Not all her roles have been large or central to the narrative arc, but, as Aibileen Clark, the maid who helps expose the folly of the white Mississippi matrons she serves, in *The Help* (2011), she was a popular success and gained a second Academy

Award nomination. 'No one had ever akst me what it felt like to be me,' Aibileen says at the end of the film. The lack of white curiosity about black life is something Davis is always tilting at. 'I've played many best friends, crack-addicted mothers, next-door neighbors, or professionals with no personal lives,' she said. 'There's a limitation to how we are seen.' When Davis took on the role of Annalise Keating, a high-profile defense attorney and law professor, in the ABC legal-drama series *How to Get Away with Murder*, currently in its third season, she addressed this cultural trivialization directly. The show and her character were hatched in close collaboration with the series' creator, Peter Nowalk. From the start, Davis pushed him to dramatize Annalise's interior world and to show the private moments of this tough, brilliant professional, who has a difficult, and promiscuous, past. 'I'm trying, within the confines of the narrative that I've been given, to show her pathology,' she told me. 'I don't see acting as hiding. I see it as stepping up buck naked in front of a group of people that you don't know. Every single time. It's about exposing. If you're not doing that, you're basically not doing anything.' Nowalk elaborated, 'From our very first phone call, she said, 'I want to be a woman who takes off her wig and wipes off her makeup, and you see who she is underneath.' She made the character frankly more complex, more interesting. Taking off her wig – that is the show's most famous moment, and it is all hers.' He added, 'I can never state too much how she elevated the character.' It was a spectacular exhibition of agency in a woman who is, as she puts it, 'darker than a paper bag.' 'Colorism and racism in this country are so powerful,' Davis told *Entertainment Weekly* last year. 'As an actress, I have been a great victim of that. There were a lot of things that people did not allow me to be until I got ... Annalise Keating. I was not able to be sexualized. Ever. In my entire career.' In 2011, Davis, with her husband, the actor Julius Tennon, formed JuVee Productions, a multimedia company that takes on everything from virtual reality to movies. JuVee began as a strategic way for Davis to try to alter the public perception of African-American life, which hasn't changed much since Zora Neale Hurston observed, in 1950, that 'the average, struggling, non-morbid Negro is the best-kept secret in America.' Davis told me, 'It's hard for people to see us beyond narratives that are didactic. I'm trying to change the landscape. And not just for me, for everyone.' JuVee's productions so far include the vigilante thriller *Lila & Eve* (2015) and *Custody* (2016), in which Davis plays a judge presiding over a custody case. The *Personal History of Rachel DuPree*, a drama about an African-American farming family in the Badlands of South Dakota in 1917, is under way. Davis and Tennon have also commissioned a bio-pic, about the politician and civil-rights leader Barbara Jordan (with a script by the playwright Tony Kushner).

In January, Davis, who is fifty-one, will get a star on Hollywood's Walk of Fame, but the real acknowledgment of her renown will come a couple of weeks earlier, with the December 25th opening of the movie adaptation of August Wilson's Pulitzer Prize-winning play *Fences* (1983), in which Davis gives the best performance – in the best role – of her career. She plays Rose, the tender and sorely tested wife of Troy Maxson (Denzel Washington, who also directed the movie), a once great athlete who is now a garbageman, cheated of his potential by social circumstance. *Fences*, which is set in the fifties, is the most commercial of Wilson's ten-play *Century Cycle*, a series that chronicles, decade by decade through the twentieth century, what he called 'the cultural response of black Americans to the world they find themselves in.' Davis and Washington, who delivered Tony Award-winning performances in the same roles in the 2010 Broadway production of *Fences*, are two of Wilson's most eloquent messengers. And the film, which was shot in the Hill District, in Pittsburgh – the working-class black neighborhood where Wilson grew up – is that rarest of phenomena, a cinematic adaptation that is better than its theatrical template.

Davis's depth and delicacy are exceptional; so is her range. 'She finds the character's song and she plays in that key and that melody,' her co-star Stephen McKinley Henderson, who plays Troy's sidekick, said. In 1995, as Vera, the sometime girlfriend of a smooth-talking forties musician, in Wilson's *Seven Guitars*, Davis was alternately shy, sassy, and saturnine; in 2001, as Tonya, the wife of an ex-con who strives to live by his own moral code, in *King Hedley II* – a performance for which Davis won her first Tony Award – she was fierce, heartbroken, and shipwrecked. In *Fences*, she is full of love and lament. When Troy reveals to Rose that he has fathered a child with another woman, she stares at him in blank disbelief; then, as understanding settles in, Davis's face begins to register Rose's roiling internal weather. 'There are moments in life where emotions are just not understated,' Davis told me. 'They're not thought out. It's a release.' Rose's grief at Troy's betrayal is one of them. She tells him:

> You not the only one who's got wants and needs. But I held on to you, Troy. I took all my feelings, my wants and needs and dreams . . . and I buried them inside too. I planted a seed and watched and prayed over it. I planted myself inside you and waited to bloom. It didn't take me no eighteen years to realize the soil was hard and rocky and it wasn't never gonna bloom.

By the end of her speech, Davis is so submerged in Rose's shame and fury that, as tears stream from her eyes, snot comes out of her nose. Of her performance in the scene, Henderson said, 'You can't go there if you haven't been there. There's no path to that.'

★

'A black person in this democracy is certain to endure the unspeakable and the unimaginable in nineteen years,' James Baldwin wrote in his essay 'The Price of the Ticket'. It took Davis half that time to understand the horror of her situation. 'If you haven't experienced poverty, you can't imagine it,' she said. 'It's so close, so tight. It's fraught with so much deprivation that it just explodes.' She added, 'Homosexuals, the transgender community, women, blacks – they're mistreated. With poor people, it's not mistreatment. You're not even there. You don't exist. It seeps into your brain.' That sense of invisibility made it hard for Davis to come to terms with her childhood. 'Our whole lives were about hiding, not sharing the secret,' she said. 'Because you're afraid of being judged. You're afraid of the shame. I just wanted to get out, to be somebody. I was always so hungry and ashamed. I couldn't get at the business of being me.'

Davis's parents, Dan and Mae Alice, married when Mae Alice was fifteen and Dan, a racehorse groom, was twenty-two. (Dan left school after second grade and was illiterate until he was fifteen; Mae Alice quit after eighth grade.) Davis, the fifth of their six children, was delivered by her grandmother in a one-room sharecropper's shack on a former plantation near St Matthews, South Carolina. 'My mom says that all the aunts and uncles, everybody was in the house, just drinking, laughing, eating,' Davis told me. 'She said, "And then when you was born everybody was yelling and cheering. Jumping up. I had a sardine-tomato-onion-mustard sandwich."'

Soon after Davis's birth, her parents decamped to Central Falls, Rhode Island, an old mill town that was close to two racetracks, Lincoln Downs and Narragansett Park, where Dan hoped to find work. Central Falls was rumored to be both the smallest and the most densely populated city in the state, and the Davises were the first African-American family to live there. Among the many dilapidated buildings they lived in, the most notorious in family legend was 128 Washington Street, a partly boarded-up, condemned building, in which the Davises lived rent-free for a time, often without heat or electricity. Rats ate the faces off Davis's dolls; from her bed, she could hear them killing pigeons in the attic. She went to bed each night with rags tied around her neck to keep them from biting her in her sleep. The precariousness of Davis's life made it difficult for her to concentrate in school. 'I messed up all the time,' she said. 'Detention every day. Nasty back talk with teachers. I pushed a teacher once. I wanted attention really bad. I felt I just didn't fit in.' She wet the bed until she was fourteen. 'We didn't have money all the time to do laundry. A lot of the time, we didn't have soap or hot water,' she said. 'We were smart kids academically' – her sisters Deloris and Diane made the Rhode Island National Honor Society – 'but we'd go to school smelling. I reeked of urine.' Davis and her sisters were lectured on hygiene by teachers and by the school nurse. But 'it wasn't an option to out ourselves,' she said. 'We just sat there with our heads down.' For most of Davis's childhood, school lunch was her main meal. 'When I say we had nothing, I mean zero,' she said. 'I remember one time a friend came over to the house and she opened the refrigerator. There was nothing in it. She said, 'Are you guys moving?" Davis and her sisters mooched off the families of friends, dumpster-dived, and stole. 'The last time I stole something, I was nine years old,' Davis said. 'I stole a brownie, but I never got it out of the store, because the store owner just told me to get away and never come back.'

Racism was as pervasive as hunger. 'People would throw things out of cars and call us the 'n' word,' she said. At school, she was taunted and chased by the white boys. When she finally told her mother about the bullying, Mae Alice handed her a crochet needle. 'I tell her, "You don't run away, you stand your ground. If they mess with you, you just take out the crochet needle and you jab them,"' Mae Alice recalled. 'I'm not gon' teach them to let someone call you names, hit you, and make you feel like you're not worth nothing, 'cause you are worth something.' Davis never had to use her weapon. 'But I tell you, the power of suggestion,' she said. 'I had my hand around it, in my coat pocket, and I had this kind of internal monologue going in my head: 'Jig 'em all, jig those motherfuckers.' At eight years old, I had a filthy mouth.' She went on, 'I could hear them behind me: 'You ugly. You black nigger, you ugly. You black nigger.' I felt them grab me, and I said, "If you touch me again, I'm gonna stab you to death." I said it methodically. I remember the first kid, Stanley, he stepped back. He was, like, "Oh, we don't mess with you anyway."' At home, however, there was no escaping the violence. Although Davis 'never for a moment' doubted her father's love, Dan was an alcoholic who had been a boxer in his youth. Every Thursday, when he got paid, he came home drunk. The havoc could be spectacular. Dan once ripped the door off the refrigerator. He beat Mae Alice on a regular basis. 'There was no peace in my household,'

Davis said. Sometimes, she recalled, after a beating Mae Alice 'would come into our room, go into a closet, and hide in the back all night and just cry.' It could take 'all night, two days, or five minutes' for Dan's anger to dissipate, Davis said. Sometimes Mae Alice ran for help, and Davis went with her. 'One time, she ran to the corner drugstore when it was real bad, when it lasted a couple of days. I stayed with her as long as I could, and then they took her to the hospital. I was about fourteen,' she said.

The idea of leaving Dan 'never occurred to me,' Mae Alice said. She went on, 'My mother never leave. My grandmother never leave. My aunts never leave. That's showing me something. You can't expect real life to be like a fairy tale.' In the last ten years of her parents' marriage, Davis said, the violence abated and they grew close. 'My mom said he apologized to her,' Davis told me. 'The way Mom phrased it was: "Mae Alice, you know all those things I did to you? You know I didn't mean it, right? You know I'm sorry."' Mae Alice, who now lives in an apartment in Providence, was Dan's caretaker until he died, of cancer, in 2006. 'The day before he died, she was bathing him,' Davis recalled. 'She said he looked up and said, "Thank you, Mae Alice." She misses him.'

On an unseasonably hot day in November, I visited Davis at her five-bedroom, seventy-five-hundred-square-foot home in Toluca Lake, a shady neighborhood of Los Angeles. She appeared at the gate, in bare feet and a black shift from Target, to escort me into the cool, high-ceilinged biscuit-colored hall. 'Here's the thing,' she said. 'Because I grew up in such tight spaces, I don't get manicures, pedicures, I'm not into cars, but I am into a fabulous house. I wanted the spiral staircase, clean sheets on the bed, to be able to take a shower.' Davis moved into her new home in August, and many of the rooms were still undecorated, but it was clear that she was still living with the ghosts of her past. 'The big "Aha!" moment is that the trauma never goes away,' she said. But now, through acting, she could release the anguish rather than hide it.

Davis was preparing collard greens for dinner, a recipe that she said she'd passed along to Meryl Streep – 'The only area where I could absolutely challenge her is my collard greens,' she said. As she chopped onions to add to the simmering pot, Davis gazed out the window at the swimming pool beyond the patio and its stainless-steel Viking barbecue console, which looked like NASA Mission Control. She and her husband like to throw parties, for which they cook together. 'Julius grew up with a mother who was ultra-clean, so everything has to be ultra-clean. I grew up with no food, so there's never enough food. "I only have enough food for forty people, what if they want two or three servings? We're gonna run out of food – they're gonna be hungry." That's me.'

The house is a kind of trophy of Davis's survival. 'I consider myself a hero,' she said. 'I don't have a cape, I don't have a golden lasso. I had a call to adventure, a call to live life bigger than myself. I found the elixir.' Davis and her sister Deloris (who is now Deloris Grant and teaches drama at the Central Falls high school they attended) started performing early. 'We wanted to dream away the problems,' Deloris said. When their father was drunk or there was turmoil, they would disappear into the bedroom and become 'Jaja' and 'Jagi,' rich, white Beverly Hills matrons, with big jewels and little Chihuahuas. 'We would play this game for hours,' Davis recalled. '"Oh my, Jaja, I bought this fabulous house and my husband bought me this beautiful diamond ring." It was so detailed, to the point where it became transcendent. We actually believed we were in that world.' Eventually, Deloris would break the spell. 'She'd always say, "You're not Jaja. You're poor. You're on welfare. You don't have diamonds,"' Davis said. 'Then we'd fight and it would be over.'

As a shy, overweight teenager, Davis discovered uncanny powers of dissociation. 'I knew how to throw myself outside my body,' she said. She would lock herself in the bathroom, focus on a body part, and, she explained, 'totally clear my head. I wouldn't let anything, any thought, any sound, in, until I felt myself literally floating out of my body. I could actually look at myself like I was maybe five steps away from myself. I did it for fun, for laughs.' Through acting, Davis discovered a healthier way to get outside herself. She showed me a photograph, on her cell phone, of a Pawtucket *Times* article, published forty-two years ago, that captured the first time she experienced the thrill of performance. She read aloud, 'Participants in Skit Day staged Friday at Jenks Park, under the sponsorship of the Central Falls Recreation Department, included nine-year-old Viola Davis (left), who played the role of Junior from the television show *Good Times*.' Davis interjected, 'They messed that up. It was the Woooo-Whee Kid from *That's My Mama*.' She went on, 'And Diane Davis, fifteen, who appeared as Fred Sanford from *Sanford and Son*.'

The sisters had approached the contest with the same tenacity with which they pursued every opportunity to escape their circumstances – model legislature, cross-country running, basketball, arts club. 'We were like hunters. Even if we didn't really have any interest, we'd do it just to get out, just to channel ourselves into something,' Davis said. For the contest, they had rehearsals, rewrites, and even a production budget of two dollars and fifty cents, which they spent at the Salvation Army on a hat and a straw purse. In the Davis children's landscape of loss, the rare victory was pivotal. 'It was just one of those perfect moments of feeling like a winner, understanding the power of your talent, having no doubt,' Davis said. 'We showed everyone.' Their prize was a plastic baseball bat, which they used to kill rats.

When Davis was fourteen, she enrolled in an acting class through the federal program Upward Bound, which helps prepare low-income students for higher education. The class was run by a young actor and coach named Ron Stetson. "'How many people in this class want to be an actor?'" Davis remembers Stetson saying. 'We all raised our hands. He said, "You know you have to work fucking hard every fucking day." A fourth of the hands went down. "Every day." More hands down. "You can go on an audition every fricking day for six weeks and never, ever, get a job. You know that, right?" More hands down. I remember thinking, Wow, that is awesome. My hand still was up. I was trying to reach the ceiling with my hand. "And you're gonna get rejected time and time and time again."' Davis continued, 'Pretty soon, I was the only one who had my hand up. He kept going at me. "You're gonna get egg on your face. You're gonna fail." I kept my hand up, staring at him. He stared at me. "O.K., let's get back to class."'

'Whatever Viola got from me, she brought,' Stetson told me. 'I just happened to be standing there when she was ready to give it.' Stetson's class proved to Davis that her dream was bigger than her fear. Acting, and the emotional release it allowed, Davis said, 'gave me great joy. Perfect joy. It wasn't like I had to search for anything else.' When you're acting, she explained, 'you're feeling everything

– every last receptor in your body is alive, one-hundred-per-cent alive, and you're not hiding anything, because everything is used as a tool to make the character a fully realized human being.' Davis enrolled at Stetson's alma mater, Rhode Island College, where she was awarded a full scholarship. She graduated with a B.A. in 1988, and was one of two dozen actors chosen from a thousand applicants to the Juilliard School, in New York City.

At Juilliard, Davis's dream wobbled. Politically, she was waking up; artistically, she was hibernating. Instead of focussing on her strengths as an actor, the teachers fixated on her perceived weaknesses. 'I wasn't light enough, too much gravitas,' she said. 'For the next four years, this woman with lots of gravitas was leaping across the stage like a ninety-pound Caucasian girl.' Davis also bridled at what she saw as the school's Eurocentric notions and its aesthetic, in which 'if you were emotional, if you were vulnerable, then that did not show technique.' But, the summer after her second year, Juilliard gave her a grant for a two-week study of dance, music, and folklore in Gambia. The experience was an antidote to the school's orthodoxy. In Gambia, witnessing traditional ceremonies – baby naming, food preparation – Davis experienced communities in which art was not separated from life. 'It wasn't about technique; it was about the soul. In their zest for life, their need to connect to each other and to God – everything they did was done with extreme passion,' she said.

Davis now compares her student days to cough syrup: unpleasant but useful. 'It was good to see how other people see me,' she said. 'Because then I began to have an inner gauge as to how to direct myself, how I'm coming off.' Three years after graduating from Juilliard, in 1993, Davis earned her first Tony Award nomination, for her performance in *Seven Guitars*. By the time that *Doubt* premièred, in 2008, she had established herself, in eight plays on the New York stage, as a major actress, with a Tony to prove it.

As Esther Mills, in Lynn Nottage's *Intimate Apparel* (2004), an expert seamstress who succeeds in her lingerie business but fails at love, Davis exhibited a particularly arresting reserve, a quality of silence that translates with equal power to her screen performances. 'What she doesn't do is (or can be) as important as what she does with a scene,' Meryl Streep wrote to me. 'She has enormous restraint as an artist. It's a big dam holding back the deluge, and that power, held in check behind her eyes – what she withholds, or lets you wait for – is evidence of real mastery.' Streep also recalled 'the softness of her patience' when filming *Doubt*: 'After she had shot her most challenging scene (what seemed) scores of times (and perfectly, sublimely), the director decided he didn't like the background. He went back to the location the next day and put her through it all over again, as inexplicably many times as the first, for hours. I thought it was abuse, and had a snit on her behalf. But she was almost blazing under the emotional yoke. She used it, as actors are meant to, in our masochistic craft.'

★

The back door of Davis's kitchen opened, and her six-year-old daughter, Genesis, whom she adopted five years ago, skittered in after a long day at school. Genesis clamped onto her beaming mother with her arms and legs. In the background, a babysitter stood with Genesis's backpack in hand. 'What do you say, G.,' Davis said. Genesis whispered a shy hello, then scampered off to do homework.

Davis put a skillet on the stove and dumped some rice and butter into it. 'When I first started, acting was very therapeutic,' she said. 'I needed it. I felt I was unfinished. Then I went into therapy. I got married to the most beautiful man.'

Three weeks before Davis met Julius Tennon, in 1999, she prayed for a husband. 'I said I wanted a big black man from the South who looked like a football player, who already had children,' she recalled. Davis was in the craft-services line on the set of Steven Bochco's *City of Angels*, a short-lived medical drama in which she played a nurse, when she was approached by Tennon, who had a recurring part as an anesthesiologist. 'I heard her complaining about Los Angeles and not knowing anybody. Being a good Southern boy, my mom always told me that, if you like a girl, just give her your phone number.' Tennon gave Davis his card. 'I don't have swagger,' Davis said. 'I'm not that gregarious woman who knows how to flirt.'

Davis was thirty-four; she'd had one long-term relationship, with an actor who had only once told her that he loved her. It took her a month to overcome her low self-esteem and, at her therapist's prompting, call Tennon. She was surprised that he recognized her voice. Tennon took her to a restaurant near the Santa Monica Pier. He liked her big laugh. 'She just had a zest for life,' he said. 'She wanted to reach out to somebody. I scared her, because I told her everything about me.'

Tennon, who is eleven years older than Davis, had a story to tell. He'd been reared in Texas, one of eight children in difficult circumstances, won a full football scholarship to the University of Tulsa, where he was a starting strong-side linebacker and the first African-American to graduate from the university's drama program. He was a single parent who had brought up a daughter and a son alone, for seventeen years. Tennon remembers Davis saying, 'Wow, you've lived a life. I've never had a life. I've just been an artist. I just wanted to do this.' By the end of the evening, according to Davis, 'basically, it was a wrap.' Three months later, they'd moved in together. 'I had anxiety attacks before I met him,' she said. 'I had no money, because I had to pay for my apartment in New York and pay to live in L.A. for seven months. My driving was crappy.' She continued, 'The moment I met my husband, all of it stopped. The worry, the anxiety. Everything.'

While Davis was attending to the rice – 'Just a little butter. I cook the onion a little. Then I add chicken broth. Delicious' – Genesis ran back in and was quickly scooped up by her mother. 'What's the best thing Mommy does for you?' Davis said. 'Cuddle,' Genesis answered in a soft voice.

'Not cook' – Davis laughed – 'because Mommy don't cook every night.' She straightened the pink bow in her daughter's hair. 'What does Mommy say to you all the time?' she said. Genesis whispered something inaudible, then, prompted, said it louder: 'No one's gonna love you like I love you.' 'That's what I tell her. She loves it,' Davis said.

When Genesis had skipped off again, Davis added, 'There are days when I give myself a D as a mom, then on some days I give myself an A. A great Mom Day is when I can bring her to school, pick her up, help with homework, cook a great meal, and put her to sleep. A bad day is when I can't do that.' Genesis has brought with her 'a different understanding of mortality,' Davis said. 'We're older parents. Julius is always trying to teach her everything he can right now.' She smiled, and said, 'There's a lot of living in this household.'

★

Davis has described marriage as a process in which 'you sort of die to yourself and you're reborn into this union.' Her perspective on her career also underwent an adjustment. The more successful she was, the more her work revolved around publicity rather than performance. The stereotypical parts she was being offered – 'I have been given a lot of roles that are downtrodden, mammyish' – were as unfulfilling as she found the Hollywood community to be. 'I've been in movies with actors I've never met,' she said. 'I felt like I needed higher meaning in my life.' Davis committed herself to motherhood and to the social issues of childhood hunger, education, and sexual abuse.

When she became the first African-American to win an Emmy for Best Leading Actress on a television series, in 2015, she quoted Harriet Tubman in her acceptance speech: "'In my mind, I see a line. And over that line I see green fields and lovely flowers and beautiful white women with their arms stretched out to me over that line. But I can't seem to get there no-how.'" Davis went on, 'The only thing that separates women of color from anyone else is opportunity. You cannot win an Emmy for roles that are simply not there.' She didn't hear or see a response from her audience. 'I didn't think it was landing,' she said. 'I wasn't so concerned with that, because my whole life I've been focussed on approval, on acceptance, on shame and all that. I've been focussed on it for so much. One day it lifted.' The audience may have been startled, but Davis sees her gesture at the Emmys as part of the 'unknown responsibility of celebrity.' 'There is no line in my life and in my spirit, but there is a line in the culture for me as a woman and me as an African-American,' she said. That ceremony marked the moment when she began to pronounce herself in public.

The next time I saw Davis was on the set of *How to Get Away with Murder*, which is shot at the Sunset-Gower Studios, at the far end of a sleepy warren of drab, enormous buildings, sprawling over a few city blocks, a sort of Levittown of entertainment. While Davis was in hair and makeup, I was directed to wait in her double-wide trailer, which was docked in the corner of a parking lot, thirty feet from the stage door. 'Star Wagon,' it said on the back. The trailer had a smart TV in each of its two rooms, both turned on. To the left was Davis's cluttered dressing room, full of tokens from her real life, including the December issue of *Essence*, with Davis on the cover, and a box of Genesis's toys. The other room was clinical and tidy – a receiving room, with a gray sofa and a small desk, where the green pages of Davis's next scene were laid out.

This episode, which would air in January, as the season première, required a sensational opening. The writers had Annalise being arraigned at the police station. A body had been found in her house, which had gone up in flames. Annalise had been arrested and was being charged with arson and murder. Did she do it? And who was the corpse? None of the producers, assistants, publicists, or crew milling around the set would tip me the wink. Eventually, Davis came into the trailer, and it turned out that she didn't know, either. 'I gather you have burned your house down,' I said, as she sat across from me in the living room. 'I hope that I didn't, because I haven't been playing it that way,' Davis said, smiling.

The show's popularity and the power that has come with it have been, for Davis, a surreal reversal of fortune. She talked about how it felt to act alongside the legendary Cicely Tyson, whom she had suggested for the role of Annalise's mother, Ophelia. With a smart TV flickering behind her, Davis recalled the small family TV set at 128 Washington Street, with its portable aerial wrapped in tinfoil, around which she and her sisters crowded to watch Tyson in the 1974 TV movie of Ernest J. Gaines's *The Autobiography of Miss Jane Pittman*. 'My sisters and I were completely transported by it,' Davis, who was nine at the time, said. 'We couldn't believe what we were looking at. The fact that she looked almost exactly like my mother. The Afro. She was a black woman. That was one thing. But the other thing was how she transformed. We could not believe that we were seeing a human being transform from the age of eighteen to a hundred and eight.' She went on, 'It was my first introduction to seeing craft at play and not just entertainment. We would try to imitate her in our rooms. We became obsessed with acting classes.'

In the first season of *How to Get Away with Murder*, Annalise faced off against Ophelia, accusing her of failing to protect her from being molested by her uncle. Davis recalled the thrill of the exchange with Tyson, who turned ninety the day the scene was shot: 'I'm working to convey all this history, this sexual assault, and all the pain. I remember her face, her look, the ease with which her response came out. She said, "It happened to all the women, that's our curse. It happened to my mother. It happened to her mother." You saw all the sexual assault that she'd witnessed – it was in her eyes, her demeanor.' Davis went on, 'She showed a very specific deep history, and that you cannot teach in school. That's just something that comes around every once in a lifetime. That's exactly why I wanted to become an actor. The depth of the emotional life she is able to convey is what I have to work on.'

Davis was called to the set, in a hangar-like structure. The crew were adjusting the wooden walls of the prison room where Annalise would be patted down and fingerprinted. A row of canvas chairs had been set up behind a triptych of color monitors that tracked what was happening on set. A stagehand was running a smoke machine to help soften the reflected light. Genesis returned from the studio playroom and hopped into her mother's arms, excited to stay late at the end of the school week and see Davis at work. For a while, Davis walked around the vast space, with her daughter in her arms, then she sent Genesis off to the trailer to shower and get into her pajamas. Davis strolled over to the cornucopia of food spread out on a table behind one of the unused sets, where we continued our conversation.

'My gift is exposing,' she said. 'Exposing mess – the humanity, the vulnerability of what it means to be human. I think that that is what acting is about, anyway.' She was putting agave nectar on some peanut butter. She added, 'At the end of the day, most people gotta put on a mask. Only in acting do people literally take it off, and it's embraced, celebrated.'

A makeup artist appeared to prepare Davis for her scene, steering her into an unused library set, where Davis sat down on a chair and pulled her skirt up above her knees. 'This is so I don't get ashy,' she said, as her legs and arms were slathered with ointment. 'African-Americans have a joke about it: "It looks like you been rollin' around in some flour."' Davis continued, 'Back in the day we just put Vaseline or lard, smeared it on ourselves, because it's sacrilege to go out ashy.'

Then Davis headed toward the set for what she said was 'a humiliation scene.' She had no lines in this particular scene. She just had to bend forward so that an unsmiling hatchet-faced policewoman could inspect her hair and probe her mouth with a flashlight. There were six or seven takes. As the director and the makeup, lighting, and camera crews fussed around her, Davis remained in character, 'being private in public,' as she calls it. Her arms held tightly across her chest, her large, heavy-lidded eyes trained on her interior, she was locked in the solitude of memory, leached of liveliness, dead in the eyes, full of the torpor of anxiety, humiliated almost to tears. As I watched, something that Tennon had said came back to me: 'She is never far away from that little girl that she talks about. She's never forgot her.'

Citizen Penn

The many missions of Sean Penn

In San Francisco one day last June, at 7.45am., an hour when even the panhandlers on Geary Street were still asleep, Sean Penn was standing in front of me, in sneakers, gray chinos, and denim work shirt, the quiff of his full brown hair catching glints of sun, alert and ready to go. 'I'm not so much an early riser as a non-sleeper,' he said, peering over the top of his sunglasses. The day before, Penn had flown back from Tehran – where, as a correspondent for the San Francisco *Chronicle*, he had been covering the run-up to the Iranian elections – in order to attend the junior-high-school graduation of his fourteen-year-old daughter, Dylan. This morning, he had dropped his twelve-year-old son, Hopper, at school. Now we headed off to Union Square, for some of Sears Fine Food's Swedish pancakes.

Penn, who is forty-five and a compact five feet eight, is at ease in his body. There is nothing hunched or furtive in his bearing – he emanates what in earlier times would have been called 'backbone.' 'The feeling you get about him is that you can't call his bluff, because he's not bluffing,' Woody Allen said about Penn, who starred in his 1999 film *Sweet and Lowdown*. At the same time, Penn has a very specific gravity: reserve is part of his strength and his seduction. He is warm but no hail-fellow, polite but without that come-hither thing. 'You see me from ten feet away, everyone thinks I'm gonna bite or something,' Penn said. On first meeting, he gave no semaphore of greeting – no handshake, no smile, no small talk. His presence was his hello.

Over breakfast, he handed me an Iranian candy. He was preparing to write an article about his trip. (The piece, which was twelve thousand words, ran in the *Chronicle* in five installments in August.) He had a tantalizing array of incidents from which to draw: he had attended prayers at a Tehran mosque, a women's-rights demonstration, meetings with dissidents, a photo op with former President (and then Presidential candidate) Ali Akbar Hashemi Rafsanjani, and, perhaps inevitably, an award ceremony for his acting, at the Film Museum of Iran. On his travels, he told me, he had been 'very aware of the ugly American,' particularly in the reportorial ranks. 'There's a consistent insensitivity,' he said. 'I watched journalists. They could only ever be seen by their subject as the person with a deadline. It's 'breaking news,' literally. By the time you get the news, you've broken it. You don't get a chance to investigate stories. These journalists live half the time in the Internet cafe, filing a story.' Penn described his own form of reportage as 'tournalism.' 'It's not an obligation of the tourist to observe experience so much as to have it,' he said.' For me, a greater accuracy of perception comes out of that.'

A veteran of some thirty-five films, Penn is renowned, in the acting profession, for the meticulousness of his research. 'Sean is a guy who doesn't want to analyze a character too much,' Alejandro

Gonzalez Iñarritu, who directed Penn in *21 Grams* (2003), has said. 'He wants to be *as* the character.' For his portrait of the stoned surfer Jeff Spicoli, in *Fast Times at Ridgemont High* (1982) – the role that made him famous, at the age of twenty-two – Penn lived out of his car at the beach; to play a cop, in *Colors* (1988), he apprenticed to an L.A.P.D. officer; for the role of Emmet Ray, 'the world's second-greatest guitar player,' in *Sweet and Lowdown*, he studied guitar fingering. In his forays into politics and journalism, Penn relies on the same strategy. 'Sean's an investigative reporter of his emotional life and our world,' Dennis Hopper, who directed Penn in *Colors*, told me. 'Sean goes to the middle of the hurricane. He's not taking a secondhand opinion. He really wants to know what's going down.' In 1992, during the Rodney King riots in Los Angeles, Penn drove into the thick of the pandemonium and got a shopping cart thrown through his windshield for his curiosity. In 2002 and 2003, he travelled to Iraq (once before the American-led invasion and once afterward), in order to observe life there – and, on the second visit, to write about it for the *Chronicle*. 'My trip is to personally record the human face of the Iraqi people so that their blood – along with that of American soldiers – would not be invisible on my own hands,' he said at a Baghdad press conference in 2002. In Penn's opinion, his shift from actor to correspondent was 'seamless'. 'You wake up in the morning with an interest in listening and expressing,' he said. 'It all feels the same to me. Acting is Everyman-ness, and loving Everyman. Finally, you're reaching out to people's pain.'

Because of his activism, Penn is often caricatured as a showboating celebrity liberal. 'It's as if Ernest Hemingway made sweet, sweet love to Jeff Spicoli before our very eyes,' the media blog Gawker said when the second installment of the Iran piece came out. In *Team America: World Police*, Trey Parker and Matt Stone's 2004 marionette film parody of Bush's war on terror, a bubbleheaded Penn puppet says of Iraq, 'Before Team America showed up it was a happy place. They had flowing meadows, and rainbow skies, and rivers made of chocolate where the children danced and laughed and played with gumdrop smiles.' Penn shot back a 'sincere fuck you' to the filmmakers, in a letter that was reprinted on the Drudge Report; he also offered to retrace his steps with them. 'We'll fly to Amman, Jordan, and I'll ride with you ... twelve hours through the Sunni Triangle into Fallujah and Baghdad and I'll show you around,' he wrote. 'When we return, make all the fun you want.'

Early in 2005, Penn completed filming for Steven Zaillian's remake of *All the King's Men*, which will open later this year, and in which he plays the mesmerizing and corrupt Louisiana kingpin Willie Stark, Robert Penn Warren's fictional version of Huey Long. His plan now, he told me, was to take a couple of years off from acting. (This wouldn't be the first time that he had taken a break from performing. In the nineties, he quit for a few years, and threw himself into directing instead.) 'I'm out of fuel,' he said, adding, 'You want to be aware of the impact in terms of just how much you put out there. You want to maintain the potency of aspects of yourself – marshal your forces, select things you can put your heart and soul into. I have time to evolve and re-inform the creature who's doing it.' He said that he sometimes has difficulty sustaining his passion over the hard slog of a film shoot. 'You turn on the news, and there's something else you want to make a movie about,' he said. On the other hand, he added, 'if there's anything really valuable for me in the craft of acting, it's maintaining the skills to hold on to the passion I started with.'

Acting, he explained, was like parachuting. 'If you jump out of an airplane, you love the first thousand feet. Now you're ready to land, but you're not gonna slow down just because you aren't interested anymore. The craft is there to make sure that when you jump you're propelled properly to keep going full speed.'

★

Penn is an entrepreneur of his own edge – a roiling combination of rage, buoyancy, tenderness, and hurt. His struggle to contain this combustible emotional package makes him at once dangerous and exciting. In his art and in his life, he takes chances. ('Sean is batty as a loon and is prone to taking extraordinary risks in foreign towns,' the late Hunter S. Thompson, who knew something about recklessness, wrote.) He has been known to hand out to friends cards on which he has printed the epigraph to William Saroyan's *The Time of Your Life*: 'In the time of your life live,' it begins, 'so that in that good time there shall be no ugliness or death for yourself or for any life your life touches.' Penn has the confidence of a man who believes that the world will provide what he needs when he needs it. 'It's trusting your instincts and your experience,' he says. 'Call it fate.'

He is also a fighter. In his guntoting, paparazzi-punching, midnightrambling Hollywood years, which spanned the eighties and early nineties, he took regular pleasure in publicly biting the hands that fed him. 'What's the difference between yogurt and Los Angeles?' he liked to joke to the press back then. 'Yogurt has a living culture.' But after Penn's wife, the actress Robin Wright Penn, was carjacked in the driveway of their Santa Monica home, with their two young children still in the car (no one was hurt), in 1996, the Penn menage decamped for the picturesque tranquillity of the Bay Area, to a tidy patch of suburban normality about forty-five minutes north of San Francisco, where they live now in a tile-and-stucco hacienda, surrounded by a large wall that Penn constructed.

Penn likes driving. He's been known to take long, freewheeling car trips around America, especially after a film has wrapped and he gets that '*big* fucken school's-out-for-summer feeling,' he told Richard T. Kelly, who published the fascinating oral history *Sean Penn: His Life and Times* last year. 'Give me a car and a country I can zigzag through . . . and I'm a bird,' he said. Even on the short trip back to his house after breakfast, he seemed to enjoy the glamour of himself in motion. He leaned forward over the steering wheel of his black S.U.V., cupping his hands around his lighter as he lit a Marlboro. I remarked that he seemed like the kind of person who would roll his own cigarettes. 'Oh, no, then I'd be a real smoker,' he said. 'These give me the illusion that I can quit.'

With the cigarette dangling raffishly from the side of his mouth, he was a snapshot of casual, at least until he spotted a police car in his rearview mirror. 'I always think it's me. 'Para-fucking-noia, Eddie,' he said, quoting a line from David Rabe's *Hurlyburly*. (Penn appeared in the Los Angeles première of the play, in 1988, and also in the 1998 film version.) He fumbled through the glove compartment. 'I have a driver's license,' he said, 'but I don't have it on me.'

Penn has had his share of run-ins with the police. In Macao in 1986, during the shooting of *Shanghai Surprise*, he was arrested for helping to deter an intruding paparazzo by hanging him by his ankles from the ninth-floor balcony of his hotel room. (Penn subsequently broke out of the jail where he was being held on charges of attempted murder and escaped from the country by jetfoil.) In 1987, he served thirty-three days of a sixty-day sentence in the Los Angeles County jail (twenty-three hours a day in solitary) for violating the probation he'd been given for punching a fan who tried to get too close to his first wife, Madonna. In 1988, Madonna herself summoned a SWAT team to the couple's house in Malibu, after the two had fought. ('She developed a concern that if she were to return to the house she would get a very severe haircut,' Penn, who was not arrested in the well-publicized incident, said later.)

For a mile or so, Penn kept careful watch on the police car behind us while he chatted about his children – Dylan's transfer to a private school, Hopper's skateboarding obsession. Then the police car swung into the express lane and pulled up alongside us, and the officer driving it motioned in Penn's direction. At first, it seemed that she was signalling Penn to pull over, but she was only pointing at his seat belt. Penn strapped himself in. The police car sped away. 'That's nice,' Penn said. He turned to me and allowed himself a smile.

Penn's office space – two capacious rooms built above the garage of his house – has its own entrance, with a doormat that reads 'Witness Protection Program.' He refers to it as his 'after-hours editorial facility'; a 'bunker' is what his close friend the musician David Baerwald calls it. This is where Penn comes to write, edit, drink, carouse, and wheel and deal. It is also a visible manifestation of Penn's guarded nature. The rooms – decorated in a sort of bordello burgundy, with burgundy velvet wallpaper, burgundy baize on the pool and poker tables, and burgundy chairs – have a crepuscular gloom; they reflect the 'downtown quality' that Jack Nicholson has said expresses 'the dark part of Sean's character ... this feeling for lost souls and the kind of green-tinted late-at-night quality.' Penn, of course, has a wide range of well-placed friends, but he seems to be happiest in the company of what Baerwald calls 'the demidemimonde – the kind of people who might follow Al Capone around.' In this demotic scrum – 'I'm just another American who appreciates a little color,' Penn once wrote – he feels safe. 'I hang out with guys who are very comfortable not looking at me and not having me look back at them,' Penn told *Playboy* in 1991. 'It's like being by yourself without being by yourself'.

'You have to protect your edges,' Dennis Hopper said, explaining why Penn keeps much of the world at arm's length. 'James Dean said to me when I was young, 'The giant sequoia tree in its beginning is very small inside but the bark is very large. The bark is a foot thick but doesn't get bigger. The bark is there to allow the inside to grow. An actor is like that.' Every time you do an emotional scene, you're exposing yourself. The second the scene's over, you have to shut it back down and put your bark back on. If you walk around without it, you're just a wounded tree – you're going to die, because there's just too much stuff coming into you. Sean goes deep into his emotional inner life. He allows you to see it, then he closes it back up. He has to, or he wouldn't be able to survive.' Woody Allen agreed. 'He's not easily accessible,' he said. 'It's hard to get through to him, and you feel that at any minute he could blow up at you. It makes it so interesting. Women want to take care of him and men find him heroic.'

Penn's elusiveness was established at an early age. Penn's mother, the actress Eileen Ryan Penn, told Richard Kelly that, as a child, 'Sean had his own private little world going.' 'I don't think that I really spoke outside my home till I was five,' Penn told me. 'I remember plenty of conversations, but they were all with myself. If I ever felt loneliness, it was in a group.' Penn's shyness, by his own admission, was also a kind of strategic retreat. 'When I realized that people could not see into me – that bothered me,' he said. 'I wanted to be transparent, so as to be understood. I knew that my intentions were good. It seemed to me I could give a lot more and be more productive with people who could see who I was.' He went on, 'I didn't want to be charming. I didn't want to have to be funny. I didn't want to have to be flawless. I wanted to be able to know that my heart was in the right place and not do a big song and dance to display it.' Penn's kindergarten teacher dubbed him 'Gary Cooper.' 'The only complaint that teachers ever gave me about him was "Is he happy?"' Eileen Penn said. 'He seemed to be so quiet.'

In high school, Penn learned that his unreachable quality could be used to both provoke and seduce. 'Being shy brings attention – it brings my subjects to me,' he explained. 'It works the same way it did on the quad in high school. There's a lot of noise, a lot of alpha dogs plying their trade. Then, there's you, bouncing your tennis shoes off the brick on the planter you're sitting on. At some point in the school year, a pretty girl reaches a moment of reflection where that becomes more attractive than the alpha dog. You've got a lot of stuff that will be new to share.'

Onscreen, Penn parses his own solitude. Almost all the characters to whom he has been drawn are to some degree cut off from the world, whether by murderous obsession (Samuel J. Byck, in *The Assassination of Richard Nixon*; Sergeant Tony Meserve, in *Casualties of War*; Matthew Poncelet, in *Dead Man Walking*; Jimmy Markum, in *Mystic River*), by mental or physical damage (Sam Dawson, in *I Am Sam*; Eddie Quinn, in *She's So Lovely*; Paul Rivers, in *21 Grams*), by drugs (Eddie, in *Hurlyburly*, Spicoli, in *Fast Times at Ridgemont High*), or by artistic self-absorption (Emmet, in *Sweet and Lowdown*). But the fury that fuels Penn's performances – 'the wonderful homicidal quality of his rage,' as the screenwriter Nick Kazan describes it – is examined in even greater depth in the three films that he has directed (he also wrote the first two): *The Indian Runner* (1991), *The Crossing Guard* (1995), and *The Pledge* (2001). On the surface, Penn's well-told tales seem disparate. However, the issue at stake is almost always his own: the desire both to connect with and to elude people to be, in other words, a kind of respectable outlaw. Penn addressed this division most directly in *The Indian Runner*, which was inspired by Bruce Springsteen's song 'Highway Patrolman.' The film tells the story of two brothers, one a dutiful family-loving deputy sheriff, the other a violent, unreachable jailbird. 'I think both things exist in me,' Penn said, adding, 'If we're of any use, then we have blood on our hands.' The film takes its title and its central visual trope from a game of hide-and-seek that the brothers play as kids in the cornfields. 'I'm the Indian runner. I'm a message, and the message is "Bet you can't find me,"' the wayward Frank tells his older brother, Joe, as their chase begins. The tale ends in a standoff, Frank is gone and Joe has given up the chase. The short-film director Matt Palmieri, who has been a close friend of Penn's since elementary school, agreed that the characters represent the two sides of Sean. 'One part of him is the responsible, clearheaded, thoughtful older brother, the guy who kind of takes charge in a crisis,' he said. 'But, on the other hand, he's angry, wild, rambunctious – definitely highly aggressive.'

As Penn and I talked in his office, he noticed me glancing at a plastic Barbie-like doll propped against the fireplace. 'An Ann Coulter doll,' he explained, referring to the neo-conservative TV pundit. 'We violate her,' he said. 'There are cigarette burns in some funny areas. She's pure snake-oil salesman. She doesn't believe a word she says. She mentions Leo in her book *Treason*.'

Leo Penn, Sean's father, was a movie actor, whose career was blighted in the early fifties by the Hollywood blacklist. (He died, of lung cancer, in 1998.) According to Penn, Leo was 'the king of comfort in his own skin.' (He was buried in his iconic mufti: sandals, Hawaiian shirt, and baseball cap.) Every Father's Day, Penn shows his children ten minutes of a video of Leo, made two years before his death, in which he recounts his eventful life to a group called Women in Film. Penn cued up the film for me, and Leo and his gentle charm filled the room:

> When I was eleven, my mother – who was maybe four foot ten – and I occupied the back seat of a Greyhound bus and drove to California non-stop, where my father had been for a year, squeezing oranges to make a living. And I'll never forget that trip. That had a large impact on my life because it was so joyous. And this was during the Depression, when the gap between rich and poor was not what it is now. We were all in the same boat, and we all had a blast on that Greyhound bus: people playing guitars and singing songs and relating to one another....
>
> I went to war. I was away four years. While I was here – came back on I guess it was overseas leave – I was invited to do a play at U.C.L.A.... It went very well, and suddenly I was getting phone

calls – and I was still in the service. I was getting calls from agents. I thought, Jesus, is it possible to turn this into a profession. . . . I did a screen test. To my amazement they put me under contract. . . . Life was very rosy for a while. . . . I worked in the theatre; for some of the time I had a soap opera on radio. . . . Then I was under contract to a B-movie company called Monogram. I did one picture. They didn't like my [last] name, and I refused to change it. . . . I changed my first name to Clifford 'cause I liked Clifford Odets. They didn't like Clifford 'cause they said he was a Communist.

Although Leo was not named in the House Un-American Activities Committee investigations, his progressive leanings, his refusal to testify, and his support of the Hollywood Ten got him labelled as a fellow-traveller. By 1952, he couldn't work on the West Coast. He moved back East, where, he said, 'it took roughly two years and I was dead in New York, too. I couldn't do either film or television.' Nonetheless, Leo built up a considerable reputation as a theatre actor; in 1957, he replaced Jason Robards in the legendary Circle in the Square production of *The Iceman Cometh*. He soon fell in love with a beautiful, outspoken actress in the company, Eileen Ryan, and they married in 1958.

The Penns were socially conscious, resilient survivors. 'We didn't have the money to get me out of the hospital when Michael was born,' Eileen Ryan Penn said of her first son's birth, in 1958. 'We laughed a lot about it.' The Penns moved to California, and settled in the San Fernando Valley, in 1959. When Leo was offered the chance to try his hand at directing for television, he accepted. He loved the camaraderie of the job, and he was good at it; over the next thirty years, he directed more than four hundred hours of prime-time TV, winning an Emmy in 1973 for a special episode of *Columbo*. But there were times when Sean heard in his father's badinage a hint of disappointment: 'I'd say, "What are you up to?" He'd say, "Ah, you know, trying to make a better piece of shit out of a worse piece of shit."'

Leo had been betrayed by the country that he'd fought for with distinction. As a bombardier in the Second World War, at a time when a pilot's life expectancy was around fifteen missions, Leo had flown thirty-one, including three over Berlin, and won the Distinguished Flying Cross and the Air Medal. 'He had about ten years of hardcore flashbacks and sleeplessness,' Penn has said. 'As a tail gunner, you saw the face of your enemy. You saw the devastation of the rounds at the end of your gun. That was a big thing for him.' Many of the hallmarks of Sean's artistic career – his fascination with outsiders, his rebelliousness, his hatred of injustice, his suspicion of authority, his flirtation with heroics – are informed by the legends of Leo's life, of both his military and his political travails. 'One thing that the children of blacklisted people know is that on many levels acceptable polite society is just another fraud,' Baerwald said. 'Leo should have, could have, and certainly wanted to do work of more substance than he did. Life was much diminished.'

Nowadays, when Penn invokes his father's memory, he recalls the smile in his eyes. 'He could have very strong opinions and see all sides of an issue at the same time, but there was always that sparkle thing,' he told me. Leo's work, however, usually took him away from home at dawn and brought him back after dinner. 'He was a good weekend father,' Penn said. 'Once Dad got home, it became about the couple. Basically, that was their time. Our family time was the weekend.' When Penn was a child, his parents' bond was complicated but palpable. 'We adored each other,' Eileen has said. 'We had a great marriage. We were never bored with each other. We grew together.' Penn remembers his mother and father sitting late at night on their patio in Malibu, looking out at the Pacific. 'If you sneaked out for a snack or something, they'd just be sitting there, lights out,' he told Kelly. 'She'd be sound asleep with her head on his lap, and he would be rubbing her hair. And that was very common – nearly every night.'

As we were driving, Penn returned to that memory, but with an additional detail: 'He'd drink a bottle of J&B at night; my mother'd polish off a bottle of Smirnoff. She never started drinking till we were in bed. They could both get up early the next morning and function.' Penn recalled a night when he was a teenager and he and his brother Michael sneaked home late. He turned off the engine of his beat-up Mazda at the foot of the driveway and they pushed it thirty yards, to where the family house was nestled beside a coral tree. As they crept up, they could see their parents on the patio in their usual entwined position. 'My mother had fallen asleep – call that "passed out,"' Penn said. 'My dad had taken the ship's wheel off the wall.' (Leo had a fascination with the sea, and the house was decorated with boating paraphernalia.) 'He had my mom's head in his lap. Above her head was the ship's wheel. My brother said, "Dad's steering the house!"' Eileen Penn told me, 'Leo and I drank equally. We enjoyed the drinks. I'm not sorry. If I was like my mother – falling down the cellar steps, me coming home from school with a friend and she'd be half hanging out of her nightgown . . . Sean never experienced any of that with me.' But Sean's younger brother, Chris, also an actor, who died accidentally, after taking a combination of prescription and over-the-counter medications, last January, at the age of forty, saw a difference between his father's attitude toward alcohol and his mother's. 'I think my father was a hard drinker,' he told me last year. 'I don't think he was an alcoholic.' And his mother? 'I won't go into it,' he said.

Eileen Penn is of Irish and Italian descent, and she has a particularly volatile intensity. After obtaining a bachelor-of-science degree from New York University to please her parents – her mother was a nurse – she followed her own dream by going to New Orleans to sing in a bar, then becoming a successful actress Off Broadway. She gave up performing when she had children. 'All the passion I had for acting went into being a mother,' she has said. She wanted only sons. When Michael was being born, she yelled at the nurse, 'If it's a girl, push it back in! I'm not going through twenty-four hours of labor for any woman!' She explained, 'My father was so protective, so worried if I ever did something that he thought was dangerous. So I just wanted boys who could go out there and do anything they wanted in the world.'

On the way to his house, Penn had suddenly pulled the car off onto a slip road and switch backed down to a spot below the Golden Gate Bridge so that he could show me where the breakers were sometimes large enough for surfing. 'I don't know this break well, so I don't know the times of the year that it shoots up,' he said. 'I've actually seen it come through these piers when it was a real crazy squall.'

When Penn was nine, in 1969, his family moved from the Valley to a ramshackle fifty-seven-thousand-dollar beach house with a view of the ocean, near Point Dume, in Malibu. Today, the plot is worth millions, and Barbra Streisand lives at the end of the road. Back then, the community was almost rural, and Penn loved it. 'The newness of the world. The smell of the creeks. That stuff did not get old to me. 1 can still smell Point Dume, 1969,' he said. He surfed throughout his teenage years, and the sport has had a lasting influence on him. 'I defined surfing then as an art form,' he said in 1991. 'It was truly about matching the energy of the wave. It was a harmony, and there was poetry to it. There was a spiritual aspect to surfing.' At the age of eleven, Penn signed up for the gruelling regimen of Junior Lifeguards, which included a sixty-eight-buoy early-morning ocean swim. ('He always put himself through tough stuff: very stoic like that,' Eileen has said. 'He can take a lot of discomfort.' 'I liked it,' she told me of his grit.) An article published in the magazine *Surfer* by the former pro surfer Alf Laws, who oversaw Penn's training, became a kind of inspirational text for him. 'I've thought about it thousands of times, it was about being able to adjust, how to apply yourself,' he said. Laws wrote, 'One must possess two important qualities: confidence and go-for-it attitude. In aggressive surfing, one must believe in himself and his ability to make it through any situation. No hesitating allowed, boy, punch it! Tune yourself to the energy the waves are creating, and create some tracks of your own. You'll feel righteous.' Surfing taught Penn both the pursuit of excellence and the habit of bravery. According to his former fiancee Elizabeth McGovern, who was his co-star in *Racing with the Moon* (1984), it 'was a sort of parable for his whole life. He's always riding the crest.'

'We were roaming kids,' Chris Penn, who also surfed, rode horses, and sometimes slept overnight on the beach, told me.

'We had a lot of freedom.' Sean said, 'From the time we were very young, it was all about expanding your imagination.' Eileen's gospel, according to her, 'wasn't "Aim high"; it was "Aim *out* – to life."' She set her children a feisty example. 'She was a lioness,' Penn said. 'Boy, she could dress down those authority figures. She was unintimidatable.' She was also tough to the point of scathing. 'She was a grinding wheel,' Baerwald said. 'I mean, to make a knife, you've got to have a hard surface.' He added, 'I get the feeling she was really, really, really, really, really, really rough on Sean.' After high school, Penn apprenticed at the Group Repertory Theatre, a ninety-nine-seat house in North Hollywood. He described his mother's visit to his debut performance: 'I played a part in a stage version of *The Young Savages*. My mom comes backstage. She took my face in her hands. She looked me in the eye, and she said, "You were just terrible. You cannot do this." Meaning acting. That's my mom.' Penn added, 'About a hundred per cent of my friends were definitely afraid of her.'

'He had to fight me growing up,' Eileen said. Penn emerged from the battle with an unusual carapace of ferocity, charm, and strength. 'When I was a young man, she was a greater source of confidence than my father,' Penn said. She was also the template on which Penn based what he calls his 'unyielding attention to what we would perceive as injustice.' To the suggestion that his mother was a kind of fanatic, Penn answered, 'I would say that lovingly, but I do confirm it as such.' 'There were times when being dramatic was needed,' she said. 'I needed to get it out. I wasn't always perfectly in control. I just blasted away.' Eileen was fiercer with Sean than with her other sons because, as she said, 'he was more like me.' He certainly had her forthrightness – 'He's nobody's candidate for Secretary of State; he's not very diplomatic,' Baerwald said – and her appetite for conflict.

'Anger feeds my brain,' Eileen said. 'If you're justified in it, it's exciting. It makes me feel alive – a good fight. It was the only problem I ever had with Leo. I couldn't get him mad. I couldn't get a fight when I wanted one. Maybe that's why I fought with Sean.' Chris, who was five years younger than Scan, spoke of his brother's 'turbulent' adolescent relations with their mother as 'a very hurtful time for me because I loved them both.' One time, when Sean was particularly cruel to his mother, Chris remembered, 'I basically told him to leave the house, after throwing him around the kitchen, smashing his head against the wall. It wasn't a kid's fight. It was a real fight.' Of Sean's tendency to close himself off, Chris added, 'I can tell you this: that unreachable thing kept me angry at him until my father got sick, in the late nineties. It was confounding. I don't think it was intentional. Now when he does it – he still does it, he always will – it doesn't bother me anymore.' 'I don't think Sean goes into depression,' Eileen told me. 'He creates pain in others so he can fix it. If it isn't there and it doesn't need to be fixed, he can't be the hero and fix it.'

'I'm damaged,' Penn told *Rolling Stone* in 1996. 'I recognize that.' Penn told me that he 'still hadn't sorted out' the source of his rage. 'A couple of girlfriends ultimatumed me into therapy things,' he said. 'I tried but it just didn't play.' Baerwald told me, 'The stuff he has shared with me indicates to me that he was a mighty, mighty confused teenager. I mean *might-y*. There's one way he could reach his parents – by becoming "Sean Penn," and fulfilling both their dreams.' Chris agreed. 'Once Sean got out and started acting, it changed,' he said.

★

Acting allowed Penn to turn his turmoil to advantage; it also allowed him to live up to his mother's notion of his singularity. ('He was her protege,' Chris said. 'She absolutely lived a lot of her career through Sean.') Once, as a child, Penn asked his mother if she loved him the same as Michael, who is now a musician and songwriter. 'No,' she said, 'you're an original. There's only one Sean and only one Michael.' Penn was obsessed with the Watergate hearings, and dreamed of becoming a lawyer, but he lacked the grades. By his senior year of high school, he was cutting classes and toting around a Snoopy lunch box full of film paraphernalia for Super 8 movies that he was making with Chris and friends like Charlie Sheen and Emilio Estevez. After a brief stint at Santa Monica Junior College, where he studied car maintenance and cinematography, Penn found himself drawn back to the theatre. 'Acting is the only field I could find where it was all about not having a precedent,' he said. 'For better or worse, it was one that depended singularly on what was different about you.' By then, Robert De Niro's performances had captured Penn's imagination. 'He made excellence a moving thing,' Penn said. 'This wasn't a guy who was born with fireworks in his pocket. He didn't have a conventionally handsome face. He didn't have the melodic voice of Gregory Peck. He didn't even have an interest in having those things. He was a totally unique creature and spoke of his time.' He added, 'One knew how invested he was in what he did. It also struck a chord in me. I needed to do something one hundred per cent. I hungered for a process that would leave no stone unturned.'

Penn recalled being backstage during his apprenticeship at the Group Repertory Theatre and watching a middleaged actor get ready to go on. 'He had a pretty good TV career going, 'he said. 'I had seen him in a lot of things. He didn't have to be at this theatre, for zero money.' Penn continued, 'I watched him take off his cowboy boots to get into his costume; I followed his eyes down to the boots, and I said to myself, "You know, I'll be O.K. at forty looking down at those boots, knowing that I'm going to do what he's going out to do tonight. I'll like this life. I know I'm good enough that I'll be an actor when I'm forty. Not a failed actor. Not a successful actor. I'll be an actor. It's an adventure."'

At the outset of his career, according to Chris, Penn 'didn't have a flamboyant or entertaining presence at all,' but he 'worked as hard as an Olympic athlete.' 'The thing Sean had was guts,' Eileen has said. 'The talent came later.' From the age of eighteen to twenty, five hours a day, five days a week, Penn trained with the diminutive methodacting coach Peggy Feury, who counted among her clients Anjelica Huston, Michelle Pfeiffer, and Jeff Goldblum. Feury was 'interested in how are you gonna bring yourself to the material rather than the material to you,' Penn said. 'I felt that Peggy was very personal with me. She'd teach you how to graph your work. I was wary of anything that was gonna fuck with my precious fucking instincts, but she just got to me. It was gentle, very gentle.'

On his nineteenth birthday, Penn got his first professional part – on *Barnaby Jones* – and his Screen Actors Guild card. A year later, in 1980, he went East looking for work; almost immediately, he landed a part in a Broadway play, Kevin Heelan's *Heartland*. When the play opened, the *Times* panned it as a 'hackneyed melodrama,' and said that Penn's character 'mopes around the house like a sick gerbil.' Still, the play marked a seismic shift in his life. 'He said that for the first time he felt like himself,' Baerwald recalled. 'He could understand what being himself was.' Two years later, he was cast in a cameo role in *Fast Times at Ridgemont High*; after the early rushes, his role was expanded into a star turn. Penn contributed his own surfing argot – 'tubular,' 'gnarly,' 'awesome' – to the script; he also brought his own wardrobe to the set, including the black-and-white Vans that became a fashion statement for a generation. Art Linson, one of the film's producers, told Richard Kelly, 'The famous scene where Spicoli comes late to class and Ray Walston rips up his card, and Sean says, 'You dick' – Ray Walston didn't know who Sean Penn was. So he says his line, 'I think you know where the principal's office is.' And Sean says, 'You *old, red-faced motherfucker* . . .' Ray Walston turned beet red and got crazy pissed-off, like "How dare this kid?" Linson continued, 'But Sean, even then, was trying off-camera to get a rise out of him that would be great for the moment. That's a pretty audacious move for a kid who no one had heard of yet.' *Fast Times* made Penn a renegade legend and won him instant membership in the fledgling Hollywood talentocracy known as the Brat Pack.

'Each time, Penn comes as a complete surprise,' Pauline Kael wrote in her review for this magazine of the 1983 film *Bad Boys*, in which Penn played a teenager in juvenile detention exacting revenge on another inmate. She explained, 'He gets so far inside a role that he can make even a sociological confection such as this hero . . . someone an audience can care about.' Penn often approached characters from the outside in, which was a bone of contention with his mother. When he was about to go on location as a drug dealer spying for the Soviet Union in the 1985 film *The Falcon and the Snowman*, Penn told Eileen that he would be changing his hair and teeth for the role. 'Just act the part,' she said. 'You don't need all that makeup.' Later that day, Penn called her and invited her over to his house. When she got out of the car, a man came to greet her. 'Hi, Mrs Penn,' he said. She vaguely recognized him, thinking 'he was probably some friend of Sean's from school.' "Remind me, I know you, I know you,"' she recalled saying. 'And he's walking toward me. "You're . . . Oh my God, you're my son."' He was wearing the makeup he planned to use for the part. 'Gotcha, Mom,' he said.

But it wasn't until 1988, when he was playing Eddie, the coked-out Hollywood casting agent in *Hurlyburly*, at the Westwood Playhouse, in L.A., that Penn achieved, in his eyes, a balance of discipline and expression. 'Charlie Parker – or one of those guys – once said he played an A chord for half an hour before he heard it,' he said. 'I was playing the chords of this stuff for some years, and then, within the course of that play, I heard what it was I was trying to say and why I was trying to say it.' At the intermission on opening night, the actor Robert Culp tapped Eileen on the shoulder. 'You've got a Stradivarius,' he said. The film version of *Hurlyburly* brought out all the emotional daring of Penn's technique. In it, he condensed the turbulence of his young adulthood into an almost visionary embodiment of Rabe's hilarious and horrible portrait of moral collapse. 'Twenty years ago, it was internal combustion,' Penn told me of his own life. 'There wasn't anything that resembled peace in my spirit.'

In 1996, Penn and Wright, after six years together, followed by a fraught period of separation, were married (their children were five and two). The newfound maturity of his private life has been reflected in the range and depth of his screen performances as well. Over the last decade, his restraint has become more elegant, his reservoir of feeling more profound. The breakdown of the death-row killer Matthew Poncelet, in *Dead Man Walking* (1995), and Jimmy's grief-crazed fury over the murder of his daughter, in *Mystic River* – for which Penn won an Academy Award for Best Actor in 2003 – are among the high-water marks of contemporary acting. Penn has drawn frequent comparisons to Marlon Brando, who was a friend of his. Brando, however, was never known for his light touch; Penn has one if he needs it. 'I know I haven't shared as much joy – pure joy – and humor as I might experience in life,' he said. 'I'm predisposed to hold back.' But, as he demonstrated in *Sweet and Lowdown*, his reticence can be spice to comedy. 'Sean can do lighter material,' Woody Allen says. 'He can deliver a line if he has to. He's just lucky that way.'

Penn was driving me back to San Francisco when his cell phone rang. Wright needed the car by two. 'So let's have dinner tonight,' I said. Penn mumbled something about making a start on his *Chronicle* article. 'I'll get back to you,' he said.

At around five, the hotel phone rang. 'Meet me at Tosca's at five-thirty,' Penn said. He told me that he had made a dinner reservation at a Vietnamese place near Tosca's, a nondescript saloon in North Beach, which serves Penn variously as watering hole, mail drop, and clubhouse. When I walked into the dim glow of the bar, he wasn't there. I took a stool, ordered a beer, and settled down to watch the only two other people at the bar, who were going through the rituals of a first date. After fifteen minutes or so, I asked the bartender, 'Sean been in?' 'Yeah,' he said. 'He and the boss went out for dinner.'

About half an hour later, Penn walked in with Jeanette Etheredge, Tosca's owner and den mother. 'Everybody needs a bar in their life,' Etheredge said; over the decades, hers has played a part in the carousing lives of Hunter S. Thompson, Francis Ford Coppola, Dennis Hopper, and William Kennedy, among others. Penn told Etheredge that he'd be back soon, and then, without mentioning that he'd already had dinner, he headed out with me to the Vietnamese restaurant. At Tower Valet Parking, Penn proffered some bills in the direction of the attendant. 'Don't let him pay,' another attendant shouted from across the lot, before persuading Penn to pose for a photo. As Penn finally approached his car, a tweedy middle-aged couple stood quietly on the sidewalk watching him. 'We're just ogling,' the woman said.

Over dinner, I repeated a story that his mother had told me, about talking to Woody Allen on the set of *Sweet and Lowdown*. 'Woody said he's always wanted to work with Sean but couldn't figure him out,' Eileen had said. 'I'll sum it up for you, Woody,' she replied. 'He's embarrassed at having had a happy childhood.' Speaking of his mother earlier that day, Penn had said, 'She has rewritten history quite a bit.' (In Kelly's biography, for instance, Eileen claimed to have kept watch while her eleven-year-old son surfed. Penn categorically denied this. 'At that age, the idea that your mother would stay at the beach to watch: impossible,' he said. 'It was a drop-off.' He added, 'Maybe she was taking too many chances with her kids. How did I survive?')

He was just about to comment on the story when his cell phone rang. 'I'm sorry,' he said. 'I'm on kid call.' After he hung up the phone, Penn looked down at his half-eaten appetizer; the sight of food led him to a meditation on 'the hunter-gatherer aspect of things.' 'Hunting isn't necessary in the world we're living in,' he said. 'A man can go and hunt elk if he wants. But the woman can get to the market sooner than that and bring home the food. So what's left? Violence. That's it. There's no identifiable venue for the system of alpha.' The waiter took away our plates. Penn pushed himself back on the banquette. 'I'm full,' he said. 'You want anything else?' I demurred. Penn called for the bill; he insisted on paying. It seemed that I was the venue for alpha.

Back at Tosca's, where the habitues were now three deep at the bar, arms were raised not to cheer on the Giants on the TV above the bar but to hold up cell-phone cameras as Penn made his sprightly progress to the back room. When he paused to talk to Etheredge at the end of the long bar, a young Asian man shoved a phone into his hand and asked him to speak to his father, who was celebrating his birthday. 'Your son really should watch his drinking,' Penn said into the phone. 'Happy birthday.'

The back room was as cramped and musty as a shebeen. The space was lit by a yellow neon sign that said 'Tosca' and the green glow of a shaded bulb over the pool table, which kept the denizens crowded against the walls. Film posters haphazardly plastered to the walls added to the room's subterranean panache. Penn was at home. After he'd had a couple of vodka-and-tonics, his mood lightened and his guard lowered. At one point, talking about his friendship with the magician David Blaine, Penn leaned across the table and said, 'Why are we close friends? I don't ask. I don't want to know. Love the mystery. Don't want to know why I'm here, per se, in life. Feel it, follow the feeling. But don't want the answer. Don't believe I'll get it. Don't want the safety net of 'Am I gonna have an afterlife or am I not?' He continued, 'Somebody says there's a God, I think it's a kind of funny notion. Somebody says there's not, I think it's a funny notion. To know is a funny notion. And so, you know, if I've got a religion, it's the mystery of the thing.'

After a while, Penn led me upstairs to another dingy inner sanctum, where two off-duty policemen were sitting at a bare table, discussing the recent suicide of one of their cohorts. Penn knew the men and asked if they minded our presence. They waved us in. We settled into a plywood alcove. Penn reached into his pocket and pulled out a sheaf of typed pages. 'First rough,' he said, and in hushed tones he began to read:

> Jet lag had cut me down around midnight the day of my return from Tehran. But my fractured body clock sounded its alarm at 4.30am, the following morning. I got up, went to the kitchen, flipped on the TV, and surfed my way through the channels, landing on CNN's *American Morning* with Soledad O'Brien ... She reported me to be currently in Tehran for the San Francisco *Chronicle* ... Then as footage of me from a well-meant farewell given me by the Iranian Film Society played, she observed that I looked to be playing a journalist. So here we begin, as I sit in my kitchen in northern California, she's reporting me to be in Tehran. She looks at the film given her by a producer and jumps on the bandwagon of attack ... Let's set the record straight, shall we? From the moment the international press became aware of my presence in Tehran, the predictable misreporting began deluging Web sites, newspapers, television, and radio in the United States and around the world. The inaccuracies ranged from claiming me a pro-Iranian, anti-American lefty, to a continuous and lazy presumption that my first and highly criticized trip to Iraq had been supported by the San Francisco *Chronicle* ... What's disturbing here goes to the heart of the misunderstandings throughout the world and to the heart of freedom. And the free press is only free when it is bold and accurate. And while the dismissive and trivial attacks on me may be the bickering of details, the number of dead and the purpose of war are not.

Penn read for about ten minutes, glancing up occasionally to see my reaction. After five pages, he was just about to disembark from the plane in Tehran. I suggested that perhaps he should get to Iran earlier in the piece. He nodded, but said nothing. (Stripped of some of its vainglory and verbosity, the edited version of Penn's essay became the *Chronicle's* most read story of the year, with more than half a million hits on the newspaper's website.)

Back downstairs, Penn made a beeline for Gavin Newsom, the mayor of San Francisco. He was soon in animated conversation with Newsom and his then wife, Kimberly Guilfoyle Newsom, a former lingerie model who was an anchor for Court TV. Penn, as the world knows, likes a good time; he is also expert at provoking one. When things get slow, according to Matt Palmieri, 'he'll tell a joke, sing a song, recite a limerick. His most famous thing is to get up and say, "Does anyone here want to see an interpretive dance?" Then he'll proceed to do a hilarious little dance.' There was no dancing that night, but, toward the end of the evening, there was a song. Penn smiled, drink in hand, and leaned close to me as he intoned the lyrics to one of Baerwald's compositions:

> Fifteen long years on a losing streak
> and a lot of bodies unburied
> and there comes a time
> when you cannot turn the other cheek
> you have got to ride the ferry
> past the battered old bodies of dead dead dreamers
> past the tethered and fettered and desk-bound schemers
> the punks and the drunks and the bad guitar players and the dewy-eyed teenage dragon slayers . . .
> ever hopeful and ever blue we
> do the things that we know we have to do
> and though we all know deep down in our hearts
> that someday this will all fall apart
> for right now, let's just be
> heroes.

The next time I saw Penn, he *was* a hero. It was September, and he was on my television screen, wading chest deep in a New Orleans sump, trying to reach a survivor of Hurricane Katrina. Over the next forty-eight hours, I caught fleeting sight of Penn brandishing a rifle; lugging old people out of his boat; bailing out the boat; and, later, just off the plane to San Francisco, cleaned up and remarkably composed, being interviewed by Larry King. By then, although Penn had helped to rescue about forty people, the press and the bloggers had done their sneering. 'Sean Penn, International Man of Action,' it was reported, had come to New Orleans with his 'entourage,' including a photographer; the boat he was seen bailing out was widely reported to have sunk. None of this proved to be true. When King pressed him about the story of the sunken boat, Penn responded with a bet. If the newspaper that had first reported the sinking – the Melbourne *Herald Sun* – could produce any evidence of it, he'd pay out a million dollars; if it couldn't, it should pay a million toward disaster relief for the Katrina victims. The story went away, but, as I discovered a few days later in San Francisco, Penn's irritation did not.

In jeans and a black bomber jacket, Penn was sprawled barefoot on his office sofa when I arrived, around midday. Dazed and unshaven, he looked rough. Bottles of vodka and red wine were open on the coffee table beside him. Before we talked, he insisted that I read something he'd written for *Rolling Stone*. 'Watching the scenes of devastation on my television set was like standing behind the tapeline at a traffic accident and watching a child slowly bleed to death unattended,' it began. 'I'm not gonna tell you I wasn't very, very pissed off,' he said about the press coverage of his rescue mission. 'The whole reason I didn't go sooner was that I worried I'd be in the way. I was not in the way. Listen, most of the rescues were done by civilians.' He added, 'It's so disheartening that people are diabolically detached.'

As the hurricane was unfolding, Penn, who had spent some time in New Orleans (and has 'NOLA Deliver Me' tattooed on his right forearm to prove it), stayed in regular contact with the political pundit James Carville, who is also one of the executive producers of *All the King's Men*, part of which was shot in New Orleans. At first, Penn was assured that everything that could be done was being done; then the Superdome lost its roof, and it became clear that the city was imploding. 'Carville at a certain point said, "Fuck it, do what you think,"' Penn said. He told his family he was going to the Astrodome in Houston and maybe to Baton Rouge. 'I didn't tell them I was going to New Orleans. I didn't know I was gonna get in but I had a feeling.' He also organized a small jet to fly to Baton Rouge with supplies: water, bug spray, athlete's-foot spray – 'a lot of people who'd come out had wet feet' – Gatorade, Balance Bars.

As Penn told his story, he still seemed to be trying to make sense of the experience; words tumbled out of him in a sort of Cubist report of fractured time and vivid details: the prop plane he took from Houston to Baton Rouge; the police car that carried him into New Orleans; the surreal darkness of the city; the empty streets; finding a boat; the adrenaline, the bewilderment ('You kept thinking, like you did watching television, Any minute now the cavalry's coming'). A preacher called Willie from Noah's Ark church, who knew of forty kids trapped in a school, became the navigator on Penn's boat while Penn manned the bow, watching for submerged cars. It was a beautiful day; the water was black. Bloated bodies floated by 'all in the same position: facedown, spread-eagled.' People waded through water, foraging. 'One guy had a big ham.' Penn, who had been vaccinated for infectious diseases for an African safari earlier in the year, had no problem spending nine hours in the contaminated swamp. 'I saw three non-civilian boats,' he said. 'What was surreal was the lack of presence of official people – the National Guard, the United States Army, the state, the New Orleans Police Department. There just weren't nearly enough of them.'

Penn didn't stop to draw breath. He recalled a two-story building that had lost its entire front wall. 'You were looking right into people's bedrooms,' he said. 'And, upstairs, in his boxer shorts, was this Middle Eastern guy with a shotgun and with Islamic symbols painted on the walls. He didn't want anything to do with us.' Penn took a drag on his cigarette. He recalled a schizophrenic woman who had been days without her medicine, chest deep in water, groping toward a helicopter as it descended noisily toward her. 'We were yelling at her to turn and come to us,' he said. 'She didn't hear us. Shingles flew off roofs and all that kind of shit. The water was like an ocean. I turned my back because the water was kicking the hell out of us. Somebody starts screaming. I turned around and she's gone underwater because of all this turbulence. That's when I ended up in the water. We got her. We got a few others on that run.'

At the end of the day on the water, Penn returned to a landing area in the Garden District where he and his friends had ferried the people they'd rescued. All of them were still waiting at the water's edge. 'Nobody was there for decontamination, nobody was there for medical relief, nobody was there to transfer these people out of there,' Penn said. He spent the rest of the night shuttling the rescued victims to a clinic. Now that the situation in New Orleans was no longer about emergency response, Penn declared himself 'a little depressed about it.' He said, 'When it was about pulling people out of water, that's a no-brainer.' But 'where do they go? How do you feed them? How do you get them to start their own lives back up again? How do you figure out who's the child molester? Now I'm as confused as the government about what to do.' He said, 'I struggle with the notion that my mind doesn't go far enough. I'm always frustrated by intellectual restrictions. My frustration's with my brain, not with my heart. My heart's clear. I don't have a problem there.'

Whether by accident or by design, Penn has cast himself on the world stage as a sort of one-man Citizen Watch. In his interview with Larry King, Penn had pulled his punches about President Bush and his late response to Katrina – 'Clearly there's a lot of political issues that are surrounding this that'll come out in the wash' was his only rueful comment. Nonetheless, over the years he has consistently sought to get right up under Bush's chin. For his pieces in the *Chronicle*, Penn tried, and failed, to interview the President; in the run-up to the invasion of Iraq, he famously paid fifty-six thousand dollars to publish an open letter to Bush on a nearly full page of the *Washington Post*. 'Many of your actions to date and those proposed seem to violate every defining principle of this country over which you preside: intolerance of debate . . . marginalization of your critics, the promoting of fear through unsubstantiated rhetoric, manipulation of a quick comfort media, and the position of your administration's deconstruction of civil liberties all contradict the very core of the patriotism you claim,' he wrote.

In the same letter, Penn invoked his father ('He raised me with a deep belief in the Constitution and the Bill of Rights'). 'My dad was a hero to all of us,' Chris Penn told me. 'I think it's easy to say that Sean wants to be a hero. I see what he does around the world, and, you know, I think that his heart's always in the right place. And is some of it wanting to have a little credit as a hero? Maybe. I think there's also a kind of innocence, which my father to a degree had. I think I'm a little too cynical. Most heroes get killed.' Baerwald agreed. 'I think there's a part of Sean that isn't gonna be happy until he gets murdered by the Republican noise machine,' he said.' 'Until he finds out what it's like to feel like his dad.'

Penn took me downstairs to the kitchen, where Hopper was studying an earth-science textbook at the vast blondwood kitchen counter, waiting for his father to check his homework. 'Give me a few minutes,' Penn told Hopper. Turning back to me, he said under his breath, 'I used to hate doing homework.' He poured some Cracker Jacks into a bowl and led me out of ear shot, to a patio overlooking a walled garden and the pool. 'I'm under investigation by the Office of Foreign Assets Control, the Treasury Department,' he said. 'It's a five-year investigation. Did I violate the embargo by going to Iraq under Hussein? Did I spend money? Did I use my American passport to get there? All those things. The answer to those questions is no.' He added, 'We know it came from the White House. My lawyer in Washington knows that.' Penn has been told by friends in the L.A.P.D. that he is under surveillance.

On the way out, Penn had paused at a side table. 'There's a cool picture of my dad here,' he said. 'That's him directing.' In the photograph, a viewfinder was hanging around Leo Penn's neck; his jaw was tight and his chin assertively thrust forward. We stood together for a moment scrutinizing the image of command, and I thought of something that Penn had told me earlier in the day. 'My dad loved humans and humanity,' he'd said. 'I'm good on humanity.'

The Sphinx Next Door

The Julianne Moore Paradox

One day in mid-March, with patches of snow still mottling Brooklyn's side streets, I went to meet Julianne Moore on the set of *Maggie's Plan*, a comedy written and directed by Rebecca Miller, in a town house on Vanderbilt Avenue. Arriving exactly on time for the 8am call, I picked my way past gaffers and gofers slouched on the stoop, working their phones and sucking on their morning Starbucks. Inside, Moore was already shooting a scene in the farmhouse kitchen, which was sealed from view by a wall of cables, cameras, and technicians. In the crepuscular hubbub, Rachael Horovitz, one of the film's producers, introduced herself and ushered me downstairs to a basement bedroom, where the production team was hunched around a video monitor wedged among ballet trophies, karate belts, and a turquoise-and-pink four-poster canopy bed.

Three weeks earlier, Moore had won an Academy Award for her performance in *Still Alice*, a movie about a high-flying middle-aged linguistics professor who is in the process of losing her memory. In *Maggie's Plan*, which premièred this month at the Toronto International Film Festival, she was playing Georgette, a high-flying middle-aged anthropology professor who is in the process of losing her family. On the monitor, Moore and Ethan Hawke, as Georgette's husband, John, an adjunct professor of 'ficto-critical anthropology' at the New School ('Nobody unpacks commodity fetishism like you do,' Georgette tells him at one point), were serving up dinner to their two children: Justine (Mina Sundwall), a bumptious thirteen-year-old, and Paul (Jackson Frazer), a dreamy seven-year-old. This very contemporary family tableau – all four were conversing while working their digital devices – was interrupted by a call offering Georgette a department chairmanship at Columbia. 'When am I ever going to get any writing done?' Georgette asked her husband. 'Look – I'm already breaking out in a rash.' The line wasn't surprising, but Moore's pitch-perfect accent – Georgette is Danish – was.

'You want to call Caleb to discuss the pros and cons of taking the chairmanship,' John said. 'Justine wants to finish texting her friend. Am I right? Paul would love to play Ninja Revinja on the iPad. And, believe it or not, I even have a minor text I'd like to write myself. What do you say we all stop pretending to have this close-knit family dinner and be honest for five minutes? Then we can go back to the bullshit.' The scene, it turned out, was the movie's inciting incident, which would send Georgette on a new career path and John on a new romantic path.

The choreography of ordinariness requires time as well as timing. The scene was played, stopped, then played again, until even the onlookers had memorized the lines, the moves, and the delivery, which got tighter with each take. When Miller stepped into the scene to discuss adjustments with the actors, the sound on the video monitor went suddenly mute, taking away any prospect of overhearing Moore's thoughts. As the shoot wore on, a sort of soporific haze settled over the spectators; around midday, I momentarily lost track of Moore on the monitor. As I tried to locate her, there was a rustling on the stairs leading to the production office. When I looked up, Moore was making her way toward me, her thick red hair knotted into a high bun that flapped like a squirrel's tail. She thrust her cheek forward to be kissed. 'You're here. How are you? So nice to see you,' she said. It was the first time we'd laid eyes on each other.

Although Moore, at fifty-four, is a current face of L'Oréal, she is no conventional glamour-puss. Hiding in plain sight is how she tries to negotiate her public life. 'I try to make myself small,' she told me. 'I try not to call attention to myself.' The novelist Michael Cunningham remembers going out for a coffee with Moore, who had starred in the 2002 Stephen Daldry movie based on his novel *The Hours*. As they stepped outside, he noticed that she changed. 'You just did something, didn't you?' he asked. 'She said, "No." I said, "You retracted your beauty, didn't you?" She said, "Oh, yeah, kind of,"' Cunningham said. 'She pulled something in. There was a glow that she'd emanated in the living room that she could retract in the street.'

Moore may have a star on the Hollywood Walk of Fame, but she exhibits none of the imperialism of celebrity; she has no desire to make a spectacle of her separation from others. 'I don't understand why that would serve you as a person or as an actor,' she said. She is contained but not reserved; her good manners are a form of non-friction, intended to pre-empt envy while inviting contact. 'I don't like playing antagonism,' Moore said to Miller, after shooting a scene in which she had to be aggressive with the title character, Maggie (Greta Gerwig), a marital carpetbagger.

'I feel I'm really like a Labrador – "I mean no harm. I mean no harm,"' she told me. 'I lead with friendliness. I feel that works for me. I don't want to be aggressive. I don't want to push to be in a dominant situation.' At the same time, she doesn't retreat into herself. She's present. She listens. 'She works by being completely open to what's outside her,' Miller said. 'When she's with another actor, she's not closing him off so she can listen to what's going on inside herself. She's actually awake.'

As Moore stood chatting in the cramped production office – about Uber, the death of Mike Nichols, Wallace Shawn, who was returning from a vacation in Spain to be in the film – the conversation turned to the Birkenstock sandals she was wearing. Horovitz professed to being a fan of that particular style. 'What size are your feet?' Moore asked. 'These probably would fit you. You could take these. I have a pair at home. So – you take these.' After some back-and-forth, Horovitz accepted Moore's shoes. Before handing them over, Moore took out her phone to show off the profile picture for her Twitter account (she has more than six hundred and forty thousand followers): an image of her Birkenstock-sandalled feet.

Then she turned abruptly to the video monitor. 'I'm just going to look at playback on the scene to get an idea of this thing we just shot,' she said. With a fierce, unsmiling focus she scrutinized the screen, like a pitcher watching for the catcher's sign. After a while, she pivoted away from the monitor. 'I just wanted to see the rhythm,' she said. 'It's O.K. It'll be better when it's cut.' The scene was over, and so was Moore's day. She was off to take her then twelve-year-old daughter, Liv, to the orthodontist. (She also has a seventeen-year-old son, Caleb.)

After she left, the video-playback operator, Max Frankston,

explained that I had witnessed something that was essential to Moore's process. 'Independent films are shot like television shows, with just a live monitor,' he said. But, for this shoot, Moore had requested the playback operator: she preferred watching video playback in the moment to sitting through dailies at the end of the day. 'I feel like then you can do something about it,' she told me later. 'At that time, I can figure it out. Dailies? Who cares. I've done it.'

Moore has a visual imagination as well as a mimetic one. It's important for her to see herself not just in the role but also in the frame. 'Acting is not all about feeling,' she said. 'It's not all about what's on the inside. There's a physicality to what the frame is. Sometimes you want to see what story it's telling.' Moore's performances, at once penetrating and succinct, come from a calibration of the character with the scale and proportion of what the camera is showing. Not long into the shoot of David Cronenberg's *Maps to the Stars* (2014), a coruscating satire about Hollywood, in which Moore played Havana Segrand, a movie star persecuted by memories of her legendary actress mother – a bravura performance, which won her the Best Actress Award at Cannes – Moore approached Cronenberg. 'I love how you're isolating us in the frame,' Cronenberg recalled her telling him. 'It really works for suggesting that all these characters are in a kind of isolated bubble and are so self-obsessed.' 'It was nothing that I'd talked to her about,' he said. 'She could just see that I wasn't doing over-the-shoulder shots. Everybody was isolated in their closeup. She saw that immediately, knew what it meant, knew why I was doing it. She's totally aware of everything.'

★

Moore may be aware of everything that happens in the process of filmmaking, but she prefers to keep her own process a mystery. When, for instance, Cronenberg offered to show me her e-mails about her role in *Maps to the Stars*, she asked him not to. 'Much of it was about the ins and outs of physical stuff... whether or not I should dye my hair blond, or if the production had enough money to make a wig, etc. etc.,' she e-mailed me. 'I just felt that the exchange demystifies the process a little.'

Moore doesn't like to rehearse. She wants to be taken by surprise, and feels that repetition can deaden the experience. 'She is protecting something extremely vital and untamed that she can unleash on camera,' Todd Haynes, in whose films *Safe* (1995) and *Far from Heaven* (2002) Moore has given two of her greatest performances, said. 'She doesn't want to overthink, overplan, overanticipate.' 'I prepare very stringently,' Moore told me. 'I really know my lines. I really think about what I'm gonna do. Sometimes people think that means I've already played the part in my head. That's not true. I know the parameters. Then, when the camera goes on, I'm ready to have an experience. I don't want it to happen in my living room. I want it to happen on camera.'

A character exists for Moore only once she exists on paper. 'I hate it when people pitch stuff,' she said. 'That doesn't help me. Let me see the words.' According to Bruce Wagner, who wrote the screenplay for *Maps to the Stars*, Moore, who never reads stage directions, is 'a brutal parser of the text.' To generate emotion, she doesn't call on sense memory from her own life, as actors are often taught to do; instead, she immerses herself in the circumstances of the character. 'I have to find the place where the character cries; I have to find the place where she's hurt,' Moore said. ('Julianne Moore Loves to Cry,' a three-minute

YouTube montage from twenty of her films, bears lachrymose witness to her claim.)

Even in the most fraught scenes, Moore's work is highly technical. 'There's nothing more awkward than scenes that deal with sexuality,' Hawke said. 'Because if you have a fight scene you have a choreographer come in and do it. But if people want sexuality they're just, like, 'O.K., let the actors go,' like you're wild animals that are supposed to just do this stuff on call. And it's very difficult to do anything that has feeling to it that reads on camera.' But, for a sex scene in *Maggie's Plan*, he said, 'Julie had a distinct sense of "This needs to be a two-shot, this needs to be a single. It cuts here." She had very specific demands about where the scene ended and where it would begin. And "No, that's not sexy, that's not funny. That's gross." And she was dead right. And what is normally difficult became really, really easy. There's a math to everything we do, to how emotions read, and she's acutely aware of it.'

Moore is fond of quoting Flaubert's dictum 'Be regular and orderly in your life, so that you may be violent and original in your work.' And she insists on that regularity. 'I'm incredibly bourgeois,' she said. 'And I don't care. I'm not wild. There's nothing outrageous about me. I'm really a pretty nice person. I am not erratic in my behavior. You know the kind of people who are really irregular – they keep people off balance that way. I'm not that kind of person.' 'Julie's great adventure is her imagination,' her younger brother, the novelist Peter Smith, said. (Moore was born Julie Anne Smith; Anne is her mother's name, and Moore is her father's middle name.) 'She understands the force and wildness of it. It's a blessing and a warning. It's this big crazy thing. It's something that makes her feel really confident.'

In a children's book that Moore wrote in 2009, *Freckleface*

Strawberry and the Dodgeball Bully (one of a trio of Freckleface tales, which have sold more than a hundred and fifty thousand copies in eight languages), her freckled young alter ego 'practices her monster,' a shadowy, horned, benign purple giant that is visible only to her and gives her the power to defeat whatever is weighing her down. Moore also created two Freckleface Strawberry apps, which teach children how to take control of their imagination – how to give their inner monsters shape, color, and sound. She can be similarly controlling with her own creativity. For instance, when she was filming *The Myth of Fingerprints* (1997), a movie about a dysfunctional New England family's Thanksgiving gathering, the twenty-six-year-old director, Bart Freundlich, who had also written the screenplay, made the rookie mistake of trying to block a scene by telling Moore, then thirty-five, her motivation for the action. 'I'll move over there,' she snapped. 'But don't tell me why.' ('The director can tell you that you do it. Your job is to figure out *how* to do it,' she said to me.)

In time, Freundlich not only came to understand Moore's protective ferocity; he married her. 'She's one of those people for whom the portal to up there is open, so you guard it the same way you would guard your family, by being very careful with your boundaries,' Freundlich told me. 'I pictured it like a pilot light – this little flame that's inside her. If she doesn't let it get blown out by all the talking and ideas that get expressed on a set, then she can ignite it at any time. Her No. 1 job is to protect that, even if it means being prickly with you as a director.' Mark Ruffalo, who co-starred with Moore in *The Kids Are All Right* (2010), described her acting as 'one hand in a boxing glove and the other in an elbow-high velvet glove.' He added, 'She has something pretty damn fierce about her, forward-leaning and aggressive. At the same time, she is filled with exquisite poise.'

Even to her fellow-actors, the emotional volte-face between Moore's off-screen ordinariness and her onscreen extraordinariness can be confounding. 'She comes from a military background,' Wallace Shawn, who co-starred with her in Louis Malle's 1994 film *Vanya on 42nd Street*, said. 'She takes a military approach to her very unusual job. Her orders are to turn into a complete maniac on Tuesday at three o'clock in the afternoon. And so she guiltlessly does that.' André Gregory directed her in the intermittent five-year workshop of Chekhov's *Uncle Vanya* that led to the Malle film. 'What I loved – and what was even intimidating at times – is that she's like a roller coaster,' he said. 'She's talking about something like decorating at rehearsal in one moment. The next moment, she's careening into some territory you've never seen before. It's not that she acts the beast, but she has access to it.' 'The nicest thing André ever said about me was "She's Beauty *and* the Beast,"' Moore told me. 'I like the idea that nobody's one or the other. You can be the regular girl and you can be the monster at the same time. They're one and the same. The beast doesn't have to be an evil or a destructive thing. It's about possibility and feeling and emotion and all of that stuff.'

That duality is actually built into Moore's face. 'She's more angular from the profile and softer from the full on,' Cronenberg said. 'So, just by turning her head, she can go from hard to soft. She knows how to use that, too.' Although Moore can be physically transformed – as she was by her red bob wig in *The Big Lebowski* (1998) and by a blond one in *Far from Heaven* – most of her shape-shifting is emotional. Watch her in Paul Thomas Anderson's *Magnolia* (1999), as Linda, the faithless, drug-addicted wife of a dying husband whom she's come to love. As Linda waits at a pharmacy for the prescription with which she intends to kill herself, the young pharmacist prattles on, 'What exactly you have wrong, you need all this stuff?' Moore's face goes from cold to stormy. '*You motherfucker! You motherfucker! You fucking asshole! Who the fuck are you? Who the fuck do you think you are?*' she snarls. 'Where is your fucking decency? And then I'm asked fucking questions . . . *what's wrong?* You suck my dick, that's what's wrong, and you, you fucking call me "lady." *Shame on you! Shame on you!*' This blistering moment, in which Linda forces her own shame onto someone else, shows Moore's almost extrasensory balance between intensity and restraint. In a scene in *The Hours*, in which she plays a suicidal housewife named Laura Brown, Laura is in the bathroom, fighting a harrowing battle with her desperation. Her credulous husband (John C. Reilly) calls to her, asking her to come to bed. 'I'm brushing my teeth,' she says chirpily, pretending normality. When her husband asks again, 'Are you coming?' a mask of resignation falls over her face and freezes there. In a barely audible voice, she forms the word 'Yes.'

Moore doesn't consider herself a theatre actress. To her, the stage experience feels too 'externalized,' and she wants what she's doing to be internal. 'I like to pretend no one's watching,' she said. 'The thing that was so wonderful for me about film acting, when I finally discovered it, was that it felt like walking into a book you wanted to be in.' For Moore, learning to read was a watershed event: she was six and sitting in a wing chair in her family's living room, in Omaha, Nebraska, with her red-haired Scottish-born mother, whom she strongly resembles, when she read her first sentence. 'And then I just read,' she said. 'I read everything. I read whatever I could get my hands on.'

Moore's parents, according to her, 'liked the life of the mind' and preached the gospel of education. They were aspirational, the first in each of their families to earn a university degree. Anne Love, who had emigrated with her family from Greenock, Scotland, at the age of ten, was twelve when she met Peter Moore Smith, at their Presbyterian church in Burlington, New Jersey; they married when she was nineteen and he was twenty. By the time Anne was twenty-five, she had had three children – Julie was the first – whom she struggled to care for alone while Peter was on a tour of duty in Vietnam.

The Smith family was a tight unit, because it had to be. In the course of Moore's childhood, they moved twenty times – North Carolina, Nebraska, Virginia, Alabama, Panama, Alaska, Georgia, Texas, New York, Washington, Germany – following the trajectory of her father's career, as he transitioned from Army helicopter pilot and paratrooper in the 182nd Airborne Division (he won a Purple Heart for his service in Vietnam) to lawyer and, finally, to judge on the U.S. Court of Appeals for the Armed Forces at the Pentagon. Moore attended nine different schools. (She recently started a petition to have her Virginia high school – which was named for a Confederate general – renamed for the Supreme Court Justice Thurgood Marshall.) But every week, no matter where they were, Anne took her brood to the library to check out books; in the shifting ground of their peripatetic life, literature was a comfort. 'We were moving all the time. I had a lot to adjust to,' Moore said. 'But you pick up a book, and you know you're going to get a story. You know how it's going to make you feel. The constancy of storytelling is a great thing.'

The continual uprooting made Moore adaptable and as adept at reading people as she was at reading words. When starting at a new school, she said, she studied the social behavior of those around her. 'I didn't want to distinguish myself. My interest was in fitting in – seeing how do they walk, how do they talk, what do they do, what are the rules here?' In her narrative of growing up, Moore accentuates her nerdiness: she was bad at sports, a failed cheerleader, a drill-team reject, a smart kid in glasses, and so on. 'All actresses love that outsider thing,' her brother said, laughing. 'She was Homecoming Queen. She was beautiful. She was a straight-A student. She was popular.' ('I wasn't Homecoming Queen. I was runner-up,' Moore insisted.) One thing, however, was incontrovertible: from sixth grade on, she was the star of all her school plays.

By the time Moore decided to become a professional actress, at eighteen, her mother, who had briefly trained as a nurse before marriage, had finally managed to cobble together a degree in social work. (When she graduated from Briarcliff College, in New York, she was the only summa cum laude in her class.) Anne went on to get master's degrees in psychology and social work. Despite her late-blooming achievements, the years she spent following behind her husband's career inevitably generated in her a sense of disappointment, a dissatisfaction that rumbled under the surface of the marriage. 'My mother felt thwarted by the world and oppressed, rightly,' Peter Smith said. 'She had ambitions that she was never able to realize. She communicated powerfully to both my sisters that in order for them to achieve success they had to be better than anybody. They couldn't just be good. They had to be excellent.' The children grew up in this ozone of expectation. (Moore's sister, Valerie Wells, is now a business executive.) 'She didn't want us to marry or have children young,' Moore said. 'She wanted us to have an education and a career.' Still, the news of Moore's career choice was about as welcome to her mother as a returning kamikaze pilot. 'Oh, Julie,' she said. 'Why waste your brain?'

'I think it was a surprise even to me that I became an actor,' Moore said. When she made her decision, she had never met an actor or seen a professional play. 'I liked television and movies, but I didn't even know there was an industry,' she said. The person who planted the notion that Moore could act for a living was Robie Taylor, her theatre teacher at Frankfurt American High School, in Germany, from 1977 to 1979. Moore was a junior when Taylor first saw her perform.' She opened her mouth in her first solo, and it was kind of primitive but it was there,' Taylor said. 'She was just so stable within herself. She could walk into a room, assess what was going on, and move right in. She knew who she was.' In her senior year, Moore went to Taylor's classroom to ask for career advice. 'I said, "Julie, you're bullet-proof,"' Taylor recalled. '"You can accept rejection and keep going. You need to go to New York, check into the Y, find a job that you can work at night, and audition all day."' A few days later, according to Taylor, there was another knock on the classroom door: this time, it was Moore's parents. 'They were aghast. "She can't do that – she's got to go to college." I said, 'Julie has the talent. It's ready to go. If you make her go to college, you will put her five years behind her peers."' The compromise that the family worked out was that Moore would apply to drama schools that also offered a liberal-arts degree, so that if she washed out as an actress she'd have the credentials for graduate school. 'My mother got on the plane with me, and I auditioned for three different schools,' Moore said. In the end, she chose Boston University, where she knew no one. In the next four years, she returned to Germany and her family only twice. 'Our parents referred to it as "when Julie ran away from home,"' Moore's sister, Valerie, said.

★

After graduating, in 1983, Moore moved to New York, where she waited tables – 'I was an excellent waitress. I'm very impatient with people who tell me they're not good at waiting tables. I'm, like, "Well, you're just not paying attention"' – and began her single-minded pursuit of her craft. In 1985, after some work in regional theatre, she landed a regular role as Frannie Hughes, and then as her evil half sister, Sabrina, on the CBS soap opera *As the World Turns*. (She won a Daytime Emmy Award for Outstanding Ingénue in 1988, the year she left the show.) Although Moore puts a happy face on this journeyman period of her professional life, 'she hated soap operas,' according to the actor Larry Pine, who worked with her on *As the World Turns*.

Moore began to understand what it meant to inhabit a character when she joined André Gregory's workshop for *Uncle Vanya*, in 1990. Tipped off by Pine, who had already been enlisted for the workshop, Gregory and Wallace Shawn went to see Moore in a production of Caryl Churchill's double bill *Ice Cream with Hot Fudge*, at the Public Theatre. 'There was one moment in her performance that was absolutely staggering,' Gregory recalled. 'She was sitting on the floor reading a newspaper and doing absolutely nothing, saying nothing. But whatever she had going on inside was terrifying.' Afterward, Gregory took her to dinner. He asked her, 'Could you tell me what you were doing when you were sitting on the floor?' She said, 'I was counting from one to sixty.' Gregory said, 'It showed a very clever actress who understood what she didn't need to do to get the appropriate response.'

'I owe a huge debt to André, because that painstaking five-year process changed how I thought about acting and what I wanted to do,' Moore said. 'He encouraged us to play each moment for action and reaction, to literally respond to what an actor gave. He allowed me for the first time as an actor not to be result-oriented. What is in front of me? What is happening? What could happen? What is different?' 'I think Julie learned over time not how to act but how to *be*,' Gregory said. He added, 'For two or three weeks, in rehearsals you could not hear a single word that she said. She was just mumbling. Or whispering. And actors would come to me on the side and say, 'I don't know what to do, because I can't hear her, so I don't know when to give my cue.' And I, being the weird director I am, said, "Just let her do it." And I think what she was doing was creating the introvert. In a very subtle way.'

Moore's focus on her fellow-actors' performances could be intimidating. 'She's like a tomb of truth. You can't fool her in any way,' Pine, who played Astrov to Moore's unhappily married Yelena, said. 'You had to be truthful before she would respond. She'd just turn off. She would emotionally go away.' He went on, 'She reads you when you're coming at her. She looks at you and decides whether she cares or not. She has a magical quality, very slippery. You can't be crude.' In one rehearsal of the scene in which Astrov tries to seduce Yelena and she fends him off, Moore 'got so fed up with Larry – he's the archetypal male chauvinist pig – that she leaned back against the wall, thrust her pelvis forward, and did the scene physically demonstrating "You want to fuck me? Go ahead,"' Gregory recalled. 'I loved it. I thought it was great. She thought it was vulgar and would never do it again. It broke my heart. Every time I see the movie, I go to the bathroom. I can't watch it. I know what I lost.'

In 1991, Gregory staged the play for invited audiences at the dilapidated Victory Theatre (where I saw it). On one of those evenings, the director Robert Altman, who was in the audience, decided that Moore was right for a part in his movie *Short Cuts*, which was inspired by Raymond Carver's short stories. 'I called her,' Altman said in a 2004 Directors Guild interview. 'I said, "Listen, Julianne, I've got a part, but before I even discuss it with you ... I have to tell you this character has to play a scene – about a five-minute scene – naked from the waist down with her husband. It's not a sex scene, it's not about sex, but she has to be there naked."' Altman went on, 'There was a little pause. She said, "I can do that." I said, "Great. I'll send you the script, and see if you like it." She said, "Bob ... I have a bonus for you – I really am a redhead."' (Moore denies having said this.) The role was one of many that she was called 'brave' for taking on, a notion she disputes. 'To say that you're "brave" connotes that you're afraid,' she said. 'I'm not afraid of anything that's imaginary. There's almost nothing I wouldn't do while acting, because it's pretend. It's narrative.'

Short Cuts (1993) was the first of a trio of outstanding Julianne Moore performances that were released within twenty months of one another in the mid-nineties. 'I went from somebody no one knew about to this new hot thing,' Moore said. *Short Cuts* made a spectacle of Moore's daring, *Vanya on 42nd Street* showcased her plangency, but the masterly *Safe* (1995), Moore's first leading role, revealed her potential for greatness. The movie, written and directed by Todd Haynes, tells the story of Carol White, a woman struggling with a mysterious disease that makes her allergic to her environment; she retreats, by degrees, to a New Age desert community of the afflicted. A brilliant study of negativity, Carol is the Bartleby of American cinema. When Moore was shown the script for *Safe* (Haynes had admired her work in *Short Cuts*), she said, 'I was, like, "Holy cow, what is this? Who is this guy? Isn't this cast?" I felt very strongly about how it should be played. How she should sound. I could hear it.' She paid her own way back to New York from Pittsburgh, where she was filming a Peter Yates comedy, *Roommates*, to try out for Haynes.

She auditioned in white jeans and a white T-shirt, with her hair tied back, because, Moore said, Carol is 'someone who won't even take up space.' She also found a register in her voice, high in the diaphragm, basically cut off from the throat. The sound had no desire in it; the words were spoken with an uplift that turned everything into a question. 'I would talk on the top of my vocal cords, so I never made any contact with the bottom of my voice, my body, at all,' Moore said. 'This is someone who is completely out of her body. Someone who is not present, who has this lack of connection to everything.'

Safe was the first demonstration of Moore's sensational ability to vacate herself on camera. 'Julianne knows how to stop signifying, how to let the viewer fill in,' Haynes said. 'There are times when she's almost blank.' In one scene, for instance, Carol stands in her kitchen drinking milk, which has become an addictive antidote to her symptoms of environmental sensitivity. The camera's shifting perspective is meant to suggest Carol's unsettling discomfort, but Moore refuses to editorialize her character's feelings. As she swallows, she stares at the lens for some time, almost without moving. Her ability to do nothing unleashes something active in the audience; her profound emptiness takes on the force of a body blow. At the finale, coaxed by the community to speak at her birthday party, Carol delivers a halting soliloquy that is by turns awful and heartbreaking. 'I don't know what I'm saying, just . . . it's true how much I . . . hated myself before I – came here, so

I'm … trying to … see myself hopefully more as I am,' she says, struggling to find breath. The very act of speaking is, for Carol, a masquerade. She cannot pronounce a self because her vocabulary has no purchase on her feelings.

Safe set the pattern for Moore's adventurous, intelligent choice of scripts. With the exception of a few Hollywood moneymakers – *Jurassic Park*, *Hannibal*, *The Hunger Games: Mockingjay* – over the years Moore has followed her instinct for strong writing and emotional complexity. She has mostly resisted positive, triumphant representations of women in order to take on roles whose ambivalence and ambiguity stroke neither her audience nor her image. 'She somehow understood that she wasn't going to be an emblem of good values,' Haynes said. He wrote *Far from Heaven* – which tells the story of a fifties housewife who strays from her bisexual husband into an affair with the black gardener – specifically for her. In Paul Thomas Anderson's *Boogie Nights* (1997), Moore plays Amber Waves, a drug-addicted porn star who loses custody of her child ('Just cum on my tits if you can,' she tells Dirk Diggler sweetly, at their first shoot); in *Savage Grace* (2007), directed by Tom Kalin, she's the alcoholic sociopath Barbara Baekeland, the Bakelite plastics heiress, who beds her schizophrenic son only to be murdered by him. The appeal of playing Sarah Palin, in the 2012 HBO movie *Game Change*, Moore said, was 'the perfect storm' of Palin's paradoxical personality: 'confidence and lack of information.' For the role, Moore went beyond the kind of mimicry that Tina Fey practiced in her scathing lampoon, capturing both Palin's comedy and her pathos (and winning an Emmy in the process). Moore said, of acting, 'It's my responsibility to find the place where I connect with that person. What is most human, what is most extreme in human behavior, is interesting to me. I like to mentally explore that.'

On the drab West Village block where Moore lives, her house – a Greek revival town house built in 1839, which Moore and her husband bought in 2003 and restored over eighteen months – is the only one with welcoming plants outside. As you enter, the first image that meets the eye is Thomas Struth's 'Paradise,' an enormous photograph of dense jungle foliage: an immanence of Moore's wild imagination. But beyond that – in a flower-filled high-ceilinged living area with art-covered walls, and an adjacent, superbly appointed kitchen dominated by three large tortoise shells on a wall – order rules. (Moore, who has a way of being soft and tough at the same time, has a particular fascination with turtles and tortoises. 'I do believe that there's a correlation to be drawn there, between that shell protecting something that otherwise would be totally unprotected and what I refer to as her fiercely protective exterior,' Freundlich told me.)

Moore is, according to her brother, 'absolutely neurotic about cleaning.' The fastidiousness, she explained, 'gives me a kind of mental clarity. If I'm trying to think, and I have all this stuff in front of me, visually, it's confusing to me. I can't stand it. I can't bear it,' she said. 'If something doesn't look right, it makes me uncomfortable.' 'She personally dragged a Chinese trunk that was my grandmother's out of my living room and told me I couldn't have it in there,' Evelyn O'Neill, her manager of twenty-five years, told me.

As Moore sat at her kitchen table, drinking a green health concoction, Freundlich, a rangy, good-looking man with a beard, a full head of brindled hair, and an easy smile, appeared at the threshold of the dining room. He was wearing long black-and-silver basketball shorts and carrying a knee brace. 'This is my husband,' Moore said. Until her mid-thirties, when she and Freundlich got together, Moore said, she did not have 'a personal life.' 'I was a worrier, someone who was always trying to get somewhere,' she said. At twenty-three, she met the actor-director John Gould Rubin, and they married two years later; it was an unhappy alliance that lasted nine years. 'I didn't know what I was doing,' Moore said. 'I was lonely. My family was still in Germany. I think I really wanted a base.' Freundlich was her luck.

She was an hour late when she rushed in for her first production meeting for *The Myth of Fingerprints*, in 1995. 'I was looking for someone who had a lot of complication, a lot of sadness under the surface, and betrayed very, very little of it in her face,' Freundlich said. Near the end of the meeting, Moore asked him why he wanted to cast her. 'Because you look completely different when you smile. I want that duality of character,' he said. 'I was, like, Huh! He's a pretty insightful guy,' Moore said, adding, 'That was probably the beginning.'

Freundlich recalled a moment, at the end of the first week of shooting *Fingerprints*, when Moore was standing outside without a coat in the Maine chill. 'I came up to her and stood with my back to the wind. I didn't want her to be cold, and I also didn't want to put my arm around her, or smother her, because I didn't know her that well,' he said. 'Even though I couldn't have articulated it then, I understood that I could keep her warm up to a point. But then the rest was going to be for her to do. We connected in that moment on an unspoken level, where she knew

I saw that flame in her, and understood it, and was willing not to suffocate it but to protect it.'

Freundlich was a week away from shooting his latest script, *Wolves*, a Lower East Side coming-of-age story involving basketball, which he himself has played a couple of times a week for the past fifteen years. At Knicks games, to which the couple have season tickets, Moore suffers courtside with Freundlich. ('I have a chronic belief that each year will be better,' he said. 'I think this'll be the last year.') 'I like basketball because I like to watch the faces,' Moore told me. At one point in the conversation, she led me into the living room to show off a large framed black-and-white photograph of the Knicks by George Kalinsky, the official photographer of Madison Square Garden, which she'd given to Freundlich for his birthday. 'And this is Willis, what's his name?' Moore said, calling back to Freundlich, who was making a smoothie. 'They're about to win the championship. This is a famous moment in Knicks history. What's the name of this guy? The one I got you. Willie?'

'That's Willis Reed,' Freundlich said. He added, 'Those were the days when they wore long pants.' It was Freundlich's wry way of telling his wife that in the photo the Knicks were still warming up and were not yet playing a game. Over the years, Freundlich's jokey approach to life seems to have relaxed Moore and made her more humorous herself. 'She had that in her,' he said. 'I just brought it out.'

At one point, their daughter, Liv, who had been watching *Valentine's Day* downstairs, came in. Moore introduced her, then made the parental gaffe of trying to brush fuzz out of her red hair, a gesture that earned her some severe adolescent blowback. Moore may be an idol to the public, but to her daughter, as

Moore said afterward, 'I'm an idiot, let's put it that way.' She continued, 'The other morning, I was making her waffles, and she got it on her sweater. She kind of went like this' – Moore flicked her hand. 'I said, "No, no, let me get that." She goes, "No." I said, "It's gonna bother you all day." And she goes, "No. It's gonna bother *you* all day."' She added, 'I always feel that your job as a parent is just to be steady. In our family, my husband's the fun one, the sporty one. I'm the mom that's always asking them to clean up, put your clothes in the laundry basket, pick up those papers, just trying to keep things clean. That's very irritating about me, they think.'

Freundlich works at the top of the house; Moore's small office, which overlooks the street, is on the third floor, off their bathroom, which has a marble tub like a sarcophagus at its center. Behind her desk chair, looking over her shoulder, is her Oscar statuette, along with a baker's dozen of other trophies. On the wall just above her computer are photographs of the children and their notes of endearment; to the side, on a bureau, are framed shots of her with her parents and an Expressionist statue of a mother and child, which used to sit on her mother's desk. Anne Smith died of septicemia, at the age of sixty-eight, in 2009, two months before her retirement, a fact that still brings tears to Moore's eyes. On the weekend that she fell ill, instead of going to a doctor Anne stayed in bed. 'If she had gone to the doctor, she would have been fine,' Moore said. 'Septic shock is one of the top ten leading causes of death. Generally, you can catch it, so it was infuriating.' The suddenness of the loss made it particularly traumatic for her. 'I think a lot in narrative. I work in narrative. I always think of that shape,' she said. 'And what you learn from the loss of someone like that is that life isn't like that. We impose narrative on everything in order to understand it. Otherwise, there's nothing but chaos.'

★

The next time I saw Moore, we had breakfast before a looping session for *Freeheld*, a movie directed by Peter Sollett, in which she plays Laurel Hester, a lesbian police officer who is dying of cancer and fighting the Ocean County, New Jersey, Board of Chosen Freeholders to allow her pension benefits to be transferred to her girlfriend. The film, which will be released in October, is based on a 2007 Oscar-winning documentary of the same title, and co-stars Ellen Page as Laurel's lover.

At first, Moore said, she couldn't understand the character she was playing: 'I didn't know who she was. I could see Laurel in the documentary. I could see Laurel in the script. But there wasn't any corollary. I was having a hard time.' Her research led her to Ocean County and to the real Laurel's girlfriend, Stacie Andree, who showed Moore photographs of Laurel that no one else had seen. 'Laurel had this beautiful blond hair, somewhat Farrah Fawcetty,' Moore said. 'When they did the documentary, she'd already lost it through chemo. Once I saw how she'd looked, I understood. It was just from the look. You don't know when you start doing the work what you're gonna find. Or how to find it. A very small thing can lead to a big thing.' Moore took out her iPhone and scrolled through photos of Stacie and Laurel and then her own startling transformation for the role. In the photo, Moore, in a wig, had disappeared into the character; she was unrecognizable.

As we set off for the recording session, at the Harbor Picture Company, in the Village, Moore blushed and said, 'I'm probably going to let you stay for, like, half an hour. I don't want you to get in my way. Because you will. You'll take up mental space, and I need to have focus.' In the recording studio, a lectern had been set up for Moore, facing the front wall, which was a movie screen. On it were neatly typed pages of the words and sounds to be re-voiced. Eliza Paley, the supervising dialogue editor, sat at a desk to the left. Peter Sollett and I took our seats on a beat-up, dun-colored sofa, just below the sound-booth window. 'He's only going to stay for a little while,' Moore said to Sollett. 'Don't say anything embarrassing.' Then she scrutinized the first page of lines – 'Funny,' 'Damn it,' 'Where'd they go?,' 'Got it.' The scene in question was played on the screen. Amid a barrage of expletives, Laurel gave chase to a couple of villains. 'I think it's better as "Where'd they go?" and then "Damn it." "Where'd they go. Shit. Damn it,"' Moore said. 'That's too many. Shit. Damn it.'

'It seems like "Damn it" should be the TV line,' Sollett said. 'We don't think that "Damn it" will get us booted off of network TV?'

'It's fine,' Bobby Johanson, the recording mixer, kicked in from the sound booth.

'You know what? Let's just take it out,' Moore said. The line was replayed a few times. 'It's a little raspy. Let me try another one,' she said, finally nailing it.

Then she addressed the issue of recording the appropriate grunts for Laurel as she is pushed to the ground in a scuffle. After the first try, Paley said, 'That's more like winded. It'd be good to have a variation.'

'I think you need an impact. That's what's missing. I think it should be' – Moore grunted – 'and you should hear the thump on the ground of the body. I think it's better to hear the body hit, right? Don't you? Let me give you another. See, John,' she added. 'It's all fun and games.'

'This is the art,' Sollett said.

At one dramatic point onscreen, Laurel and Stacie, who recently met, kiss for the first time and are set upon by some local thugs. 'You two a couple of dykes?' one of them brays, and demands their money. Laurel draws her gun and backs them off. Afterward, she tells Stacie that she's a detective.

> STACIE: You always carry a gun?
> LAUREL: Most of the time.
> STACIE: On a date?

The line made me laugh out loud. 'That's why we kept it in,' Sollett said.

Watching the moment where Laurel points her gun at the thugs, Moore didn't like the sound of her voice. 'I want to bring my pitch down, because it makes no sense for me to keep yelling like an idiot. "Walk away. Keep moving. Did you hear me? Go!"' After a few more tries, Moore turned toward me. It was time for me to go.

She walked me out of the studio and sent me on my way uptown. As the car eased into traffic, I turned to see her hurrying back to her play world, and I remembered something that the screenwriter Bruce Wagner had said about Moore: 'She's got a secret, but we're never going to find out what it is. She's so affable. She presents as the girl next door. But she's the Sphinx next door.'

The Director's Cut

How Todd Haynes rewrites the Hollywood playbook

At 7.30am on a frosty March Saturday in downtown Cincinnati, the director Todd Haynes was on the sixteenth floor of the corporate law firm Taft Stettinius & Hollister, and he was already, as he puts it, 'in the weeds, dealing with every little piece in every shot in every scene.' The firm's lawyers and secretaries had been banished for the weekend, and the maze of cubicles and passageways was cluttered with cameras, cables, extras, and a drowsy crew. Haynes, a trim, boyish fifty-eight, with dishevelled brindle hair, was standing at the epicenter of his newest drama: a small corner office, whose west-facing windows looked out on skyscrapers and a sliver of the Ohio River.

It was from here, in 1999, that Robert Bilott, a partner in the firm and a specialist in helping corporations negotiate environmental regulations, switched sides and sued DuPont, a chemical leviathan, whose plant in Parkersburg, West Virginia, was thirty-five times larger than the Pentagon. In what became a class action suit on behalf of seventy thousand residents of West Virginia and

Ohio, Bilott pursued the company for having knowingly dumped in those states more than seven thousand tons of perfluorooctanoic acid, or PFOA, a toxic, nonbiodegradable chemical used in making Teflon – thereby poisoning hundreds of acres of land, deforming and killing hundreds of animals, contaminating the water supply, and doing long-term, irreversible damage to the health of the community. Bilott's fight pitted him not just against DuPont but against his own firm; he was the legal insider turned outsider, a poacher turned gamekeeper. A herculean, eighteen-year legal struggle followed. In 2017, Bilott won a six-hundred-and-seventy-million-dollar settlement for thirty-five hundred of the people who had filed claims relating to illnesses linked to the PFOA in their drinking water. (Additional personal-injury claims against the company are still in progress.) For Haynes's eighth feature film, *Dark Waters*, Bilott's battle had been broken down into a two-hundred-and-forty-six-scene jigsaw puzzle that the director was now painstakingly piecing together.

Haynes, in T-shirt, jeans, and sneakers, sat down on the office sofa to discuss the morning's scene with his stars: the towering Tim Robbins, who plays Bilott's boss, Tom Terp, the head of the firm's environmental group, and the shortish, stocky Mark Ruffalo, as Bilott, the saga's unlikely hero. Ruffalo was not only the film's marquee attraction; he was its lead producer, and he had initially sought out Haynes to direct and deepen the screenplay, by Mario Correa and Matthew Michael Carnahan, which was inspired by Nathaniel Rich's 2016 exposé on the subject in the *New York Times Magazine*, and which Ruffalo felt had been written too strictly as a procedural thriller. 'You're trying to find the balance between character and story,' Ruffalo told me. 'If you go heavy on the plot, you lose character.' He added, 'I love the inner space of Todd's work with actors and characters. I always feel he's interested equally, if not more, in what's happening below the lines.' Haynes, who is a gifted screenwriter – he was nominated for an Academy Award for the screenplay for his movie *Far from Heaven* (2002) – made sure that Bilott's wife and his family relationships were given a real presence in the shooting script.

As a student at Brown University, in the mid-eighties, Haynes studied painting and semiotics in a program that, he said, 'kind of combined Freud, Marx, and feminism.' He emerged, as he wrote in the introduction to an edition of three of his screenplays, with 'a strong interest in popular form, combined with a strong desire to invert it.' In earlier films, he played on the bio-pic (*Superstar: The Karen Carpenter Story*, 1988), the horror movie and the tabloid documentary (*Poison*, 1991), the 'disease of the week' film (*Safe*, 1995), the melodrama (*Far from Heaven* and *Carol*, 2015), and even the silent film (*Wonderstruck*, 2017). *Dark Waters*' subverts by taking the legal thriller – a form that traditionally concludes with the triumph of good over evil – into areas of psychological complexity and ambiguity. All investigative stories, he told me, when we met in Los Angeles in June, have the burden of revealing a truth. 'What I love so much about the genre,' he explained, 'is the *cost* of revealing the truth. The drama of that, and what it does to people. That is the part that kills you.'

On the set, the camera perched on the threshold of Bilott's office, and a scrum of technicians outside formed a second barricade, so I watched the filming from a conference room, where a large monitor had been installed for the production staff. 'I have no actual time beyond the shoot itself – every day is a mortal trial,' Haynes had warned me before I flew in to watch him work, but

I had no idea then just how fiercely he inhabited his imagined worlds. 'He's got himself in a bubble,' one of the film's producers, Christine Vachon, said of the laser-like focus that he exhibited on the monitor. A co-founder, in 1995, of Killer Films, Vachon is the doyenne of independent producers; she and Haynes met at Brown, where she, too, studied semiotics, and she has produced all his feature films. She sat across from me, working the phone, in her customary getup – black T-shirt, pants, hoodie, and combat boots (which gained some notoriety when she wore them on the red carpet at Cannes for the première of *Carol*). 'He's always very passionate,' she added. 'He's not good at juggling a lot of balls in the air.'

I was thinking of myself, sadly, as one of those balls when Haynes's director's assistant, Lucas Omar, suddenly materialized with a large black leather portfolio. 'Todd wanted you to see the Image Book,' he said, and disappeared. The incident was proof of Haynes's attention to detail; even in the early-morning hubbub, he'd kept my presence on the set in mind. Haynes is renowned in the business for his preparation: rigorous shot lists, hundred-page editing notes, and his Image Books, which remain close at hand throughout his shoots. These books are key, Haynes has said, to his 'psychic process.' Before beginning each film, he distributes a magazine-size version to the head of each department, to insure that all his collaborators have a sense of the film's emotional terrain.

The *Dark Waters* Image Book consisted of forty-six laminated pages that followed the linear and thematic trajectory of Bilott's crusade, a sort of map of Haynes's ideas for the movie's visual language. The images, many of which were shot with foreboding lighting or from unsettling angles, included derelict West

Virginia landscapes, DuPont billboards, and screen grabs from other movies (*Silkwood*, *The Insider*, *The Parallax View*, *Invasion of the Body Snatchers*, and *All the President's Men* – a primer for the postures of fear and frustration in Bilott's battle against corporate corruption). Into this visual stew, Haynes had mixed photographs of Bilott as a boy, and of his family (his grandmother lived in West Virginia, not far from DuPont's most toxic dumping site); a wall of boxes holding the hundreds of thousands of pages of relevant correspondence and documentation that Bilott had extracted from DuPont; the worn faces of West Virginia farmers; the severed head of a wild-eyed contaminated cow; polluted streams. The album also included a list of the painters and photographers Haynes had chosen to inform the film's palette and perspective, among them Gerhard Richter, Gordon Parks, Andreas Gursky, William Eggleston, Stephen Shore, and Joel Meyerowitz. Haynes's visual challenge in *Dark Waters* was to elevate the legal offices, storage rooms, and middle-class homes where most of the drama of the movie takes place to an expressive backdrop for Bilott's internal struggle, which, he said, was infused 'with anxiety, dread, futility, and despair.'

Around noon, while Robbins and Ruffalo were horsing around between takes – Robbins: 'You were horrible.' Ruffalo: 'Wait till I'm off camera. I'm gonna be horrible to you' – a slight middle-aged man, in a plaid shirt and jeans, slipped into the conference room and took a seat against the back wall. It was Rob Bilott. I introduced myself. Ruffalo, in his round-shouldered, restrained performance, seemed to have uncannily captured Bilott's trout-lipped solitude, a standoffishness that made him seem permanently braced. The one physical quality that no actor could capture was his sunken, forlorn eyes. Bilott said that he was nervous about the next scene on the schedule. I asked why. 'Neurological issues,' he said.

In the scene in question, which takes place thirteen years into Bilott's legal battle, Bilott's boss tells him that he has to wrap up the suit and take a pay cut. 'Tom, that's my fourth. I'm down a third now,' Bilott replies quietly. Terp says, 'You don't have any clients. No one will take your calls. What am I supposed to do here? Now, I'm on your side, but, Rob . . .' At this point in the script, Bilott starts to stand up, his legs give out, he grabs at the desk and collapses. Haynes went to work on the choreography of the fall.

During the next four hours, with the three-page scene in hand, Haynes kept popping out from where he was crouching behind the door, to explain the motivation of the moment. 'You think he's going to get up,' he said to Robbins at one point, then, turning to Ruffalo, 'You're fighting waves of nausea.' They explored the scene's dynamics, then, satisfied, moved on to the next beat. Systematically, Haynes ramped up Bilott's tension: his blinking eyes, his twitching hands, his juddering feet, his fumbling for the chair, and his flailing spasms on the floor. By the fifth take, Ruffalo's portrayal of Bilott's psychological struggle to contain his collapse had become as sensational as the physical one. Afterward, in the conference room, I turned to the real Bilott, who had been joined by his wife, Sarah (played by Anne Hathaway in the film), to ask what he thought of it. 'Hard for me. Disturbing,' he said, adding, 'I'm not being very articulate.' He scratched his forehead, searching for more words. 'Never realized I didn't smile,' he said.

The caravan of lights and cameras moved down the partitioned corridors to the next location. The dark passageways, the contrasting bright sources of light, and the outside vistas with no direct horizon all served Haynes's effort to create a landscape of obfuscation and menace. 'Barrier upon barrier upon barrier. It's so smart,' Ruffalo said later of what he calls Haynes's 'geometrics,' as he waited to be filmed from another disconcerting angle, below a stairwell. 'He's laid the music down, and I'm the piano player. I can move within the structure. It's a complex game. He's challenging you, and he won't walk away until it's impeccable.'

The first of three children, Haynes was born in 1961 to Allen and Sherry Haynes, who had married at nineteen. Haynes grew up amid the suburban buoyancy and abundance of Encino, California, just a few miles from Hollywood, during one of the industry's most vital periods. At three, ravished by the movie *Mary Poppins*, he fell into what he called 'a total imaginative rapture': he didn't just want to rewatch the movie; he wanted to enter the story through 'a fanatical, creative, obsessional response where I had to replicate the experience,' he said. He drew hundreds of pictures of Poppins, performed the Poppins songs, even persuaded his mother to dress up as Poppins. ('You gotta put the flower hat on, Mom.') 'I had to satisfy the hysteria I felt for this experience creatively,' he said. In *Dottie Gets Spanked* (1993), Haynes's remarkable thirty-minute map of his boyhood inner world, he depicted his spellbound self, sitting cross-legged in a bathrobe in front of the TV with a pad and colored pencils in hand. In the background, his parents contend sotto voce with his fixation. 'I could feel my parents behind me, worrying about what this might mean, or worrying whether they should be worried, and I always felt defiant of their concerns,' he said.

Haynes was a kind of prodigy, who was lucky enough to have been born into a cultured and progressive extended family, presided over by his liberal-thinking maternal grandfather, Arnold Semler, 'the Almighty Bompi,' as Haynes called him, and his charismatic, artistic wife, Blessing, with whom Haynes sometimes painted. Sherry, whose own ambitions were deferred until her later years, when she studied theatre with prominent teachers, including Salome Jens at the Stella Adler Studio, encouraged all her son's art-making. Within the family, Haynes's constant engagement with creativity turned him into a 'child of God,' according to his father. (In *Dottie Gets Spanked*, the boy is depicted as a little king, complete with paper crown, ruling over his imaginative domain with his superpowers.) 'We'd come home from a movie and my wife and I'd be fixing dinner, and he'd be sitting at the piano and playing one finger, one finger, one finger,' Allen told me. 'Forty-five minutes later, we'd come in and he'd be playing the whole melody from the movie. Now, where that came from I don't know. I mean, he was a little scary to me. I was awed by the multitalents that were part of his everyday being.'

When Haynes was seven, his grandfather, who had been the head of set construction at Warner Bros. – until the late forties, when the HUAC investigations and the blacklisting of his friends made the position untenable – arranged for him to meet his TV idol, Lucille Ball, and watch her rehearse. (That event became the erotically charged inciting incident of *Dottie Gets Spanked*, in which the boy sees the aloof, no-nonsense Ball preparing offscreen for a scene in which her ditzy, caterwauling alter ego is spanked by her husband.) In addition to taking Haynes to concerts, plays, and museums, his grandparents took him, at age nine, to New York and to Washington, D.C., and, at fourteen, to Asia. Their support extended into adulthood. Bompi invested more than a hundred thousand dollars in *Poison*, Haynes's first feature.

In 1968, the seven-year-old Haynes appeared on *The Art Linkletter Show*. In response to the inevitable question 'What do you want to be when you grow up?,' he replied, 'An actor and an artist.' The same year, his parents took him to see Franco Zeffirelli's film adaptation of *Romeo and Juliet*. It was a seismic experience that 'absolutely changed my life,' Haynes said. At nine, he made his first movie: a fifteen-minute Super-8 version of *Romeo and Juliet* in which he played almost all the parts. 'I made the tunics out of towels, tied a rope around the middle, got tights,' Haynes said. 'My dad would run the camera, and hold the sword offscreen when I was playing Mercutio. And then we'd do the other side and I'd dress in Tybalt's outfit.' Haynes drew the backdrop for the Capulet ball with crayons on a big piece of butcher paper. The Nurse was played by his six-year-old sister, Wendy, who also performed in the after-dinner plays that Haynes regularly conceived and staged. When Wendy was very young, he would drape a blanket over her bedroom table and light the space with a reading lamp, creating a mini-amphitheatre in which he acted out melodramatic tales with her toy horses. 'She was my audience,' he said. 'I remember just loving to make her cry.' Wendy Haynes, now a therapist as well as the lead singer of the glamrock band Sophe Lux & the Mystic, was charmed by her brother's mind. 'Who was this creature?' she said. 'What's going on in there? It wasn't stopping. It was a train. It left the station when he was born. It's a beautiful thing to see someone who knows his destiny.'

For a decade, Haynes attended weekend classes at Virginia Rothman's Art School, in Studio City, and he used his art to make contact with the show-biz icons he adored. When he drew a picture of Diana Ross with six arms, according to his father, he managed to deliver it to her backstage at the Universal

Amphitheatre. When he was in high school, his mother drove him to Joni Mitchell's home in Bel Air so that he could give her his illustrations of some of her lyrics. 'I knocked on the door, and a sort of Joni clone came to the door, in a bikini with long blond hair,' Haynes told me. 'And she said, 'Oh, that's so sweet. Thank you. I'll give them to her."' The actress Elizabeth McGovern, who was Haynes's best friend at the progressive Oakwood School, in North Hollywood, remembered him being indignant that Mitchell never responded. She added, 'He had that sense of himself – to think that it was rude of her. He was just a high-school kid.'

'Eyes should be seen not hid' are the first words spoken in *Dottie Gets Spanked*, and the phrase seems to hold a clue to Haynes's obsessive art-making. 'I know that I enjoyed being seen – performing and putting on shows for the family, impressing people with my drawings and paintings,' he said. 'But there may have been something beyond that, where what I was really interested in was replaying my own pleasure in seeing: returning to that moment of seeing *Mary Poppins* on film, seeing *Romeo and Juliet*. The rapture was in the process of re-creating it, over and over.' Other films, including *The Miracle Worker*, *Anne of the Thousand Days*, and, especially, *The Graduate*, fed his excitement at how a lens could tell a story. 'I remember feeling stimulated through my entire body. I would walk around looking at the world literally through frames,' he said.

From the outset, Haynes was a sort of escape artist, compulsively immersing himself in art. But to escape *to* is also to escape *from*. Haynes was, in part, fleeing his parents' 'absolutely terrifying' arguments, which left him in 'a constant anxiety that the family unit was imperilled.' One brouhaha spilled into Haynes's bedroom while he was asleep. 'She was pulling her ring off, and she threw it into the yard from my upstairs window,' he said. 'I remember them looking through the ivy the next day on hands and knees. Never found it.' Sherry, whose public manner was genteel, 'knew how to get what she wanted,' Haynes said. Allen could be moody and had a temper. Haynes's relationship with his father as a child, he said, was sometimes 'distant and competitive,' but these days he refers to him as a 'mensch.' The transformative event was a nearly fatal aortic rupture that Allen suffered when he was in his forties and Haynes was in his twenties. For a month, Haynes and his brother, Sean, slept on the floor of their father's hospital room. 'He wanted me there more than anybody. More than my mom – he wanted me there,' Haynes said.

Haynes's immersion in art was also the result of a kind of apprehension of his own otherness, an undertow of estrangement that he felt long before he understood it. Sherry was a perfectionist, both in her personal style – 'She always had perfect hair, perfect nails, perfect, perfect, perfect,' McGovern recalled – and in the clean lines, white walls, and spotless, plastic-covered furniture of her home. 'My mother would literally pour Clorox bleach on the kitchen tiles each night,' Haynes said. He, on the other hand, 'desired contamination. I wanted it.' As a boy, he was constantly drawing women: 'I loved doing the lips and the eyelashes or the cleavage.' When he badgered his father to buy him a new sketch pad, his father said, 'I'll buy you a drawing pad if you draw men.' 'It was the most remarkable thing, because it was so clear and precise,' Haynes said of his father's request. On another occasion, while playing Cinderella's Fairy Godmother in one of his after-dinner performances, Haynes made a limp-wristed gesture that earned him an immediate, unexpected rebuke. 'They were, like, "Don't do that!" I was, like, "I'm playing the Fairy Godmother, you guys." I was angry. I wasn't ashamed. It stirred up a kind of revolt in me,' he said.

At Oakwood, which placed a strong emphasis on the arts, Haynes was a class star, and he and McGovern were inseparable. 'He was my first experience of loving,' she said. When they weren't staging their own performance pieces, they were acting in school productions. After school, at Haynes's house, they played theatre games, improvised sketches, rehearsed scenes from plays. 'He was a work machine,' McGovern said. 'You'd never see Todd just hanging out. If he was sitting down, he was drawing or writing. Seven days a week. Every waking hour he was making something.' In one of many poems he wrote for McGovern, he envisioned a joint future:

> ... I will be the
> Famous film director and you will be
> The actress. I will write scripts for you.
> Ingmar and Liv, she smiled. Someday, I said

McGovern often slept over in Haynes's room, but they were never together 'in any remotely physical way,' she said. 'He had a fairly clear idea that he was attracted to boys, although not exclusively.' Haynes's parents maintained 'a fantasy for happy heterosexual closure' with McGovern, he said. He didn't come out to them until he was in college and in his first relationship with a man. 'My dad assured me that it was all right with him,' Haynes said. But his mother found the news hard to accept. 'She freaked out,' Wendy said. 'She had a meltdown. She was concerned about what the world would think. She was concerned about him being hurt in the world. It shattered her dream.' Later, however, according to Haynes, 'she would say that my being gay made her grow as a person and rethink the world.'

At Oakwood, Haynes's intellectual 'exceptionalism,' as he called it, was matched by his exceptional appearance – he kept his hair in a long blond mane. 'He did look like a girl. Everybody thought he was a girl,' McGovern recalled. 'It never bothered him.' Haynes's androgynous look was the outward sign of his increasing ambivalence toward middle-class convention. 'I always felt identification with the outcast, fragile, vulnerable people in the classroom,' he said. 'I had an empathy for kids who had a harder time fitting in.' In a high school-era letter to McGovern, Haynes spelled out his own sense of separation:

> Sometimes my life is so desperately alone and full of sorrow. It sounds self-centered to say, so pretentious, but I feel so truly different from anyone I've met. Sometimes I can barely imagine seeing things the way people do. I do not feel better or worse than them, but apart.

In ninth and tenth grades, he made a twenty-two-minute film, titled *Suicide*, which depicted a similarly troubled outsider, Lenny, who is terrified of making the transition from junior high to high school. He is 'enraged at the world for making him feel so afraid and subjugated and minimized, and uses his body to exorcise his rage,' Haynes said. The film grew out of a humanities assignment to write a hero myth. Haynes wrote the competing voices in Lenny's head with different-colored pens. Lenny's first words, written in red, were 'I carefully and intricately began cutting myself into several pieces' – a prescient line for the incipient filmmaker. 'The teachers were quite impressed with the method, the style, and the sort of Modernist construction' of the written piece,' Haynes said, and he and a few friends decided to turn it into a Super-8 movie. The film crosscut scenes of Lenny stabbing himself with scissors in an all-white bathroom with scenes of schoolyard humiliation and maternal consolation. Lenny's last voiced-over words are 'Really hard to live.' Although Haynes maintains that *Suicide* wasn't his story, some of its motifs have endured in his work: the montage structure and the idea of a derangement of identity as a form of liberation.

The movie looked good but didn't sound good. Through connections to a Hollywood producer, Haynes and his cohorts were able to get the sound remixed on a soundstage at the Samuel Goldwyn Studio. 'We were the session booked after *The Last Waltz*,' Haynes said. 'We brought our little Super-8 projector and synched up to a mixing board, with all our tracks of 35mm sound, the music, the effects, the dialogue. We did it in a real way. It was crazy.' When the movie was done, they staged an ersatz Hollywood première at a theatre in Westwood, with a limo hired by one boy's parents. The experience, however, gave Haynes second thoughts about the template of studio filmmaking. 'I kind of turned against that in my head,' he told me. 'I said, "I don't want to replicate that system. I want to make experimental films, and I want to do them alone."'

When Haynes was in eleventh grade, his film teacher, Chris Adam, told him 'that films shouldn't be judged on how they conveyed reality, that films were not about reality,' Haynes said. Cinema was a trick, almost like Renaissance perspective: a two-dimensional event that represented three-dimensionality; it created the sense of direct, unmediated life, whereas, in fact, everything in it was mediated. The notion, Haynes said, was 'a revelation to me.' He began to interrogate our 'endless presumptions about realness and authenticity. It started to make me think about stylistic and formal changes and deviations.'

★

Haynes's graduation project at Brown, in 1985, was *Assassins: A Film Concerning Rimbaud* – a forty-three-minute rambunctious mashup of artifice and anachronism, in which glimpses of the libertine lives of Arthur Rimbaud and Paul Verlaine are crosscut with scenes of the film's construction, all set to the sounds of Iggy Pop and Throbbing Gristle. In voice-over at the end, Haynes reads the last line of Rimbaud's 'Morning of Drunkenness,' a salvo directed at bourgeois stability: 'Now is the time for assassins.' The words are a kind of aesthetic battle cry against cinematic convention. 'I was never going to crawl into the Hollywood world of feature film-making,' Haynes said.

The world of experimental filmmaking, however, was changing. In the wake of such groundbreaking works as Sally Potter's *Thriller* (1979) and David Lynch's *Blue Velvet* (1986), narrative began to leach into experimental films, and experimental technique was leaching into narrative films. Haynes's first major offering, which he produced in 1987, while he was in the M.F.A. program at Bard College, was the forty-three-minute *Superstar: The Karen Carpenter Story* (co-written and co-produced with Cynthia Schneider, another friend from Brown). The film set out to tell a straightforward story of the singer's life, tracing Carpenter's trajectory from her early success to her slow death, of anorexia, at thirty-two – but dramatized it all with modified Barbie dolls. As Haynes wrote in the introduction to his screenplays, the question he was trying to answer through this radically artificial conceit was: What would happen 'if the narrative gears subsumed by our identification were quietly revealed'? Would viewers' 'desire to identify even succumb to an ensemble of plastic'? Haynes made meticulous sets and props for his Lilliputian world, and structured his story using documentary tropes – talking heads, newsreel footage, performance clips, laxative ads. Of the first screening, Vachon wrote, 'When it began, there were gasps and laughter from the audience, because it was so funny and perfect to have Karen Carpenter played by a Barbie doll. But at the end, when the doll turned around and half her face was gone, carved away by weight loss, it wasn't so funny anymore, and some people burst into tears.'

Superstar was a success at the 1988 Toronto Film Festival, and played at a few venues in New York, getting unexpectedly good notices in the *Village Voice* and *Artforum*. Another unexpected indicator of its impact was a cease-and-desist order served by Karen Carpenter's brother and musical partner, Richard Carpenter, the estate of Karen Carpenter, and A&M Records. Haynes had failed to acquire the rights to the Carpenters' songs. 'My orientation was that of guerrilla filmmaking, where music rights were historically ignored, never assuming a film would have a commercial life of any sort,' he said. At first, he tried to deflect the demands, but the lawyers prevailed. In 1990, *Superstar* was ordered withdrawn from exhibition and all copies destroyed. Nonetheless, bootleg copies still circulate; and in 2003 the film made it onto *Entertainment Weekly*'s list of the Top 50 Cult Movies.

In 1988, Haynes, Vachon, and another college friend, Barry Ellsworth (who had collaborated on *Superstar*), set up their own company, Apparatus Productions, in New York. The goal, according to Vachon, was 'to change people's perception that "experimental" was synonymous with "excruciating."' In the late eighties and early nineties, the AIDS epidemic in New York was nearing its peak. 'Our lives were so defined by that kind of death and fear,' Vachon recalled. 'It felt like we were constantly going to memorial services.' Haynes became a founding member of Gran Fury, a group of artists who devised visual campaigns for ACT UP, and he was acutely aware, he said, 'of how gay people with HIV were being depicted by the media.' He started to examine the cinematic tropes of other forms of 'deviant' behavior – the outcast, the castigated, the criminal. He was trying to locate 'the ways that our culture orients the insider and the outsider through our storytelling,' he told me, adding, 'These are not benign practices.'

The result of this inquiry was *Poison*, which Haynes co-edited with his then lover Jim Lyons, who also acted in the film and later edited and co-wrote the story for Haynes's *Velvet Goldmine* (1998). A daring, irreverent triptych, *Poison* is organized into discrete segments – 'Hero,' 'Horror,' 'Homo' – in each of which society rejects the main character and destroys his sense of belonging. 'Hero,' which is shot in faux-documentary style, tells the story of a troubled seven-year-old, who killed his father for abusing his mother, and then apparently flew out an open window. His escape plays as an ironic daydream of romantic transcendence, elevating him from the stigmatized to the sanctified. In 'Horror,' filmed in black-and-white, a scientist invents a sex-drive potion. When he drinks it himself, he becomes an incarnation of contagion, his skin mottled with oozing pustules, a walking embodiment of alienation who disgusts himself and others. Rejected, spat on, enraged, and enraging, he is hunted and finally cornered in his apartment, where he jumps to his death from a fire escape in front of a gawping crowd. 'Homo,' which is shot in color, reverses the angle on otherness. Drawing on Jean Genet's work, it depicts a lyrical, elliptical gay prison romance in which transgression is embraced as a weapon against cultural convention, 'the ink that gives the white page a meaning,' as Genet wrote.

At the 1991 Sundance Film Festival, *Poison* beat out movies by Stephen Frears and Richard Linklater to win the Grand Jury Prize. 'He has restored my faith in youth,' John Waters said of Haynes, who at thirty became the poster boy for the budding queer-cinema movement. Haynes said, 'The thing I dug about New Queer Cinema was being associated with films that were challenging narrative form and style as much as content. It wasn't enough to replace the boy-meets-girl-loses-girl-then-gets-girl with a boy-meets-boy version. The target was the affirmative form itself, which rewards an audience's expectations by telling us things work out in the end.' He went on, 'Queerness was, by definition, a critique of mainstream culture. It wasn't just a plea for a place at the table. It called into question the table itself.'

Inevitably, a graphic rape depicted in the 'Homo' chapter of *Poison*, and a 'gobbing scene' – a ritual humiliation in which prisoners spit into another inmate's open mouth – got the movie into political hot water. The Reverend Donald Wildmon, of the fundamentalist Christian group the American Family Association, brought it to the attention of some members of Congress, who then protested the twenty-five-thousand-dollar N.E.A. grant that had made it possible for Haynes to finish the film. Haynes found himself drawn into an ongoing congressional debate about government funding of the arts. He appeared on *Larry King Live* and other talk shows to defend himself and artists in general against the right-wing outcry over taxpayers' money being used to fund art that offended public sensibilities. A special screening of *Poison* was held in D.C. for senators and their spouses. An editorial in the Washington *Times* afterward declared Haynes 'the Fellini of fellatio.' 'A proud moment!' Haynes said.

★

Despite his new acclaim and the fact that *Poison* turned a profit, it took Haynes four years to raise the million dollars he needed to make his next feature, *Safe*. A restrained, masterly tale about a rich San Fernando Valley housewife, the well-named Carol White (played by Julianne Moore), who finds herself allergic to her environment, *Safe* was Haynes's attempt to take on the discourse of recovery. As a heroine, Carol is sensationally uncharismatic: thin-voiced, remote, desireless, a stranger to herself. Her identity is defined by the bourgeois perfection of her material world. Unlike traditional 'disease movies,' which, under the guise of teaching about illness, as Haynes put it, 'are really the story of people's personal victories over the odds,' *Safe* provides no clear explanation for Carol's malaise. Is it chemical? Biological? Psychosomatic? 'I was coy, I was tricky,' Haynes said. 'I wanted to touch that little bit in everyone where you just aren't convinced that who you think you are is really who you are – that moment when you feel like a forgery.' *Safe* also refuses the moral certainty and the redemptive narrative resolution of the genre, which, according to Haynes, would have been 'contingent on the central character coming to accept her illness, "finding herself."' 'There's no achieving perfect health,' Haynes said. 'There's no resolving the conflict of desire and oppression. There's no resolving the individual and the civilization.'

'One of the things that's interesting to me about Todd is that he's always examining our position within certain social structures,' Julianne Moore told me. 'Is identity purely your own? Or is it something that you've assumed?' Carol ends up at a ramshackle New Mexican community of fellow-sufferers, who purvey the mantra of self-love. (The film does not explicitly address AIDS, but does wink at the New Age recovery language adopted in such books as Louise L. Hay's 1988 *The AIDS Book: Creating a Positive Approach*, whose argument Haynes summarizes as 'If you loved yourself more, you wouldn't have gotten sick.') At her birthday celebration, Carol, surprised by a cake, is asked to make a speech. In Haynes's script, she is not only lost for words; she is entirely lost. Her sentences are a scaffolding that holds up a nonentity:

> I don't know what I'm saying, just . . . it's true how much I . . . (*she stumbles, her eyes filling unexpectedly*) hated myself before I – came here, so I'm . . . trying to be more – aware . . . seeing myself more as I hopefully am. More positive, like seeing the pluses – like I think it slowly opens people's minds, it's like educating and AIDS and other types of disease – and this *is a disease* . . . 'Cause it's out there. It's just making people aware of it and even our own selves. I mean we have to be aware of it . . . reading labels going into buildings (*Carol stops, suddenly forgetting what she was saying.*)

At the finale, Carol, cut off from all connection to the outside world, sits inhaling oxygen in her white, ceramic-tiled 'safe room.' It's a moment of almost lunar loneliness. She walks over to a mirror and stares into it. 'I love you, I really love you,' she whispers. Then, a little louder, 'I love you.' She waits in front of the mirror for something to happen, as if her words will somehow inflate her into being. 'Nothing happens' is the last line of the script, before the film cuts to black. In that devastating moment, *Safe*, which won the *Village Voice*'s 1999 poll for the Best Film of the Decade, becomes a coruscating metaphor for the negative.

In *Safe*, the chaos is internal; in Haynes's subsequent works, including *Far from Heaven*, *Mildred Pierce* (a 2011 HBO miniseries adaptation of James M. Cain's novel), and *Carol*, the battle between social norms and repressed desires is filtered through the external tumult of the melodrama, a much criticized form that he has enthusiastically adapted to his own expressive needs. 'We don't live in Westerns, noirs, murder mysteries, and shit,' he said. 'We live in families and we have relationships that come and go; we suffer under social constraints and have to make tough choices. And that's really what all these stories are about.'

In *Far from Heaven*, Haynes put a semiotic shellac on his homage to Douglas Sirk's rococo fifties domestic weepies, which featured lush, saturated color, claustrophobic décors, and attractive stars in gorgeous clothes speaking in vapid full sentences, who nonetheless played ordinary people struggling to be happy and stand up to society. 'From the outset, I think it was about embracing this beautiful, almost naïve language of words, gestures, movements, and interactions that were totally prescribed and extremely limited – not condescending to it, but allowing its simplicity to touch other feelings that you can't be over-explicating,' Haynes told the *Village Voice*. In his meta-melodrama, the beautiful Cathy Whitaker (Julianne Moore, playing the flip side of Carol White) is living the Populuxe dream in Hartford, Connecticut. But her paradise is soon lost to the conflicting desires of those who inhabit it. Her husband, struggling in vain with his homosexuality, divorces her, and she falls for her African-American gardener only to see him forced out of town by bigotry.

'To me, the most amazing melodramas are the ones where, when a person makes a tiny step toward fulfilling a desire that their social role is built to discourage, they end up hurting everybody else. It's like a chess game of pain, a ricochet effect where everybody gets hurt but there's nobody to blame,' Haynes said. The pragmatic restaurateur Mildred Pierce (Kate Winslet, who earned an Emmy for her performance in the miniseries), for instance, wins wealth and social standing in the midst of the Great Depression by turning her domestic skills into a business, but it costs her her relationship with her daughter. Likewise, in *Carol*, an adaptation of Patricia Highsmith's 1952 novel *The Price of Salt*, the suave Carol (Cate Blanchett), who is going through a difficult divorce, and the jejune Therese (Rooney Mara) act out a kind of Kabuki of normality, while the signs and signals of their attraction are being sent, received, and returned. In the aftermath of their connection, Therese loses her fiancé and Carol loses custody of her daughter.

Haynes calls his melodramas 'assaults' in which 'identity as a natural and stable property is the target.' By contrast, his music films celebrate the protean self. Haynes's goal in the glam-rock fantasia *Velvet Goldmine* (1998) was to construct a 'parallel universe in which the self-created fictions and high camp of glam rock become the raw material of a *Citizen Kane* structure, in which no depiction of the 'famous subject' is unchallenged.' His Cubist interrogation of Bob Dylan, *I'm Not There* (2007), shows how Dylan turned the strategy of shifting identities into what Haynes calls 'a glorious life's work.' A sort of patchwork of Dylan's transformations, the movie has six actors playing different personae, including an extraordinary Academy Award-nominated performance by Cate Blanchett of Dylan's tousled-hair sixties folk 'ramblin' man.'

★

Haynes hit upon the subject of Dylan's shape-shifting as he himself was facing an identity crisis. *Velvet Goldmine* had been a critical and commercial disappointment. He had also been unmoored by the collapse of his long-term relationship with Jim Lyons and by other romantic tribulations. He was, he said, 'bummed out and exhausted': 'I tried to take a break and paint and travel. I went to Hawaii alone and finished Proust. But I wasn't very inspired.' Haynes's Brooklyn apartment, on the outskirts of Williamsburg, was so seedy and messy that, in thirteen years, he never invited his parents to visit. By his own admission, he lived those years 'mostly out of boxes,' in a room that he'd turned into a workspace, dominated by a flatbed editing machine. 'By the end, there were rats,' he said.

In January, 2000, Haynes took a road trip to visit his sister in Portland, Oregon, where he planned to work on a script. As he drove west, he found himself craving Dylan's music, which he hadn't listened to seriously since he was a teenager. He was looking, he said, for 'a great physical, emotional, and psychological change.' By the time he reached Portland, he was filled with the kind of excitement 'that makes me want to make something,' he said. 'I wrote *Far from Heaven* in two weeks, started work on the Dylan movie, and by summer the landlord had taken over my apartment in Williamsburg.' Portland gave Haynes 'a kick in the pants in every possible way,' and he began to envision a different life.

'I think Todd arrived in Portland at a good moment both for himself and for the town,' the novelist and screenwriter Jon Raymond, who worked with Haynes on the screenplay for *Mildred Pierce*, told me. 'Portland was still a relatively undiscovered enclave, with a lot of good, bohemian energy.' In this laid-back world, where, according to Wendy, 'everybody gets to let their freak fly' – signs and bumper stickers proclaim 'Keep Portland Weird' – Haynes blossomed. Although, for a long time, a portrait of him hung in Portland's city hall, the lowkey rhythm of the place allowed him some respite from the burden of acclaim. When Haynes arrived late to a huge Halloween party in 2002, he was refused entrance. 'He was so delighted to be turned away,' Raymond said. 'That would never have happened in New York.'

An old friend, the director Kelly Reichardt, was also living in Portland, and she and Raymond formed the collegial core of Haynes's new creative life. 'Just being friends with Todd is like being in a seminar sometimes,' Raymond said. (The two nicknamed him El Creador Seminal.) In 2002, when Haynes threw an Oscar party, he met his current partner, Bryan O'Keefe, then an aspiring writer. (He is now an archival producer on one of Haynes's projects, a documentary about the Velvet Underground.) Portland's other great gift to Haynes was to put him back in touch with nature and his own lightheartedness. Raymond remembers him 'romping around the woods in a Bigfoot costume,' during a photo shoot on Mt Hood, and 'slathering himself with mud to scare his friends by some creek.' During the summer, Haynes swims in the Washougal River almost every day. He and Wendy often hike to Wahclella Falls, in the Columbia River Gorge. 'You see the intellect fall away,' she said. 'You see the creativity fall away. You see a peace come across him. He's a very innocent human being on a lot of levels.'

Eventually, Haynes settled into a 1907 gray-blue Arts and Crafts cottage with boxed beams and dark-wood panelling; his furniture was salvaged from the set of *Far from Heaven*, which gives the place a cozy mid-century flavor. On the wall of his study, he keeps a gallimaufry of images – among them Dylan, Freud,

David Bowie, his mother, and Brian Eno. Since 2005, he has shared the house with O'Keefe.

In 2010, Haynes's mother, Sherry, choked on a cheese sandwich and couldn't be revived. Within half an hour of her death, in Los Angeles, Haynes, who was in New York, had a stroke. 'The whole thing was inexplicable. I had no real symptoms,' he said. (He later discovered that he had antiphospholipid syndrome, a hypercoagulable condition.) 'The event was uncanny and frightening, but the loss of my mother is what survives,' he said. 'He doesn't like to talk about his losses,' O'Keefe said. 'It's not easy to know what's going on with Todd emotionally a lot of the time. He is very careful about public display.'

At work, however, Haynes's emotional radiance – what Raymond calls 'the golden thing inside him that is untouchable and unvanquishable' – is palpable. There is no grandstanding: Ruffalo refers to him as 'the consummate collaborator.' Fairness and equality are core values; in his mind, as Raymond put it, 'we are all children together, we need to play fair, everyone deserves their turn.' On the set, Raymond added, 'he creates environments where people don't feel harmed. He's very strict in his gentleness.'

Kate Winslet remembered that, while shooting *Mildred Pierce*, 'his energy would never fail.' At one point, she added, 'he had salmonella, and he just carried on working. We would do a take and he'd throw up. We would do another take, and he'd throw up again. He would sit in his chair, sweat for a bit, stand up, throw up again, and do another take. This lasted for four or five days. He was very, very unwell.' Winslet went on, 'Then there was another day – oh, my fucking God. He had to have a dental surgeon come to the set and pull a tooth out. "Thank God, that's out. O.K., let's go!"'

★

On a stifling New York morning in mid-July, Haynes was sequestered in an editing room at a postproduction facility in Chelsea with his burly, bearded Brazilian film editor, Affonso Gonçalves, whom he affectionately calls Fonzi. They were down to the wire editing *Dark Waters* for an early test screening for the studio, Focus Features, and they worked away with the kind of steady intuitive understanding that's usually reserved for a quarterback and his wide receiver. This was their fourth collaboration.

Fonzi was hunched over the Avid console; Haynes sat on a sofa eight feet behind him, his production notes at his side, staring at a large monitor as they applied a fine filigree of rhythm and clarity to the scenes. The dizzying speed of the production schedule and the fact that *Dark Waters* was Haynes's first film developed by a studio had him on edge. They were tweaking a scene in which Bilott first tells his wife about DuPont's dumping drums full of toxic sludge into the Ohio River and the Chesapeake Bay which soon began to wash up onshore. 'So DuPont starts digging ditches,' Ruffalo's Bilott says. 'Huge open pits on the grounds of the Washington Works plant. And, in those pits, they dumped thousands of tons of toxic CH sludge and dust.'

'I don't know if this is gonna track, Fonz, but try "started digging ditches,"' Haynes said. 'We're cutting out 'huge open pits.' It's not much, but try it.'

Fonzi reran the scene with the few words scrubbed out. 'He's emphasizing "ditches" so much,' Haynes said. 'You could do "so DuPont started digging huge, open pits on the grounds of their plant, Washington Works." Try that.' Haynes thought for a moment. 'Maybe "ditches" is better. He says "pits" in the next sentence.'

'Let me show you,' Fonzi said, swivelling back to the console. 'No, no, the other's better.'

'The way we just had it?' Fonzi said. 'Yeah, I think that'll work.'

Fonzi reinstated the previous trim, then briefly left the room. 'I have more fun with Fonzi than I ever do on set,' Haynes said. He compared the intimacy of editing to the process of painting together. 'You're producing results. You're problem-solving,' he said. 'You have to be surrendering all the time, letting go, looking at what you have in front of you, which is not what you imagined.' Haynes, who is concurrently editing his documentary on the Velvet Underground and developing a twelve-part TV series on Sigmund Freud, has contrived to keep himself almost continually in that climate of surrender.

As part of their process, Fonzi first edits a version of the film without consulting Haynes. Meanwhile, Haynes assembles his detailed notes to form a sort of outline of the film as he sees it. 'What's really interesting is that he and I find our own favorite takes separately, and they're often the same,' Haynes said. Once the two are in the editing room, they start again from Scene 1. From then on, the collaboration is more or less a mind meld. 'Are you feeling what I'm feeling?' Haynes asked at one point. 'Uh-huh, uh-huh,' Fonzi said.

Haynes subscribes to Rainer Werner Fassbinder's contention that revolution belongs not on the screen but in the world. 'To provide an audience with a solution – to give them the revolution – is to deprive them of creating their own,' Haynes said. His films ask viewers to contend with ambiguity, which is part of their sly subversiveness. In *Dark Waters*, Bilott is not only an unlikely hero. He's an unlikely messenger for one of Haynes's most deeply held Freudian convictions: 'There is no resolving of conflict. The conflict is the process of life.' Haynes considers the movie 'a primer on how to live with as much knowledge and awareness as possible.' He added, 'There's no silver bullet, no magic solutions. There's no way to just end corporate greed and corruption. But there are steps to take, and we just have to keep taking them.'

Bilott's struggle to take those steps was what Haynes and Fonzi were trying to punch up next, in a terrifying scene: after deposing DuPont's C.E.O., Bilott walks slowly through a brightly lit underground parking garage to get to his car – Haynes's homage to the Deep Throat garage scene in *All the President's Men*. As the camera tracks Bilott through the concrete pillars, for a split second a stranger appears against the back wall. 'I don't think Rob literally had death threats,' Haynes said. 'But he really did have that experience in the parking garage. Rob said that, once the *New York Times* article came out, in 2016, he knew that he would at least not be killed. The cat was out of the bag.' On the screen, Bilott sits at the wheel of his car, looking around with dread in his eyes, as he cautiously inserts the key into the ignition and turns it.

'Stay in the same low angle of him, intercutting with the key,' Haynes said. 'Going to another angle then back to the first angle breaks the tension for me.' 'I think the tricky part is where he's closing his eyes,' Fonzi said. 'Because once he closes his eyes it's done. I'm using an extra shot to stretch the moment, delaying that action.'

Haynes's cell phone flashed with a 'Breaking News' alert, and Haynes, a news junkie, couldn't resist peeking at it. '"The E.P.A. will not ban a widely used pesticide associated with developmental disabilities in children and other health problems,"' he read. 'There you go!' He tossed his phone on the sofa and got back to work.

Disappearing act

Cate Blanchett branches out

In Sydney, Australia, on the bright, blustery morning of November 10th, 2007, toward the end of Pier 4, a 'finger wharf' that reaches out two hundred yards into the harbor and houses the Sydney Theatre Company, a little bit of show-biz history took place. There, inside a cavernous former wool storehouse – now a dusty gray rehearsal room – amid a cluster of cameras, lights, and local journalists, the actress Cate Blanchett and her husband, the playwright Andrew Upton, announced their appointment as co-artistic directors of the S.T.C., Australia's most prestigious theatre, which operates three stages. Theatre history is studded with examples of renowned actor-managers – Molière, Shakespeare, and Sir Laurence Olivier come to mind – but never before had a movie actress of Blanchett's calibre, at the height of her powers and popularity, made this kind of commitment to the theatre community that launched her. Blanchett and Upton will officially begin their three-year appointment in 2008, after a year of shadowing the current artistic director, Robyn Nevin. They also happened to be in the process of staging a double bill at the theatre: Harold Pinter's *A Kind of Alaska*, directed by Blanchett, and David Mamet's *Reunion*, directed by Upton, both of which opened to strong reviews at the end of November. 'Andrew and I are galvanized by a challenge,' Blanchett said. 'Frankly, this is the most exciting thing that has happened to us, apart from marriage and having children.'

'I feel the need to move forward,' Blanchett, who is thirty-seven, told me later. 'I know it's going to broaden me as a human being. I hope it broadens me as an actor.' She added, 'Movie-making becomes a little pointless after a time. You think, Well, yes, that's an incredible role, and, yes, it would probably stretch me as an actor. But performance is not, and never has been, really, all of who I am.' Still, it is through film that most of her fans have come to know her. Blanchett's list of twenty-seven movies is notable for both its range and its ambition. In her most recent collection of character studies, she plays a predatory Nazi collaborator (Steven Soderbergh's *The Good German*), an American tourist who is shot in Morocco (Alejandro González Iñárritu's *Babel*), a British schoolteacher who has an affair with a fifteen-year-old student (Richard Eyre's *Notes on a Scandal*, a performance for which she was just nominated for an Academy Award), and a version of Bob Dylan, complete with big hair and sideburns (Todd Haynes's *I'm Not There*). 'I wanted to *be* him,' Blanchett said of the singer. 'It's the first time I ever had that feeling. I actually wanted to be Dylan. Ultimately, he just really didn't care. He's on his own path.'

At the S.T.C., Blanchett, who calls herself a 'theatre geek,' was following her own path. Her appointment was also a strategic coup for the company: with Blanchett and Upton as artistic directors, its productions will attract international press and talent. (Philip Seymour Hoffman, for instance, will direct Upton's play *Riflemind*, later this year.) And for a theatre company that, in 2005, found itself in the red for the first time in twenty-seven years, Blanchett's stardom will draw lucrative sponsorship. None of this sense of promise and purpose, however, seemed to catch the imagination of the local press back in November. When it was time for questions, the journalists seemed nonplussed. What if Blanchett got a movie role? they asked. Would she have time, in her busy film schedule, to undertake such a job? Did this mean that she and her sons – five-year-old Dashiell and two-year-old Roman – were going to live permanently in Sydney? How would her celebrity affect the running of the theatre? 'Celebrity is a by-product,' Blanchett replied firmly. 'If that by-product can be harnessed to the company's name, fantastic.' After the final question of the proceedings – which, like many before, was directed only at Blanchett – she put her hand on Upton's shoulder. 'We're a team,' she said.

Upton, like his wife, seems to know himself without insisting on himself; he exudes a sort of ironic equanimity. In 1997, the newly married couple spent three months apart while Blanchett was shooting Shekhar Kapur's *Elizabeth*, and vowed, Blanchett said, to 'never ever do that again.' In the decade since then, they have travelled together whenever possible. The S.T.C. offer coincided, serendipitously, with their sense that they needed, for their children's sake, to settle somewhere. Over lunch, at the theatre's restaurant later that day, Blanchett turned to Upton and said, 'If it wasn't for you, I think I probably would have imploded. Acting takes its toll on people. There's a kind of madness in it that's thrilling and wonderful but also can be incredibly destructive.' She turned to me. 'Andrew is an incredibly strong person,' she said.

Strength – or the outward appearance of it – is not the first thing that comes to mind when you meet the impish Upton, who is forty-one. His sinew lies in his good-humored stability and in his allegiance to his wife's talent. Upton studied playwriting and directing at the Victorian College of the Arts School of Drama, in Melbourne, and has already done a series of successful stage adaptations for the S.T.C., including a tempestuous version of Ibsen's *Hedda Gabler* (2004), starring his wife. He and Blanchett got to know each other in 1996, while working on one of her lesser-known Australian movies, *Thank God He Met Lizzie*. 'We were both taken by surprise,' Upton said. 'I mean, it could have been a one night stand. We just kept going. Three weeks into our relationship, Cate says she thought, Oh, God, he's gonna ask me to marry him. I'm gonna have to say yes. I asked her three weeks later.' Their decisions to marry and to run the S.T.C. seemed to share an adventurous sense of optimism. 'Our spirit is jump in, then just keep going until you can make the thing work or not,' Blanchett said. 'If it's not making sense, you pull it apart and try to put it back together again.'

'Walking a tightrope' is how Blanchett once described the experience of acting. A similar metaphor came up over lunch, when Upton described his view of their family life. 'There's someone on top riding a bike with a bar and a ball balancing the thing,' Upton said. 'I think we're in there.'

'In the ball?' Blanchett said.

'Me and the boys are in there.'

A flicker of distress showed in her eyes. 'That's not true,' she said.

'In a balancing way.'

'You're not in the ball with the boys.'

'I mean, there's balancing in it,' Upton said.

The exchange, in its matter-of-factness, seemed evidence of the clarity that Upton brings to Blanchett's thinking, which, she has admitted, is 'very meandering – nothing is linear.'

When I asked Blanchett if she agreed with Upton about their family dynamic, she said carefully, 'There's something about being an actor that is shaman-like. It can produce a great amount of superstition in terms of how you connect to it. To talk about that is very private. Before Andrew, in previous partnerships, even friendships, I couldn't go there. I didn't want to break some spell.' She turned to Upton. 'I met you and I finally could talk to somebody else about that stuff. I feel like every time I make a film or go into a rehearsal room I've already collaborated with you on it. The hardest thing is to get up there and voice what it is that you're feeling, for fear of being misunderstood or locked down too early or just plain ridiculous. I think that to be able to sort of air that stuff with you . . . allows it to grow,' she said.

From the outset of her acting career – she studied at the National Institute of Dramatic Art (NIDA), in Sydney, from 1990 to 1992 – Blanchett exhibited an uncanny ability to enter the kind of egoless state that her former teacher the director Lindy Davies calls 'transformational.' In work and in life, Blanchett, whose favorite word is 'fluidity', has a kind of inconclusiveness that lets her remain receptive. 'I don't like everything to be tied neatly in bows,' she told me. 'If it's flowing, you don't arrest it.' Keeping things open when you're acting, she explained, reinforces the mystery and the intensity of the moment. 'I think it's important to pin questions down,' she said. 'Sometimes you can answer things definitively within a character, within a moment. And sometimes it's important that you don't.'

'Cate is willing to throw herself into a chaotic state out of which something will arise,' the director Shekhar Kapur told me. 'The fluidity you get in Cate is also because of the contradictions inside her.' Blanchett is both candid and private, gregarious and solitary, self-doubting and daring, witty and melancholy. It was these contradictions that prompted Kapur to cast her as Elizabeth I, in *Elizabeth*, one of the films that made Blanchett an international star. 'I was looking for somebody who could portray not only a reality but an ethereal quality,' he said. 'This ability to be both of the earth and of the spirit was very attractive to me – the ability to be both vulnerable and totally ruthless. Cate's absolute ruthlessness is with herself, an obsessive ruthlessness about her craft.'

'There's something tightly wound inside her, something hidden,' the British director Jonathan Kent, who worked with Blanchett on the Almeida Theatre Company's 1999 revival of David Hare's *Plenty*, said. 'An uncontrolled core that she's not entirely in charge of, which, when it's harnessed, makes her riveting.' In *Plenty*, Blanchett played Susan Traherne, a woman whose life after the Second World War is a slow diminuendo into despair. The production was controversial, and some of the reviews were catty – the *Independent* suggested that only Dame Edna could have done more to expose the weaknesses of the play. Blanchett was distraught. 'She didn't weep like a prima donna,' Upton said. 'She wept like a betrayed woman.' Since that incident, Blanchett has never read a review; Kent, for his part, has never quite believed in her apparent confidence. 'That grounded self that you and I perceive – the directness, the straightness, the lack of nonsense – in a way I think that's a performance,' he said. 'I think the hidden chaos of Cate is so interesting.'

Scott Rudin, a co-producer of *Notes on a Scandal*, told me, 'She's very shrewd about what capital she gives up and when. When she gives you the tiniest bit of insight into why the character's behaving the way she is, you gobble it up. I think it's a combination of alluring and elusive.' He added, 'It is the elusiveness that is the key.' Blanchett herself made the same point. She was describing her character Lena, a Nazi collaborator in Berlin in 1945, in Soderbergh's *The Good German*, which she began shooting, without any rehearsal, the Monday after she'd completed *Notes on a Scandal*. The scene Blanchett filmed that day had Lena sitting on a bench with an American military attorney from whom she's hoping to get the papers she needs to leave Berlin. 'I thought, The biggest thing I'm gonna do is cross my legs,' she told me. 'I'm not gonna give anything away to this man. I knew everything that Lena was concealing. But it was, like, I'm not going to let Steven Soderbergh know. I'm going to be completely, utterly ambiguous.' She continued, 'Ambiguity is not absence. It's a wildly contradicting series of actions, emotions, and intentions. There was a line where Lena said, 'No one is all good or all bad.' And I thought that she was referring to herself. So I let a tiny little bit of her own self-hatred come through.' (Soderbergh got his shot on the first take.)

What Blanchett hides from her directors and her audience she also hides from herself. 'I do like to preserve the mystique of the thing, for myself as much as anyone else,' she has said. Over the years, she has repeatedly dodged autobiographical questions by claiming, 'I've sort of forgotten my childhood.' These ellipses in conversation help Blanchett to trick herself out of self-consciousness. 'I'm not interested in the character I am in myself,' she told James Lipton on the television series *Inside the Actors Studio*. 'Any connection that I have to my characters will be subliminal and subconscious.' The first time Blanchett realized that she might have talent is associated in her mind with this ability to make herself disappear. She was in her second year at Melbourne University, appearing in a play by Kris Hemensley called *European Features*, at Melbourne's La Mama. 'My sister, Genevieve, came to see the play,' Blanchett said. 'My sister's a harsh critic. She said, "That's the first time I couldn't see you." I understood what she meant.'

Blanchett grew up in Ivanhoe, a leafy suburb of Melbourne, beside the Yarra River. She was the middle child, between an older brother, Bob, who had a mild case of cerebral palsy, and Genevieve. (Bob works as a computer programmer; Genevieve is studying architecture, after a successful career as a stage designer.) Of the siblings, Blanchett was, by her own admission, the most adventurous. 'I felt very free as a child,' she said. Together, she and Genevieve invented characters, which Blanchett would play, for days at a time, around the house. 'My sister and I would dress me up in something,' she said. 'I'd pull a face or a stance; she'd give them names and an identity.' When Blanchett was around nine, her enthusiasm for performance took the form of knocking on strangers' doors to see if she could talk her way inside their homes with a tall tale about a lost dog. 'It was the adrenaline rush, really,' she said. 'My friend hid in the bushes. I remember the woman at the door saying, 'I haven't seen a dog. Come in. I'll ask my husband.' I looked at the bushes thinking, Oh, my God, what am I doing? I remember the look in this woman's eyes when she started to think, You haven't lost a dog, have you? It suddenly had become a real thing.' Blanchett continued, 'My whole childhood was like that. If someone dared me, I'd do it.'

Blanchett's mother, June, was a jazz-loving schoolteacher. Her Texas-born father, Robert, who met June when his Navy ship broke down in Melbourne, had, according to Blanchett, 'a very dry sense of humor.' He had quit school at fourteen – 'I went to the school for bums,' he told his daughter. Robert put himself through night school, worked at a television station, returned to Australia to marry June, and got into advertising. Then, when Blanchett was ten, he died. 'I was playing the piano,' she has recalled. 'He walked past the window. I waved goodbye. He was going off to work. He had a heart attack that day. He was only forty.' The fact that she hadn't embraced him before he left haunted Blanchett. 'I developed this ritual where I couldn't leave the house until I could actually physically say goodbye to everyone,' she said.

The ritual continues, according to Upton. 'She will never forget to say goodbye,' he said. 'When you're going off to work, if you're going overseas, that point of departure is really important to her.'

When asked about her father now, Blanchett generally brushes the questions aside. 'I don't necessarily need to consciously understand my past,' she said. She went on, 'Drama school was a place where a lot of these things came up, but in a way that one could deal with them in a visceral sense. You move them through your body and out your fingertips. Then you keep the bits that are useful and throw away the junk.' Still, the loss was clearly a transforming one, for her and for her work. She has called bereavement 'a strange gift.' In many essential ways, she told me, her father's death was the shadow that informed her brightness. 'It's chiaroscuro,' she said.

After Robert died, Blanchett developed a passion for horror movies. 'I loved being terrified,' she said. 'It used to be a badge of honor if you could sit through *Halloween II*.' Some of the appeal of horror movies lies in the thrill of surviving them, of, in a sense, cheating death. It's a thrill that carries over, as Upton pointed out, to acting. 'You go onstage and you're alive,' he said. 'You walk offstage, then the character's gone. You survive the experience. It's scintillating.' He added, 'I think that's why Cate's not one of those Method people who carry the role offstage with them.' Over the years, Blanchett has turned her appetite for this form of transcendence into a kind of life style. 'You can't say no to things because you're frightened,' she told a group of students in 2005.

The idea of performance first captured Blanchett's imagination when she was about five and saw a production of *The Mikado* in which an actor's long mustache fell off onstage. 'You could feel the whole audience go, 'Oh, my God, something real just happened,'' Blanchett told Lipton. 'He said, 'Oh, you can never trust these Japanese,' or some joke. I remember that moment – seeing the actor handling a real moment in a completely surreal and unreal production. I thought, I wish I could be up there with him.' Throughout her childhood, on Saturday afternoons, Blanchett attended a drama class in a musty warehouse, with a costume box full of 'things that were slightly frayed around the edges.' 'I would often spend the whole class by myself, or with another girl, trying on this stuff and making little things up,' she told me. She was, she added, 'the child of whom everyone said, 'Oh, she's gonna be an actress.'

Still, Blanchett started out at the University of Melbourne as an art-history and economics major. After two years, she auditioned, on a whim, for the three-year acting course at NIDA. Her most celebrated performance at NIDA was one for which she wasn't originally cast. She was playing Clytemnestra in a production of Sophocles' *Electra*; two weeks into rehearsals, the woman playing Electra withdrew. The director, Lindy Davies, asked, 'Who can work over Easter?,' and Blanchett raised her hand. 'One of the things that she can do,' Davies told me, 'is move into the realm of metaphor, but without being histrionic.' Davies recalled Blanchett weeping during rehearsals. 'She sobbed on the floor in the sunlight. She was talking about Menelaus. The sense of grief was like a waterfall cascading. The thing is that she understands loss.'

'When I came out of drama school, I wasn't that hot young thing,' Blanchett told me. But she gathered heat soon enough. In 1993, at the Sydney equivalent of the Tony Awards, she was voted Best Newcomer, for her performance in Timothy Daly's *Kafka Dances*; the same year, for her appearance opposite Geoffrey Rush in a memorable production of Mamet's *Oleanna*, she was named Best Actress. (She was the first person ever to win both categories at once.) Three years later, Blanchett auditioned to play the role of the mercurial title character in Gillian Armstrong's *Oscar and Lucinda* (1997). The movie, which was based on the novel by Peter Carey about two obsessive gamblers, brought Blanchett's 'chalky phosphorescence,' as the director Anthony Minghella called it, out of the Southern Hemisphere and into the international arena. After her next movie, *Elizabeth*, the world, and every film director in it, knew her name.

At NIDA, one of Blanchett's teachers gave her some advice that she took to heart. 'When you're performing, always keep your lights on,' he told her. 'When you're home, turn them off.' Blanchett and Upton have settled down in the sleepy heart of Sydney normality, the sedate suburb of Hunter's Hill, about fifteen minutes northwest of town, where the noisiest thing in the street is an explosion of purple jacarandas. Ten minutes from their rented sandstone house, they are renovating a house on three acres of land seeded with Norfolk pine and eucalyptus trees, which hide the neighbors and muffle the sound of cars. To Blanchett, the place, which she calls her 'oasis,' has 'a feeling of being completely in the bush.' Even in her current cramped residence, Blanchett has established a sense of calm order. The living room is dominated by a television, photographs of a windswept Upton and Blanchett on the New Zealand coast, and, in the corner, a small children's table, where, on the day I visited, Roman was proudly learning how to maneuver his knife and fork over some fish sticks. Nowhere was there any sign of Blanchett's line of work. (A converted closet off the dining room serves as her office; a bevy of her awards – Academy, Golden Globe, and BAFTA among them – is pushed to the far corner of her desk by a morass of papers, books, and photographs of the children.)

When he was finished with his lunch, Roman came over to discuss the possible modes of transportation to the playground, where his nanny was about to take him. He was leaning toward taking the stroller. Blanchett listened closely to his argument, then said, 'Maybe you should walk. What do you think? Walk on your little feet?' Roman considered for a moment, then agreed to leg it. Later, Blanchett negotiated with the inquisitive Dashiell, whom she'd just picked up from the local Montessori school and who had gone from voluble curiosity in her gray BMW ('What are guts? What are the guts of the house?') to visible fury over his lunch menu of soup and fish sticks: 'I don't want it; they're disgusting!'

'That's his favorite word of the moment – "disgusting,"' Blanchett said, as Dashiell's complaints escalated. She leaned down to speak to him. 'Hang on,' she said. 'You're giving conflicting messages. You're saying you don't want fish fingers, but all of a sudden you do want fish fingers.' Dashiell mumbled something about wanting a sandwich and not soup. 'If you start to eat your meal, darling, then we can make you a sandwich,' Blanchett said.

Dashiell said, 'I'll eat the bread but not the soup.'

'This is the new Dash,' Blanchett said, smiling. 'He thinks he's living in a hotel and wants to order room service all the time.'

'I don't want to,' Dashiell said, and slapped at Blanchett's hands. She calmly scooped him up and took him to his bedroom at the back of the house. A few minutes later, the sound of his grievance ceased, and Blanchett returned. 'There's a whole thing with my generation about having the children like you,' she said. 'Most parents want to be friends.' Her role at home, she made it clear, was mother, not pal.

At home and at work, Blanchett has a talent for listening. When she studies a script, she often writes down everything that her character says about herself and about other characters, as well as everything that other people in the script say about her character. 'You get an objective sense, within the story, of how they're perceived and how they perceive themselves,' she said. 'You get a sort of three-dimensional sense of what they are doing.' She went on, 'Each project you encounter reveals to you the way to work on it. It's all about the text. Some pieces need to be invented, or reimagined, or teased out. Some just need to be unlocked.'

She has the capacity to see herself as part of a larger landscape. Her form of storytelling, therefore, lies not just in the dialogue but in the dance of the character. 'She has a constantly amorphous physicality,' Geoffrey Rush told me. 'That's why she seems to transform from role to role.' She also has the acuity to sit inside an emotion and parse it. In Tom Tykwer's *Heaven* (2002), for instance, she played Philippa, an English teacher in Italy, frustrated by the failure of the corrupt carabinieri to stop the drug lord who is selling to children at her school and whose drugs killed her husband. In an act of rough justice, Philippa plants a bomb in the drug lord's office. We watch Blanchett place the device in his waste-paper basket before escaping from the building; we also watch a cleaning lady empty the contents of the basket into her cart, which she wheels onto an elevator carrying a man and two girls. The scene in which Philippa is confronted with the news that she has killed four people, including two children, is perhaps Blanchett's greatest emotional moment on film. Her expression goes from blankness, to shock, to sorrow, to disbelief, to moral horror, to a grief so overwhelming that she finally faints in anguish.

In her career, Blanchett has played Australian, American, Scottish, Russian, English, Irish, French, Italian, and German characters. 'She can do a voice in soprano, a baritone voice, a nasal voice, an adenoidal voice, a three-octave voice, or she can do something quite tinny and twangy,' the dialect coach Tim Monich told me. 'People use the phrase 'I'm gonna make it my own.' With Cate, it's quite the opposite; it's about adapting herself.' The key to Blanchett's characterizations is not so much the imitation of sound as the penetration of syntax. 'An actor's job is partly anthropological,' she told me, and the character's idiom is where she does much of her excavation. 'The way people speak reveals how they think,' she said. 'The rhythm reveals emotion, it reveals intention.' When she was at Melbourne University, working part time as a waitress at the Old Homestead Inn to pay her way, Blanchett would jot down overheard conversations on her pad; those 'found moments' went into a play that she wrote with another student, about life in the city and how people's conversations are often 'a way of avoiding rather than communicating.'

Over the decades, her methods have become more cunning and more detailed. When preparing to play the title role in Joel Schumacher's *Veronica Guerin* (2003), a portrait of the Irish journalist who was murdered for her investigations into the drug trade, Blanchett listened to every interview that Guerin had ever given. 'You could hear the way she was thinking,' Blanchett said. 'You could hear the missteps; you could hear when she wasn't telling the truth; you could hear when she was unsure of something. I thought, Ah, she's not sure about her own intelligence.' 'Every seemingly little trivial piece of information is something that can feed her,' said Monich, who worked with Blanchett on her version of Katharine Hepburn's imperious, vowel-strangled Yankee barrage of words in Martin Scorsese's *The Aviator* (2004). It was Monich who first told Blanchett about Hope Williams, a socialite and actress for whom Hepburn was an understudy in *Holiday*, on Broadway, in 1928. 'She was a genuine rich girl whom Philip Barry wrote a couple of plays for,' Monich said. 'I had this theory that Hope Williams was a role model for Hepburn as a person, as a character, as an actress. They called her the Park Avenue Stride Girl. Later, it became clear she was a lesbian. She had very short hair ... Cate was completely intrigued with my theory. We both became obsessed with Hope Williams.' Monich and Blanchett told Scorsese, who screened for them Ben Hecht and Charles MacArthur's *The Scoundrel*, in which Williams makes an entrance in a stylish hat with a breezy 'Hello, hello.' In *The Aviator*, Blanchett pays homage to that scene, when Hepburn arrives at her family's New England summer lunch party. 'Cate is imitating Katharine Hepburn imitating Hope Williams,' Monich said.

At her first meeting with Scorsese for the film, Blanchett brought a coffee-table book containing studio stills of Hepburn. 'She said, "Look, I looked at some stills of Katharine Hepburn,"' Scorsese told me. 'And she got in a certain position, sort of crouching down. Cate said, 'I think she was like this.' Sure enough, she just had it. She had the gesture, she had the body lines, the look of Katharine Hepburn.' In her research, 'the most fantastic resource,' Blanchett said, was Dick Cavett's 1973 two-part interview with Hepburn, then in her mid-sixties. 'She was older and her voice had calcified and her whole personality had become a burlesque of itself, but it was fascinating to see how she behaved, and how uncomfortable she was,' Blanchett told the *Times*. Her portrayal of Hepburn, for which she won an Academy Award, managed to suggest a defensiveness behind the brusque bravado, especially in the vocal restrictions of her machine-gun laugh.

In a preproduction discussion for last year's *Notes on a Scandal*, Richard Eyre says he got off to 'a slightly sticky start with Cate.' He told me, 'She'd had one session with a dialect coach, and was she going to have another? I was worried about whether she'd be class-specific. Her character is kind of upper-middle bohemian. I wanted the distinction between her and Judi Dench's character, who is petit bourgeois, to be clear.' Eyre continued, 'I think she thought I was overconcerned with the externals instead of the psychology.' 'He was really worried about the issue of class,' Blanchett explained. '"Richard," I said, "I need to work on it because I'm not a mimic. I need to sit down and work on it." So the accent became an issue, when I didn't want to focus on the accent but on the meat of things.' No sooner were Eyre's words out of his mouth than he realized that he'd made a mistake. 'I was sitting in my kitchen and talking. She said, "Don't you think I can do this?"' Eyre said. 'She was upset. I must have been eroding her self-confidence. I felt as bad as I've ever felt. I apologized. She didn't extract revenge.'

In fact, Blanchett turned in one of her most thrilling performances, as the art teacher Sheba Hart. 'She was quite ruthless in the way she approached that role,' the British playwright Patrick Marber, who wrote the screenplay, said. 'This was a woman whom she was not going to explain or apologize for – she was just going to play it. She never asked me to write something that would make her more sympathetic or her predicament more understandable.' On the other hand, Blanchett was willing to disagree with lines that she felt didn't match the character she had in mind. In one scene, after Sheba's affair with her fifteen-year-old student is made public and she has taken refuge with her teaching cohort and confidante, Barbara, she discovers Barbara's toxic diaries, full of twisted sexual obsession with her, and taped-in mementos of the infatuation. Sheba melts down. Marber recalls, 'I put this line in it, "Where did you get my hair? Did you pluck it from the bath with some special fucking tweezers?" She said, "I don't want to say that line. It's too funny. It will corrupt the tone of where Sheba's at." We hammer-and-tonged it for about ten minutes. Eventually, I said, "Oh, please, just please." I think she felt compelled to concede to the writer, even if he was a bloody idiot. I think that's because she's come from the theatre.'

On the day that Blanchett and Upton announced their artistic leadership of the Sydney Theatre Company, she assured the wary journalists, 'We've got good instincts and a good eye.' Her visual sophistication is apparent in her art collection, which includes works by Paula Rego, Howard Hodgkin, and Tim Maguire. After tea, she suggested that we visit a gallery that featured artists in whom she had an interest. There was a provocative show by the Chinese conceptual artist Zhang Huan, that included disturbing images of the artist buried beneath a mound of books and appearing to sodomize a donkey. At the same gallery, Blanchett studied the Chinese-born Sydney artist Guan Wei's 'Echo,' a series of forty-two panels painted as mythological maps of Australia, which appropriated figures from European colonial exploration, as well as Chinese landscape painting. On the periphery of another Guan painting, a wild seascape in black, were iconic emblems of Australia's past and present: galleons, soldiers, Aborigines, and kangaroos. At the center were roiling waves and clouds, in which pink figures fell from boats and bobbed in the surf. At the edge was the desert.

Blanchett scrutinized Guan's works. 'He's very witty,' she said. 'Towns called Dread and Bathe. It seduces you with one feeling, then it undercuts it. He's got actual creatures, then mythological creatures. He's got Chinese characters, to which he's added little brushstrokes that make them not quite those characters, so it's an invented language.' She went on, 'It's about the way we tell ourselves stories: how we handle failure, how we handle success, how we place ourselves against the rest of the world. All these things are at the core of who I am, who we all are. It's somewhere bound up with this journey inward.'

Two days later, Blanchett, Upton, and I met at the S.T.C.'s three-hundred-seat main stage, to look at the set for *Reunion* and *A Kind of Alaska*, which had just been constructed. Blanchett regarded the moody, brackish gray-green backdrop and the walkway that led to an angled square in the center; she and Upton intended to flood the space so that the performing area would appear to be a floating island. 'One thing I do understand is space,' she'd told me earlier, and so it seemed. The design was playful and daring, poetic and timeless. 'It really liberates preconceptions,' she said. She said that she had seen a similar effect used at the Saatchi Gallery, in London. 'I asked the curator how deep the water was. He said, "It's as deep as you want it to be."'

In *Alaska*, which is inspired by *Awakenings*, Oliver Sacks's study of several survivors of 'sleeping sickness,' the heroine, Deborah, after having been 'asleep' for thirty years, awakens, struggles to get her bearings in this strange new world, then sinks back into darkness. 'I've always been interested in the emergent consciousness – that point between wakefulness and slumber, that place where the sense of one's self is extremely malleable,' Blanchett said. 'She's a broken person who's trying to reassemble herself.' Toward the end of the play, Deborah starts to feel her mind receding. 'Oh, dear,' she says. 'Yes, I think they're closing in. They're closing the walls in. Yes.' On the play's last beat, Blanchett and Upton planned to have the water seep upward. 'It somehow formally completes the evening,' she said.

Later that day, I met up with Blanchett again to accompany her to the opening night of *Keating!*, a musical revue about the trials and tribulations of Australia's flamboyant former Prime Minister Paul Keating, directed by Neil Armfield. Before we left, she insisted on playing for me the soundscape she was devising for *A Kind of Alaska*. 'Chris Abrahams is an amazing pianist and plays in a jazz trio called the Necks. Abrahams did this music – sort of a hybrid form,' she said. With her elbows planted on the desk and her face in her hands, she leaned forward, concentrating on the insistent pounding that was both funereal and celebratory, like a heartbeat getting stronger. Voices and archival sounds were layered into it: a piano played a snippet of 'If You Were the Only Girl in the World'; a voice growled 'piss in your face.' The cursing voice was authentic – taken from a video of Sacks's patients, which Blanchett had tracked down, she said, after noticing a footnote in *Awakenings*. She listened awhile longer, then hit 'Pause.' 'The theme is good,' she said, 'but it's just too present. You don't want to give it all away in the soundscape. There are all these memories, inventions, planes of supposed reality. If you describe them literally, then it depletes them. The audience has to listen with their reaching ears.' Blanchett shoved the CD into her bag. 'We're gonna have to fuck with it,' she said.

When we arrived at the Belvoir Street Theatre, a converted tomato-sauce factory, the lobby was a scrum of people, with blinking red lights strung around the low ceilings and the exuberant buzz of a beer cellar. Blanchett pushed her way through the well-wishers and news-hounds until she ran into Gillian Armstrong. In the hubbub, it was impossible to hear what she was saying. Instead, as the cameras flashed, I watched her easy smile and thought about a story that Armstrong had told me on the phone the night before. 'I ran the first answer print of *Oscar and Lucinda* at the lab for the color grader, Arthur Cambridge, whom I worked with for many years,' she said. 'You sit in the dark. You watch the film at mute, with no sound at all. No one had ever heard of or seen Cate before.' She went on, 'We're halfway through the film when Arthur said, "Is she a nice person? It just comes through that she is." I thought, Isn't that great? He's the first audience.'

After we took our seats, a tall, handsome older man in a blue sports coat stopped beside us. 'Hello, Cate,' he said. It was Keating himself. The lights dimmed. 'I love it when it goes dark,' she said. 'It's like a slumber party.' She settled back to be, for once, a member of the audience. The show had a fine set of impudent lyrics and an inventive staging; it seemed to release Blanchett's robust sense of humor. The sultry face of the glamour pages gave up its famous composure; the poised lips dissolved into guffaws. Blanchett rocked in her seat. At one point, in 'Freaky,' a song about Alexander Downer, the current Australian Minister for Foreign Affairs, who became a figure of fun after he was photographed in fishnet stockings and women's shoes for a charity event, Blanchett was surprised to find herself part of the joke. Downer was played by the show's lyricist and composer, Casey Bennetto, a large man with a hairy back who swanned onstage in the tight-fitting garter-belted mufti of a dominatrix. He looked, more or less, like a bratwurst in heels. Bennetto worked the room with gusto:

I'm a greasy-cheek freak
A leader of tomorrow,
But I won't be 'round next week
'Cause I'm too freaky.

As he marched up the aisle loudly lamenting his volatile career, he came upon Blanchett. He looked at her for a split second, then flopped into her lap and, invoking the singer Barry White, ad-libbed, 'It's S.T.C./When you're next to me.' The audience, and Blanchett, howled.

When the show was over, she made her way toward the exit. Just before we got there, Blanchett was asked to return to be photographed. When I turned around, she had vanished, swallowed up by the milling crowd. For a moment, I thought I'd lost her; then it occurred to me to follow the popping flashbulbs, which, like the landing lights of an airstrip, led inevitably to Blanchett. About forty-five minutes later, we made our way back through the theatre, through the dressing rooms, past the laundry room, the wardrobe, and out into the rain-cooled air.

Blanchett had made a reservation at an Italian restaurant she liked. From the table, she phoned home to check on the boys, which led to a discussion of parenthood. 'I find it's made me more economical, more focussed, more generous, less self-centered,' she said. 'I'm grateful for it.' She went on, 'I remember embarking on *Veronica Guerin* after Dash was born, thinking I have nothing to give this project because I'm so filled up with this creature we've created. But I've become a better actor because of it. I think parenthood is knowing what cards you've got and then throwing them up in the air. You need to let go. It's like when you experience intense grief – you often have the deepest insights because the dead wood's been cleared out. When you're absolutely exhausted, somehow the work you've been consciously trying to do gets done on a different, deeper level.' Earlier, Upton had told me that Blanchett was 'in a constant battle between optimism and pessimism – the futility of all the effort.' As Blanchett tucked into her *fagottini di carne*, I asked her about this. 'We sort of liberate one another from melancholy,' she said of her husband. 'At least, he certainly does with me. The only thing that gets in the way is lack of time.' Nonetheless, they have considered having another child. Just that day, Blanchett said, Upton had taken a Pilates class at home with a female instructor who had a newborn baby. Blanchett held the baby while Upton ran through his stretching regime. 'I was in my pajamas,' she said. 'I held this seven-week-old baby. He came out looking at me like "Don't." And I did.' Blanchett looked away for a moment. 'The reality of what three children would be like?' she said. She turned back to her pasta. 'We like a bit of chaos,' she said.

Showman

Sam Mendes and the art of directing

The British director Sam Mendes doesn't like to act, but he frequently finds himself in front of an audience, taking a bow. For the forty-eight stage productions and seven feature films he has directed, he has collected thirty-four awards. In 2013, at the Empire Awards, where he received No. 28 – for *Skyfall* (2012), which grossed more than $1.1 billion, making it the highest-earning of the twenty-five James Bond films to date – Mendes spoke to the assembled:

> I want to thank Stanley Kubrick for the war room in *Dr. Strangelove*, Billy Wilder for C.C. Baxter in *The Apartment*, Kurosawa for the death of the king at the end of *Throne of Blood*, Martin Scorsese for panning a camera down an empty corridor in *Taxi Driver*, Joel and Ethan Coen for the last scene between Marge and Norm in bed at the end of *Fargo*, Paul Thomas Anderson for the deafening of H.W. Plainview in *There Will Be Blood*, Bergman for the visit of Bibi Andersson to Liv Ullmann in the dead of night

in *Persona*, Francis Coppola for the killing of Fredo Corleone in *The Godfather II*, David Fincher for the first scene in *The Social Network*, Bob Fosse for the audition sequence at the beginning of *All That Jazz*, Quentin Tarantino for Christopher Walken's speech about the watch in *Pulp Fiction*, Woody Allen for the fireworks over *Manhattan*, Clint Eastwood for making it rain at the end of *Unforgiven*, Michael Powell for the moment Moira Shearer steps into the ballet of *The Red Shoes*, David Lynch for the car journey with Frank Booth in *Blue Velvet*, Mike Nichols for Benjamin in the swimming pool in *The Graduate*, François Truffaut for the moment the boy looks into the lens at the end of *400 Blows*, and Wim Wenders for the moment Harry Dean Stanton sees Nastassja Kinski after all those years at the end of *Paris, Texas*.

In April, at London's Royal Albert Hall, Mendes was at it again, taking the stage to accept the Olivier Award for his direction of Jez Butterworth's *The Ferryman*, which also won an Olivier for Best New Play. (Mendes's staging of *The Ferryman* will open on Broadway, at the Bernard B. Jacobs, on October 21st.) This time, when Mendes accepted his award, he dedicated it to 'a relatively unsung hero of British theatre,' the director Howard Davies, who died in 2016. 'I lost count of the number of times while I was directing this that I thought, How would Howard do this?' he said.

Mendes feels that 'you can't mimic your mentors, you can't copy them, but you've got to understand where you are.' His place – as the master showman of the British theatre scene, whose emotional and analytic intelligence, swiftness, and command are more or less unrivalled – is secure. 'When you get into trouble, he is hardwired to get you out of it,' the producer Scott Rudin, who has worked with Mendes on both stage and screen projects, told me. 'You don't stay in trouble very long.'

Mendes's skill as a fixer doesn't make him conservative; it makes him daring. On the first day of shooting his début film, *American Beauty*, for DreamWorks, in 1998, when he was thirty-three, Mendes was so callow that he had to ask his cinematographer, Conrad Hall, when to say 'Action': 'I'm thinking, Oh, my God, that's amazing! I'm in Los Angeles, California, and I actually said, "Action!"' Mendes told the *Guardian* in 2008. 'And the whole crew is standing there and looking at me and I say, "What?" I'd forgotten to say, "Cut!"' At the dailies that night, he told me, 'My luck was that every single thing was wrong. Every. Single. Thing. I saw it with great clarity, very quickly.' Mendes went to the head of DreamWorks and gave a forensic account of his missteps: bad performances, bad costumes, bad use of locations, badly shot. He asked to begin again. That moment had a huge impact on the rest of his life. The studio let him reshoot.

'Coming on the front foot about what was wrong bred so much confidence, they left me alone,' he said. *American Beauty*, which went on to gross more than three hundred and fifty-six million dollars, was nominated for eight Academy Awards and won in six categories, including Best Director.

Mendes's trust in his instincts and his preternatural self-assurance still allow him to cheerfully seek out new challenges. On a chilly overcast morning last March, he found himself, coffee in hand, at a BBC recording studio, standing in as a d.j. for Iggy Pop, the Godfather of Punk, on his 'Iggy Confidential' show. With a gray muffler double-knotted below his raffish salt-and-pepper beard and a blue Breton cap tilted back on his thinning silver hair, Mendes sat at the console, ready to indulge his passion for eighties rock, which he still plays and collects on vinyl. 'I'm a bit sad like that,' he said, before the green light flashed and he was on the air. 'This is Sam Mendes on Six Music sitting in for Iggy Pop,' he said, leaning into the mike, before playing what he termed 'music from when I cared about it the most – when I was in my teens and early twenties and the enemy was still alive. *Top of the Pops* was still on television. I'm justly and rightly nostalgic for that period.'

Mendes spun his golden oldies, which included 'Blank Expression' (the Specials), 'Clever Trevor' (Ian Dury), 'Sgt. Rock (Is Going to Help Me)' (XTC), and 'Totally Wired' (the Fall). When he played 'Felicity,' by Orange Juice, he noted, 'This is the sound of happiness. It really is. The live version of that, released on 1979 flexi disk, long before the album's major studio release on Polydor – anyone who has that flexi disk, I'd be very interested in purchasing it.' After Lloyd Cole and the Commotions' 'Hey, Rusty,' Mendes confided to the audience his worst directing nightmare, which, he explained, usually involves his sitting in the auditorium while the actors onstage dry up. 'They turn to the audience looking for my help, and I'm unable to give them help,' he said, adding, 'The most common production in these dreams is a production I did at university called *The Changeling*. Right at the end of the production, I did the only good thing – which is to play this song by Tom Waits from his album *Rain Dogs*, from 1985. See if you can spot the ironic title. It's called 'Clap Hands.''

The nightmare of being unable to help others stems, in large part, from Mendes's childhood. 'Sam grew up as a caretaker,' Rudin told me. 'He doesn't have to think about it. He's basically been built to make sure everybody's O.K.' When Mendes was three, his mother, Valerie, had the first of several breakdowns and was taken to Kingsley Hall, in London's East End, a psychiatric treatment center run by the Scottish psychiatrist R.D. Laing. 'My dad took me to visit her,' Mendes said, in the handsome brick-walled Covent Garden office of Neal Street Productions, the multimedia company he co-founded in 2003. Behind his desk was a large poster for *The Ferryman*: 'This family can take care of its own,' it read. 'We went up on the roof to look out over London. My first memory is holding my dad's hand and my mother's hand. I tried to pull them together.'

For Mendes, this image remains a metaphor for his childhood, when everything he'd imagined would be stable in his life turned out to be 'a mirage.' Valerie, an editor and a novelist, was ambitious and fragile. Mendes's father, Peter, was a laid-back Portuguese-Trinidadian English professor (the son of the West Indian novelist Alfred H. Mendes). A gentle man who wanted a quiet life, Peter grew terrified of his wife's 'black-eyed intensity,' as Mendes refers to his mother's manic state. 'At the height of her first breakdown, she forced my father to call the White House, to tell the President to stop the Vietnam War. And he did try,' Mendes recalled. (Valerie Mendes refused to speak to the magazine for this article.)

The couple divorced in the early seventies, and Mendes and his mother left Manchester, where they'd been living until then, to settle in Primrose Hill, in North London. 'A single woman bringing up a child – no help, no nanny, no money. Couldn't cope,' Mendes said of his mother, who had a more severe breakdown when he was nine. He walked into the front room of their apartment one morning to find her standing by the window. 'I said to her, "Mum, Mum, Mum,"' he recalled. 'She wouldn't turn around.

I got dressed. I couldn't find my shoes, so I had one shoe on. I went to school crying. My dad picked me up, and I went to live with him for three months.' Mendes continued, 'I had to deal with the swing from the vivacious, extremely hyper, extremely articulate person to the sedate, almost wordless, low-self-esteem, slightly overweight person she was when she was medicated.' Added to his mother's erratic behavior, he said, was her 'not wanting, or being able, to talk about what happened, which was a very big thing, bigger than the illness itself.'

Inevitably, Mendes was a difficult child, 'unstable and emotionally needy,' as he put it. 'I was constantly in tears about something,' he said, recalling himself at the Primrose Hill Junior School playground, watching two kids, whose names he still remembers – Stewart and Jackie – whispering about him. 'They walked over to me. I was shaking with fear and tension. Stewart leaned in. He went, "Cry!" I burst into tears. Then he turned to Jackie. "See, I told you," he said.' Once, his mother sent him to buy candy with a potential boyfriend. 'She said, "Tell me what you think of him." I gave him such a hard time, he just left me on the doorstep and went,' Mendes said.

In 1976, when he was eleven, Mendes and his mother moved to a modest two-up-two-down house in a modern housing estate in Woodstock, on the somnolent outskirts of Oxford, where she had found work as a senior editor at Oxford University Press. Mendes was a latchkey kid, attending the swank Magdalen College School, a change that widened his intellectual horizons but socially isolated him even more; he was his mother's constant companion. Her mantra was 'Nothing is impossible.' But the real impossibility was living up to the role in which she had cast him: as a kind of savior, but with no power to redeem.

Even in the happy, settled stretches of their coexistence, Valerie was always, Mendes said, 'just inches away from being slightly out of control.' Living with his mother, he learned vigilance, which later became a talent for paying forensic attention to the details of his actors' performances – 'the quality of noticing, full beam,' as Josie Rourke, who was the assistant director of London's Donmar Warehouse, under Mendes, for a year and has been the artistic director since 2011, put it. 'Imagine that you're alone with a person for a year,' Mendes said. 'You eat every meal together. Every day, she shifts one inch back toward madness, one inch back toward sanity. As you eat, your radar reads every moment, analyzing whether she's moving backward or forward.' The spectacle was indigestible: Mendes rushed his meals to avoid 'the pain of having to observe for any longer than I had to.'

'She would almost deliberately kamikaze herself,' he said. 'Doing brilliantly for a year or two. Become embroiled in some weirdly political issue with her job, generally an authority figure. Start losing sleep. Start doing crazier and crazier things.' Valerie would become dishevelled. There would be food on the floor, writing on the wall. 'From the moment that you spot your mum is gone and can't be pulled back, there is probably a week or two of horror where you have to watch her disintegrate in order for her to get so bad that the social services take her into hospital,' Mendes explained. 'Every time this happened from the age of thirteen, I called up social services. It was me, and only me, who could.'

Social services would alert Mendes before their arrival so that he could leave the house. 'I would go back and clean up,' he said. The mess wasn't always physical. Once, Mendes found that in her manic state his mother had put in a bid on a two-million-pound estate in North Oxford, and the offer had been accepted. 'I had to unpick that,' he said, adding, 'Once trust has waned, you build up great reserves of containment and resilience. You become quite broad-shouldered. Whatever the world throws at you, it can't possibly be as bad as that.'

Mendes took refuge in his imagination. 'I was a troubled fantasist,' he told the *Independent*, in 2002. 'My friend was the television.' He was indifferent to education – 'terrible at maths, sciences, languages, pretty much everything that wasn't English, history, or art' – but he went to school on British sitcoms (*Fawlty Towers*, *Dad's Army*, *Rising Damp*) and comedians (Tommy Cooper, the Goons, the Pythons, Morecambe and Wise). He was equally avid about film. When he was fifteen, he insisted that his first girlfriend, Pippa Harris, who now runs Neal Street's film and television divisions, go to London with him to see *Taxi Driver*. 'I didn't know why we had to go and see this film,' she said. 'I remember him sitting in the cinema drinking it in. I didn't know anyone like that.'

On an unseasonably warm afternoon last May, Mendes made his way down Oxford's Woodstock Road in his gray Range Rover. He was back in town as the Weidenfeld-Hoffmann Visiting Professor in Humanities, and was taking a break from various honorary duties. As he passed the luminous greensward of Keble College's cricket field, players in their whites could be seen throwing up their arms as a wicket was taken. The distant sound of jubilation filled the air. Mendes, who is an expert batsman, played there as a boy, immersing himself in the game. 'It's not necessarily the batting or the bowling,' he said. 'It's the hours spent in the outfield just being part of the game, being both inside and outside of it, allowing the mind to wander and yet being there as part of the team. You step into a little bubble. Nobody can get you.' He went on, 'You watch the plots and subplots develop. The individual battles between players, but also the overall shape of the match. It's like reading a novel.'

For two years at school, Mendes captained his side. (He still plays for the Oxfordshire Over-Fifties.) The game taught him 'how to get the best out of a disparate group of people.' He became obsessed with the idea of team psychology. (He wrote the foreword to *The Art of Captaincy*, by Mike Brearley, who led England's team from 1977 to 1980.) 'I learned how to issue instructions, to be respectful and at the same time clear. It gave me the confidence to exert authority, and that was a massive thing,' he said. 'I can't exist alone. I can't achieve anything while I'm alone.' Much to his union's chagrin, Mendes refuses to benefit from the hard-fought battle for 'possessory credit' – you won't find 'A film by Sam Mendes' in the credits for any of his movies. A film, he said, 'is written by someone else, shot by someone else. It's not all me. It's *because* of me.'

Cricket was Mendes's first taste of leadership and also his first ticket to ride. When he was eighteen, he went on a cricket tour to the West Indies with his school team. For the program bios, the players were asked to state their ambitions. Mendes wrote, 'To be remembered.' He told me, 'In some way, what happened to me in those years between thirteen and eighteen shifted me from being underconfident to being extremely driven.'

Strapped for cash as a teenager – 'He was always cadging money off me,' Harris said – Mendes could rarely afford theatre tickets.

By the time he entered university, he'd attended only a handful of plays, including the Royal Shakespeare Company's *The Merchant of Venice*, with David Suchet, *Antony and Cleopatra*, with Helen Mirren, and *The Life and Adventures of Nicholas Nickleby*, with Roger Rees, which he calls 'the single best piece of storytelling I had ever seen.' He was first drawn to film not as an art form but as 'a subject that would get me out of having to read anything vaguely academic.' He applied to Warwick University, which had the only film-studies course in the U.K. at the time. He was turned down. A year later, he went to Cambridge instead, with the vague ambition 'to do something I loved.' Having spent a summer working at the Peggy Guggenheim Collection, in Venice, he'd intended to study art history but soon switched to English. At the Freshers' Fair, where the university societies set out their stalls for incoming students, Mendes perused the Drama Society's booth. Who'd want to be an actor? he thought.

Then, one day, a friend asked him if he'd ever heard of David Halliwell's *Little Malcolm and His Struggle Against the Eunuchs*, a play about a student rabble-rouser who leads a revolt against the college authorities who have expelled him. Mendes hadn't. The friend read out loud one of the play's hilarious tirades. 'I'm thinking of directing it,' the friend said. '"I think I should direct it, and you should be in it,"' Mendes recalled saying. 'And that was kind of it.'

On the first day of rehearsals, in a lecture hall that had been converted into an occasional theatre space, Mendes explained to one of the actors how the scene should be played. 'He looked at me – I can't do the look – but the look was: "How do you know all this, you wanker. Fuck you, you're right." I looked back at him and shrugged.' Once Mendes had grasped the live wire of theatre, he couldn't let go. 'I had a literary bent, but there was something about creating an alternative universe and then populating it,' he said. After his confounding childhood, he had found a world where he could be always in control and in mind. 'I had no family, and here is this family,' he said. 'I need the sparks that fly when two people collide. Clearly, I wanted to be seen, but, weirdly, I wasn't a showoff. I don't find the applause particularly satisfying. I knew I liked it because it brought me in regular contact with people. I also knew I didn't know what I was doing.' He set about getting his education in public. In his three years at Cambridge, he directed sixteen plays.

By the time he graduated, in 1987, Mendes had acquired a reputation as the Great Persuader. He was casting a production of *Cyrano de Bergerac* for the Marlowe Society, a Cambridge theatre club, and two friends, who would go on to become professional actors – Tom Hollander and Jonathan Cake – were vying for the lead. Mendes went to Cake's rooms at Corpus Christi College. "'I'm giving Tom Cyrano. I want you to play de Guiche,'" Cake recalled Mendes saying. 'Of course, my world fell apart.' When he protested, Mendes replied, 'Do you know who played de Guiche when Ralph Richardson played Cyrano?' 'No,' Cake said. 'Alec Guinness. Stole the fucking show – that is what you're gonna do,' Mendes said. 'By the time Sam left my room, I was running around. "I got de Guiche!"' Cake said. 'But de Guiche has only four scenes.'

In 1989, Mendes learned that the Donmar Warehouse, which had once been a studio theatre for the R.S.C., was part of a redevelopment project in which the historic venue had to be preserved. He saw an opportunity. He arranged a meeting with the developers. 'I strode in and said, "I can run that theatre,"' he recalled. On New Year's Day, 1990, he signed a contract to take over the Donmar, with Caro Newling, a seasoned theatre administrator eight years his senior, who had previously been the head of press for the R.S.C. Mendes was twenty-five. By then, two of his productions had been mounted in the West End – Anton Chekhov's *The Cherry Orchard*, with Judi Dench, and Dion Boucicault's rollicking *London Assurance*, a transfer from the Chichester Festival Theatre, which he'd taken over when the play's previous director abruptly quit. Mendes was not only collaborating with such high-stepping performing workhorses as Dench but also sometimes reining them in. In her memoir, *And Furthermore*, Dench recalled saying in response to Mendes's instructions, 'I'm not going to do that, I'm going to try something else.' He said, "Well, you can if you want, but it won't work," and he turned his back and refused to watch.'

But others were watching. Nicholas Hytner, the future artistic director of the National Theatre, recalled seeing Mendes at a party just after his West End success with *The Cherry Orchard* and saying to a fellow-director, Declan Donnellan, 'We're all gonna be working for that fucker.' Even the notoriously sour playwright Edward Bond, whose work *The Sea* was directed by Mendes, at the National, in 1991, confided to Richard Eyre, then the head of the National, 'He's got something. I'm not sure what it is.' Eyre wrote in his diary afterward, 'What it is is a very astute mind, a preternatural self-confidence, and a willingness to learn by observing other people.'

The Donmar Warehouse opened boldly for business, in 1992, with the British première of Stephen Sondheim's *Assassins*, a carnival of carnage that had failed Off Broadway two seasons earlier. The revamped version – Mendes set the show entirely in a fairground and asked Sondheim for a new song, 'Something Just Broke,' to give a choral perspective on the horror – scooped up all the British theatre prizes that year, setting the standard for a series of innovative Mendes productions, most of them revivals, including *Cabaret*, *Richard III*, Alan Bennett's *Habeas Corpus*, Brian Friel's *Translations*, Tennessee Williams's *The Glass Menagerie*, and Sondheim's *Company*.

The two-hundred-and-fifty-one-seat Donmar is an intimate, oblong space that puts the actors right up under the noses of the paying customers, a sort of court theatre, whose stalls are only four rows deep. The theatre demands a certain minimalism, which streamlines productions and intensifies performances. 'My directorial style was inextricably linked to the building,' Mendes said. 'There was no proscenium. I couldn't do scene changes. There was no pit, so the band had to be up and visible. There was no point in miking, because the theatre was too small.'

Among theatricals, Mendes is known for creating a 'safe room' for rehearsals. 'People are free to have a bad idea. Frequently, the bad idea illuminates where the great idea is,' Rudin said. 'Sam makes the room embracing, warm. He's very open about what he perceives to be his own mistakes. If he doesn't know something, he's entirely comfortable asking the questions. That makes people feel incredibly well protected.' By extension, the Donmar was also a safe room for Mendes: a home he built to keep his stage-managed family together. As producer and creator, he was father and mother to the group, at once controlling and nurturing. 'I will find out what the actors need,' he said. 'My language to each of them has to suit their brain.' To Hilton McRae – who, as a hard-bitten reporter in Mendes's production of *The Front Page*, had to shout, 'My God, she's dead!' when a woman jumped from the newsroom window – Mendes said, 'After you say the line, pick up your camera.' It was, McRae told me, 'the best note I ever had.' The Irish actress Dearbhla Molloy, who is one of the stars of *The Ferryman*, recalls being directed by Mendes in Gorky's *Summerfolk*: 'I was playing Maria Lvovna, and I had this long speech, which I had no idea how to get into, and I thought, I'll eat an apple while I do the speech. It will kind of deflect. So I brought this into rehearsal. We went on and on. I had an apple every day until we got to the first preview. Sam came to my dressing room and said, "Now you don't need that apple."'

'Each actor is different,' Mendes said. 'On a film set you have to be next to them all, touching them on the shoulder, saying, I'm with you. I know exactly how you're working. Now try this or that.' To put his actors in the right frame of mind, he sometimes makes tapes of songs that suit their characters: for Annette Bening's manic real-estate broker in *American Beauty*, he chose Bobby Darin's 'Don't Rain on My Parade'; for Javier Bardem's sniggering cyberterrorist in *Skyfall*, he opted for weird and haunted songs, such as 'Boum,' by Charles Trenet, and 'Everything in Its Right Place,' by Radiohead. 'It shows the actors that you're thinking about their character's journey,' he said.

Sometimes, to pull actors back into character, Mendes provides more provocative notes. In 1997, a three-month tour of his much praised production of *Othello* was rumbled by critics in New Zealand, and the cast sent an S.O.S. to Mendes, who was in New York directing *Cabaret*. He asked for a video of a recent performance and faxed them his notes. His note to Simon Russell Beale, one of Britain's great Shakespearean actors, who was playing Iago, was 'Simon, what time of day does Iago have his first drink?' 'It just set up a constellation of ideas,' Beale said. 'Iago is an alcoholic. By three minutes into the scene, I was wanting my drink.' He added, 'To Montano, the governor of Cyprus, who gets into a brawl with Cassio, his question was "Does Montano enjoy his job?" That's all that's needed for a tired actor after three months.'

'The most difficult thing when you have early success is to keep yourself open,' Mendes said. 'Actors see directors work all the time. Directors see precisely no directors at work.' In 1989, he took himself to Berlin to sit in on the rehearsals of Peter Stein, the director of the Schaubühne Theatre. The experience was eye-opening. 'I think I labored for a long time under the pressure of trying to prove to everyone that I was fair and democratic,' Mendes said. Stein would walk up to actors and speak the lines and make the gestures alongside them. Sometimes he would stand behind them and lift their arms into the postures he wanted. 'What was amazing is they just carried on. It didn't break their concentration,' Mendes said. 'It's much more dictatorial than I would ever attempt, but it did teach me not to be afraid of it. Sometimes what you need to be is prescriptive.'

Flow – the carving up of space and energy – is the name of Mendes's game. Ethan Hawke, who appeared in *The Cherry Orchard* and *The Winter's Tale* under Mendes's direction, said, 'He thinks like an athlete. Sam knows how to move the ball. When the ball is moving well, good things happen.' When Mendes started rehearsals for *The Ferryman*, a play with twenty-one characters inhabiting a large kitchen in a Northern Ireland farmhouse, he trusted the emotional life of the play but didn't know whether its physical life would work. 'I'm going to test the externals of this play before I test the internals,' he told the cast. 'So you are my guinea pigs. For two weeks, I'm simply gonna tell you where to stand and I'm gonna tell you who to look at when you speak a line. Day one of week three, you can tell me it's all wrong. Let me do this and do it exactly as I see it.'

In Mendes's eyes, his immersive production of *Cabaret* (1993), which began at the Donmar and went on to run for six years on Broadway, the third-longest-running revival in Broadway history, came as close as any of his revivals to achieving the pace, precision, and technical dynamism of his original vision. He took his concept from a tart sentence in David Thompson's *A Biographical Dictionary of Film*, slapping down Bob Fosse's 'slack and shabby' movie version: 'One has only to imagine all of *Cabaret* within the club and seen through the m.c.'s eyes, to recognize how it compromises.' Mendes disagreed with the criticism, but it inspired an idea: Why don't we do *Cabaret* in the club? he thought. Why doesn't the club hold the scenes, rather than the club being held within the piece? All that followed – the audience seated at the Kit Kat Klub tables having drinks, the actors playing instruments, the story told with only a few props, Alan Cumming's louche and lubricious star turn as the m.c. – grew from that idea. The success of the production gave the musical a new life and set Mendes on a path to Hollywood.

Outside the window of a seminar room at New College, Oxford, where Mendes faced about a dozen aspiring student filmmakers around a horseshoe-shaped table, the city's original wall and the college chapel, both built in the fourteenth century, glowed in the sunlight, impervious to the vagaries of time. Mendes, in contrast, was bringing news of change. 'The director as a concept, as a cultural phenomenon, is dying,' he said. 'Coppola of *The Godfather*,

Scorsese of *Taxi Driver*, Tarantino of *Pulp Fiction* – these figures are not going to emerge in the way they did in the twentieth century. The figures who are going to emerge will come out of long-form television.' He continued, 'Now is an unbelievable time to be alive and a storyteller. The amount of original content being made, watched, talked about is unprecedented. You're in the strongest position if you write. If you're a writer, you can also be a showrunner. A showrunner is the new director.' Mendes invoked David Simon (*The Wire*), Vince Gilligan (*Breaking Bad*), and Matthew Weiner (*Mad Men*). Then, like a cinematic Moses coming down from the mountain, he reeled off the eye-watering amounts that will be spent annually on original material in the next few years by the streaming companies: Netflix, $10 billion; Amazon, $8 billion; Apple, $4.2 billion. 'These streaming companies are going to steamroll the traditional studio system,' he said. (Hollywood, during the same period, will spend about $2 billion.)

In show business, form follows money. The boom of the streaming services has also changed the shape of filmed stories, shifting the old theatrical formula of 'two hours' traffic' into a new guideline of ten to sixty hours. 'They want one neverending movie,' Mendes said. 'The model they're chasing is *Game of Thrones*.' As a producer, Mendes understands the market forces; as a filmmaker, he resists the attenuated narrative. 'I was brought up to believe that a movie should have a beginning, a middle, and an end. For me, a narrative is something you tell an audience in an evening. You can put your arms around it. It's singular.' He added, 'Even though my company produces a lot of television, I don't feel comfortable not knowing if an audience is watching, or whether they're watching all ten hours or ten minutes at a time. That's where my theatre roots, I suppose, are most clear.'

Although he is realistic about Hollywood's devotion to action and adventure movies – 'They don't give a shit about Academy movies and critics' darlings' – Mendes takes heart from such ambitious studio films as *The Revenant* and *The Life of Pi*. 'You can only make them if you can marshal the forces and the money from the studios,' he said. 'For that, you have to have had a career over the past twenty years. The problem with these young directors is that the only way they can get that cachet is by doing a franchise film.'

When Mendes set his cap at Hollywood, he knew that he didn't want to adapt a classic or make a film of a play he'd already directed – the usual Hollywood path for British directors. 'The movies I wanted to make were like the ones I'd seen at the art cinema in Cambridge – *Paris, Texas*, *Repo Man*, *River's Edge* – that had access to a mythic landscape, where the audience doesn't know what's going to happen next.' In 1998, he flew back to London from L.A. with a book bag full of potential projects; the first script in his pile was Alan Ball's *American Beauty*. 'I thought, Either I'm mad or this is one of the best scripts I've ever read,' he said. 'I didn't read any of the others.'

The external landscape of *American Beauty* may have been new to Mendes, but the internal one wasn't. The film maps the ructions of isolation, frustration, teenage anomie, and madness in a suburban family whose façade of normality is shattered by chaotic desire. It tracks the gradual unravelling of the dyspeptic, middle-aged lost soul Lester Burnham (Kevin Spacey), a telesalesman who is unmoored first by his hate-filled household and then by his lust for his daughter's kittenish friend. Although Mendes feels that he hasn't yet made his best film, *American Beauty* is the most emotionally complex and compositionally elegant of his movies to date. At once poetic and humane, humorous and harrowing, it informs and delights the heart in equal measure. 'I felt that movie in the pit of my stomach,' Mendes said. 'I understood the vulnerability and sense of loss of a forty-two-year-old man. I understood the isolation of his only child. I understood the mother who was hyperactive and on the verge of a mental breakdown, and the woman who lived next door who was drugged, in order to avoid a mental breakdown. They were people I knew very well, and in some cases were me.'

Winning an Academy Award for his first film was thrilling and 'slightly ridiculous,' he said. 'I decided to treat it as a bank loan I was going to be paying back over the years.' To that end, he has consistently challenged himself to work in different genres. His choice of films is intuitive and highly personal. 'Every Sam Mendes production has the magic of a secret,' Ethan Hawke said. 'It's hidden somewhere in the fabric, this little something sewn into the material that you can't see.'

Road to Perdition (2002), a coming-of-age story played out within the gangster genre, is about a young boy who hides in the back of a car and discovers that his father kills for a living. 'A child steps into an adult world before he's ready to understand it – that was the heart of it for me,' Mendes said. *Jarhead* (2005) tells the story of a young Marine sniper in Iraq, who is looking for an adventure and finds a disaster. 'The movie is about someone who's lost, and I think that's not a coincidence,' he explained.

In 2003, Mendes moved to New York with the actress Kate Winslet, whom he married that year. Initially, they were there for the filming of Michel Gondry's *Eternal Sunshine of the Spotless*

Mind, which starred Winslet. But, as a celebrity British couple, they found the anonymity of New York a release. They stayed, and for the next six years, while they concentrated on rearing their son, Joe, and Winslet's daughter from her first marriage, Mia, Mendes made only two movies. During those years, he experienced a 'slight sense of slipping,' he said. He was disappointed with his work. 'I never quite landed anything. I just missed the runway,' he said. *Jarhead* wasn't exactly the movie he wanted it to be. His Broadway productions of *Gypsy* (2003) and David Hare's *The Vertical Hour* (2006) were poorly received. 'I should have stepped aside,' Mendes said, recalling his contentious relationship with *Gypsy*'s 'scary' book writer, Arthur Laurents, and 'the poisonous hatred that exuded off this tiny homunculus.' In the case of *The Vertical Hour*, Mendes couldn't coax a credible performance out of Julianne Moore, who was making her Broadway début, as an Ivy League professor and TV pundit in favor of the Iraq War. 'I think I was more depressed than I knew I was,' he said. 'I felt a little lost, lacking in things that gave me inspiration: London theatre, my theatre family, my folks. All of those things made me feel progressively more alienated.'

By the time Mendes made *Revolutionary Road* (2008), a coruscating study of a failing marriage, based on the novel by Richard Yates, his own marriage was in disarray. Making the movie was 'the ultimate meta experience,' he said. 'I was not very comfortable being married to a celebrity. I could never throw it off. It made me feel self-conscious. Many times I wanted to be invisible. You sort of suppress your natural personality.' *Away We Go* (2009), a romantic road movie about a hippieish couple trying to find a place to settle, have their baby, and build a happy life, embodied 'the relationship I wanted to have,' he said. He and Winslet divorced in 2010.

Just as his family was collapsing, Mendes inherited the James Bond franchise. His innovation in *Skyfall* was to add angst to Bond's patented action. 'Partly by accident and partly by design,' the existential questions that Mendes was asking himself went straight into the movie. The new James Bond, played by Daniel Craig, was more or less Mendes: returning to a changed Britain, aged, alone, racked by doubt and loss. *Spectre* (2015), Mendes's second Bond film, was a juggernaut that grossed eight hundred and eighty million dollars. After that, he declined to direct a third. 'Those movies were a siege,' he said, of the four years he spent making them. 'I wanted my life back.'

Onstage, control is Mendes's prowess; offstage, it has been his nemesis. 'To me, the biggest learning curve is to let go,' he said. 'I was absolutely unwilling to surrender.' Mendes attributes his pattern of attraction and retreat to his childhood. He was, he said, 'drawn to vivacious, complex, dynamic women,' among them the actresses Jane Horrocks, Calista Flockhart, Rachel Weisz, and Rebecca Hall. 'It wasn't that I pushed those women away,' he said. 'I was attracted to them, then found myself deeply uncomfortable in a relationship where I was really trying to solve them. The best thing you can do in a rehearsal is solve the problem; it's the most unhealthy thing to do in a relationship. It took me a long time to understand that.'

It took Mendes a long time, as well, to learn that a romantic relationship between an actor and a director is unlikely to be a healthy one, because of the power imbalance between them. There's also a disjunction between home life and professional connections. 'The most stimulating relationship for an actor is often with a director,' he said. 'Nothing to do with flirtation. It's just very intimate, very exciting. As a director, you feel weirdly guilty at not lavishing on your family the energy and focus you've given in large part professionally all day. You begin to be dishonest about how much you're giving, because you know, in a way, that the person will become jealous. You pretend it's less intense. It becomes a little bit of a masquerade.'

Two weeks after *Spectre* was released, Mendes, then fifty, met Alison Balsom, a thirty-seven-year-old classical trumpet player, recognized in the musical world as one of Britain's finest brass instrumentalists. Balsom was, crucially, not an actress. On one of their early dates, Mendes took her to a film première. 'Ali said that, as they walked up toward the door, obviously no one recognized her – and all these people were shouting, "Sam! Sam! Sam!"' Pippa Harris recalled. 'She found that extraordinary. She said that she suddenly thought, Oh, you are really, really big in this world.' Harris sat with Mendes at a sold-out Royal Albert Hall concert where Balsom was playing: 'You watch Sam in the audience and he's totally transfixed. I remember him sitting there, beaming, radiating pride.' Intimacy requires equality. 'He's in awe of Ali both as a person and in her achievements,' Jez Butterworth told me. 'I think it's very useful that those achievements aren't in the same field as his.' Both Mendes and Balsom understand the obsession with excellence – 'We share a similar tenacity,' he said – and its perils. They married in January, 2017, and their daughter, Phoebe, was born in September. 'Without a shadow of a doubt, it's the best relationship of my life,' Mendes told me.

In the early years after separating from Winslet, Mendes said, he felt that his son needed him, but he couldn't always be there, because of the divorce; now, he said, 'that feeling that somehow

I'm never quite where I'm supposed to be has gone.' He has found a kind of balance to ambition. In the past three years, he has directed only two plays. But he has found time in his domestic idyll to co-write, with the TV and film writer Krysty Wilson-Cairns, his first screenplay: *1917* – a hard-charging First World War saga, loosely based on a story told to him by his grandfather, who was gassed in the trenches but survived – which he will direct and Steven Spielberg's Amblin Entertainment will co-produce. The film will be shot in Britain next spring. 'Phoebe is starting nursery, Joe and Charlie' – Balsom's son from a previous marriage – 'will be in secondary school,' he said. 'I don't want to be away for that.'

Still, Mendes is, by his own admission, 'addicted to the creative process. I'm built to move on. Pleasure is in the doing.' By mid-June of this year, he was back in the cavernous National Theatre Rehearsal Studio 1, directing a streamlined version of Stefano Massini's *The Lehman Trilogy*, adapted by Ben Power. (The eleven characters of the original script were now being played by three actors.) Although the opening was still a month away, the re-imagined production was already sold out. With the help of a revolving stage and projections, the play was a kind of theatrical kaleidoscope – an expressionistic blend of characterization, exposition, and visualization, which told the story of the rise of the immigrant Bavarian brothers from Southern peddlers to finance capitalists and then of the collapse of their bank. 'I'm the happiest I've ever been at rehearsal,' Mendes said, as the actors – Simon Russell Beale, Ben Miles, and Adam Godley – took up their positions in a wooden mockup of the boardroom. 'I don't have any idea how it will come out,' he added, smiling.

Mendes hankers for the exhilaration of discovery. 'The small triumphs, the victories every day, are what you live for,' he said. With *The Lehman Trilogy*, he worked to excavate the play's rhythms and its storytelling shorthand. 'Animate *the idea*,' he wrote in his first notes to his stage designer, Es Devlin. 'Make concrete *the shape of history* ... Understand in your head ... because you can feel it in your gut.' Every nanosecond of the production – the actors' glances, their gestures, their positions, their crosses between scenes, the counterpoint of image and action, the music – was shaped by Mendes. At one point, Beale stood on a table playing a 'piano' made of cardboard boxes. 'Let's just block it out,' Mendes called up to the actors, who did as they were told. 'Sit,' he said. He stood back and pondered the tableau. 'Now stand.' He studied the stage picture again. 'I think that's better,' he said. 'Let's see what happens in the next scene.' 'It's like a dance and Sam's choreographing it,' Beale told me during a break. But the experience was more revelatory than that. Mendes's work was like sculpture – a continual molding and remolding of space, speech, and gesture. (The show, which opened to rave reviews, will transfer to New York's Park Avenue Armory next March.)

On September 3rd, the first day of rehearsal for the Broadway-bound *The Ferryman*, in London's Welsh Center, two things were different. There were twenty-one actors in the room, not three, and Mendes was working with a script in which every character was fully imagined. Here his job was orchestration, not interpretation. 'The detail, the ear for dialogue, the rhythm of the whole thing – it's all him,' he said of Butterworth. 'You very rarely encounter writing of that quality.'

Mendes was in his usual mufti: black jeans, black sports

shirt, black-framed glasses, black FitFlop sneakers. As he eased his way into the scrum of actors meeting and greeting around the coffee urn – most of the cast from the London production had signed on for New York – he clapped his hands loudly. The hubbub stopped. 'Holiday's over,' he said. 'We've come back to the first day of school. You will unfortunately have the same boring teacher.' Butterworth was pressed against a sidewall, holding a bottle of water. He 'literally felt chills,' he said, at seeing his play begin a new life, headed for a new land. On September 24, 2016, at an Arsenal-Chelsea match, Butterworth had left a draft of the play – which dramatizes the intersection of politics and private life in Northern Ireland in 1981, at the height of the Troubles – in a cupboard in the Arsenal Football Club box the two men share. Even with the ending still unwritten, Mendes quickly agreed to stage the play.

Butterworth, who has three brothers and considers Mendes his fourth, is a sort of Mendes Maxi-Me: the same salt-and-pepper beard, the same swarthy skin, the same tonsorial style, but not the same metabolism. Mendes likes an early night; Butterworth is a carouser of note. Mendes is organized; Butterworth is chaotic. 'All you have to remember with Jez is that he grew up in an eccentric family,' Mendes told me. 'His father was very, very nervous of outsiders. When they rang the doorbell, he instructed the boys and their sister to hide in the bathroom until the person had gone. With Jez, you have to be in the bathroom with him. All the figures of authority in his life are knocking on the door. You can't be the person knocking on the door. I just don't want to be the guy saying, "Eat your peas."'

Mendes had a model of the set at the Bernard B. Jacobs Theatre. He steered Butterworth over to it to explain some adjustments, which he later addressed with the cast: 'American theatres are built with wider prosceniums. The distance between you and the farthest audience is much shorter. The set has been pushed forward, with the ceiling lowered, so you're physically closer to the audience. It makes it feel more intimate.' Mendes stopped and looked over at Fionnula Flanagan, a newcomer to the cast, who would play the doolally Aunt Maggie. 'Have you seen the set before?' he asked. 'No,' she said. 'Welcome to your new house,' Mendes said, smiling. Later, he pointed to a flight of stairs that had been moved forward on the sidewall of the farmhouse kitchen. 'The staircase is steeper,' he said. Genevieve O'Reilly, who, as Mary Carney, the frail, reclusive wife, has to make all her entrances and exits – many of them carrying a baby – via those precipitous steps, buried her head in her hands. 'Joke,' Mendes said.

With Mendes reading the stage directions, the cast cantered through the first act, then broke for lunch. Before they left, he asked them to write down answers to two questions and hand them to him at the end of the break: 'When your character goes out in the morning, what's in your pocket? What's in your bedroom?' 'It gets them thinking about their parts in a non-textual way,' he explained to me. 'It stops them from going back to just muscle memory, so they reimagine each other and themselves.' At the end of the day, rather like a teacher reading student essays, Mendes leaned back in his chair and read out some of the answers while the actors vied to identify the characters they belonged to. 'I wouldn't dream of having a handbag,' he began. 'Aunt Pat!' someone shouted, identifying the feisty firebrand played by Dearbhla Molloy. Mendes inspected another. 'This is good,' he said. 'My best handkerchief, the one with lace around it.

A lump of sugar, in case I meet a horse on the road.' It turned out to be Flanagan's vision of Aunt Maggie.

As I watched Mendes engage with the actors, savoring the nuances of their reading and issuing clear strategic instructions, I recalled something that his father had told me. When Mendes was nine and staying with his father, he had the use of a reel-to-reel tape recorder. 'I would come up and find him acting out things from *The Goon Show*, Peter said. 'He would be acting them out on tape.' Mendes, it seemed to me, was still doing the same thing: figuring out how stories worked and giving voice to all the parts. For him, theatrical exploration has always contained an element of consolation. His long career suggests an Albert Camus line that he sometimes quotes: 'A man's work is nothing but this slow trek to rediscover, through the detours of art, those two or three great and simple images in whose presence his heart first opened.' 'There is a grief that can never be solved,' Mendes told me. 'And that's what fuels you and confounds you in equal measure. It gives you a motor.'

Varieties of disturbance

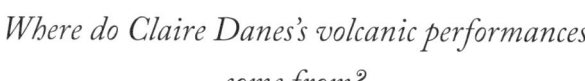

Where do Claire Danes's volcanic performances come from?

On a muggy June morning, in a sprawling, unnamed, and unnumbered red brick building near downtown Charlotte, North Carolina – which serves as the headquarters for Showtime's political-thriller series *Homeland* – tornado warnings were being broadcast on TV. Outside, torrential rain brought traffic to a standstill on the highway. Inside, the cast and crew of *Homeland* were hard at work by 8am, calmly building their own storm for the first episode of the much awaited third season. In the finale of Season 2, the characters had survived 'the worst terrorist disaster since 9/11': a car bombing at C.I.A. headquarters that killed more than two hundred people. The emotional weather buffeting them now was contained within a behemoth enclosed wooden set, where the homes of the show's two central figures – the bipolar, transgressive C.I.A. operative Carrie Mathison (Claire Danes) and her suspect, Sergeant Nicholas Brody (Damian Lewis), a captured marine sniper turned Al Qaeda sleeper – had been meticulously designed, right down to the

CDs on Carrie's bureau (the Temptations and John Coltrane's *Newport '63*).

In the vastness of the studio, the only sure way to know that acting was taking place was to huddle near the twin monitors behind the set. On the screens, Carrie sat on her living-room sofa, her eyes fixed on her television, where her longtime mentor, Saul Berenson (Mandy Patinkin), now the head of the C.I.A., was being strategically sandbagged at a congressional hearing on the bombing. Danes had no lines in the scene, but as Berenson's testimony shifted from showboating to scapegoating – he referred to a 'case officer' who was 'unstable' – her face was a barometer of Carrie's interior. Incredulity, sorrow, and humiliation swept over her. The director Lesli Linka Glatter, a noisy dynamo in a T-shirt, vest, and cargo pants, stood so close to a monitor screen that her nose almost touched it, her head rolling with each shift in Danes's expression, as if urging her into every unsettling transition. When Carrie finally sat back on the sofa, with a gesture of abject disbelief, Glatter's arms shot high above her head, as if Danes had scored a goal, which, in a way, she had. 'Cut! That's great!' Glatter called, while Danes quietly dried her eyes.

After four takes, four huddles, four different versions of Carrie's chagrin, Glatter declared herself satisfied. She was excited by the spectrum of feelings that Danes had laid out for her to choose from in the final edit. 'We talked about how it could land,' she explained. 'One was anger. The other was a kind of betrayal. To me, the one with the tear – my heart hurt. But I don't know where that's gonna take us.' Glatter, who is also a co-executive producer of the show, added, 'I always come with a clear plan, but then you have an actress like this who is fearless, and you really want to see what she's bringing to the party.'

Eleven director's chairs were arranged in a semicircle around the monitor screens. On some of them, emblazoned in white, were the names of staff grandees. The chair meant for the Emmy award-winning Danes, however, was marked simply 'Carrie' – a sign, if more were needed, that the agitated, wayward espionage agent was more real to those present than the thirty-four-year-old actress who had given life to her in twenty-four previous episodes. Danes, still dressed in Carrie's unassuming mufti of black slacks and white shirt, strode resolutely off the soundstage and settled into her chair. 'I didn't think the scene would be very emotional,' she said. 'But, in the actual playing of it, hurt is sort of unavoidable. I don't really edit as I go along. I leave them to decide.'

Although there is nothing domineering in Danes's demeanor on the set – she creates no commotion around herself – onscreen she is capable of what David Harewood, who played the stonewalling deputy director of the C.I.A. in the first two seasons, calls a 'tsunami of emotion.' In extremis or out of it, her body semaphores feeling. As one *Saturday Night Live* cast member commented during a recent lampoon by Anne Hathaway, 'It's like she makes her mouth turn fully upside down. Her eyes seem to be looking five directions at once. It's like her whole face is chewing gum.' Danes, speaking of her portrayal of Carrie's manic moments in Season 3, told me, 'I don't even know how it happens, but I start shaking. My body expresses it. It's really fun when it starts becoming physicalized. It's not necessarily a conscious decision. It's a little mysterious to me.' That kind of porous physicalization comes, in large part, from Danes's early training in dance, which she began at the age of six. 'Dancing is a kind of drawing,' she said. 'I'm interpreting what I'm hearing with my body. Acting is like that, too.' She added, 'I use my body to generate feelings a lot.

If I have a very emotional scene, I'll often walk in circles before. It gets you out of your head. I'm not afraid to use it.'

Danes is frequently accused of being over the top. '*Homeland* is actually TV's best post-9/11 metaphor yet, where Carrie is America and America is a mad, paranoid, overacting blonde,' one TV critic wrote of *Homeland*'s first season. But, then, people suffering from psychological disorders often are melodramatic. 'We are so much bigger in life than we realize,' Danes said. 'We're betraying so much more than we think.' Over the decades, in her performances, she has explored a full spectrum of disturbance, from spousal abuse, autism, and paralysis to Carrie's bipolar disorder and the paranoia of adolescence. At Harvard last year, to accept the Hasty Pudding Theatricals' Woman of the Year award, she joked about her penchant for roles that turn acting into an extreme sport. 'I'm just working my way through the *DSM-V* – the *Diagnostic and Statistical Manual of Mental Disorders* – she said. 'So whatever mental condition you have for me . . .' But, in its silliness, the Hasty Pudding roast – which required Danes to parade down Massachusetts Avenue wedged between two burly drag queens, to read a faux-Shakespearean speech sending up her brief appearance in *The Vagina Monologues* ('To be or not to be an angry lesbian'), and to challenge-dance with a gangly, moon-walking 'Virus' – revealed more of her personality than her acting roles do.

In her work, Danes flirts with the darker forces; in her life, she exhibits a wacky charm and a swift, playful mind. She has a particular affection for puns. When she first went to dinner at the home of her friend Jenette Kahn, who was a producer of *The Flock* (2007), in which Danes co-starred with Richard Gere, she arrived with a gift of bespoke lingerie: a camisole with an image of Sigmund Freud printed on it – a Freudian slip. When Patinkin recently sent out an S.O.S. for Danes's roast-chicken recipe, he received a forensic two-page e-mail on how to cook the bird, which ended, 'I hope this arrives in time (thyme?).' In June, on a visit to an antique store in Charlotte, Danes couldn't resist buying a hamburger timer in the shape of a hand, with a clock embedded in the palm – a hand burger timer. 'I've never seen in any other actor such a divide between the performance and the person in the room,' the novelist Michael Cunningham, who became friends with Danes in 2004, during the filming of his screenplay *Evening*, said. (In 2009, he officiated at her wedding, in the South of France, to the British actor Hugh Dancy, whom she met on the set of *Evening*.) 'Claire's buoyancy is real. She's not impersonating a buoyant person.' One of the lessons of her adulthood, Danes has said, was 'that there is real honor in being a total goofball.'

'The central mystery of Claire is, where does she come from?' Cunningham said. 'She doesn't match her family. If you gathered into a room two dozen parent-aged people and said, 'O.K., spot the Daneses,' you couldn't do it.'

Danes's parents, Chris and Carla, met at the Rhode Island School of Design, in the early sixties. Chris was scrawny, bespectacled, funny, and analytical; he studied engineering and biology at Brown, before transferring to RISD's photography department. Carla was earnest, intuitive, eccentric, and prolix. (One of Danes's friends refers to her as the Queen of Too Much Information.) Both were liberal, former VISTA volunteers, and adventurous, and both had been marked by problematic childhoods. Chris's mother died when he was ten; his father, Gibson Danes, a former dean of the Yale School of art and architecture, was distinguished but distant. He committed suicide in 1992, along with his third wife, the artist Ilse Getz. Chris 'just kind of grew himself up,' Carla told me. Carla was the eldest of five children; she spent her childhood helping her mother wrangle her siblings.

The Daneses moved to New York in 1969, and a few years later bought a seven-story building on Crosby Street, in SoHo, with another RISD couple. In order to pay the bills, they had to put their artistic ambitions on hold. Chris became a building contractor. Carla, a textile designer and painter, started a day care that she called the Crosby Street Toddlers Group. 'For me, a lot's been about survival,' Chris said. 'I've been clinging to the edge of the boat and only fairly recently do I realize that I'm inside the boat and I can relax.'

Still, Danes's parents retained a playful side. The two-thousand-square-foot loft on Crosby Street, where Danes, who was born in 1979, and her older brother, Asa, grew up, featured a trampoline, a trapeze near the long kitchen table, and a swing suspended from the living-room ceiling in front of high windows. 'It felt like you could just fly out onto Lafayette Street,' Danes recalled. For the day care, Carla installed a large box of rice, which served as an indoor sand pit, and containers of dress-up clothes. 'A huge emphasis was placed on art and creativity,' Danes said. At the same time, Danes found herself re-creating Carla's childhood – sharing her mother and her home with a gaggle of younger children. 'You get a little lost in the shuffle,' she said.

Below the antic surface of family life was an indigestible anxiety. Chris and Carla were lumbered with a sense of not having lived up to their own potential; 'both of us were smarter and more imaginative,' Carla said. The Daneses felt that they should treat their own children as 'unfinished equals,' and Danes picked up the message of autonomy early on. 'I played grownup – a child's idea of grownup. A little too strict, a little too arch,' she said. At the age of three, Danes demanded and was granted the power position at the head of the dinner table. When she was four, and a rogue haircut left her with bangs that she didn't want, she turned furiously to her mother. 'Why did you let them do that? It's *my* body!' she said. 'Claire seemed always ready to play the adult,' Carla said. 'She always seemed to want to be on to the next stage.' As a child, Danes became, as she put it, 'parentified' – a kind of parent to her own parents, a role that was infuriating, impossible, and irresistible. She described her mother as 'very childlike,' adding, 'She needs mothering herself.' Her father, she said, had 'lost every parent he ever had. Everybody kind of held vigil over him. I wanted to rescue him from those awful feelings.' Danes carried another burden: the name of her father's late mother, of whom he has no memories. Calling his daughter Claire, Chris admitted, was 'big' for him. '"Repair" would be too strong a word, but it had a satisfaction to reach out to this memory I didn't have,' he said.

Danes, however, who was 'riding the subway alone at the age of eleven,' sometimes felt unprotected. 'I think they realize that they did ask too much of my brother and me. They regret that,' she said. A couple of times in her childhood, Danes had a 'dalliance with madness.' Terrifying visions of ghosts and gargoyles emerged out of the showerhead and from shapes in the woodwork. 'Very O.C.D.,' she said. 'They were gonna suck me into some horrible place.' She briefly saw a psychiatrist. Later, when she was nineteen, famous, living in her own SoHo loft (with a ceiling swing), and coming down from her first and last hit of Ecstasy, Danes was again visited by these emissaries of her unconscious aggression. 'They were the same, except smaller,' she said. 'I was, like, "Really, guys? You're still here? I'm a grownup. I'm done."'

Danes discovered the joy of dissimulation at the age of three, when, a chronically bad napper, she passed herself off as asleep. 'I'd observed my mother sleeping, and she twitched,' she said. 'So I kind of did that. It was a pretty refined imitation. I really loved the experience of pretending.' When she was five, dancing and singing on her parents' bed while watching Madonna on TV, she first 'registered that performing could be a job' and decided that that was what she wanted to do. The next year, she signed up for a class with Ellen Robbins at Dance Theatre Workshop, starting a weekly ninety-minute regimen, which she kept up for a decade. Even then, Danes was drawn to theatrical extremes: she danced a shipwreck, a moth drawn to a flame, a 'lazybones' hauling an enormous sack. 'She was a risk-taker and improvised full blast,' Robbins said.

Around the age of eight, Danes, exasperated by a boy in her class, was spooked by the pleasure she got from her revenge fantasies about him. 'Can people read your thoughts?' she asked her mother. 'Your imagination is your own. You can do whatever you like with it,' Carla answered. The knowledge that 'you could be a good person and host lavishly violent acts in your imagination' was, Danes said, a kind of liberation. 'I was so happy,' she added.

A year or so later, after her best friend, Ariel Flavin, appeared in a film made by a graduate student at New York University, Danes, 'burning to have the experience,' put herself forward for the student's next project, *Dreams of Love*, a film about child abuse. (She auditioned for one of the movie's executive producers, Milos Forman.) Danes thought it 'interesting to think about' the rage, loss, and bewilderment a girl would feel at being molested by her father. Onscreen, she found an outlet for her own forbidden feelings. 'I loved discovering the camera. It was like a confidant,' she said. 'To be seen is a crucial part of my attraction to acting.' She began to imagine a life as an actress. 'Someone told me that actors don't typically make much money,' she said. So when people asked her what she wanted to be when she grew up she'd say, 'I'm going to be a therapist and act on the side.' At ten, however, she formally announced her vocation at the dinner table. 'I said, "You know what? Money or no money, I have to be true to my art. I'm gonna take the risk. There is no plan B. I'm going to act."'

At twelve, after two years at the Lee Strasberg Institute, Danes was offered a part in the soap opera *One Life to Live*. She turned it down. 'I was a malleable, unformed actor. I didn't want to develop bad habits,' she explained. Then, in December, 1992, on the basis of an appearance on an episode of *Law & Order*, the thirteen-year-old Danes was one of two young actresses – Alicia Silverstone was the other – who were called to audition in Los Angeles for a show about American adolescents. The show was being developed by Ed Zwick and Marshall Herskovitz, who had previously hit the mother lode with their exploration of another age group, *Thirtysomething*, along with Winnie Holzman, who had been a member of the *Thirtysomething* writing team. 'In our heads was some notion of trying to write a more accurate representation of the teenage experience,' Zwick said. Holzman was enlisted to write the pilot, which she began by keeping a journal in a teenager's voice, the funny, thoughtful, naïve palaver of fifteen-year-old angela Chase:

> – My mom's a slob. She'll go for like weeks without making her bed, then all of a sudden it'll become like her religion. Make your bed! Make your bed.
> – This summer I began to feel really terrible about being white. It just seems like black people have this really hard time. And yet everybody wants to be like them.

Silverstone auditioned first. Zwick, impressed, told Herskovitz, 'It's done. Just cast her.' But Herskovitz thought she was too pretty for Holzman's messy high-school universe, which included subplots about drug addiction, bullying, binge drinking, promiscuity, and homosexuality. 'Alicia is so beautiful that that would have affected her experience of the world. People would have been telling her she was beautiful since she was six years old. You can't put that face in what's been written for this girl,' he argued. Linda Lowy, the casting director, suggested that they see Danes before deciding. 'From the minute she walked in the room, Claire was chilling, astounding, and silent,' Lowy said. 'There was so much power coming out of her without her doing much.' One of the scenes that Danes read – which involved a nervy bathroom breakup with Angela's best friend, Sharon – required her to cry. 'Tell me what I did, Angela. I mean, I would really like to know,' Sharon says. 'We get to that line and Claire's face turns entirely red,' Herskovitz said. 'Her body starts to vibrate and tears come into her eyes. You realize that she's having a physical experience that is beyond acting.' Even then, Danes's defining quality as an actress – a combination of thoughtfulness and impulsiveness

– was on display. 'She seemed to have been born fully grown, you know, out of a seashell,' Herskovitz said. Zwick claimed that Danes was his first sighting of a 'wise child,' a rare species that show business occasionally tosses up. As he put it later, 'What she knows cannot be taught.' Danes also satisfied another quality that Holzman's script called for: her face could transform in an instant from beautiful to ordinary.

Holzman's pilot for *My So-Called Life* (then titled *Someone Like Me*) was meant to trap 'a naked quality, not a person but a feeling of freedom and bondage, shyness and fearlessness,' she said. Holzman found herself staring at this protean paradox in the flesh. Danes 'was sexy and not sexy, free and bound up, open and closed, funny and frighteningly serious,' Holzman recalled. Her performance freed Holzman's imagination. 'We gave birth to each other,' she said. 'I was looking at someone who literally could do anything, and so I could, too.' The novelist and television writer Richard Kramer, who worked on *My So-Called Life*, places Holzman's writing for the show on a continuum of original television voices that leads from her to mike White, Larry David, and Lena Dunham. 'Winnie wouldn't be Winnie without Claire,' he said. 'And Claire wouldn't be Claire without Winnie. There was something mythological about their meeting.'

After Danes left the audition room, Lowy recalled, 'no one could really speak.' In the excitement of the moment, the production team found themselves faced with a conundrum. Silverstone was sixteen and 'emancipated,' meaning, in Hollywood's piquant terminology, that she could work very long days. Danes was thirteen and, by law, had to go to school. If they cast Silverstone, they could move ahead with the show they'd written; if they opted for Danes, they'd have to adapt later scripts to accommodate her schedule. 'We turned to Winnie,' Herskovitz recalled. 'Winnie said, "Let's change the nature of the show."' He added, 'In that moment, we decided to include the lives of the parents more.'

★

Danes arrived in Los Angeles on January 18, 1994 – the day after the Northridge earthquake. The relocation was thrilling for her, but harder for her parents, who had to cope with suburban isolation. 'The power and attention that come with a successful Hollywood thing are like a big wave,' Chris Danes said. 'For me, a level of success was not letting any one of us get pummelled by it.' Carla closed down her day-care business to become her daughter's full-time manager and on-set 'supervisor,' a role she characterized as 'a dog and a shadow.' 'She'd experienced terrible frustration as an artist and she didn't want me to go through that,' Danes said. 'She wanted me to have as much creative freedom and opportunity as I could have. I'm so grateful that she did that. I don't know if I would have been able to do it for my child.'

My So-Called Life, which débuted on ABC that August and won Danes the first of her four Golden Globe awards the next year, more or less mirrored her own stressful experience of junior high in New York, where she had difficulty 'navigating the social seas.' She changed schools twice, 'fleeing one mean girl only to find another incarnation of that same girl in the next school.' She was targeted for her looks, her nerdy curiosity, her refusal to conform. 'I thought it was a crock of shit, all these social games. I couldn't deal,' she said. 'She was not cool,' Flavin recalled. 'She just always said what she thought. She raised her hand every time she knew the answer, and she knew the answer every time. So people didn't like her.' At school, Danes could also be mouthy and a bit of a hot-head. 'I went through this vigilante period,' she said. 'I would see somebody being bullied, and I would get really righteous and intercept.' Once, seeing a boy berating a girl after class, she slapped him. 'He slapped me back, and we went to the principal's office,' she said. When she got the role in *My So-Called Life*, Danes said, 'I remember being so relieved that I had an opportunity to voice my complaints about my time at school so perfectly and so eloquently, with the right amount of rage and humor.'

She continued, 'Angela and I were the same age, so we could dance around each other. Sometimes I would have an experience and then it would be articulated in the show. Other times, I would play it out, then experience it personally later.' When the script called for Angela, who was besotted with the granite chinned Jordan Catalano (Jared Leto), 'to kiss his face,' Danes said, 'I was, like, 'kiss his face'? What is that? I had no idea what it meant. Jared had to coach me.' In the first Angela-Jordan onscreen meeting, Angela slips and falls in mud at a party and, to get away from everyone, rushes into a room where she comes face to face with her heartthrob, who is watching television. She panics and tries to leave, but the door is stuck. She lets her body go limp, as if she were going to fall to the floor, then pulls herself back up, smiling, and sits down awkwardly beside him. 'The whole thing takes a second and a half,' Herskovitz said. 'It's full of a lifetime of irony and ruefulness and embarrassment. She was fully equipped as a master craftsman.' Danes's resourcefulness intimidated the creative team. 'I went five days before I gave her a direction,' he added.

In 1995, despite an online campaign (the first in the history of television) to save the cult hit, ABC cancelled *My So-Called*

Life. The show had put Danes into the dream life of the nation; it had also brought her to the attention of film directors. Gillian Armstrong had cast her as the terminally ill Beth in *Little Women* (1994); Francis Ford Coppola hired Danes to play the brutalized wife Matt Damon rescues in *The Rainmaker* (1997); and Baz Luhrmann gave her the chance to play opposite her teenage crush, Leonardo DiCaprio, in a modern reimagining of Shakespeare's tale of first love, *Romeo+Juliet* (1996). 'She was the only girl that looked me in the eye in auditions,' Di Caprio said. Danes's performance as Juliet is the most luminous of her early years, an effortless exhibition of her modesty, exuberance, and sensuality.

In 1999, after making thirteen films in five years, Danes enrolled at Yale. She was twenty, celebrated and rich, but she 'didn't feel finished as a person.' 'I didn't have a sensibility, a value system, an aesthetic. I needed that time in school to be clear on who I was and what kind of career I wanted to have,' she said. But by the time she left Yale, in 2001, without completing a degree, she felt, she said, removed from acting and from the film industry. 'I just felt outside it,' she said. 'I started to think, How do these actors do it? It seemed alien and incredible. I became self-conscious.' Danes found it hard to get roles that tested her range and her resources. She had a couple of solid outings: as a female Shakespearean wannabe in the all-male world of Elizabethan theatre, in Richard Eyre's *Stage Beauty*, and as a vulnerable aspiring artist behind the glove counter at Saks, in Steve Martin's *Shopgirl* – both strong performances in weak scripts. But, increasingly, she was cast around the edges of the story (in *Me and Orson Welles*, *Evening*, *The Hours*, *The Family Stone*). Between decent roles, she did business chores, appearing in such movies as *The Mod Squad* and *Terminator 3*.

Despondent over the roles she was and was not being offered, she resumed her dance training, after a decade's hiatus, working now with the choreographer Tamar Rogoff, who was the mother of her friend Ariel Flavin, 'to learn her body' as a grownup. The two developed an exercise in which one of them danced as the other watched and wrote down free associations; then, after a few minutes, they'd reverse roles. Rogoff challenged Danes to trust her body to communicate for her. 'You don't have to tell us what you think,' she said. 'Just feel it. Your whole body's dramatic.' Referring to Danes's long neck and spine, Rogoff told me, 'She has a very unusual body. Her spine really bends. She can bow, and then she can be like a warrior. She's willing to abandon style for the essence of something.'

Over time, they devised *Christina Olson: American model*, an hour-long solo piece about the paralyzed woman memorialized in Andrew Wyeth's painting 'Christina's World,' who refused her wheelchair and insisted on crawling everywhere. 'I wouldn't let her use her face,' Rogoff said. 'I said, "You're gonna be acting with your body."' Danes performed the piece at P.S. 122, in New York's East Village, in 2005. In footage intercut with a video of the performance, Danes, as Olson, slithers along First Avenue on her belly. Pulling herself up the stairs of P.S. 122, step by step, on her elbows, she crawls into the theatre. 'Nobody noticed,' Danes said. 'Some scrawny white chick dragging herself on the floor in basically no clothing. I thought, Wow! You can get away with a lot more in this town than you realize.' ('Make no mistake: She's a dancer,' Deborah Jowitt, the dance critic of the *Village Voice*, wrote.)

A couple of years later, while in London, Danes, then twenty-eight, took a call from the British director Mick Jackson, who told her about an HBO movie that he wanted her to star in, a bio-pic of the autistic professor and animal-welfare activist Temple Grandin. In an interview with the Directors Guild of America, Jackson recalled telling Danes that, in order to play a person with such a limited emotional range, she would have to deny herself 'all the things which you use as an actress, the ability to make the audience empathize with you, because this is a character who doesn't empathize with anybody, even her own mother. She cannot bear to be hugged by her own mother.' He went on, 'You're going to look very unattractive, because it's a person who's loud in conversation, can't modulate her voice, is very awkward in society . . . because she can't think of how other people are looking at her. You're going to have to work without a safety net.' Danes, who was speaking to Jackson from a seventeenth-floor apartment, told him that she was looking down to the street below. 'I realize that what you're asking me to do is to jump that distance,' she said.

Temple Grandin was in her early sixties at the time. 'When I heard that Claire Danes was gonna be playing me in the movies, I went to the Internet and looked her up. I saw the long blond hair, and I thought, You gotta be kidding!' she said. Danes invited Grandin to lunch in her New York loft as Grandin explained what it felt like to be autistic, Danes filmed her and recorded her voice to study. 'Temple was so candid, so guileless,' Danes said. Grandin could not hear consonants well; she overcompensated by hitting them hard, something Danes picked up on in her voice work. Danes enlisted Rogoff to help teach her Grandin's rigid movements, undergoing a regimen of physical realignment that went on for weeks. 'Claire is totally the opposite of Temple. She projects out,' Rogoff said. 'We had to change the way she held her head. I had to pull her chin all the way back, because if you're autistic you're not communicating with the world – you're communicating within.' Together, Danes and Rogoff developed a 'panic lock': a hunched, fearful posture, in which Danes's pelvis and rib cage were yoked together so that she moved 'like a cow bent heavy under you.' To this, they added gestures: hand wringing, leg shaking, hair stroking, downward searching eyes, hyperventilation. To test Grandin's body language, Danes took walks through Wall Street traffic and into the subway. Being caged inside this unstable physical frame brought her new insights. 'Your internal world becomes really vast when you're that disengaged,' she said. 'I thought that it would be lonely playing Temple, because she's socially isolated. But she's so turned on by her ideas that she has the company of the ideas. She didn't have the same needs that I had. That was an interesting lesson. What I perceive as a loss isn't necessarily a loss for her.'

As the first day of shooting approached, Jackson repeatedly asked Danes if she'd like to show him anything. 'She said, "I don't think you'll be disappointed, but I'm not ready to show you yet,"' Jackson recalled. For the first scene of the film, Danes looked at the camera and announced, 'My name is Temple Grandin.' At that moment, Jackson said, 'the hair stood up on the backs of our heads. Not only had she got the booming voice, but when she walked from one corner of the room to the other she strode leading with the shoulders, and I thought, Oh, my God, that's Temple Grandin.' Danes didn't imitate Grandin; she channelled her. She found delightful moments of humor in Grandin's gaucheness, and her protean face worked its weird magic. 'There are scenes where she looks like a young Grace Kelly and scenes where she looks like an old horse-faced English duchess,' Jackson said. Danes refused to watch the rushes. 'I think she very much wanted to be in the moment and not to have that moment broken by thinking, How do I look? Is my right profile showing to my best advantage?' Jackson said. 'She wants that moment to be sacrosanct – the moment when you're in the character and nothing else in the world matters.'

Of the many accolades Danes received for the performance – an Emmy and a Golden Globe among them – the ultimate one was bestowed offstage. When Danes's name was called at the Golden Globes and she rose slowly from her seat in a backless salmon-pink gown, Grandin, seated next to her in Western regalia, stood and embraced her. Grandin keeps a framed note from Danes in her house. 'Through you I think I have become a better person,' it says.

The day after 'Temple Grandin' aired, in early 2010, the television writer-producers Alex Gansa and Howard Gordon, who had worked on *24*, sat down to discuss their idea for a new psychological thriller based on the Israeli series *Prisoners of War*, by Gideon Raff. *24*, a series about the male intelligence officer Jack Bauer (Kiefer Sutherland), a go-it-alone hero who spent as much time fighting red tape as he did fighting terrorism, had premièred two months after 9/11. But eight seasons later, in the world of Abu Ghraib, Guantánamo, and drone strikes, the political landscape was murkier, and it had become increasingly difficult to tell the cowboys from the Indians. 'There was this wonderful irony,' Gordon said. 'The thing that we had to be most afraid of was a monster of our own creation.' When he and Gansa conceived their show, which became *Homeland*, their primary concern was America's fear fatigue. 'The law of unintended consequences had created all this collateral damage,' Gordon said. 'There were no good answers. We just wanted to dramatize the complexity.' Their story, embroidered from the headlines of the day, gave shape to the country's growing skepticism and fear of blowback.

One of the nation's greatest losses on 9/11 was its illusion of invincibility. Carrie Mathison, poised between breakthrough and breakdown, personified the country's deracinating confusion. Both Carrie and Sergeant Brody, who was held hostage by Al Qaeda for eight years, see themselves as patriots; both, in different ways, risk their credibility. 'We knew we wanted to create an unreliable narrator, or, at least, someone whom most other people looked at as being unreliable, in part because of her youth, in part because of her record, and in part because of her gender,' Gordon said of Carrie. 'Unlike Jack Bauer, she is a woman who was marginalized. We reverse-engineered her. We pathologized her to account for her gift.'

Gordon and Gansa's early screenplay drafts made no mention of bipolar disorder. 'We created Carrie's behavior, then stumbled on the diagnosis,' Gordon said. although the illness elevated Carrie into the realm of the extraordinary – 'They fly closer to the sun than the rest of us,' Gansa said of bipolar-disorder sufferers – it also gave her a defining obstacle to negotiate, a double time bomb, which threatens at every moment to blow up her mission and her life. 'It's her kryptonite,' Gordon said, a natural weakness that maximizes her loneliness, her secrecy, and her fear of intimacy.

Gansa and Gordon had seen how in *Temple Grandin* Danes walked the razor's edge between competence and unbalance. 'There's something in her that feels a little bit broken,' Gordon said. Their new heroine was, similarly, 'an extremely intelligent woman freighted with a real emotional problem.' The writing team envisaged Danes in the role from the beginning – for the first six drafts of their pilot they called their character Claire. The network argued for an older woman to play Carrie. At the time, TV series such as *Weeds*, *Nurse Jackie*, and *The United States of Tara* were finding success with actresses in their late thirties and forties. But Gansa and Gordon were adamant. 'We wanted Carrie to have this flaw, this illness, but to give her the opportunity to maybe rise above it, to fashion her life in a way that opened up the possibility that she would have another chapter,' Gansa said. 'If you're forty-five or forty-six, and you've been living with bipolar illness all this time, the story is already written. The audience cannot root for the character in the same way.' Gansa and Gordon finally met with Danes on November 1, 2010, over drinks at the London, in West Hollywood. 'We were prepared to have our hearts broken when she said no,' Gansa recalled. For her part, Danes was beginning to believe that she'd never again be offered a challenging film role. In the nearly two years since she shot *Temple Grandin*, her career had languished. 'It was getting painful. I was starting to kind of cry a lot. Sort of uncontrollably,' she said. 'I'd had such a deeply fulfilling experience that I just was not gonna settle.' at the time of her meeting with Gansa and Gordon, she was up for a supporting role as J. Edgar Hoover's secretary, in Clint Eastwood's *J. Edgar*. 'Here was this F.B.I. story and I was thinking about it in the same weekend as this C.I.A. story,' she said. 'I was thinking, you know – I could be the secretary or I could be Hoover.'

The show's first season opened, in 2011, with an establishing shot of an agitated Carrie Mathison beseeching her controllers to protect her source while impatiently negotiating Baghdad traffic.

Viewers were thrust directly into the center of *Homeland*'s two dramas: the one outside Carrie's mind and the one inside it. Danes's job on the show, Gansa said, 'was to be an open wound.' In the postmodern TV crime thriller – *The Killing*, *The Bridge*, *Monk* – it's not enough for the detective to solve the problem; the detective also has to *have* a problem, to struggle both with society and with the self. 'It's micro and macro,' Danes said. 'I thought about it in those terms.'

To prepare for the role, Danes read medical texts, consulted with therapists and bipolar patients, and followed the blogs of people in hypomanic states. (Her own bipolar acquaintances, she complained, were all 'annoyingly medicated.') 'I have always been curious about people who are wired in a fundamentally different way from most of us and was eager to integrate the bipolar condition into the character, without turning it into a gimmick,' she told me in an e-mail, adding, of Carrie, 'I also appreciated the dichotomy between her obvious flaws and transgressions and her strong moral core. For all her recklessness, she is surprisingly earnest and honest. another fun paradox: she dedicates herself entirely to the noble cause of protecting her country, but she doesn't do it simply for noble reasons. She is terrified of forging intimate relationships with others – which is, basically, what constitutes a life – because she knows the kind of damage that her condition can wreak. Because she has such an anemic life, it is easier for her to risk losing it on behalf of her cause. While this is an advantage of sorts, she must live with the pain of her loneliness. She is, basically, a classic superhero. Who wouldn't want to play that?'

In Season 3, Carrie blames the C.I.A. car bombing in the Season 2 finale on a lack of vigilance caused by her medicated 'normality' and goes off her meds. Danes welcomes the narrative volte-face. 'I want to see more of the boring work involved in just maintaining a healthy plateau,' she said. 'I think we have to see her slog through the daily grind. I think we owe it to audiences.'

It is Carrie's fear of intimacy, paired with promiscuity, that shapes the show's steamy romantic subplot – a mystifying game of cat and mouse between Carrie and Brody. 'It's a way of getting out of their heads,' Danes said of the sexual compulsiveness of some bipolar sufferers. 'It's another kind of self-medication.' Danes refers to Carrie's exhilarating rounds of slap-and-tickle with Brody as a 'slalom.' Part of the characters' sparky charisma is due to the transparent opaqueness of Lewis, an Old Etonian playing an American marine. 'He has a slightly cheeky, naughty on-set demeanor, which I'm missing now that our characters are so physically estranged in the third season,' Danes said. 'I can throw hard and fast and he'll always catch the ball and return it in surprising ways.' Gordon recalled, 'The chemistry between them we saw the first day they were together, but they were adversarial. It really wasn't until Episode 4 in the car park, when Claire puts herself in front of him and plays him, and he scrutinizes her and doesn't quite know what to believe about her – that was where we thought that this was going to be special. It was dangerous; it was electric; it was alive.'

The pilot of *Homeland* aired on October 2, 2011, and drew more than a million viewers – the highest-rated début of a Showtime drama in eight years. More than 1.7 million people tuned in for the première of the second season; by the finale, that number had grown to 2.3 million. Danes, who had become an icon for a generation as a teenager, reclaimed that stature as an adult. Fans began to approach her 'with a rabid look in their eyes.' The admiration reached as far as the White House. According to Danes,

President Obama, who was given an autographed boxed set of the series, told her when they met, 'You're a finer actress than I am President.' Danes has a seven-year contract for *Homeland*, but she has learned to take nothing for granted. 'Who knows if it will last that long,' she said. 'No character is safe.'

On the last day of shooting for the Season 3 première, Danes sat working her iPhone outside a liquor store in the Plaza Midwood area of Charlotte. She had just taped a scene in which Carrie panic-buys tequila, her current self-medication of choice, and is approached by a hunky shopper. Glatter darted out of the store's crepuscular gloom. 'I'm gonna miss you,' she said to Danes.

'You're around, right?' Danes said, glancing up at her director.

'Oh, yes. Forever. You're stuck with me till November.'

Danes was leaving the next day for a trip to her farmhouse, in the Hudson Valley, where she would spend time with her parents and Dancy and their son, Cyrus, who was born last December. (Danes had to use a 'belly double' for the final episodes of Season 2, when she was eight months pregnant.) In addition to a newly purchased town house in the West Village, Danes also keeps an apartment on the forty-second floor of a Charlotte skyscraper, and a place with Dancy in Toronto, where he films the NBC series *Hannibal*.

'That's perfect,' Glatter said. 'It'll be nice to have that break before all the emotional stuff to come.'

'Yeah, I know,' Danes said, fixing her with a look.

Glatter disappeared back into the liquor store, which was also a treasure trove of novelty items: stickers ('Unattended Children Will Be Given Espresso and a Free Puppy'); exotic coffees (Booty

Call, Bad Hair Day, and Sexy Power, the blend that Danes bought for Dancy); and specialty wine labels, some of which Glatter broadcast from the air-conditioned store to the sweltering world outside (Naked on Roller Skates, Yard Dog, Broke Ass). After filming her last scene, Danes had lingered in the store to snap a shot of a sticker, which she planned to post to Instagram: 'If Women Ruled the World There Would Be No Wars Just a Bunch of Jealous Countries Not Talking to Each Other.'

'I'm away from everybody in my life,' she said, to explain her attachment to her phone. 'Wherever I am, I'm estranged.' She elaborated later, 'You just have to accept that you're always going to be missing someone. But, as you're missing one set of people, you're getting reacquainted with others. I have dear friends in L.A., in New York, upstate, friends now in Toronto. I had to create a community there when I became a mom.'

At her New York town house, Danes keeps drawers full of glitter, pipe cleaners, and fabric paint, and frequently has craft days with friends. Dancy won her heart a few years ago when he helped her throw a Christmas-ornament-decoration party and cut out an intricate pattern of cowboy paper dolls with 'Holiday' written on them. 'I thought, You can craft? That was it. I was done. I concede myself to you totally and forevermore,' she said.

Danes is also an enthusiast of the costume party. 'In New York, people tend to party-hop,' she said. 'If they're in a costume, they're stuck there. It loosens them up.' For her thirtieth-birthday party, which was Easter-themed, she dressed up as thirty pieces of silver; Dancy was a severed ear; her father wore an Easter basket on his head; and Michael Cunningham, in a suit, sunglasses, and stigmata, walked around saying, 'No, don't thank me. It was nothing. I was glad to do it.'

Danes holds an annual Eggathon, in which about a dozen friends come to her place to create exotic Easter eggs. The best of them are photographed for albums curated by Dancy. 'It's very competitive who makes the cover, sort of like the swimsuit issue of *Sports Illustrated*,' Danes said. On an April visit to her town house, she took me to the second-floor living room to show off her contribution to the most recent volume, 'Oh-Very' – an egg wedged inside a russet Twinings English Breakfast tea-bag wrapper, a bit of Pop art irony. By general agreement, Dancy's tribute to Marcel Duchamp – an egg in the form of a urinal, signed 'R. Butt' – is the high-water mark of the competition so far. But the album had some strong contenders: an Obama egg, an I.M. Pei egg, with large circular spectacles, and a Donald Trump egg, with a shock of big hair.

At some point in the conversation, as the willow tree in her small courtyard played tricks with the afternoon light and Cyrus woke up from his afternoon nap, Danes leaned back on her upholstered sofa and reflected on the career she had chosen as a child. 'I think the more whole you are as a person – the more integrated – the deeper you can go into scary territory,' she said. 'It's just amazing that we have a means of doing that safely. What better thing is there? It's so cool to get that much more of an understanding of what it is to be a person.'

The Player Queen

Why Judi Dench rules the stage and screen

In the opening sequence of *Iris*, an extraordinary film about the late novelist Iris Murdoch's descent into the limbo of Alzheimer's, Murdoch and her loyal man-child of a husband, the Oxford don John Bayley, are shown swimming like two plump sea lions through the murk of the Thames. They're happy in their underwater playground, which distorts light and form and contains the sediment of ages. They float freely but are always in contact, dodging among the rocks and weeds in joyful, directionless exploration. Water was Iris Murdoch's primal habitat; by no accident, it is also the favorite element of the woman who plays her here, Judi Dench. 'There's a wonderful abandonment you feel in water,' Dench says. 'It's very liberating. It's like the unconscious. You're just floating around there and trusting that you're going to come up to the surface.'

This is not the only point of intersection between the two women: the adventure of the unknown, the salvation of the imagination, the promotion of happiness, and a lifelong inquiry into goodness are all themes in the elusive lives of both Murdoch and Dench. Sir Richard Eyre, the director and co-author of *Iris*, says that while writing the screenplay he tried to instill his sense of Dench into the character of Iris. 'There was never a question of how do you bring Iris and Judi Dench together,' he says. 'Essentially, the character is Judi Dench-stroke-Iris Murdoch.'

Dench, who has played both Queen Victoria and Queen Elizabeth I on film and was made a Dame Commander of the Order of the British Empire in 1988, is beloved by the English public for her quintessential Britishness. 'I think that in a lot of people's eyes she is the equivalent of the Queen – she inspires such phenomenal affection,' says the director John Madden, who launched Dench's late-blooming film career in 1997 with *Mrs Brown*. (Significantly, last month the seventy-seven British families that lost relatives in the Twin Towers catastrophe chose Dench to read at the memorial service at Westminster Abbey.) But she and Murdoch share an Anglo-Irish heritage, and each, in her own way, is a paradoxical amalgam of propriety and wildness.

With a leafy home in Surrey, a silver Rover, a taste for simple if expensive clothes, a commitment to charities (she is a patron of a hundred and eighty-three of them), and her obbligato of drollery – what Billy Connolly, who starred opposite her in *Mrs Brown*, calls 'that light, posh, self-effacing humor' – Dench, who is sixty-seven, cuts a deceptively sedate, suburban figure. At work, however, she trolls her turbulent Celtic interior, a vast tragicomic landscape that ranges between despair and indomitability. 'There's a sort of crimson place deep within her – a fiery dark-red place that stokes all the things she does,' Connolly says. 'You don't get to see it. But you occasionally get glimpses of how tiresome she finds the doily-and-serviette crowd. You know, those English twittering fucking women – they think she's one of them, and she isn't.' This complexity is what Dench brings to her acting, which is nowhere more inspired than in her depiction of Murdoch. Her performance parses every nuance in the writer's trajectory of decline – from embarrassment to bewilderment, from terror to loss, from nonentity to a final connection with an enduring life force, where, in the shuffle of dementia, Murdoch somehow finds a dance.

Dench is not much of a reader, but she has read most of Murdoch's novels, and before filming she went so far as to sit outside Bayley's house while he was away to absorb the shambolic atmosphere of the place. (She found his car in the driveway, unlocked and with a window open.) 'I didn't want to miss that snapshot in my mind,' she says. But her uncanny portrait emerged out of her own process, a combination of technical rigor and imaginative free fall, in which, according to Eyre, 'she doesn't put anything of herself between her and the character.' He explains, 'I was really staggered at the way she transformed herself. Toward the end of the film, when Iris's mind has gone, and you look at Judi's face and see that implacability, the sense of peace and the absence in her eyes, that is alchemy. She didn't go to old people's homes. She didn't sit and study. It's intuitive. She's quick. I mean, *really* quick.'

Except for time out to have a child and to nurse her husband of thirty years, the actor Michael Williams, who died last January of lung cancer, Dench has been performing almost constantly for four and a half decades. She appeared in the first season of the Royal Shakespeare Company, in 1961, and in the eighties was a founding member of Kenneth Branagh's Renaissance Theatre Company, for which she has also directed plays. Under the auspices of the Old Vic, the R.S.C., and the Royal National Theatre, she has turned in some of the greatest classical performances in recent memory. Her Juliet in Franco Zeffirelli's 1960 stage production *of Romeo and Juliet*; her Titania in *A Midsummer Night's Dream*, directed by Sir Peter Hall in 1962; her Viola in *Twelfth Night* in 1969; her Lady Macbeth in Trevor Nunn's magnificent 1976 production; her Cleopatra in Hall's 1987 *Antony and Cleopatra* — all are exemplars of contemporary Shakespearean performance. Her working in the modern repertoire – as Anya in *The Cherry Orchard*, as Juno Boyle in *Juno and the Paycock*, as Lady Bracknell in *The Importance of Being Earnest*, and as Christine Foskett in Rooney Ackland's rediscovered fifties classic *Absolute Hell* – has also had a huge impact on English theatregoers. And Dench has inspired allegiance as well through her television career, which includes thirty-four films and two popular long-running comedy series, *A Fine Romance* and *As Time Goes By*.

'See you on the ice, darling,' she has been known to callout from her dressing room to an actor headed toward the stage. For Dench, 'the crack' – the Irish term for fun – is riding the exhilarating uncertainty of the moment. To that end, she is famous (some would say notorious) for not having read many of the parts she accepts. Instead, she has someone else paraphrase the script for her. (Williams usually had this duty before he died; now it has fallen to Dench's agent, Tor Belfrage.) 'Michael said, "Just read that one line,"' Dench recalls of *Pack of Lies*, Hugh Whitemore's successful spy story, in which she and Williams starred. 'It was just one line. I read it, and I knew then that it would be all right.'

'It often seems absurd to me that a woman as intelligent as Judi could roll up at the beginning of the rehearsal not having read the play,' says Branagh, who directed Dench in his films of *Hamlet* and *Henry V* and has, in turn, been directed by her on stage in *Much Ado About Nothing* and *Look Back in Anger*. Although this method allows Dench to arrive at rehearsals with, as Branagh puts it, 'the right kind of blank page to start writing on,' 'from a professional point of view it is also sensationally reckless. 'I don't know what it is in me, this kind of perversity,' Dench told me when I visited her at home last July. 'I don't understand it myself. I think some people think it's an affectation. It's thrilling, though, isn't it? You don't know what's coming.'

The habit of not reading scripts has, over the years, landed Dench in a few sticky theatrical situations, such as Peter Shaffer's turgid *The Gift of the Gorgon*, in 1992. And at first she wasn't keen to take on her current West End outing, in a revival of *The Royal Family*, the slim 1927 Edna Ferber and George S. Kaufman satire of the theatrical Barrymores, but her mind was made up for her when she received a call from the director, Peter Hall. 'It's entirely a roll of the dice, but it has to do with friends, with people I love and admire,' she explained several weeks before rehearsals of *The Royal Family* began. 'So if Peter rings me up and says, "You ought to do this play," I say, "Sure." I swear before God I have not read the play.'

Dench's risk-taking onstage is in inverse proportion to her vulnerability off it. 'When I go into a rehearsal room, my coat and bag have to be nearest the door,' she said in a recent television interview. Performing, for Dench, is an antidote to chronic insecurity; it gives her, she says, what the Cockneys call 'bottle': 'It's courage. You know, like jumping into icecold water. If it's to be done – do it. Go!' Recently when Trevor Nunn offered her a role at the National, she replied, 'I want to come back to the National, but not in that part. Would you ask me to do something more frightening?'

Dench's derring-do also seems necessary to keep her nearly perpetual routine of rehearsal and performance a fresh and vigorous challenge. 'Her desire is to recreate each time, to re-experience, and not simply reproduce,' Branagh says. To that end, she refuses analysis. Without preconceived notions, she tries to let the character play *her*.' She absolutely hates to rationalize,' Eyre says. 'When you're working with her, she'll ask a question about a scene or a character, and when you go to talk about it, at some point she'll say, "Yeah, O.K., I understand." She doesn't want it spelled out. She has to find it herself.' A long time ago, when Eyre was doing a play with Dench at the National, where he was the artistic director for ten years, she left her script in the rehearsal room; the next day, Eyre handed it to her. '"Oh, you look terribly shocked,"' he recalls her saying. '"Is it because I didn't take my script home with me?" I said, "Well, I guess so."' She talked to me about how she learned lines. The work that she does outside rehearsal is not sitting down with the script. She just sort of envisions the scene and colors it in her mind.' Dench's method of bushwhacking through her unconscious to find the emotional core of a character is, she says, completely instinctive: 'The subconscious is what works on the part. It's like coming back to a crossword at the end of the day and filling in seventeen answers straight off.' In one scene of *Iris*, the senile Murdoch goes walkabout in the rain on a motorway and slips and falls down an embankment into the under brush. This is the first and only scene in the film in which Dench's Murdoch, whose eyes are always turned inward, really sees and acknowledges Bayley. 'I said to

Judi, "You have to find a way of doing it that reconciles a sort of rationality with the fact that her brain is more or less gone,'" Eyre says. 'That's all she wanted to know.' When the distressed Bayley (played by Jim Broadbent) finally finds her, Dench is covered with mud and laughing to herself. Out of her solitude, her eyes come to rest on Broadbent's face. 'I love you,' she says, and with a startling glimmer of clarity Dench manages to invoke the blessing and heartbreak of a lifetime of connection.

Dench describes herself as 'an enormous console with hundreds of buttons, each of which I must press at exactly the right time.' She adds, 'If you're lucky enough to be asked to play many different parts, you have to have reserves of all sorts of emotions. When I was rehearsing a part I'd never, ever, ever discuss it with Michael, because I had that pressure-cooker syndrome. If I once open that little key – *pffft!* – the stuff goes.'

In nature, as in art, the secret of conservation is not to disturb the wild things. Dench's brooding talent has its correlative in her five-acre Surrey domain, Wasp Green, and in the low-slung, woodbeamed 1680 yeoman's house where she lives with her twenty-nine-year-old daughter, the actress Finty Williams, her four-year-old grandson, Sammy, nine cats, and several ducks. The front of the house is bright, tidy, and picturesque in a *Country Life* sort of way; the back acres, however, have been left alone, with only a small path cut through a thicket of brambles, nettles, and wild orchids. 'You have to see the back garden to understand Judi,' Franco Zeffirelli says. 'She puts up a façade sometimes, but for herself she reserves a private garden. You discover there treasures that you don't see at the front of the house.'

On the day I visited her there last summer, Dench, in Wellington boots, stepped lively on the overgrown path. 'I've got to cut these back,' she said, swiping at the nettles. She pointed out new plantings: a black poplar to commemorate a row that had blown down the previous year; 'Sammy's oak,' a tree planted in honor of her grandson's birth; and the place she'd chosen for 'Mikey's oak,' a sapling that was originally an opening-night present from Williams to the director Anthony Page, whose production of *The Forest* was Williams's last acting job. 'What's important to me is continuance – a line stretching on,' Dench said. 'I hate things that start and finish abruptly.'

If the wild back garden is a kind of memory theatre for Dench, the theatre itself puts her in touch with her family, which she calls 'a unit of tremendous encouragement.' 'All the qualities that Judi has as a person, and, indeed, as an actress, come from the very close family background,' Williams said on a 1995 *South Bank* TV biography of his wife. Dench's love of work, painting, swimming, jokes, and especially acting are passions she absorbed from her father, Dr Reginald Dench, a physician who served as the official doctor for the Theatre Royal in York before he died, in 1964. 'I remember going visiting with him,' Dench says. 'When we turned into a road, children would run and hold on to the car. That's the kind of doctor he was. He was a wonderful raconteur. He had the most incredible sense of humor – just spectacular.' When Dench was about fifteen, on holiday in Spain, she admired a pair of expensive blue-and-white striped shoes. 'Well, I think you could probably have those shoes,' she recalls her father saying. 'Let's go to lunch. We'll discuss it.' At lunch, Dench – a fish lover – scanned the buffet of prawns and lobsters. 'Daddy looked at me and said, "Would you like that?" "Yes, please." So I had four big prawns and enjoyed every minute of it. Daddy said, "You've just eaten your shoes."'

The Dench children – Judi, Jeffrey, who is now an actor, and Peter, who became a doctor – grew up in York, in a sprawling Victorian house, where Judi, the youngest, had the attic room and was allowed to draw on the walls. 'She got her own way,' Jeffrey says. 'Judi was Daddy's Beautiful Lady.' According to her daughter, Finty, the only discrepancy between the public Dench and the private one is her temper. Her volatility is an inheritance from her flamboyant, sharp-tongued mother, Olave, who once threw a vacuum cleaner down the stairs at a representative who had called to inquire about it. 'You didn't cross her, or *pow!* – not hitting, but a tongue-lashing, and you stayed lashed,' Jeffrey says. Dench's contradictory nature – with its combination of mighty spirit and 'non confidence,' as she calls it – appears to have been forged as she tried to negotiate her mother's combustible personality. 'She loved admonishing Judi,' Trevor Nunn says of Olave. 'I mean the kind of admonishment that comes from absolute worship. The privilege of being able to be the one who could put her in her place. "Judi, you mustn't say that!" "Judi, you're such an embarrassment!"' Dench says, 'She was outrageous.' In the late seventies, by which time she was having trouble with her sight, Olave had lunch with Nunn and Dench at a sophisticated, self-congratulatory Italian restaurant called the Lugger. 'Olave ordered tomato soup, which came in a huge bowl,' Nunn recalls. 'A waiter arrived with a little sachet of cream, with which he spelled out the name of the restaurant on the soup and then left Judi. Olave said, "a man has just come and written 'bugger' in me soup!"'

Dench's parents took a keen interest in amateur dramatics and, when Dench became an actress, their support verged on the overprotective. They saw their daughter in *Romeo and Juliet* more than seventy times; once, Reginald got so involved in the play that when Judi, as Juliet, said, 'Where is my father and my mother, nurse?' he was heard to say, 'Here we are, darling. In Row H.'

Whereas most stars seek a public to provide the attention they failed to get in childhood, Dench's commitment to the theatrical community is, she admits, an attempt to reproduce the endorsement and excitement of her first audience – her family. She claims not to be 'good at my own company'. Rather, to understand her own identity she needs to be in the attentive gaze of others – as the psychologist D.W. Winnicott put sit, 'When I look I am seen, so I exist.' Dench is clear on this point. 'I need somebody to reflect me back, or to give me their reflection,' she says. Ned Sherrin, who directed Dench and Williams in *Mr and Mrs Nobody* in 1986, says he was so aware of Dench's need 'to create a family with each show' that he added a couple of walk-ons to what was otherwise a two-person play.

Dench, who keeps a collection of Teddy bears and hearts and a doll's house at Wasp Green, somehow contrives, as Branagh says, 'to feel and be in the moment, as a child.' In the collegial atmosphere of a theatre company, she is an adored and prankish catalyst, inevitably, as her brother Jeffrey points out, 'at the center.' 'Eight going on sixty-seven' is how Geoffrey Palmer, her co-star in the nineties TV series *As Time Goes By*, characterizes the innocence and spontaneity she brings to the daily routine of self-reinvention. Her process – her abdication of responsibility to intuition, her need to be told the story – is not so much about being lost as it is about being held. She casts the director as her father and exhibits an almost filial devotion. 'When we did *A Midsummer Night's Dream*, she did this extraordinary Titania,'

Hall says. 'I said to her, "One day, you'll play Cleopatra. I want you to make me a promise that when you do it you'll do it with me." We shook hands on it.' Hall goes on, 'Twenty years later, she rang me up and said, "I've just been asked to play Cleopatra by the R.S.C. I said I was promised to you. Now, do you want to do it?"'

From her first sighting onstage – as a seventeen-year-old Ariel in a production of *The Tempest*, at the Mount School, in York, where she boarded from 1947 to 1953 – Dench was transparently a natural. But neither Dench, who then aspired to be a set designer, nor her teachers took her ability very seriously. The novelist A.S. Byatt, a schoolmate, recalls, 'I used to talk to Katharine MacDonald, the English mistress who taught her. "You know, Judi will probably be content," as she put it, "to dabble her pretty feet in amateur dramatics."'

Dench enrolled at London's Central School of Speech and Drama simply because her brother Jeffrey, who went there, had told her appealing stories about the place. Vanessa Redgrave, who was in Dench's class, and who was then self-conscious and gawky, remembers being both 'admiring and jealous' of Dench's naturalness. 'She skipped and hopped with pleasure and excitement up the stairs, down the corridors, and onto the stage,' Redgrave wrote in her autobiography. 'She wore jeans, the only girl who had them, a polo-neck sweater, and ballet slippers that flopped and flapped as she bounded around.' The turning point in Dench's ambition came during a mime class in her second term, when she was required to perform an assignment called 'Recollection' that she'd completely forgotten to prepare. 'I don't remember thinking anything out,' she says. 'I walked into a garden. I bent down to smell something like rosemary or thyme. I walked and just looked at certain things. I picked up a pebble, and threw it into what I imagined was a pond and watched the ripples going out from it. I looked over and sat on a swing. And I swung, you know, like you do on a swing that isn't there. Then I walked out of the garden. That was my mime.' Her teacher, Walter Hudd, gave her, she says, 'the most glowing notice I think I've ever had. What is more, he said, "You looked like a little Renoir doing it." I thought, Well, I think that I will enjoy what I'm going to do, hopefully get work, go for it.'

Dench graduated with a first-class degree and four acting prizes. According to her biography the unfortunately titled *Judi Dench: With a Crack in Her Voice*, by John Miller a notice was posted on the school's bulletin board naming her the student most likely to become a star and when the Old Vic offered her the role of Ophelia opposite John Neville's Hamlet it seemed a self-fulfilling prophecy. 'ENTER JUDI – LONDON'S NEW OPHELIA – OLD VIC MAKE HER A FIRST-ROLE STAR,' the *Evening News* announced. When Neville heard about his tyro Ophelia, 'I blew my top,' he says. He begged the theatre's publicity department not to hype her before the opening. 'I thought, and still think, that it would have been best just to let the media discover her for themselves,' he says. Dench was more or less annihilated by the press. 'Hamlet's sweetheart is required to be something more than a piece of Danish patisserie,' Richard Findlater wrote in the *Sunday Dispatch*; in the *Observer*, Kenneth Tynan swatted her away as 'a pleasing but terribly sane little thing.' At the end of the season, when the production toured America, the role was taken away from Dench. 'That was a kind of dagger to the heart,' she says. 'I remember John Neville saying to me, "You must decide what you're doing this for." And I made my mind up, and I think that's what keeps me going.' The answer remains Dench's secret. 'The only part of her that is totally unreachable for me is that she's never told me why she's an actress,' Finty says. 'I would love to know what motivates her.'

Dench came of age just as the definitions of femininity were being rewritten, and she was an incarnation of the freewheeling, bumptious independence of the eternally young New Woman. With a cap of close-cropped hair, a strong chin, rough cheekbones, big alert eyes, and a wide smile, the five-foot-two Dench cut a gamine figure on stage. Zeffirelli still thinks of her as 'a kind of irresistible bombshell.' He says, 'She was funny and witty and biting. You had to be very careful what you said because she would answer back promptly. She was a dynamo, this girl. She just was an extraordinary surprise, because I was accustomed to Peggy Ashcroft and Dorothy Tutin, that style of acting.'

David Jones, who directed one of the high-water marks of Dench's TV career, *Langrishe, Go Down* (1978), remembers her quicksilver quality in Zeffirelli's *Romeo and Juliet*. He describes her 'darting-like a bird coming onto the stage and going off again. You weren't quite aware of the feet touching the ground, this extraordinary agility of body and of mind.' Dench's kinetic quality onstage finds different but no less startling expression in film. 'She has a kind of sprung dynamic with her eyes,' John Madden says. 'They don't move gradually and settle or shift. They dart, then dart back, then settle again on the place that they just avoided looking at. It's almost like a double take, which suggests a kind of current flowing in an opposite direction from what she is saying.'

When you meet Dench, it's hard not to feel the engine running inside her. She's nervy. Her fingers play across her lips; her feet tap under the table. Her lightness and quickness are very much a part of her metabolism as an actress and lend credibility to her performances. 'She is the perfect Shakespearean, because the great characters in Shakespeare have fantastic speed of thought,' Nunn says. 'They have speed of wit, speed of response, speed of invention of the image. That only works if the actor convinces the audience that that language is being coined by that brain in that situation.' He adds, 'You live in the moment with her. There's never a sense that she's doing a recitation.'

Dench's combination of insight and inspiration, charisma and cunning has made her one of Britain's two marquee players whose names guarantee West End commercial success. (Her friend Dame Maggie Smith is the other.) Even with the drastic fall-off of tourism after September 11th, *The Royal Family* had half a million pounds in advance bookings, and, despite a tepid press, is still doing brisk business. Dench's drawing power, for which she is paid a five-figure salary every week, plus up to ten per cent of the gross, has been greatly enhanced since the mid-nineties by her emergence as an international film star. Before being touched by what she calls 'the luck of John Madden', who directed her in both *Shakespeare in Love* and *Mrs Brown*, Dench had not shown much interest in films, though she'd appeared in twelve. When she was starting out, she was told by an industry swami that she didn't have 'a movie face.' 'It put me completely off,' says Dench, who nonetheless nearly got the starring role in Tony Richardson's 1961 film *A Taste of Honey*. 'But then I only ever really loved the stage. It's only recently that I've got to like film so much.' For the last three James Bond films, Dench's severe side has been siphoned off into M, Bond's no-nonsense boss; and among the fifty-five awards she lists in her bio are three Oscar nominations in the past four years – for *Mrs Brown*, *Shakespeare in Love*, and *Chocolat*. (The command and wit of her seven-minute cameo as Elizabeth I in *Shakespeare in Love* earned her the 1999 Academy Award for Best Supporting Actress.)

Among theatre people, Dench's popularity is a source of some curmudgeonly grousing – 'If she farted, they'd give her an award,' one playwright said – and some good jokes. Eyre recounted a conversation he once had with the playwright Alan Bennett, who had seen a man wearing a heavy-metal-style T-shirt that read 'Hitler: The European Tour.' They tried to imagine a T-shirt in worse taste. Recalling the thirty-nine Turin soccer fans who had been killed at a match against Liverpool in 1995, Eyre suggested 'Liverpool 39-Turin 0.' 'Yes, that's ghastly,' Eyre recalls Bennett saying. 'But the worst-taste T-shirt, the very, very worst, would be "I Hate Judi Dench."' One clue to Dench's appeal is her husky voice, which has a natural catch in it; certain notes fail to operate. When Dench was at the Nottingham Playhouse in the mid-sixties, she had the box office display a notice that said, 'Judi Dench is not ill, she just talks like this.' Dench's sound is idiosyncratic but not mannered; it is full of intimations that, as Alan Bennett says, 'open you up to whatever she's doing' and allow various interpretations. Sir Ian McKellen, who has performed with Dench in four plays, most memorably as Macbeth to her Lady Macbeth, calls it 'a little girl's voice – the crack suggests she's not in control.'

Another reason for Dench's popularity is her warmth. She communicates a palpable, deep-seated generosity. 'You feel somehow, even as a member of the audience, that if you were in trouble she would help you and laugh you out of it,' Hall says.

Dench pays close attention to her audience. During the half hour before a show, she keeps the loudspeakers in her dressing room turned up, both to take the measure of the house and to pump up her adrenaline. 'I have to hear the audience coming in,' she says. 'I need to be generated by it – for the jump-off. It's like a quickie ignition.' Once, an American student asked Dench if the audience made a difference to her; Dench replied, 'If it didn't make a difference, I'd be at home with my feet up the chimney. That's who I'm doing it for.' 'It's a little unnerving when you're working with her,' McKellen says. 'What's happening is that she's making love to the audience – not making love but providing the focus of attention to an audience that wants to love. You could be wrapped in Judi's arms onstage and acting as closely with her as possible, and she's capable of betraying you, because her main reason for being in your arms is for the audience's delectation. It isn't upstaging. That isn't taking away the focus. Her spirit is flowing, and it's a decision she's made that it will flow. And when I'm in the audience I want her to do that.'

In performance, Dench is a minimalist: no gesture or movement is wasted. Richard Eyre refers to what he calls her 'third eye': 'It's the ability to walk on fire and yet be completely unburnt, to be red-hot with passion and at the same time there's this third eye that is looking down thinking, Am I doing this right?' Billy Connolly told me about filming one scene in *Mrs Brown*: In the first meeting between the widowed Queen Victoria and her Scottish manservant, John Brown, Brown's forthrightness catches the Queen off guard 'Honest to God, I never thought to see you in such a state,' Brown says. 'You must miss him dreadfully.' In an astonishing closeup, the austere formality of Dench's visage suddenly transforms – a cloud of grief sweeps over her and she breaks up. 'Judi did that twelve times,' Connolly says. 'Every time, I thought I'd really wounded her. You see me looking all bewildered. Well, I actually was.'

'Dench has a kind of glamour when she performs,' says Hal Prince, who directed her as Sally Bowles in *Cabaret* in 1968 and considers her 'the most effective of all the people who played the part.' Glamour – the word has its root in the Scottish word for 'grammar' is an artifice of elegant coherence; it requires distance. Dench, who is no Garbo or Dietrich, manufactures this not through stagemanaged aloofness but through a natural sense of containment. David Jones says, 'Her gift is to step down the throttle, so you don't get the full impact of her passion; you just know there's an enormous amount in reserve. It's like a wave suspended.' McKellen observes, 'She goes *out*, but she doesn't always invite you *in*.'

On a bright July morning, Dench picked me up outside Gatwick Airport to ferry me back to Wasp Green. She arrived with a story – one that she retold three times during the day. She hadn't known what I looked like, she said – though I later noticed on her desk a book I'd sent her with my jacket photo prominently displayed – and she'd stopped two men before I loomed up in her windshield. 'I slowed down and this man says, "I know you. Are you with American Airlines?"' she said. At a stroke, she had levelled the playing field, by making herself appear just an ordinary, unrecognized citizen. The story got us talking and laughing. Disarming others is one of Dench's great social gifts, and one of her most skillfull defenses. 'She was successful very young,' Eyre says. 'She developed some sort of tactic that stopped people from disliking her.'

As a diva Dench is something of a disappointment. Her dislike of public display – what Branagh calls her 'puritanical scrutiny of anything showy' – can be attributed at least in part to the tenets of her faith. She was introduced to Quaker practice as a teenager at the Mount School, and she still goes to Quaker meetings. 'I have to have quietness inside me somewhere, otherwise I'd burn myself up,' she said in a recent television interview. Quakerism requires its followers to look for the light in others, as well as in themselves, and this, in a way, explains Dench's view of acting as a service industry. 'It's a very unselfish job,' she says. 'It's about being true to an author, a director, a group of people, and stimulating a different audience every night. If you're out for self-glorification, then you're in the wrong profession.'

'There are a lot of people who are very willing to put my mother on a pedestal, which is a lonely existence,' Finty says. 'She wants to dispute that so much that she will literally do anything for anybody.' For twelve years, Dench and Williams lived with all of their in-laws in one house, and Dench is a legendary sender of postcards and birthday cards; by Finty's reckoning, she gives about four hundred and fifty Christmas presents a year. She once gave Eyre a wooden heart carved from a tree trunk; and, for as long as Hall can remember, on his birthday Dench has managed to have delivered – as far afield as Australia – his favorite meal: oysters, French fries, and a bottle of Sancerre. 'Comes my seventieth birthday, and there's no oysters, no Sancerre,' Hall says. 'I said to my wife, "Well, I must be off the list." We had my dinner' – a party for fifty, with Dench at his side – 'and there's a Doulton china plate from Judi, specially made, with six oysters and chips painted on it.'

This hubbub of good will and connection, however, skirts the issue of intimacy. 'Judi has always found safety in numbers,' says

David Jones, who was involved with her briefly in his twenties. 'When we were dating, I would arrange what I thought was a one-on-one meeting to go to a museum or the theatre. Quite often, I would turn up and find two other people invited. And Judi would say, "Isn't it fun? They're free! They can come with us."' Some of Dench's schoolmates, like the writer Margaret Drabble, found her buoyancy 'a little Panglossian.' Even Dench's husband, a man prone to the kind of melancholy that he called 'black-dog days,' and which could stretch into months, sent up her effervescence. 'With Judi, it's bloody Christmas morning every day,' he told Branagh.

'I'm a person who off-loads an enormous amount onto people,' Dench told me. 'Inside, there's a core that I won't off-load.' According to Finty, Dench 'doesn't like to talk about very emotional things,' but throughout our day together at Wasp Green her gallant cheer was tested by small unsettling moments. Although her charm never faltered, I was left with mixed messages, as if I had wandered into some Chekhovian scenario full of distressing secrets. Our extended conversation at a garden table on the lawn was interrupted first by a series of visitors (the mailman, a next-door neighbor, and two secretaries, each of whom got Dench's full attention), then by phone calls from Anthony Page and Peter Hall, then by someone delivering a single pink rose (I learned later that it was from Finty – carrying on Williams's tradition of having a single red rose sent to Dench every Friday of their marriage), then by Dench's need to feed the herd of cats, and then by a panic over a credit card that might or might not have been stolen.

Finally, and most perplexingly, Finty, who moved back into her parents' house when Michael fell ill, walked over unbidden with a provocative and bewildering announcement 'Your granddaughter is being played by an eighteen-year-old,' she said. Dench's bright face collapsed. 'Oh, Finty, I'm so sorry.' 'It's all right,' Finty said, with a wave of her hand. 'I'm all right.' She turned back to the house, leaving her mother to struggle with her obvious disappointment. After a while, Dench said, 'It'll be for a very good reason.' Then, finally, she explained: '*The Royal Family*. She saw Peter.' Finty, who had recently finished filming Robert Altman's *Gosford Park*, had hoped for a part in the play.

A few minutes later, Finty came out again to say goodbye. 'It doesn't matter about that, you know,' Dench said. 'It doesn't matter.' Finty agreed. 'She's only a little eighteen-year-old, and maybe it's her first job. Maybe she'll be celebrating with someone and getting very excited,' she said. 'Maybe you will have something else to do, you never know,' Dench said. 'Never know,' Finty said, nodding. 'My audition's been cancelled on Tuesday.' There was a long, fierce silence as she exited for the second time. 'It's impossible being the child of an actor,' Dench said. A certain gravity fell across her face as she seemed to push down feelings of remorse and guilt and got on with the professional task at hand.

Onstage, Dench has found her bliss; offstage, that bliss has cast a shadow on others – on her brother Jeffrey ('There is jealousy,' he admits. 'She's had the breaks. I'm a jobbing actor. You know that niggles'), on Michael ('In some way, his heart was broken by Judi's success,' Eyre says), and now on Finty, who seemed, in a way that neither of them quite acknowledged or understood, both to adore her mother and to wish to subvert her. A few months later, Finty told me a story that reminded me of this. While she and Dench were watching television together one night, Finty said, 'Oh, I think Kylie Minogue' – the Australian pop singer and former soap-opera star – 'is so talented.' According to Finty, Dench got 'massively uptight.' 'Define "so talented," she said. "She's a singer, isn't she? She looks good." She got really cross with me. She was, like, "If you think that's talented, what are you aspiring to?"'

In her time, Dench has been serenaded by Gerry Mulligan from beneath her New York hotel window. She has watched, in West Africa, as, at the finale of *Twelfth Night*, people in the audience threw their programs into the air, then jumped to their feet to sing and dance for several minutes. She has clowned with the comedians Eric Morecambe and Ernie Wise. She has locked herself in a bathroom with Maggie Smith to escape the advances of the English comic character actor Miles Malleson. She has refused Billy Connolly's offer to show her his pierced nipples. As for her own nipples, she has stood in front of the camera, naked to the waist and unabashed, dabbing meringue on them. She has cooled herself on a summer day by jumping fully clothed into a swimming pool. At Buckingham Palace, she has scuttled away from the ballroom with Ian McKellen to sit on the royal thrones. In a Dublin restaurant, when Harold Pinter, a theatrical royal, barked about the tardiness of their dinner, Dench, according to David Jones, actually barked back, 'Mr Pinter, you are not in London. Would you please adjust.' She has made David Hare a needlepoint pillow as a Mother's Day present, with the words 'Fuck Off' intricately stitched into the tapestry. On the day she became Dame Judi, Dench pinned her D.B.E. insignia on the jacket of the actor playing Don Pedro in a production of *Much*

Ado About Nothing that she was directing. It is a barometer of her louche and lively life that, not long after that, the first ten rows of the National's Lyttelton Theatre heard Michael Bryant, who was playing Enobarbus to her Cleopatra, say to Dench under his breath, 'I suppose a fuck is well out of the question now?'

Still, as Zeffirelli says, 'She has known suffering.' At the corner of her Surrey property is a rowan tree, planted on an exact axis with the back door of the house, which, according to folklore, is supposed to protect the house from witches; it has not been able to protect Dench from the caprices of life. Soon after Michael died, in January, an electrical fault in the garage – an old barn – started a fire that gutted it to the frame. That charred skeleton is the first thing that rolls into view as you enter the property, and it stands in eerie contrast to the tranquillity behind it – wisteria by the front door, a sundial, a swimming pool, a flotilla of plastic slides and Winnie-the-Pooh toys tucked underneath the warped cantilevered timbers of the porch. Seven years earlier, Dench's house in Hampstead had burned down and a lifetime's memorabilia went up in flames. And in 1997, in a weird instance of life imitating art, Dench, like her character Esme in *Amy's View*, which she was rehearsing at the time, learned that Finty, then twenty-five, was eight months pregnant and hadn't told her. She went immediately to Eyre's office at the National. 'She stood in the doorway and just collapsed,' he recalls. 'She exploded. I'd never seen that. Unbelievably painful. She was massively wounded that the person she had thought of as her best friend in the world had not confided in her the not insignificant fact of her pregnancy.' (Finty hadn't wanted Michael, a conservative Catholic, to know that she was having an illegitimate child.) Nevertheless, rehearsals of *Amy's View* went on. Eyre says of Dench, 'Deep within her is the ethos that you don't let people down. If you're an actor, you go on. As Tennessee Williams says, you endure by enduring.'

On July 9th of last year, a muggy Monday, at St Paul's Church in Covent Garden, a standing-room-only crowd heard Trevor Nunn eulogize Michael Williams as a fine actor and partner. 'I remember them courting,' he said, standing opposite an enlarged photo of Williams, who was five feet four and puckishly handsome. 'When they got married, Mike said to me, he was in the grip of feelings "beyond any happiness he had ever dreamed of." He told me more than once that his favorite line in Shakespeare was "You have bereft me of all words, lady." Because when he was with Jude, he knew the full extent of what Shakespeare was saying.'

By the time Dench and Williams were married, in 1971, when she was thirty-six, Dench had done a lot of living. 'When she likes something, she wants it like a wild animal,' Zeffirelli says. Eyre adds, 'She was prodigiously falling in love with the wrong man.' One such man was the late comic actor Leonard Rossiter, who was in another relationship when they had an affair. 'Some days, she'd come in and she'd had a wonderful day with him,' recalls McKellen, who was then co-starring with her in *The Promise*. 'Other times, he'd have to leave early or hadn't turned up, and she was desperate. Tears, tears, tears. She was helpless and hopeless. What I was seeing was utterly vulnerable.'

In 1969, on an R.S.C. tour of Australia, Charlie Thomas, a talented young actor with a drinking problem, who was playing the lovelorn Orsino to Dench's Viola, died under mysterious circumstances. Thomas had been very dependent on Dench, Nunn told me. 'It was a shattering situation,' he said. Williams, who was also a member of the R.S.C. and had become, in Nunn's words, 'probably more than a friend,' flew out to comfort her. 'What was between them deepened enormously during that time,' Nunn says. 'Mike arriving made a fantastic difference.' On that trip, Williams proposed, but Dench demurred. 'No, it's too romantic here, with the sun and the sea and the sand,' Williams remembered her saying. 'Ask me on a rainy night in Battersea and I'll think about it.' One rainy night in Battersea, in 1970, she said yes.

Williams, who came from Liverpool, had a more working-class pedigree than Dench, and he had the right combination of sturdiness and faith to both tether Dench and contain what her agent calls the 'Dizzy Dora' side of her personality. 'Michael was all-calming,' Dench says. By every account, they were good companions. Dench recalls, 'He used to say of himself, because he was Cancerian – the crab – and I'm a Sagittarian, I'm scuttling away toward the dark, and you're scuttling toward the light. What we do is we hold hands and keep ourselves in the middle.'

But, as the decades wore on, and despite *A Fine Romance*, the sitcom they starred in together in the early eighties, Williams was increasingly in Dench's shadow. 'In a sense, every one of her successes was a diminution of him,' Eyre says. Dench was acutely aware of the problem. 'Judi was protective of Michael like a lioness,' Geoffrey Palmer says. 'I don't think Michael was an easy man. But the fact that all his married life he was Mr Judi Dench – that's difficult for any man. He used to get very low. He sat at home feeding the bloody swans while she was doing three jobs a day.' According to Dench, during these depressions Williams would become remote and 'very, very silent.' She says, 'I had to give an incredible amount of confidence to Michael, who was very unconfident indeed.'

On the inside of Dench's wedding ring is inscribed a modified line from *Troilus and Cressida*, which Williams included in the first note he wrote to her: 'I will weep you, as 'twere a man born in April.' It proved to be somewhat prescient. On their twenty-fifth anniversary, Dench spoke of 'just missing the rocks.' The marriage, she says, was volatile. 'I throw things,' she adds. 'I threw a hot cup of tea at him and his mother. And the saucer. I didn't hit either of them, unfortunately.' Williams enjoyed spending time at the local pub. On several Sundays, when they had guests for lunch, Williams and the male guests rolled back from the pub late for the meal. 'Mum's like "Fine. Lock all the doors,"' Finty recalls. '"No, he's not coming in unless he can get through the top window."' Williams and his crew climbed to their lunch on a thirty-foot ladder. And once, just before Christmas in 1983, an argument about the boiler sent Dench and Williams into such a blind fury that they refused to talk or look at each other on the long ride into London, where they were performing in *Pack of Lies*. 'The air was black, and we're bowling down Shaftesbury Avenue and not speaking and this person knocks on the window and begins to sing "A Fine Romance,"' Dench says. 'We howled with laughter. Howled. I realized it very much in the last year – he was a tremendous anchor to me. A real, proper anchor.'

Just months before Williams died, the family took a trip to Aberdeenshire, where Billy Connolly had gathered some friends at his castle. The week before, Williams had asked Dench whether he was going to die, and she told him he was. 'When Judi told me about it, she started by looking me in the eye and ended up fiddling with the cutlery, then just went very quiet,' Connolly recalls. 'She went to a place in her head where she obviously feels much more comfortable and didn't say a thing.' Connolly is a banjo player, and when Dench and Williams were in residence he and his other guests – Steve Martin (banjo), Eric Idle (guitar), the Incredible String Band's Robin Williamson (mandolin), and a local fisherman who played the fiddle – would go to a clearing in a nearby wood, build a fire, and sit on tree stumps to play, sing, and sometimes dance into the night. Connolly has a picture of the revels, with two green wicker chairs brought into the circle for Williams and Dench. Williams is laughing and holding a large glass of whiskey. He's looking beyond the fire at the fiddler; Dench is looking at him. 'They were like young lovers,' Connolly says. 'They touched all the time. The wicker chairs are still there. We can't move them. Nobody wants to. 'Cause it's Judi and Michael.'

'I have a huge amount of energy,' Dench told me when we met at the Union Club in Soho for lunch in November. 'Grief produces more energy, and all that needs burning up.' In the ten months since Williams's death, Dench's herculean workload – *The Royal Family* and three films, *The Importance of Being Earnest*, *The Shipping News*, and *Iris* – had brought some of the shine back to her pale-blue, almond-shaped eyes. Her face was both animated and calm. 'When my father died, it was almost like she was curiously liberated,' Finty says. And although Dench still feels 'lopsided,' she said, 'I just want to learn new things all the time,' and was full of news of her accomplishments in gardening, archery, and pool.

She had also learned to ride a Zappy scoot – sort of a skateboard with handlebars. Kevin Spacey, who before making *The Shipping News* told the director, Lasse Hallström, that he had two goals – 'to give a good performance and to make Dench laugh' – had taught her in Central Park on his scooter, which has a turbo engine that goes up to about twenty miles per hour. 'I was running along with her as she did it,' Spacey says. 'People were kind of recognizing us, particularly her. Someone said, "Didn't you have something to do with James Bond?" And she said, "Yes, I'm his boss," and kept moving.' From her gold-leafed diary, Dench produced a photo of Spacey on location; he was wearing a black baseball cap with 'Actor' embroidered above the visor and a sweatshirt she'd had made for him with the legend 'The Caramel Macchiato of Show Business,' in honor of the coffee he'd brought her each day on the shoot. That evening, she told me, Spacey was coming to *The Royal Family*.

On performing nights, Dench leaves Wasp Green by car at quarter to five and arrives at the Theatre Royal Haymarket in London at six-fifteen. Her dressing room – No. 10, on the third floor, John Gielgud's favorite – has a blue carpet, high ceilings, an antechamber, and a gold plaque on the front door with her name on it. First, Dench reads and responds to her letters. Her next order of business is to talk with the company. 'We always will check up with each other,' she says. 'Essential. It makes you laugh if you see them for the first time onstage. I don't know why. I'm on a knife edge in this play.' Her ritual for getting dressed never varies. She puts on a bodystocking, then black tights and a dressing gown. She bandages up her hair and does her face and, finally, her nails. Above her is an oval mirror festooned with greeting cards; to her right, a photo of Williams; and to her left a photo of her grandson, Sammy. Beside her on the dressing table are two lucky pigs, two trolls, and a snail (a memento of her very first role, at the age of four).

After our lunch, on the way out, I mentioned to Dench that I hadn't yet seen *The Royal Family*. She paused at the front door of the club. 'Will you tell me when you're coming in?' she said, holding out her cheek to be kissed. 'And I'll overact for you.' It was an exquisite exit. The line came so fast and was played so deftly and spoken with such warmth that, for a moment, I believed she'd never said it before.

Making It Real

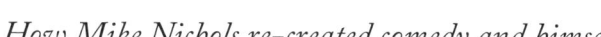

How Mike Nichols re-created comedy and himself

Once, in the early seventies, Mike Nichols was sitting in a commercial jet as it took off from J.F.K. Moments after it was airborne, the plane went into what Nichols recalls as 'an unnervingly steep bank. Everybody looked at each other. Nobody knew what it meant.' The pilot came on the intercom. 'We are experiencing –' he began in his best *Right Stuff* drawl. Then, suddenly, he said, 'Just a minute!' The mike went dead. In the long silence that followed, the people on the airplane started to panic. A woman a few rows in front of Nichols turned around and looked squarely at him. 'What do we do now, Mr Success?' she said.

Nichols, who has a sharp American wit but courtly European manners, bit his tongue. 'All those "Mr Success" years would have been hard to explain to anybody if I tried,' Nichols, now sixty-eight, says. 'What I really wanted to say to that envious woman was "Don't worry. There's still nothing happening inside me. I'm not experiencing success or anything much."'

But feelings aren't facts. From the moment Nichols made his

name, in the late fifties, as the lanky deadpan half of the comedy team Nichols and May, he took up residence in success. As early as 1961, a letter addressed to 'Famous Actor, Mike Nichols, U.S.A.' reached him. And, by the seventies, Nichols represented the high-water mark in not just one but three areas of American entertainment. As a comedian, he improvised routines with Elaine May which are among the treasures of American humor; as a stage director, beginning in the early sixties, he had a string of commercial hits that made him the most successful Broadway director since George Abbott; as a film director, he made the bold, intelligent *Who's Afraid of Virginia Woolf?* (1966) and *The Graduate* (1967). The latter, for which he won an Academy Award and which both summed up and influenced his generation, got him off the Hollywood blocks perhaps faster than any director since Orson Welles.

Nichols has made seventeen films in the last three decades. Success, however, as Winston Churchill said, is never final. On May 3, 1999 – just one day short of sixty years since Nichols, then Michael Igor Peschkowsky, the son of a White Russian emigre and a German beauty, arrived in New York by boat from Germany – he found himself at one of those occasions he likes to call a 'ratfuck,' at Lincoln Center's Avery Fisher Hall, where more than three thousand citizens had gathered to celebrate his lifetime achievement in film. The first part of the evening was a cinematic homage. Just before it began, Nichols and his wife, Diane Sawyer – the most observed of all observers – took their seats in the front row of a box just beside the stage and surveyed the illustrious guests below, among them Richard Avedon, Steve Martin, Itzhak Perlman, Stephen Sondheim, Caroline Kennedy Schlossberg, and Barbara Walters. Nichols assumed the runic crooked smile Elizabeth Taylor describes as 'that smile that tilts up at one end, that you can read so much into – a shared joke, a certain skepticism.' Then, one by one, various grandees of American popular culture – Meryl Streep, Paul Simon, Elaine May, Harrison Ford, Buck Henry, Nora Ephron, Candice Bergen, Art Garfunkel, Matthew Broderick, Nathan Lane – filed into the box, too, and flanked the evening's sovereigns. They were part of Nichols's story; later in the ceremony, in their encomiums from the stage, they would individually swear allegiance to him like courtiers to a king – which, in a way, he is.

'He knows that all the Versailles stuff is bullshit,' says the screenwriter Buck Henry, a close friend who has scripted three of Nichols's films, including *The Graduate*. 'He knows when his ass is being kissed, and he knows when it isn't, although it is most of the time. He casts a baleful eye on all of it, but in his heart he wants it and needs it.' In its deluxe panoply, the Lincoln Center extravaganza fulfilled one of Nichols's lifelong fantasies. 'He's on an island that belongs to him, manned on the turrets by men with machine guns,' another close friend, Richard Avedon, explains. 'People can only get in with a passport, and then only his friends.' The need for a seamless armor is the legacy of Nichols's friendless, despairing refugee childhood. When he arrived from Berlin, at the age of seven, he was totally bald; he'd been permanently denuded of all body hair at the age of four, a reaction to a defective whooping-cough vaccine. He knew just two English sentences – 'I do not speak English' and 'Please do not kiss me.' He'd lost his homeland, his language, his class pedigree, and, by the age of twelve, he would also lose his father. 'I was a zero,' Nichols says now. He adds, 'In every way that mattered, I was powerless.' Nichols sought something to counteract his paralyzing sense of inadequacy and to disarm a world that he saw, and still sees, as predatory and cruel. 'The most useful thing is if your enemy doesn't know he's your enemy,' Nichols told me, setting out the rule of dissimulation by which, over the years, he has kept the world in his thrall. 'Never let people see what you want, because they will not let you have it. Never let anybody see what you feel, because it gives them too much power. You're probably better off not showing weakness whenever you can avoid it, because they'll go for you.' With its aspects of detachment, generosity, and control, the imperial posture has served him well.

On the night of Nichols's gala, Elaine May couldn't resist a wink at his jerrybuilt crown.' So he's witty, he's brilliant, he's articulate, he's on time, he's prepared, and he writes,' she said. 'But is he perfect? He knows that you can't really be liked or loved if you're perfect. You have to have just enough flaws. And he does. Just the right perfect flaws to be absolutely endearing. And my three minutes are up, but if I had another four seconds I'd tell you everyone of those flaws.'

Nichols is a purveyor of aplomb, a rare commodity these days. He lives like a pasha and long ago took up the kingly pastime of breeding Arabian horses. (In 1972, he had the national-champion stallion and mare, Elkin and Elkana.) Over the years, Nichols, who calls himself 'a Dionysian who gets tired easily,' has also been romantically linked to a variety of goddesses – goddesses of literature (Robert Graves's Black Goddess, Margot Callas, who was Nichols's second wife), goddesses of glamour (Suzy Parker), activism (Gloria Steinem), society (Jackie Onassis), and the media (Sawyer, who became the fourth Mrs Nichols, in 1988). Well before Nichols grew into his grandiosity, his hauteur had him typecast in college plays as the Dauphin and the emperor.

With his long Russian nose, he emits a kind of mandarin snottiness – what Woody Allen calls 'his superb contumely,' adding, 'It's supercilious in the way we all wish we had the genius for. He's a nice version of George Sanders in *All About Eve*.' At a dinner party in the sixties, Nichols corrected Norman Mailer, who had declared that his favorite line of poetry was Dylan Thomas's 'Do not go quietly into that good night.' 'Actually, it's "gentle,"' Nichols said. '"Quietly" wouldn't scan, would it?' Mailer rounded on Nichols, calling him a 'royal baby,' a put-down that Nichols thought was 'pretty good.' (In jollier circumstances, Sawyer has been known to refer to her husband as 'His Royal Cuteness.')

At the finale of the gala, Nichols had planned to go on stage and say to the assembled, 'Well, that's all very well and good, but what about my humanity? What about my *fucking* humanity?' But Art Garfunkel scuppered the joke by speaking earnestly to that very point. So when Nichols stepped before his audience – a tall man with big, gnarly hands and an indulged belly that precedes him by some inches – he resorted to another gripe. 'Where the hell is Dustin Hoffman?' Nichols said. 'He was nothing when I found him.' His straight face caught the audience off guard and made the joke ambiguous. 'It's like the monster not showing up at the tribute for Dr Frankenstein,' he continued. 'Actually, I suspect that his not showing up is related to my not going to his A.F.I. tribute, although that was all the way across the country. . . . Well, it's all blood under the bridge now.'

But blood has a way of sticking to things; even the solvent of Nichols's wit can't wipe out certain dark spots. In his movie career, things have not all gone Nichols's way. There was a string of flops in the mid-seventies: *Catch-22* (1970), *The Day of the Dolphin* (1973), *The Fortune* (1975), and *Bogart Slept Here*, which

Nichols closed down in production; there followed a seven-year hiatus before his next film, the excellent *Silkwood* (1983). Some of his later movies – *Heartburn* (1986), *Regarding Henry* (1991), *Wolf* (1994) – were more or less rumbled by the critics. In 1995, after Nichols had shown the final cut of *The Birdcage* (which went on to gross more than a hundred and eighty million dollars worldwide) to his editing team on Martha's Vineyard, he sat down with them for a celebratory meal. 'I was very emotional and very angry. l couldn't speak all through lunch,' Nichols told a friend. 'The film was so good, so strong. I realized I'd had no inkling of my anger at the people who had written me off. My reaction, instantaneously, was "Fuck you, bastards. You thought I couldn't do this anymore. Well, look at this."'

So, here at his retrospective, Nichols both masked and displayed his vindictive triumph. As a parting shot, he announced that he was leaving the next day for Los Angeles, to go into pre-production on his new film – a comedy called *What Planet Are You From?* And he left the audience with a slightly altered version of W. H. Auden's acid envoi – a ruler's deadpan rebuke to those young upstarts 'who think they could do it better' and who might dismiss the proceedings as merely 'geezer aggrandizement':

> Death takes the innocent young,
> As poets have frequently sung,
> The rolling-in-money,
> The screamingly funny,
> And even the very well-hung.

★

In mid-July, I caught up with Nichols in his current kingdom, Sound Stage 15, at Culver Studios, in Culver City, where a broken ankle and crutches – the result of a spill on the set – in no way impeded his show of good spirits. 'Life is difficult and fucked up and complicated,' Nichols says. 'The cutting room isn't.' At the studio, his power is absolute. 'I really need to control it. Every aspect of it, every nuance of the reading. How long every second of every shot is,' he says. 'Partly because that's the job, and partly because I just have to. I'm happy when I'm controlling it and uncomfortable when I'm not and crazed when it's out of control.'

On the set, Nichols's wit serves him well both as a social lubricant and as an equalizer. In conversation, he lays out his colorful word hoard like a vender at a bazaar – a delightful abundance of erudition, playfulness, and surprise, which helps take the odor off his Eeyore-like nature. His voice, which is nasal and comes from the back of his throat, can wring all sorts of sardonic music from the sounds of words. 'A retreat? How *moving*. It's not a sweat lodge, is it?' he says, taking a call on his portable phone as the crew prepares for a scene with Garry Shandling and Ben Kingsley. 'Come and see me. We can have a *tiny* retreat in my trailer.'

While the shot is being set up, Nichols hobbles away toward his trailer, which is parked opposite the sound stage; the makeup man standing at the shadowy threshold of the building cautions Nichols about the ledge he's standing on. 'Thankyou, Roy,' Nichols says. 'Where were you when I fell in that hole?' Among the myriad problems facing Nichols on this particular cerulean day, as he clambers up the steps to his trailer, is what to get the cast as an endof-production present. 'My assistant came up with a silver – what do you call it – vibrator,' he says. 'I'm not sure. Maybe if it has *Ars Gratia Artis* on it.' Inside, the trailer is dominated by photos of his handsome children – Daisy, thirtyfive, who dubs movies into French; Max, twenty-five, who is a record-company A.&R. man; and Jenny, twenty-three, a student at Brown – and by food (See's Candies, jelly beans, nuts, chocolatechip cookies). Nichols, who has never met a calorie he didn't like, is, as Candice Bergen says, 'a poster child for unhealthy living.' Because he's currently immobilized and can't climb up onto the spacestation set, a gizmo called a 'god box' has been installed in his trailer, just opposite the sofa. A microphone allows Nichols to talk directly to his players as he watches them. 'It's annoying,' he says. 'It's like wearing a condom. You're there and you're not there.'

What Planet Are You From? is about an alien, played by Shandling, who, as part of a plan to dominate the universe, is sent to earth to impregnate as many women as possible and take over the planet from within. Nichols inspects a replay of the just completed scene in which Ben Kingsley, the leader of Shandling's planet, taps him for the procreative mission. 'The success of our planet's domination of the universe rests in your hands,' Kingsley says, in his gravest British Received Pronunciation. 'Now, if you'll come this way we'll arrange your transfer and attach your penis.' A big, chesty laugh rumbles through Nichols's body. 'Kingsley was put on earth to say that line,' he says, and laughs some more. Nichols has as many kinds of laughs as he does ironic inflections, but his high-pitched Big Laugh is like no other. His eyes widen, his body stiffens, his pale skin reddens as hilarity crashes over him. In that moment of wipeout, all of Nichols's power, self-consciousness, and royal command vanish into childish delight. This wheezy, teary collapse has been captured on record ('Nichols and May at Work'); and anyone who has been in its force field knows the strength of its infectiousness. 'It's incredible when you get it,' Neil Simon told me.' It inspires you to show him more material to get it again.'

In the next shot, which is the movie's finale, Shandling goes into a righteous harangue – 'Why are we taking over earth? Is that what it's about? More, more, more?' – and Nichols stops him in mid-flow. 'It's a moment from an operetta,' he says. 'We don't want that gesture. It's too Jewish." Speech, like the portrayal of a character, is in the details; Nichols watches over it with vigilance. 'I constantly have to edit the things I want to say,' he adds. 'Shambling and I get into this kidding thing, but then it gets a little bit out of hand.' 'He's called "Shambling," is he?' I ask. Nichols fixes me with a lidded glance. 'Well, now and then,' he says. Nichols continues, 'He's playing the game of student with the master, which is partly meant to disarm me. He's not without self-knowledge. He knows how to use me to make certain things happen to him in scenes. The game is useful to us both.'

But the previous week, for what Nichols said was the first time in his directing career, he had screamed at his star, who is also the film's co-author. Nichols knows that he can be withering. There was a moment during the filming of *The Day of the Dolphin* when Nichols saw himself becoming a tyrannical bastard. 'I remember that I told the D.P.' – director of photography – 'toward the end that I was not proud of the way I had treated the guys and I wanted to apologize,' he says. 'And he – a very mild man – said, "It's too late for that." It took my breath away. It made me realize that I had to put the brakes on completely. Because nobody can fight back, the director has an absolute obligation to treat people decently.' By his own admission, he had gone "totally nuts" at Shandling, in an outburst that sent people scurrying off the set. He explains, 'Garry came in and didn't know the scene, although he'd written it. Annette Bening, of course, knew it perfectly. After it was over, I said something to her about her character.' Bening plays a ditzy recovering alcoholic, with no knack for picking Mr Right. 'Garry said, "I think she should be kooky." I said, "You do? Her clothes are kooky, the set is kooky, her lines are kooky you want her to *act* kooky, too?" I said, "Why don't you come in prepared and do your own work?"'

'It was mean,' Bening told me. 'He was attacking Garry inappropriately. It was really out of line.' Shandling apologized for being unprepared, and Bening then met with Nichols in his trailer to defend Shandling's right to have a creative conversation, a point that Nichols conceded when he, in turn, apologized to Shandling. In Nichols's remorse, Bening saw a 'fierce superego.' 'He's not as generous to himself as he deserves to be,' she says. 'He's got a voice in him that's very harsh, and unnecessarily so.' In his surprising anger – he now says he was 'much angrier than seemed warranted' – Nichols saw 'the dim racial memory of rage,' that little boy in himself who is still angry and whom he constantly struggles to keep down. 'He's the one,' Nichols says. 'He's somewhere saying, "Don't fuck with me." And I can't stop him.'

'All the shit was in the beginning,' Nichols says of his life. Hitler – or his voice, broadcast from speakers on dockside lampposts – literally saw Nichols and his three-year-old brother, Robert, off to America in 1939. Nichols remembers not being allowed to board the Bremen, which was leaving from Hamburg, until the traffic-stopping speech was finished. The brothers, each with ten marks in a purse around his neck, made the journey alone across the Atlantic. Their mother, Brigitte, was ill and stayed behind for a year and a half before rejoining the family; their doctor father, Paul, who had left Russia for Germany after the revolution in 1917, had gone ahead to New York in 1938, just before the Nazi takeover, to set up a practice on the prosperous Upper West Side. On their first night off the ship, Nichols remembers seeing Hebrew writing on a delicatessen and asking his father in German, 'Is that allowed?' He also remembers watching his brother throw a tantrum while his father 'pretended to call the police on the pay phone to deal with him.' 'He had no experience as a father,' Nichols says. 'He had no idea what to do.' Paul saw his boys only intermittently during their first year in America. He placed them with an English family, some patients of his who agreed to care for them while he was establishing himself. 'They were awful,' Nichols says. 'They would kiss their own children good night, then shake our hands. We'd get a spoonful of milk of magnesia and go to bed.' Things didn't improve much when the Peschkowsky family was reunited. 'My parents fought all the time,' Nichols recalls. 'They would have divorced if my father hadn't died – something that my mother immediately forgot.' Much later, Nichols learned that his father 'was impotent with her and not with many other women.' Both parents had a series of lovers.' There were always other people, in Germany and here,' he says. 'It was just the way things were.'

Nichols felt 'landlocked' in the family, trapped in the battle between his warring parents. A lot of the contention was about him. 'I wouldn't go to school. I wouldn't get up in the morning. I answered back,' Nichols says. He 'had a mouth,' which made both his schoolmates and his family wary of him.' My father wasn't too crazy about me,' Nichols says. 'I loved him anyway. One of the things I regretted for a long time was that he died before he could see that he would be proud of me. I was actually more what he wished for than he thought.' He adds, 'He could rage.' (Nichols still remembers his father, in the heat of an unhappy family moment, saying to him and his brother, 'I'll be glad to get rid of you two.') 'But he also told funny stories, and he used to dance for us in his underwear. He did routines at parties that people loved to hear.' In later life, Nichols was told by the impresario Sol Hurok, who had been one of Paul's patients, 'You're not as funny as your father.' And it's through his father that Nichols feels he understands the stoic bravado of Chekhov's characters. 'He was the Russian as entertainer,' he says. 'What I loved him for – even when he wasn't noticeably loving me – was that he had great vitality and joy of life.' Paul never let his darkness show in public. 'I feel linked to him in many ways, and that's one of them,' Nichols says.

By contrast, Brigitte, who was thirty-four when her husband died, at the age of forty-four, became 'a nightmare of accusation,' someone who collected injustices. 'She was one of those people who would hold you responsible for everything that happened to her and how bad she felt now,' Nichols says. He would try to kid her out of her misery. 'Everything wounded her,' he says. 'She was always wounded to the quick. "I raised you so you could say that to me? Thank you very much, I deserve that." It went on for hours, days.'

Brigitte, who had no profession, no money, no proper English, and only a few friends, would go to the Stanwood Cafeteria, on Broadway, and sit alone for hours. Over the years, she worked in a bakery, a bookshop, even set up a translation agency to support her boys. But after Paul was gone they found themselves plummeting well below the level of middle-class gentility to which they had been accustomed. Although Nichols blocked out the degree of their humiliating poverty, his brother subsequently reminded him of 'bug-infested apartments' and of their mother 'giving up to the point where she didn't do the laundry. We weren't clean.' 'She always had some mysterious illness,' Nichols adds. When he went home after school to their drab rooms at 155 West Seventy-first Street – 'one of those tiny apartment houses with podiatrists on the first floor' – he frequently found Brigitte propped up on her living-room sofa bed (the boys shared the bedroom) with a table of pills, 'maybe a hundred and fifty bottles of medication, and the phone, on which she always was.'

In time, Nichols discovered that he could make people laugh by telling stories about his mother. In fact, Nichols and May's definitive sketch, 'Mother and Son' ('Someday . . . you'll have children of your own. And, honey, when you do, I only pray that they make you suffer the way you're making me. [*Sobs.*] That's all I pray, Arthur. That's a mother's prayer') was inspired by one of Brigitte's lethal phone calls. As Nichols recalls, it went, '"Hello, Michael, this is your mother. Do you remember me?" I said, "Mom, can I call you right back?" Literally. And I called Elaine.' He and May were playing at the Blue Angel then. 'I said, "I have a piece for us." I told her the line. She said, "We'll do it tonight." And we did it pretty much the way it is now. She had the identical mother.'

Before he found a way to make light of his difficulties, Nichols was swamped by them. From his first day at the Dalton School, on the Upper East Side, the clouds of exclusion and isolation glowered over him. 'The kid was as far outside as an outsider can get,' says Buck Henry, who was in his class. 'He was Igor Peschkowsky when he was at Dalton. He did not speak English. He wore a cap all the time.' Nichols says, 'I remember being on the school bus in New York and saying, "What means '*emergency*'?" By the time he reached high school (the progressive school Walden, from which he graduated in 1948), Nichols had mastered English, had a make-do wig, and had learned the idiom and style of his peers, but his assessment of himself during these 'searing, painful years' was that he was 'the most popular of the unpopular kids.' 'That was cast in bronze, that's where I was chained in the galaxy forever,' he says. 'I thought about revenge a lot in those days.'

A lazy and lacklustre student, Nichols had a quick mind and a formidable intellectual inheritance. (His maternal grandmother, Hedwig Lachmann, did the translation of Oscar Wilde's *Salome* that Richard Strauss used for his opera; his grandfather Gustav Landauer, among whose best friends were Martin Buber and B. Traven, was a writer turned activist, who was a leader of the German Social Democratic Party, and whose brutal execution by the Nazis had been the reason for the family's exodus.) Nichols filled his solitude with activities that took him out of himself and into exotic other worlds. At sixteen, he went with a date to the second night of Elia Kazan's production of *A Streetcar Named Desire*. 'We just sat there,' Nichols says. 'We didn't talk. We couldn't believe there was such a thing.' He adds, 'I just wanted to be around theatre.' He also read voraciously (all of Eugene O'Neill by the age of fourteen, James Joyce's *Ulysses*, E.M. Forster's *A Passage to India*); he was a constant moviegoer; he hung out in Central Park and at the Claremont Riding Academy. 'I got to exercise people's horses; sometimes, when people were thrown off, I would catch the horses on the bridle path and ride them back.' Animals calmed Nichols; unlike his classmates, they were responsive, unselfconscious, and unable to pass judgment. 'The refugee ear is a sort of seismograph for how one is doing,' Nichols says. At high school, he explains, 'I *heard* what they thought of me – 'nebbish,' 'poor boy' – and what they thought of each other. A thousand tiny victories and defeats in an ordinary conversation. I didn't know what to do with it.'

To this day, even though Nichols wears a wig, the intrusive, objectifying eyes of others continue to be a threat. 'Staring is something that still makes me absolutely nuts,' he says. He thinks of the public as 'something to be controlled and tamed.' 'The first person to come up to me at a party is in danger to this day,' Nichols says. 'My reflex is to attack the first couple of people. I can't stop. Diane is right there, taking off the edges, fixing it. By the third or fourth person, I can be friendly.' To Nichols, the audience has always personified Them – the annihilating mob of his childhood, whom he characterizes as 'the beast' with 'too much power.' He says, 'I was so impaled on what people thought. I had to train myself away from that. I never had a friend from the time I came to this country until I got to the University of Chicago. I was seventeen.'

He ended up there by a fluke: it was one of the only schools in America that didn't require the College Boards, and Nichols hadn't taken them. 'Once I got there, I had a very specific and powerful sense of "Oh my God, look, there are others like me. There are other weirdos."' The publisher Aaron Asher, who shared college digs with Nichols, says, 'We were all freaks. We were way ahead of the country. There was sex. There was dope. There was a subculture.' Asher was just one of Nichols's new friends, who were 'refugees or first-generation Jewish intellectual guys.' When Nichols mentioned to Asher that his grandmother had written the libretto for Strauss's *Salome*, Asher joked, 'Oh, really? Was she Hugo von Hofmannsthal?' Nichols says, 'I was looking at somebody who knew who Hofmannsthal was and that he wrote libretti for Strauss. No such thing had ever happened to me before.'

The first person Nichols met at registration was Susan Sontag; they struck up a lifelong friendship. 'I thought he was terrific,' Sontag says. 'I adored him from the start. He was totally alive and incredibly verbal. We talked about books, about feelings, about how to get free of our pasts. Because we were interested in theatre, we were interested in observing people. I would happily have become his girlfriend physically, except I was intimidated by the hair problem and felt he was untouchable.' (Thirty years later, Sontag confessed to Nichols that she couldn't accept the scars from her mastectomy: 'I have this thing, and every time I take a bath I'm horrified.' He said, 'Susan, now you know how I have felt all my life.') Asher characterizes Nichols's look as 'something out of a German Expressionist movie,' but says that, 'despite the strangeness of his appearance, he did very well with the girls. He was courtly, and he was well read, which got you a long way at that university.'

Nichols, who had begun therapy, was also deeply depressed. 'I would spend long times in my room and just not come out,' he says. 'Sometimes I would step over all the dishes and the Franco-American spaghetti cans and hang out with some friends, then go back to my lair.' Nichols d.j.'ed a popular show of classical music and chat at WFMT, but his depression almost cost him the job. 'He was funny and knowledgeable but totally unreliable,' says Asher, whose cousin owned the station. 'They fired him a number of times.'

'I couldn't be a *person* that many hours a day,' Nichols explains. 'I needed – still need – a lot of time lying on the bed absolutely blank, the way I assume a dog is in front of the fire. A persona takes energy. I just needed a rest from it. Not to be anything in relation to anyone else.' When Nichols did emerge from seclusion, he worked up his losses into a kind of legend. According to one of his theatrical cohorts, quoted in Janet Coleman's *The Compass*, Nichols behaved like 'a princeling deprived of his rightful fortune.' Nichols was so poor that he took to eating the leftovers from the coffee shop where the director Paul Sills was then a waiter. 'He rattled his tin cup,' Nichols's friend Hayward Ehrlich, now an associate professor of English at Rutgers, says. 'When Mike appeared, you knew that he needed a cup of coffee or a sandwich or something. It became his way of relating to people, to have them sort of help him out of his impoverishment. I think Mike loved to magnify his sense of adversity so that in some way he could triumph over it.'

Much to Nichols's surprise, during his sophomore year he found himself 'near the center of the in-group' and 'a minor celebrity.' The theatrical talent pool at the University of Chicago was extraordinary: Sills, Ed Asner, Severn Darden, Anthony Holland, Zohra Lampert, Barbara Harris, Gene Troobnick. Nichols directed his first play, Yeats's *Purgatory*, with Asner, and he performed in a number of plays, among them *Androcles and the Lion*, *St Joan*, and *La Ronde*. He played Jean the valet in a production of Strindberg's *Miss Julie*, directed by Sills. 'He wasn't the working-class man and couldn't come close to it,' Sills says now. Nichols agrees; it was, he says, a 'pathetic, awful production.' He remembers 'this evil, hostile girl in the front row staring at me throughout the performance. I was about four feet away from her and she stared at me all through it, and I knew she knew it was shit, and there was no way I could let her know that I knew.'

A few days later, the show mysteriously got a rave review in the Chicago *Daily News*. Nichols recalls rushing up to Sills on the street with the paper; Sills was with the girl who had unsettled Nichols from the audience. He scoured the review, while the girl read over his shoulder. 'Ha!' she said, and walked away. Nichols, who was already toying with the notion of a theatrical career, had just met his future: Elaine May.

Some weeks later, on his way back from his disk-jockey gig, in the spring of 1954, Nichols caught sight of May in the waiting room of the Illinois Central's Randolph Street Station.

Their friendship began with an improvisation. 'May I sit down?' he asked. In a thick Russian accent, May replied, 'If you *veesh*.' 'Off she went,' Nichols says. 'She started us on that.' They played out the scene, which Nichols characterized as 'half spy, half pickup,' all the way home. 'I think I went home with her and she made me her specialty, which was hamburger with cream cheese and ketchup – the only thing she cooked,' Nichols recalls. 'She didn't know conventional dishes. She was utterly a rebel. That was part of the fun of it.'

May was also a femme fatale. 'Everybody wanted Elaine, and the people who got her couldn't keep her,' Nichols says. But, even at their first meeting, which led to a brief romance, he remembers feeling that 'we were safe from everyone else when we were with each other. And also safe from each other.' He goes on, 'I knew somehow that she would not do to me the things she'd done to other guys. I knew she wouldn't lose interest and move on. I knew instantly that everything that happened to us was ours.'

May's life had been as painful and complex as Nichols's.

'It's almost hard to convey how neurotic we were,' Nichols says. Although she had dropped out of high school at fourteen – the only thing she enjoyed there was diagramming sentences – May was, as Edmund Wilson noted in his diary when he fell under her dark-eyed spell in the late fifties, 'something of a genius.' She had grown up in a nomadic acting family, spending a good part of her childhood playing a little boy named Bennie in a travelling Yiddish theatre run by her father, Jack Berlin. According to her second husband, Sheldon Harnick, who wrote the lyrics for *Fiddler on the Roof*, the death of May's beloved father when she was ten left her to a future of apprehensive relations with men. She was married for the first time at sixteen; by eighteen she had a child, Jeannie Berlin, who was about four years old when Nichols met May and was being raised in Los Angeles by May's mother. By the time she reached Chicago, May had studied acting, performed a hillbilly act under the name Elly May, and written advertising copy. May, who saw herself primarily as a writer, was unofficially auditing courses at the University of Chicago and trying to develop a screen treatment of Plato's *Symposium*. (She once convinced a philosophy class that everyone in the *Symposium* was drunk and that that was the point of Plato's discourse.) 'The only safe thing is to take a chance,' May always told Nichols, who was ravished by her daring and her quirkiness.

Nichols and May had talent, but, more important, they had chemistry. They were quick; they were guarded, they were crazy. They were also 'insanely judgmental' snobs, bound together, Nichols says, 'by tremendous hostility to everyone else but never to each other.' (May once said, according to Nichols, 'that if somebody told her that I had burned down her house with her whole family in it, she would say, "Oh, I must ask Michael why he did that.'") 'I feel in opposition to almost everything,' May, who no longer gives interviews, said in a Profile of the duo published in this magazine in 1961. Like Nichols, she used wit as a pesticide, and her juicy good looks were a particularly disconcerting contrast to her sharp tongue. Once, Nichols recalls, when two men followed her down the street making kissing sounds, May turned on them and said, 'What's the matter? Tired of each other?' 'Fuck you!' one of them shouted at her. May turned and faced the guy. 'With what?' she said. Nichols dropped out of college in 1953, and, in 1954, he decamped to New York to study the Method with Lee Strasberg. 'I have decided that if I don't make it as a nervous young man,' he wrote to a Chicago friend, 'I will wait and become like Robert Morley, who is clearly the funniest man in the world.' But in 1955, with no prospect of work, he returned to Chicago with the promise of twenty-eight dollars a week as part of a new company called the Compass Players, of which Sills and May were founding members. The goal of the Compass, which would evolve into Chicago's legendary Second City, was to do away with conventional plays and make theatre by improvisational means. 'I was terrified of improvising,' Nichols says. 'I didn't even know what it was. I hated it, and I was very bad at it.' Nichols cried in his scenes for months 'because that's what I thought I'd learned from Strasberg. Paul and Elaine kept me going. The fact of Elaine – her presence – kept me doing it.' In the first successful scene they did together, Nichols played a riding instructor, and May his pupil. 'We both realized as we got into the middle of the scene that I would get to stand in the middle of the stage and watch her cantering as both horse and rider around me.' During the scene, a member of the cast ran into the bar where the other actors were congregated, shouting, 'Come quick! Mike has a character!'

Nichols reflects, 'what is implied in that story – and it was true for the first time in my life – is affection. They had some affection for me. I began to understand that I could be kidded, and people could be fond of me, and that this would all be a pleasurable thing.'

As intellectual high-wire acts go, there is no riskier or more astounding enterprise than going out in front of an audience and creating something out of nothing. 'You're showing off how smart you are, how good you are,' Buck Henry says. 'You have the pleasure of having not only performed it but written it at the same time.' Improvisation – a process, Nichols says, that 'absorbs you, creates you, and saves you' – allowed the actors to stay on the edge of emotion and character without connecting deeply to their interior lives, and this suited both Nichols's and May's private natures. 'I would never have been a performer without her, and I don't think she would have without me,' Nichols says. 'Elaine and I are, in some weird way, each other's unconscious.' Nichols made the shapes; May filled them in.' She was shockingly, endlessly inventive. She could go on and on – I couldn't,' Nichols says. 'I did my jokes, and then I was through.'

Within the Compass Players, May could be funny with several different actors, but Nichols could be funny only with her. 'I never did a good scene of any kind with anybody else,' Nichols told Jeff Sweet, in 'Something Wonderful Right Away,' an oral history of the Compass Players. 'For me, it depended on a certain connection with Elaine and a certain mad gleam in either her or my eyes when we knew something was starting.' The mad gleam meant, as he explained to me, 'Oh, fuck, I know where you're going. That's a great idea you've just had, and when you get there I'll be ready.' That focus – reminiscent of a parent's empowering gaze – was inspiring. 'We had to figure out something or we would disappear, each of us,' Nichols adds. (He would later find a similar containing attentiveness in Diane Sawyer. 'All of her is available all the time,' he says.) With May, Nichols could drop his mask 'I interested me when I was with her,' he says. 'It wasn't only that she was so great but that when I was with her I became something more than I had been.'

Onstage, in their own version of Truth or Dare, Nichols and May kept upping the ante on each other. Once, in an improv about an egotistical d.j. and a starlet called Barbara Musk, Nichols quizzed May about her next movie. 'My latest motion picture is … called *Two Gals in Paris*. It is the life story of Gertrude Stein,' May said. 'What do you play in the picture, sweetheart?' Nichols asked. 'Well, I was really just lucky enough to get the part of Gertrude Stein,' she said. 'I had heard that Gertrude Stein was going to be played by Spencer Tracy,' Nichols said, manoeuvring her into a tough spot. 'Only as a child,' May shot back. When the conversation got onto the soundtrack of the movie, May said that she'd recorded the title song. Nichols promptly asked her to sing it. On the spot, May ad-libbed an entire song, which ended

> There was dashing Dmitri, elusive Ivan
> And Alyosha with the laughing eyes.
> Then came the dawn
> The brothers were gone
> I just can't forget those wonderful guys.

The University of Chicago proved the perfect place for nurturing their particular ironic and informed voices. 'It was the most referential community that I think ever existed in this country,' says Nichols, who improvised entire scenes in the style of writers suggested by the audience. 'At the Compass, we could drop "Dostoyevsky" as a name and get a laugh. We were living in the context in which the referential joke was just the highest currency.' They were also coming of age in a 'safer, quieter place' than New York. 'Chicago is not a city of fashion, nor is it full of pride and excitement over its art,' Nichols says. 'They were very calm about Compass. They came. They laughed. They went home.'

Nichols and May were beginning to find resources in themselves that they hadn't known they had, including the ability to make anger work for them. 'Rage is the best engine, of course, if you have a tremendous gift to employ it properly,' Nichols wrote to a friend. Once, when Nichols was performing a sketch about pretentious snobs at a private party, the actor playing the effete host offered to put on a record. 'Would you like to hear *The Four Seasons*?' he asked. 'Perhaps just "Winter,"' Nichols replied. 'To freeze his ass was a pleasure,' says Nichols, who found that with jokes he could 'cow the shit' out of the public. 'When a joke comes to you, it feels like it's been sent by God.' He adds, 'What it is, really, is discovering your unconscious.'

There were other discoveries. When Nichols was onstage, even the 'curse' of imagining what others thought of him became an asset: 'I could hear what the other actors were thinking, where they were going, what the audience was thinking.' Nichols also learned 'the Aristotelian things' about the building of a scene – conflict, theme, resolution. He and May found ways to 'grab the opposite.' 'There had to be a core to a scene,' Nichols told Jeff Sweet. 'It didn't matter how clever the lines were. If they weren't hung on a situation, you were only as good as your last line . . .

But if you could grab a situation, whether it was a seduction or a conflict or a fight, once you had that spine, then things could come out of it.' And when the jokes were found, Nichols husbanded them. 'If there was a laugh to be gotten and Elaine didn't set up the feed line, Mike would work with her until she did,' another Compass member, the comedian Shelley Berman, said. 'He did everything but lasso her.' For a while, according to Janet Coleman, Nichols and May worked with Berman, a trio that May suggested they call 'Two Cocksuckers and Elaine.' 'I actually liked Shelley,' Nichols said. 'But one day he came offstage and said, 'Hey, guys, Mike had three scenes in that set, and I only had two.' It was a whole new idea in Eden to count. The group was finished in six months."

Nichols and May themselves nearly foundered in 1958, when they were working in St Louis, where a new Compass Players venue had been launched. Nichols had recently married the Chicago TV personality and singer Pat Scot ('Isn't it a beautiful first wedding?' May said at the ceremony), who joined him on weekends. During the week, on a strictly platonic basis, Nichols and May shared a room, which she vacated when Scot arrived. On those days, May stayed with another company member, Del Close. Nichols was jealous of Close, not for romantic reasons but because May was so much a part of his identity that he couldn't share her. 'I persecuted the shit out of Del,' Nichols says. 'Nothing could stop me. Elaine finally said to the producer, "I can't stand it anymore – you've got to fire Michael."' Nichols was summarily fired.

Some weeks later, from New York, where he had gone with Scot (though, as May had predicted, the marriage didn't last much longer), Nichols called to ask May if she'd like to audition with him for the New York agent Jack Rollins. Rollins handled such cabaret talent as Harry Belafonte and Woody Allen. 'They were immediately astounding. They were complete,' Rollins says, of the first time he set eyes on the team, at his office in the Pierre Hotel. 'He is Mr Practical. She is insanely creative. But Mike is the one that made the act live in this world.' By the following Tuesday, Nichols and May were playing the Village Vanguard. 'A couple of weeks later, we were on *Steve Allen*,' Nichols says. 'Then we were on *Omnibus*, and we were very famous. The whole thing took about two months.' After the *Omnibus* show, Nichols remembers calling May at 4am to say, 'What do we do now?'

As McCarthyism, the Cold War, and racial unrest made their generation anxious, Nichols and May struck a new disenchanted chord in American life. 'Nobody was doing any humor about post-Korean War young people, that urban generation,' says the cartoonist and playwright Jules Feiffer, who, when he first heard them, 'didn't dare laugh, because I was afraid of missing something.' He adds, 'Humor was Bob Hope still. When I saw Mike and Elaine, suddenly you felt not just that this is funny but that this is true.' Woody Allen, who wanted to write for Nichols and May, says that comedians like them 'were touching on some kind of truth – truth of character, social truth, truth of wit. And, suddenly, part of that whole new sense of truth was that they wrote their own material.' With Nichols and May, Jewish angst, Freud, literacy, irony, and sex were ushered into the discourse of mainstream comedy. They, along with Mort Sahl, Jonathan Winters, and, later, Lenny Bruce and Woody Allen, were the renegades who led comedy away from the ersatz to the authentic. 'The nice thing is to make an audience laugh and laugh and laugh and shudder later,' May said. The frisson was the shock of recognition. Nichols and May had the uncanny ability at once to comment on character and to fill it from within. 'They were like music,' Steve Martin says, referring to the swift intimacy of their overlapping rhythms, the deft interplay of May's soft, breathless voice and the reedy clarity of Nichols's sound. For instance, in their sendup of public outrage over Charles Van Doren and the 'Twenty-One' scandal:

NICHOLS: Thank heaven for the investigation.
MAY: Oh, yes.
NICHOLS: When I feel worst I say to myself, 'At least the government has taken a firm stand.'
MAY: Oh, yes. Well, they can't fool around with this the way they did with integration.
NICHOLS: No.
MAY: This is a . . .
NICHOLS: . . . moral issue.
MAY: Yes.
NICHOLS: A moral issue.
MAY: Yes! Yes! It is a moral issue.
NICHOLS: A moral issue.
MAY: And to me that is so much more interesting than a real issue.

'Smart is not necessarily funny,' Martin says. 'You can go through a whole evening of smart and have laughed completely perfunctorily.' But Nichols and May could be approached from either a dopey or a smart place. For example, their classic sketch about two teenagers smoking and making out in the front seat of a car contained two pieces of inspired physical business: May in the middle of a passionate kiss opening her mouth to breathe and emitting a puff of smoke (a joke Nichols later used in *The Graduate*), and the clinching lovers trying to pass a cigarette from one trapped hand to another.

However, sometimes smart alone could bring down the house. Nichols began his send up of Tennessee Williams – a high-pitched, hard-drinking Southern playwright called Alabama Glass – with the playwright explaining his newest work to the audience. 'Before the action of the play *begins*,' Nichols drawled, 'Nanette's husband, Raoul, has committed *suicide* on bein' unjustly accused of *not* bein' homosexual.'

'Most of the time, people thought we were making fun of others when we were making fun of ourselves,' Nichols says. 'Pretentiousness. Snobbiness. Horniness. Elaine was parodying her mother, as I was mine, and a certain girlishness, flirtatiousness in herself.' He adds, 'It was utterly freeing.' And redeeming. In the teenager sketch, for instance, Nichols and May were sending up the cheerleader and the football star, those high-school paragons they never were but now got to play. 'We *were* those people, and it healed something, weird as it sounds,' Nichols says. Onstage with May, Nichols felt, 'I could be anybody I needed to be. I used to have a mental image of cracking a whip when I was talking to the audience. I could control them with jokes.' Offstage, the person he presented as Mike Nichols was another version of his stage persona – witty and apparently able to handle everything. 'We'd like to say a few words about adultery – it's coming back.' That's who I was.' He adds, 'You start imitating somebody who is calm about all that. You imitate it long enough, and it becomes true.'

But, while his public persona stanched old anxieties, success brought new ones. May cared more about process, Nichols more about results. 'She was always brave,' he says of her desire to improvise. 'But I became more and more afraid. I wasn't happy with getting paid a fortune for something and not having tried it out in advance.' By the late fifties, Nichols was earning more than half a million dollars a year. He adds, 'The audience didn't give a shit whether you were improvising or not. They'd come to see good comedy.'

The team's creative differences came to a head in their brilliant Broadway show, *An Evening with Mike Nichols and Elaine May* (1960), which I saw during its yearlong run. 'We were irreproachable,' Nichols says. 'We never got a negative review. We never had an empty seat. Everybody loved us. Everybody felt they had discovered us.' But discovery – the fearless adventure of creating in the moment – was gradually being leached out of their performances by the repetition of set routines. May grew increasingly unhappy. 'Sometimes she'd be late. What is so difficult? Two hours out of twenty-four. It's a perfect job. It wasn't that way for her,' Nichols says. 'We had huge fights about it. I never could understand why she found it so difficult.'

The most stunning moment of the evening – a kind of augury of their collapse – was a sketch called 'Pirandello,' a twenty-minute exercise in which Nichols and May began as two little kids, playing at insulting each other like Mom and Dad, then became Mom and Dad yelling at each other, and then turned into a pair of actors having trouble with each other onstage. Suddenly, in a terrifying shift, Nichols and May were in the middle of some ugly private squabble. At one point, in what Buck Henry characterizes as 'a moment of unbelievably intense embarrassment for everyone,' Nichols turned to the audience and said, 'My partner and I . . .' May said, 'Well, screw this,' and started to walk off stage. Nichols grabbed at her, ripping May's blouse as she pulled away. She started to cry. 'Michael, what do you think you're doing?' she said. 'I'm doing "Pirandello,"' Nichols said. Breaking into smiles, they took their bows. But at one performance Nichols and May actually came to blows: Nichols hit her back and forth across the face, May clawed at his chest until it bled, and the curtain had to be brought down. 'We cried together. It didn't happen again,' he says. 'I think, in many ways, I persecuted her. I went on at her, "This is too slow, this has to go faster."'

The end was slow in coming. In October, 1962, Nichols took the lead in May's play *A Matter of Position*, which opened in Philadelphia. 'It was sort of about me, which she never quite admitted,' Nichols says. But, with him on the stage and May in the audience, the balance of their relationship irrevocably shifted. 'Suddenly, Elaine was not next to me, doing it with me, but out there judging me,' Nichols says. 'It was horrendous.' The play itself added to the atmosphere of fiasco. As the Philadelphia *Sunday Bulletin* wrote, 'Those members of the audience who had not already beat a hasty retreat before the final curtain, as many did, were left with a sensation of numbness that was too far down to be attributed to heartburn.' Nichols and May were no longer two against the world. May was looking for a replacement for Nichols, and Nichols was saying to people, 'Get her to cut the play or I'm leaving.' The play died in Philadelphia; and, although they didn't exactly speak the words, so did their friendship. 'It was cataclysmic,' Nichols says.

'Mike was in a state of deep depression,' says Robby Lantz, Nichols's theatrical agent at the time.' He really wasn't functioning. He went to bed. Period.' Nichols was now half of a comedy team. He had lost his best friend, his livelihood, and the scaffolding of his identity. 'Mike has no tolerance for failure,' says a former collaborator who tried to rally him after May's departure. 'I didn't know what I was or who I was,' Nichols explains. His predicament was summed up one afternoon on Park Avenue by Leonard Bernstein, a member of the deluxe set he'd become part of. Bernstein put his arm around Nichols. 'Oh, Mikey,' he said, 'you're so good. I don't know at what, but you're so good.'

What Nichols was good at, it turned out, was something that his acting classes with Strasberg, his improvising, and his comedy act with May had all been a preparation for: directing. In 1961, in New Jersey, he'd directed a collection of Jules Feiffer cartoon sketches, 'The World of Jules Feiffer,' with music by Stephen Sondheim. 'It was clear to me that he was extraordinary,' Feiffer says. But it was not clear to the producing fraternity or to Nichols. As an apprenticeship, Lantz sent him on what Nichols calls 'the lamest possible job,' to direct Wilde's *The Importance of Being Earnest* and play the Dauphin in Shaw's *St Joan*, at a Vancouver theatre festival. 'Every night at midnight he called and said, "Get me out of this. I don't want to do this,"' Lantz recalls. 'I said, "This is precisely what the doctor ordered."' And so it proved. The Broadway producer Arnold Saint Subber was shopping for a director for Neil Simon's *Nobody Loves Me*. Although SaintSubber didn't have enough confidence to guarantee the tyro director the Broadway show, he was prepared to let Nichols try out the play in Bucks County, Pennsylvania. Nichols had only seven days to mount *Nobody Loves Me*, which was later retitled *Barefoot in the Park*.

After the first reading at Saint Subber's house, when none of the actors laughed, the notoriously nervous Simon, known as Doc because of his ability to swiftly rewrite a line and make brilliant comic fixes, wanted to call off the play. Nichols was unruffled. 'The play was so light, so sweet, so funny, that my job was to make it real,' says Nichols, who impressed Simon with his extraordinary calmness. 'I was absolutely confident about what everything should be and where everybody should be.' Nichols told his talented cast – Robert Redford, Elizabeth Ashley, Mildred Natwick, Kurt Kasznai – to treat the play as if it were *King Lear*. 'Let's do it as though we don't know what's going to happen,' Nichols remembers telling the cast. 'Let's not let them know it's funny.' But it was Simon who didn't know that his play was funny. At the first Bucks County rehearsal, he sat outside the rehearsal hall. 'Suddenly, I heard a roar,' Simon says. "Thank God, they must be up to a good part.' I went inside. It was Mike telling them a story during the break. Then we went back to the play – no more laughs.' 'Doc said, "Let's call it off. This is not a play. I never thought it was a play,"' Nichols recalls. 'I said, "Let's decide after the first preview. Let's just see how it is with an audience." Of course, they yelled and screamed and fell out of their chairs. Doc never worried again.' Nichols adds, 'I had instant maturity.'

This marked the beginning of what is probably the most successful commercial partnership in twentieth-century American theatre. 'We were obsessed in the same way,' Nichols says of Simon. 'I could wake him up at two in the morning and say, "I've figured out what's wrong with the third act," and he would curse me and then come down and meet me in the lobby to listen to it. It was the joy of discovering things together.'

As a comedian, Nichols had watched himself become what he

calls 'a showbiz baby.' 'I was narcissistic,' he says. 'I would get mad. I bitched about our billing. I did all the things I dislike. Comedy is the only work in the world in which the work and the reward are simultaneous. Comedians get it on the spot. They get the laugh. It's very corrupting to your character.' But as a director Nichols got to play adult instead of baby. 'There was something about serving something that wasn't me,' Nichols says. Within fifteen minutes of starting rehearsal for *Barefoot in the Park*, he had a life-changing revelation: the experience of taking care of others made him feel taken care of. 'I had a sense of enormous relief and joy that I had found a process that both gave me my father back and allowed me to be my father and the group's father,' he says.

Nichols's love for his actors was palpable; he created a protective environment for them. 'They're giving everyone the right to assess, evaluate, criticize everything about them – their noses, their asses, their intelligence, their worthiness or lack of worthiness,' he says.' They're really out there.' Nichols was a shrewd father – clever about wielding his authority and about maintaining boundaries. During *Barefoot in the Park*, Redford came to Nichols in a quandary: he was being upstaged by the showy Elizabeth Ashley. 'I can't bear it,' he told Nichols. 'Every night when l kiss Ashley, she kicks her leg up behind her. I feel like I've been used. I'm embarrassed.' 'Why don't you do it, too?' Nichols suggested. Redford did as he was told and got a huge laugh; Ashley promptly stopped her upstaging.

Some of Nichols's charges could be notoriously bumptious. Sometimes he tamed them with his high-definition humor. Once, during a heated rehearsal of *The Odd Couple*, Walter Matthau looked out at Nichols in the auditorium and said, 'Mike, can I have my cock back now?' 'Props!' Nichols said. With other wayward actors, like George C. Scott, he knew when to be politic. During the rehearsals of *Plaza Suite*, Scott disappeared for three days. 'We're in the middle of a scene, and George walks in. Collar up – it's winter-hands in coat pockets. He's just standing there looking at us,' Simon recalls. 'I look at Mike, and I'm anxious to hear what he's gonna say. Mike said, "Hi, George. We're on Act II, page twenty-one."' On the other hand, Nichols could be strict about certain kinds of behavior. At an early rehearsal of *The Prisoner of Second Avenue*, the cast, which included Peter Falk and Lee Grant, was blocking a scene on the stage of the Plymouth Theatre. 'One of the actresses said, "Mike, if she stands over there, I don't think this part of the house is gonna see me,"' Simon recalls. 'Mike turned and whispered to the producer, "Fire her."'

Nichols's authority rested, in large part, on his unique understanding of the audience. Onstage, and later in film, his work sought – some would say too eagerly –to speak to the audience in a popular way. At its best, this sensibility produced *The Odd Couple*, one of the century's classic comedies. At its most indulgent, it allowed Robin Williams, as Estragon in *Waiting for Godot* (1988), to break the play's artifice of isolation and ad-lib with the paying customers. 'The experience of living in front of the audience for all those years in Chicago did something to me,' Nichols says. 'It gave me some closeness to them, some trust.' His sensitivity to audience reaction was the issue in a dramatic falling-out he had with David Rabe, whose play *Streamers* was probably Nichols's greatest artistic triumph – a beautifully staged and terrifying barracks tale of homosexual baiting. When it came to Rabe's next play, the powerful *Hurlyburly*, Nichols explains, 'I was desperate for him to cut. I kept saying, "I won't do this to the audience." I could not get him to see the show from the audience;

he only saw it from the light booth.' Rabe, who finally went mute in protest ('He couldn't reach me. I was not listening,' Rabe told me), stayed with the show until it opened but spoke hardly a word to Nichols. Nichols won the argument and the cut play was a success, but it cost him their relationship.

Improvisation had given Nichols another invaluable directorial impulse: 'To damn well pick something that would happen in the scene – an Event.' As Nichols explains it, the Event in any scene subliminally seeks an agreement with the audience on the human experience. 'While you're expressing what happens, you're also saying underneath, "Do we share this? Are you like me in any way? Oh, look, you are. You laughed!"' The building of this agreement through observation and detailed comic business was Nichols's signature: Art Carney, in *The Odd Couple*, suddenly single and so nervous on his first date that when he lights the woman's cigarette he closes his Zippo on it; the newlywed Elizabeth Ashley, in *Barefoot in the Park*, who knows nothing about housekeeping, holding a match to a log in the fireplace, or slamming from room to room in a passionate argument with her husband while simultaneously undressing.

Nichols has a gift for making things real. During the tryouts for *Barefoot in the Park*, he and Simon stood at the back of the theatre watching a scene in which the bride, after a week of marriage, screams that she wants a divorce. 'I said to Mike, "I don't think we should be watching this,"' Simon recalls. 'He said, "Why not?" I said "It's too personal, what they're doing on the stage." And Mike says, "Good, I'm glad you like it."' Between 1963 and 1984, Nichols chalked up about a dozen Broadway hits in a row, half of them with Simon. 'Over and over again, he'd say when everybody was getting nervous, "It's only a play. They're not going to be waiting for you in front of your house with torches,'" recalls Simon, whose hit play *The Sunshine Boys* was a script that he had abandoned until Nichols encouraged him to complete it. But one thing about theatre did make Nichols nervous: seeing his stage business and his contributions to scripts go into movie versions without remuneration. He was the first director to demand, and get, a share of the author's royalties, which, when added to his director's royalty and his piece of the subsidiary rights, quickly made Nichols a very rich man. (According to his accountant, if all his stock and film income were lost, he could still 'live comfortably' on his production royalties.) 'I wasn't pleased with giving it to him, but I can't argue with it,' Simon says. 'I would rather have him do it and have the play be great. I never worked with anyone in my life – nor will I ever work with anyone – as good as Mike Nichols. And, when you talk about percentages, what Mike asked for was more than made up for by what I made on *The Sunshine Boys*.'

Money played a large part in how Nichols measured his achievement. 'He always pushed with agents – I speak for us all: more money, more power, more billing,' Robby Lantz says. 'Eventually, the demands became cruel. Artists in the theatre should not take from each other things that are not necessary.' But Nichols, who had almost been wiped out in his first showbiz incarnation, was building an unassailable second career. 'The butterflies in my stomach won't stop fluttering until I have thirty million dollars,' the producer Lewis Allen overheard Nichols telling Lillian Hellman. 'He's ruthless when he wants to be, or sometimes maybe even when he doesn't want to be,' Lantz says. 'He doesn't let anything stand in his way.'

★

Nichols was also avid for artistic excellence, which he needed power to protect. He learned this lesson in his first taste of Hollywood, in the mid-sixties. Elizabeth Taylor had chosen Nichols to direct her in *Who's Afraid of Virginia Woolf?*, even though she had never seen or read the play: she trusted, she said, Nichols's sense of the tragic, which she'd intuited from their friendship. And it was Taylor whom Nichols invoked when Jack Warner, reversing production plans, insisted on shooting in color. As Nichols recalls, 'I said, "Mr Warner, it's impossible for several reasons. The sets are built. Elizabeth's thirty-three years old – her makeup will never withstand color. How can she go from thirty-three to fifty-six and have us believe the make up in color?' But Warner insisted. The screenwriter and the producer, Ernest Lehman, whom Nichols sardonically nicknamed Slugger, said nothing. 'Well, O.K., I'll tell you what,' Nichols told him. 'You make it in color. I'll go home. I like it at home.' Warner immediately conceded: 'All right, black-and-white,' he said. 'After that, he treated me very kindly,' Nichols says. 'Until he threw me off the picture at the end. When it was mixing time, he saved time and trouble and just had his crew mix it.'

But even here Nichols had unexpected leverage. Each night from the set, the editor, Sam O'Steen, would play him the sound mix over the phone and Nichols would give him notes on what to change. Finally, Nichols got word to Warner that he wanted to cut a deal. Warner was worried that the film, which was about adultery, drunkenness, and brutal family battles, would not be approved by the powerful Catholic Legion of Decency. In exchange for being allowed back on the set, Nichols came up with a plan to deliver the Legion: 'When the Monsignor sees the picture, Jackie Kennedy will sit behind him. When it's over, she will say, "How Jack would have loved it!"' Jackie Kennedy did as her friend asked; Warner got the Legion's blessing; and Nichols duly finished his film, the first film ever for which all of the four leading players were nominated for Oscars.

Nichols, whose film technique is not showy, is a director's director. 'He tends to get actors to give him their finest hours,' Steven Spielberg says, citing Kathy Bates's long monologue in *Primary Colors*. For Nichols, who himself gave a tour-de-force performance in Wallace Shawn's *The Designated Mourner*, at London's Royal National Theatre in 1996, the director's job is to help the actors turn psychology into behavior. When Nichols talks to actors and to students at the New Actors Workshop, which he founded with Paul Sills and George Morrison, in 1988, he is generally oblique, offering up examples from his own life to clarify a theatrical moment. 'You kind of just free-associate all day long,' says the writer-director Nora Ephron, who worked with Nichols on *Silkwood* and *Heartburn*. 'Then suddenly you get something that actually is good enough to find its way into the thing you're working on.' The veteran director Billy Wilder says, 'Mike's scenes have a kind of inner content, which the audience feels and follows. He's very lucid.' 'What you're looking for every day is one little surprise,' Nichols told Charlie Rose about directing. 'It's like seeding a cloud and hoping it will rain.'

The process requires patience, luck, and a gentle touch. Once, during the casting of *Carnal Knowledge*, Jules Feiffer, who wrote the script, told Nichols that he was worried about putting the twenty-three-year-old Candice Bergen in the lead. 'Can she act?' Feiffer asked. 'Mike said, "She'll act for me." And she did.' In his recent biography of Edward Albee, Mel Gussow quotes Richard Burton (who played the harried professor in *Who's Afraid of Virginia Woolf?*) on Nichols. 'He appears to defer to you, then in the end he gets exactly what he wants. He conspires with you rather than directs you, to get your best,' Burton said.

Nicols's goal is to match the actor to the part. 'If I can cast the right people and figure out the things they should be doing in the scene, they don't have to do anything but show up,' Nichols says. 'Nobody has to act.' Over the years, Nichols has made some particularly daring, less than obvious choices – Art Garfunkel in *Carnal Knowledge*, Adrian Lester in *Primary Colors*, Hank Azaria in *The Birdcage* –but the outstanding example of inspired casting is Dustin Hoffman in *The Graduate*, since Hoffman was both unknown and physically wrong for the preppy Benjamin Braddock, a Wasp college athlete who has an affair with one of his parents' friends. 'There is no piece of casting in the twentieth century that I know of that is more courageous than putting me in that part,' says Hoffman, who considers the film 'the most perfect movie I've ever been part of,' adding 'I was a paralyzed person. I had come from a paralyzed background – the suffocation of that family. I was not acting.'

What Nichols saw in Hoffman – 'a dark, Jewish, anomalous presence'– was, of course, himself. Through improvisation, Nichols had learned to 'treat yourself as a metaphor'; Hoffman gave him the same opportunity in film. 'If the metaphor is powerful, it's always underneath you and you're always surfing it. You're always serving it,' says Nichols. Even Hoffman's whimper, Nichols says, 'was my little whimper when Jack Warner would tell a joke – in fact, people had to tell me to try not to whimper when he told jokes, that he would notice.' Hoffman remembers Nichols taking him aside when he was listless in front of the cameras, a couple of months into the shooting, and saying, 'This is the only time you'll ever get a chance to do this scene. It's going to be up there for the rest of your life.' Hoffman adds, 'He really meant it. It makes me cry, because he had that kind of passion, and it had that importance. I've never forgotten it. Mike worked like a surgeon every second.'

Steven Spielberg calls *The Graduate* 'a visual watershed,' and invokes the moment when Benjamin races home ahead of Mrs Robinson to tell her daughter Elaine, whom he loves, about his affair with her mother. 'All of a sudden, the mother appears in the door behind Elaine, Elaine turns, and the focus racks to the mom. But when Elaine turns back the focus stays – Elaine is actually out of focus – and very slowly comes back until she is sharp and she realizes that Benjamin and her mother have been shtupping. I had never seen long lenses used that way to illuminate a character moment.'

In Spielberg's encyclopedic appreciation of Nichols's cinematic innovations, he lists the handheld camera in *Who's Afraid of Virginia Woolf?*, which 'further complicated' the anxiety and turned the couple's war into 'a dance'; the 'brilliant use of light' in *Day of the Dolphin*, when the aquarium lights are turned on and a dead body is discovered floating inside the tank; the way Nichols built, bit by bit, the paranoia and terror in *Silkwood*, which was, for Spielberg, 'one of the most frightening and suspenseful things I had ever seen in a movie'; the long opening shot in *Carnal Knowledge*, at the college party, and the way he 'made love to Ann-Margret through the lighting.' That controversial film, which Nichols considers his darkest, was a coruscating look at predatory sexual chauvinism and at women's suffering, themes that resonated with Nichols's own life at the time. 'He was not nice to his girls,' says a close friend of those middle years, when

Nichols was married to his third wife, the Anglo-Irish novelist Annabel Davis-Goff, who is the mother of two of his children, Max and Jenny. (He had split up with Margot Callas in 1964.) 'He was a terrible household tyrant.'

Carnal Knowledge dramatized this tyranny. The night before Nichols was to shoot the crucial scene – the bedroom fracas between Jonathan (Jack Nicholson) and the depressed Bobbie (Ann Margret), in which Jonathan goes berserk trying to force Bobbie out of his house and calls her 'a ball-busting, castrating, son-of-a-cunt bitch!' – Feiffer sat with Nichols as Nichols explained why the scene had to go. 'It's just so ugly, it's so awful, people are gonna hate it, and they're gonna hate the movie,' Feiffer remembers him saying. 'We went for a bite,' Feiffer adds. 'I just sat in the car listening to him go over and over why he couldn't shoot it. Finally, he just looked at me and said, "No, we've got to do it, because it's true."'

But after the box-office failures of both *Carnal Knowledge* and the ambitious but misguided *Catch-22* – a story whose surreality was not Nichols's strong suit – Nichols began, by his own admission, to lose his way. Once, during this period, he sat idling in his Rolls-Royce at a Beverly Hills traffic light when a pimp in a flashy car pulled up beside him. 'That's a Silver Cloud,' the pimp said. 'And you, man, are the silver lining.' And so it had seemed, until, after his third miscue, with *Bogart Slept Here*, it wasn't. Nichols told the world that he'd lost his appetite for making movies, but what he'd lost was a vital sense of connection to what he was doing and what he wanted to say. 'Usually it happens right away, when I'm reading a script – I see a moment, and I know what that moment is, and it's my hook into the whole thing,' Nichols says. In the years between closing down *Bogart Slept Here*, in

1975, and starting *Silkwood*, in 1983, those moments of compelling inspiration eluded him. In the interim, besides developing a film version of *A Chorus Line* (which he subsequently abandoned), he produced the musical *Annie* and the one-woman Broadway show that launched Whoopi Goldberg's career.

Then, sometime in the middle of the eighties, visions of an altogether different kind appeared to Nichols: for about six months, he experienced a Halcion-induced psychotic breakdown. He became delusional – he was convinced, for example, that he had lost all his money, and that he'd turned from being 'the hero of the story' into the villain. 'Because I'd lost the money, I was the bad guy. I'd brought shame and unhappiness to my family,' he says. 'It was a horrible feeling of abject despair and self-loathing.' He was wide-eyed and gaunt. Nothing seemed to help. He called Buck Henry to ask if he'd give him enough sleeping pills to end his life if it was absolutely necessary. 'Of course, I said I would,' Henry says. 'I was lying.' At one low point, Nichols sat with the producer, John Calley, now the head of Sony Pictures, and tallied up his assets item by item on a foolscap pad. Calley says, 'I'd add the numbers up and at the bottom it would have thirteen million six, and I'd say, "Do you see thirteen six?" He'd say, "Yes." I'd say, "Now, can you accept that?" He'd say, "The only thing I could accept would be you telling me that when I go into debtors' prison you will take care of the children."' (Max was then eleven and Jenny was nine.) By the time Halcion was identified as the chemical source of his problem and Nichols stopped taking it, he had learned, he says, 'what people are like when you're not so shiny and you don't have your powers.' (His marriage to Davis-Goff broke up shortly thereafter.)

His collapse proved cautionary, and his subsequent movies, from Neil Simon's *Biloxi Blues* and *Working Girl* to *Primary Colors* and *The Birdcage*, were an aggressive reassertion of his commercial shine. With the exception of *Primary Colors*, a subtle dissection of power and marriage, the films are crowdpleasing fables. Nichols's impulse was clearly to build himself as solidly as possible into the Hollywood system. 'Every development executive, every studio president, has a list of directors,' Spielberg says, 'and Mike has never been off the A-list.' This puts Nichols's survival at the top of the Hollywood tree at thirty-four years and counting – longer than such legends as Preston Sturges, Billy Wilder, John Huston, and Frank Capra. Spielberg adds, 'You want him because you know that he's going to tell the story better than it was told in the screenplay you bought. You're going to be getting basically two scripts for the price of one.' Nichols knows the value of stories like *The Remains of the Day*, *All the Pretty Horses*, and *The Reader*; they are works he has produced, or will produce, but wasn't interested in directing. He loved the intellectual showboating of Stoppard's *Arcadia*, a play about chaos theory, and wanted to make it into a film, but he couldn't make the numbers work. 'You don't want to take advantage of your friends and say, "Would you mind doing this at a quarter of your price?"' he says. 'If movies hadn't changed so radically what Mike would have been, perhaps should have been,' Jules Feiffer says, 'is the successor to a director like George Cukor – working in romantic comedy with urbane wit and style. But those times passed. So he had to shuffle around to find something to replace that.' In choosing his projects, Nichols needs to feel, he says, that 'only I can do this.' When he picked *What Planet Are You From?*, he thought, Yes, this is for me. I know what to do with it. Nichols's next film, starring Robin Williams and with a script by Elaine May, will be a remake of the classic Ealing comedy *Kind Hearts and Coronets*. 'I can only follow my excitement,' Nichols says. 'Sometimes I wish it were more high-minded, and sometimes I'm glad that it's not. I have no choice either way. I don't think *The Graduate* and *Carnal Knowledge* were any different from what I'm doing now.' But the fact remains that the early pictures said new things in an ironic, challenging way, and the later work ruffles no feathers.

In any case, Nichols's asking price for mainstream movies has gone up: he now gets about seven and a half million dollars just for taking on a film, plus approximately twelve per cent of the gross. 'So it's hard for him to say no,' John Calley says. Some of his friends wish he would. 'He knows I don't like a lot of the stuff he does. I think it's beneath him,' Buck Henry says. 'He should be doing more *Hurlyburlys*.' But Nichols, who has heard the arguments, is unmoved.

'All movies are pure process,' he says. 'A commercial movie isn't less process than an art movie. You can't make your decisions about a film on the basis of "Is it important enough? Is it serious enough?" It's either alive or it's not for me. If it's alive, I want to do it.' He adds, 'If you're funny, and you stay funny, I think that's already doing pretty good.'

In the pale-gray calm of his midtown editing suite, Nichols sits behind his editor, Richie Marks, who works away at an Avid console, tweaking the finale of *What Planet Are You From?* on a triptych of screens. Bening and Shandling – the earthling and the reconstructed alien – stand facing each other to reaffirm their marital vows. Bening is saying, 'Harold, meeting you has taught me the universe is one big screwed-up place where everyone's just trying to work out their problems, but I'm honored to work them out with you, because ... I think ... I love you.' When the lights come on, Nichols says, 'I have this experience over and over. I make a movie because it draws me, and when I get it all finished I think, Christ, look, it's about me.' The alien, who comes to earth merely to exploit women, has been humanized by love and he becomes, as Nichols points out, 'simultaneously the leader of his planet.' In Nichols's eyes, his marriage to Diane Sawyer has wrought the same miracle. 'True love made Pinocchio a real boy,' Nichols said in a TV interview. 'We all sort of feel like we're contraptions, like we pasted ourselves together – a little bit from here, a little bit from there – and then, if you're very lucky, along comes someone who loves you the right way, and then you're real.' 'Mike spent many years without happiness. I mean, there were dark years where it wasn't quite working in relationships,' Calley says. 'He was in them but they weren't giving him a lot of joy. With Diane, he doesn't have to pretend not to be who he is to make a partner comfortable.' Intimacy requires equality; and Sawyer, who has her own constituency, checkbook, and clout, is in every way an equal to Nichols, whom she first met while waiting to board a Concorde flight from Paris. Even today, if asked to shut her eyes and picture him, Sawyer sees Nichols as she did that first day: 'All that light in his eyes and some sort of invitation. He's just full of invitation. It's like, "Let's be young together. Let's see things for the first time and tell each other the absolute truth, want to?"' After their chance meeting, Sawyer approached Nichols for a TV interview: 'I just had this idea of wild intelligence and that there'd be some surprise there,' she says. The surprise was, she says, 'that there was no end to the surprises.'

Nichols and Sawyer live on the seventh floor of a handsome Fifth Avenue apartment building with a view of the Metropolitan

Museum of Art from their library. Most of Nichols's art collection was sold off at bargain-basement prices in his Halcion panic; at one point he owned six paintings by Balthus, including the infamous 'The Guitar Lesson,' which hung over his bed. ('I had to get rid of it,' he says. 'It pissed off too many women.') But there is still a Stubbs, a Fischl, and a beautiful Morandi study of bottles whose hard-won peace echoes the current mood of its owner. He is on record as saying that the best definition of happiness appears in Tom Stoppard's *The Real Thing*. 'Happiness is equilibrium,' the main character says. 'Shift your weight.' 'It's good, and it's true,' Nichols continues Stoppard's thought. 'You have to stay light on your feet and remember what's important and what's not.' These days, Nichols teaches; he attends meetings of Friends In Deed, an outreach charity for people with AIDS and other life-threatening diseases, which he founded with the actress Cynthia O'Neal; and he keeps up a proliferating e-mail correspondence. He visits his horses, and he even cooks now: his specialties include lemon pasta, risotto with smoked mozzarella, and sour cream peach ice cream. Sawyer leaves notes on the floor beside their bed when she slips off to the network every day at 4am to anchor *Good Morning America*; before going back to sleep, according to Sawyer, Nichols 'opens one eye and says, "Tell it like it is."'

On the chaise longue in the bedroom is an embroidered pillow, with words that play on a line from one of Nichols's favorite movies, *Lawrence of Arabia*, in which an Arab tells Lawrence to abandon a straggler in his party. 'It is written,' the Arab says. The cushion gives Lawrence's answer: 'Nothing Is Written.' It seems an apt motto for Nichols's journey. Nichols, who keeps no diaries and few mementos of his extraordinary life, is still all future. 'He can go on and on until he chooses not to go on anymore,'

Spielberg says of Nichols's movie making career. But the greatest of Nichols's mise en scene is himself: he has created a person who lives well in the world.

At the end of our time together, he sat back on the sofa and declared himself pleased with the conversation. 'I do well with the fundamentally inconsolable,' I said. The words seemed to surprise Nichols and to press him back in his seat. His eyes fluttered shut for a moment, then opened. 'We get a lot done, you know,' he said.

Acting up

Emma Thompson's third act

Emma Thompson has what she calls 'the habit of continuity,' an impulse hardwired into her by her parents, Phyllida Law and Eric Thompson, who were both jobbing actors and children from broken families. Thompson, who has been dubbed a Presbyterian in the high church of celebrity, still lives on the West Hampstead street where she grew up. She shuttles between London and a lush remote glen above Loch Long, in Scotland – where, in 1959, her parents paid three hundred pounds for a cottage – which was the rural idyll of her childhood. Those two places provide her with an 'unassailable context' that protects her, she says, from her 'capacity for self-deception.' 'I'm surrounded by people I've known since I was a child. They're not going to put up with me being grand,' she said.

Her road in London is a sloping quarter mile of comfortable semi-detached houses, a football field away from the swankier dwellings across noisy Finchley Road. Among those currently residing on it are Thompson's extended family: her now ninety-year-old mother; her informally adopted son, Tindyebwa Agaba, and his wife, He Zhang; and a collection of A-team actors, most of whom she's worked with through the years – Imelda Staunton, Jim Carter, Derek Jacobi, Jim Broadbent. 'We're terrible gossips, but "gossip" in the sense that Phyllis Rose described it, the first step on the ladder to self-knowledge,' Thompson said, adding, 'Gossip is discussion about life's detail. And in life's details are all the little bits of stitching that you need to hold it to-*fucking*-gether.'

The somnolent street has no distinguishing architectural features until you come to a house whose overgrown front garden is dominated by an eye-catching pink-and-white bathtub full of plants, with a mannequin's shower-capped head protruding at one end and a pair of shapely wooden legs dangling over the edge at the other. This gesture of caprice – a whimsical raspberry blown at the sedateness of the surroundings – sits among an equally droll collection of miniature stone animals: frogs, turtles, cats, dogs, and a lone bird affixed to the garden wall. The tableau, which is Phyllida Law's playful creation, offers a clue to her daughter's blithe spirit. Asked once what was the most important thing her parents had taught her, Thompson replied, 'To laugh in the face of disaster.'

The first of fourteen axioms in 'Thompson's Theatrical Laws,' a typed memo composed by Thompson's father, which hangs in his daughter's guest bathroom, is 'It is better to have a hit than a flop.' On the overcast October day, in 2021, when Thompson welcomed me into her living room for the first time, she was hard at work concocting a commercial stage extravaganza, a musical version of *Nanny McPhee*, which is scheduled to open in the West End in 2023. Thompson wrote and starred in the two film iterations

– *Nanny McPhee* (2005) and *Nanny McPhee and the Big Bang* (2010) – which were based on the *Nurse Matilda* book series, by Christianna Brand, and grossed two hundred and sixteen million dollars at the box office. She had now spent five years developing the musical with the composer Gary Clark (of *Sing Street*), who had provided a kind of Victorian punk sound, which she described as a 'cross between the Tiger Lillies and Tom Waits's *Swordfishtrombones.*'

Thompson was writing the book and co-writing the lyrics with Clark. As she handed me a mug of tea featuring a photograph of the Queen and the motto "I eat swans," she said that she was considering whether to direct the production herself. It would be a herculean task, made even more daunting by the fact that Thompson had never directed a musical, or anything else. She'd been seeking advice from an array of theatrical high rollers, including Stephen Sondheim, or 'the Old Man of the Mountain,' as he referred to himself in their correspondence. 'Whatever you decide, good luck,' Sondheim e-mailed her a few weeks before he died, that November. 'And remember what Larry Gelbart said: "What I would wish Hitler is that he be out of town with a musical."'

Why did Thompson want to climb this particularly forbidding theatrical mountain? She didn't need the money or the acclaim. Her obsession seemed to be personal. The idiom of Thompson's storytelling in the musical, which involves puppets and possibly ventriloquism, as well as winking outlandishness, was directly linked to her father's work, decades earlier, on the successful BBC children's program *The Magic Roundabout*. Eric Thompson, who began working as a butcher's apprentice at thirteen before finding his calling as an actor and a director, was an autodidact. He reimagined a French stop-motion series featuring a collection of animal characters, creating new narratives for them and injecting his dry wit into daily five-minute installments that aired from 1965 to 1977. The show attained cult status in Britain, at its peak reaching eight million viewers a night. 'Eric believed that children were adults who just hadn't lived as long,' Thompson told me. 'He didn't talk down to them. He'd use phrases like "hoist on your own petard" and would get letters from irate parents going, "You shouldn't use this sort of language with children." He would say, "I'm not writing for children. I'm writing for people."' With *Nanny McPhee*, Thompson had the same mission.

While her daughter's cat napped on the window seat, she played me a snatch of one song, which asked a question surely not raised before on the musical stage: 'Is it wrong to eat a baby?' The song continued, ''Cause they're pointless little creatures / And they just get in the way / Their doughy little features / Will depress you every day.' Thompson let the rollicking number play, then closed her computer. 'I'm telling my agent I'm not doing any filming,' she said. 'I'm just gonna focus on this.'

Nanny McPhee is a nanny with mystical powers, an angel of repair, who takes on a family with seven children who have scared off all other babysitters and makes order out of domestic anarchy, and whose own blemishes – a snaggle tooth and facial warts – disappear in the process. She is a sort of dowdy Lone Ranger whose silver bullet is the harmony that she leaves behind her. Her runic mantra is 'When you need me / But do not want me / Then I must stay. / When you want me / But no longer need me / Then I have to go.' Although Thompson claims not to recognize herself in Nanny McPhee ('She's the opposite of me – a Zen mistress, a wholly balanced individual,' she told me), the character is, in many ways, her avatar.

McPhee's adventures playfully confront not only Thompson's social concerns – justice, civic responsibility, community, female agency – but the core of her personality. Like McPhee, Thompson is a shape-shifter. Just this year, she has inhabited two radically different personae. Beefed up in a fat suit and Storm Trooper drag, she is almost unrecognizable as the virago Miss Trunchbull, the commandant-slash-headmistress of Crunchem Hall Primary School, in a rumbustious movie version of the musical of Roald Dahl's *Matilda*. (Trunchbull is the latest in a line of Thompson's bravura grotesques which includes the hard-shouldering Baroness von Hellman, in *Cruella*, and the four-eyed Professor of Divination Sybil Trelawney, in the *Harry Potter* franchise.) And, in *Good Luck to You, Leo Grande*, a performance that ranks among her best, Thompson plays an inhibited widow whose stifled life has left her a stranger to her own body and to herself, who hires a sex worker to help her live out her sexual desires. In the film's final beat, Thompson stands naked before a hotel mirror, contemplating the lines and folds of her then sixty-two-year-old body. (She is now sixty-three.) Offscreen, Thompson joked about herself as a 'Lucian Freud pinup,' and confessed to a 'lifelong shame and non-acceptance of my own body, which grieves me deeply, but there it is.' Onscreen, however, the scene plays as a poignant flash of revelation. 'It's not approval – "Oh my God, I look great." And it's not, "Oh my God, I look horrible." It's, "That's my body. And I know that it can bring me joy."' she told the *Washington Post*.

Joy is a choice, and a subject that came up when Thompson took me across the street to meet her mother. Law has had Parkinson's since 2015, but her charisma is still palpable behind her halting speech. Like the bathtub in her garden, everything in her home broadcasts jollity. Running diagonally across the inside panels of her front door is packing tape marked 'Fragile' in bold red lettering. Above the bath is a sign that Law designed when someone stole a figurine from her garden: an image of herself with a witch's hat and a putty nose and the caption 'please return the children's statue otherwise curses will occur.'

Thompson told me that, when she was in her twenties, 'I was domestically unbound, so I spent a lot of time with my mother, and our relationship moved sideways, away from the typical mother-daughter thing.' That collegial bond was apparent in their forthright banter. Asked if she'd ever worried about anything relating to Thompson when she was a child, Law paused, and said, 'Probably boys. You have to have a boyfriend that fits.'

'But I did lose my virginity at fifteen and didn't tell you,' Thompson replied. 'You wouldn't tell your mother that,' Law said, sipping a glass of the wine that Thompson had brought.

'I told Eleanor' – a cousin of Law's – 'who was more available for comment than my, as I thought, deeply upright mother,' Thompson said. 'And then you took me to the most extraordinary gynecologist, who was in her nineties, and who sat in front of me in this office and said, "What do you think the birth-control pill was invented for?" And I said, "To stop people from having babies." "No, that's not the answer I'm looking for. Try again." I said, "I don't know. Does it do something else?" And she said, "Yes, it allows people to have sex for joy and pleasure." That is a ninety-year-old woman speaking to a fifteen-year-old girl. That's incredible.'

On the way out, Thompson guided me through her mother's bathroom, which was festooned with photographs. She pointed to one of herself at Cambridge in a black academic gown. 'This is me at graduation,' she said. 'You were supposed to have black shoes, and I didn't have any. My shoes were tap shoes. The hall floor was made of marble, so I made quite a lot of noise.'

We were always looking for occasions to laugh,' Thompson said of herself and her younger sister, Sophie. But amid the comedy there were also tragedies, the gravest and most character-shaping of which involved her father's health. When Thompson was eight, Eric, then thirty-eight, had a serious heart attack. Ten years later, he suffered a severe stroke that left him half-paralyzed. 'I felt a tremendous amount of anxiety,' Thompson recalled. She and her sister were 'not allowed to have rows or misbehave. We were not allowed to be angry,' she said. Sophie retreated into acting and art-making, Emma into books. 'I read literally all the time. I was all words. All words,' Thompson said.

Eric himself 'wasn't morose, but he was silent,' she said. 'When he was in the house, he'd either have his back to us or be watching football. When he engaged with us, it was heavenly.' She went on, 'He was very gifted, so desired. Our need for him was intense, and we didn't get much of him, really.' (When asked what Eric liked doing with his daughters, Law said, 'Not enough.') And, as loving and attentive a mother as Law was, according to Thompson, she 'could never say the P-word.' Pride, for her, was hubris. As a result, for the best part of her coming of age Thompson felt, she said, only 'partially seen.' To get her father's attention, she tried 'to be witty, to return his wit. The love of words was a real connection.' Another strategy was to excel at school. When she received excellent O-level results, she called her father in Los Angeles, where he was directing a play. In response, he wrote her a letter:

> Darling Em – ... You don't need me to tell you that you have a very good brain and are highly intelligent ... but you also know how to use it, and that's vital to a really lively intellect. I'm sure all of your exam papers had originality of one sort or another and you know how I go on about the importance of that. I think you also know that Ma and I are very proud of you but to fuss about that or go on about it is a bit fulsome, if you know what I mean, and I think it is enough for you to know that you are quietly understood.

After his stroke, Eric lost language. When he came home from the hospital, the only words he could say were 'fuck' and 'shit.' Using flash cards, Thompson worked with her father all day, every day, for an entire summer. 'I was fierce with him,' she said. 'Once, I must have pushed him a bit too hard. He was weeping slightly. He said – this struck me to the core – "I can't do it, Emma." I said, "You can, you can, you *can*." That's when I thought, Everything is upside down.' Eric's death, in 1982, when Thompson was twenty-three, was a 'cataclysmic loss,' she said, adding, 'He left no money. We all had to earn our livings from then on.'

Thompson doesn't remember having wanted to be in show business as a girl. At fifteen, she contemplated signing up with the International Voluntary Service. When she was seventeen, her parents sent her to the Vocational Guidance Association for aptitude tests. The V.G.A.'s suggested careers, in order of preference, were social services ('e.g., Probation Service'), teaching ('After some experience you could well aim for an appointment as Housemistress or Headmistress, etc.'), and dramatic art ('This could lead to your exploring opportunities on the Production side of such an association as the BBC'). The report went on, 'You should certainly cultivate your writing in your spare time, for this could become a profitable hobby.'

During the sisters' years at the prestigious Camden School for Girls, Sophie was the actress – she dropped out at fifteen to begin her professional career, starring in the TV miniseries *A Traveller in Time* – and Emma was the academic highflier, who appeared in only one school production. Her final exam results in English literature made her 'one of the top students in the country,' according to the school's current administrator. By then, Thompson had already tried her hand at sketch-writing, producing material for a charity show with the boys at the nearby University College School. Her writing partner was Martin Bergman, who, when Thompson went to Cambridge, in 1978, was the president of Footlights, the university's renowned theatre club. 'He just got me straight in and said, "This girl's funny. She can do funny,"' she said.

Thompson's parents attended the Footlights Christmas pantomime, *Aladdin*, and were stunned. 'You just looked at her and thought, My God, where did she hide that?' Law said. At one point, Eric Thompson left his seat and walked to the stage. 'He wanted to confirm that it was her,' Law said. 'He had no idea she could do anything of that sort.' Even to her contemporaries, Thompson seemed to emerge fully formed as a performer. 'She stood out like a good deed in a naughty world,' the comedian and actor Stephen Fry wrote in his memoir. (Thompson coaxed Fry to join the Footlights; she also introduced him to his future comedy partner Hugh Laurie, with whom she was stepping out.) 'There was no doubt that Emma was going to go the distance,' Fry told me. 'In fact, we used to write sketches for her to be in, and we always had a private joke because the surname of whoever she was playing would be Talented.' By the end of her second year at Cambridge, Thompson had acquired a London agent.

★

In 1981, the year she graduated, a Cambridge Footlights Revue production called *The Cellar Tapes* won the first Perrier Comedy Award, at the Edinburgh Fringe Festival. 'Wears baggy trousers . . . refuses to be stereotyped,' Thompson's program note read. Onstage, she capered as a Sondheim chanteuse, lampooning 'Send in the Clowns' ('Just as you think / I'm stuck in G / I suddenly speed up the lyric / and end up in C'), and spouted clipped vowels from a chaise longue, as the invalid Victorian poet Elizabeth Barrett beside her suitor, Robert Browning (Fry), in a spoof of *The Barretts of Wimpole Street*. 'Emma was the secret sauce. She brought it together,' Fry said. The revue subsequently toured England and Australia. 'We weren't alternative,' Thompson said. 'We were posh cunts, basically, who didn't know anything. I use the word because we took the Footlights up to Bradford and played the university. We came on, and they just shouted, "Cunt! Cunt!," all the way through the performance.' She added, 'They threw cans of beer. We were shell-shocked.'

Nonetheless, Thompson and her cohorts were picked up almost immediately for *Alfresco*, a short-lived TV comedy series, which brought Thompson into contact with a more eclectic crew of talented funny men, including Robbie Coltrane and Ben Elton. At the time, her ambition was to become a sort of British Lily Tomlin, writing and performing her own characters, but the siren song of alternative comedy, which was just emerging in Britain, lured her briefly into standup. 'Middle-class people didn't do standup,' Elton said. 'It was very much seen as a working-class art form. It took place, traditionally, in working men's clubs. It was almost exclusively male-dominated.' He added, 'We found ourselves together in Croydon, appearing on the same bill. I think it was her début. She did a routine about thrush, talking about the various flavors you might choose to apply to your vaginal areas. She was big and bold.' Thompson recalled of the performance, 'It was my twenty-fifth birthday. I did the first forty-five minutes. Then Ben, a far more seasoned comedian, did the second half. We took our bows together at the end, and I felt accepted. Someone from the audience came up afterward and said it wasn't often he heard a woman being funny. Then, on the train home, we divided the cash. I got sixty pounds in a brown envelope, and I cannot stress how much it meant. I was economically independent. I could live on words.'

Thompson's standup routine was one of the first to bring women's issues into Britain's comic arena. 'Women haven't been allowed to make jokes about themselves,' she told the press. 'It's been the men who have made the jokes about us, jokes we haven't liked. And I'm fed up with it.' She had her own theories about gender-based storytelling. 'The joke is a patriarchal form of humor, which basically requires you to pay attention, prepare to laugh, then laugh, whether you are amused or not,' she said, during a talk at Cambridge. 'It's quite a tough form. There is no spontaneity.' Whereas the joke was like the male orgasm, she argued, female humor was a simulacrum of the female orgasm, 'with no need to go to all this ejaculation. You simply don't know when it is going to happen and it can go on and on and on or be over terribly quickly.'

Standup, however, required a kind of self-exposure that played against Thompson's strengths: her humor was observational, not confrontational or confessional. 'If she's going to try and get laughs, she's an actress. It will be in character,' said Humphrey Barclay, who directed Thompson's first solo show, *Short Vehicle*, at the Edinburgh Fringe Festival, in 1983. In 1984, at a Campaign for Nuclear Disarmament rally that she was helping to co-ordinate, Thompson stood at the base of Nelson's Column, in Trafalgar Square, in front of more than a hundred and fifty thousand protesters, and did a five-minute comedy monologue. 'Absolutely the worst moment I ever had,' she said, recalling a woman who came up afterward and hissed, 'If you can't say something sensible, *shut up!*' 'I just *died*. I would have been quite happy for a bomb to drop on me immediately.'

The failure taught her that she was 'just not cut out for standup.' But, as it happened, she didn't have to fight for another space at the entertainment table. When Barclay produced a half-hour sketch-comedy TV special based on her Edinburgh show, it caught the attention of the controller of BBC 1, Michael Grade. 'He rang and said, "I assume you've got a series,"' Barclay recalled. 'I said, "No, nobody's interested." And he said, "I'll have it for the BBC."' By the time Thompson took up that project, in June, 1987, she had sung and danced in the West End, in the musical *Me and My Girl*, and starred in the BBC miniseries *Tutti Frutti* and *Fortunes of War*, winning a BAFTA award for the two performances. She was Britain's golden girl, short-listed among the 'Women of the Year,' and one of the first sightings in British entertainment of a new kind of woman: thinking, sparky, unapologetic, secure in herself and her desires. 'I deeply admired her combination of intelligence and silliness,' Lucy Prebble, a playwright and currently an executive producer and a co-writer of HBO's *Succession*, said. 'She's a literary polymath, but without taking herself too seriously. That's a cultural role we rarely allow women.' No matter how parlous or hilarious the circumstances of her characters, Thompson radiated a subliminal solidity, 'a sort of "fuck it" that is the opposite of neurosis,' as Prebble put it.

As a teenager, Caitlin Moran, the London *Times* columnist and author, was captivated by Thompson's daring. 'If you were a woman and trying to succeed in the eighties, you had to pretend you were one of the guys,' she said. 'You've got to come in with a cigarette and go, "Fuck you, Dexter." Super-bitch, super-powerful, out-boy the boys. Somewhere deep inside, Emma was so confident in who she was that she didn't have to present as an eighties business bitch.' Moran tore out of the *Radio Times* a photograph of Thompson pulling 'a slightly silly face' and pasted it at the center of the 'god wall,' in the room she shared with her sisters. When she was fifteen, and about to make a life-changing trip from Wolverhampton to interview for a 'young reporter' position at the London *Observer*, she stared at the picture until she reached what 'seemed like the only logical and correct conclusion.' Moran took Thompson's photo off the wall and ate it. 'It's, like, I'll have her in me. I will be that girl. I went down to London and slammed the interview,' she said.

The BBC gave the twenty-eight-year-old Thompson her own series – carte blanche over six half hours of comedy. Thompson dubbed what followed her 'Hedgehog Summer.' She put in ten-hour days, trying to come up with three hours of material. The schedule was gruelling and unmooring. 'I locked her in a small office in my scruffy offices near Regent's Park,' Barclay said. 'She says she would emerge crying. She was pretty vulnerable.' Her working title for the project was *A Big Mistake*, and she charted it in her diary:

> June 20: I can't do this. Why am I doing it? . . .
> July 20: Dreadful day. Worked until 10pm.
> Nothing. Beyond belief awful.
> August 20: Somebody help me. . . .
> September 20: None of it's funny. None of it. I want to die.

The completed series was a variety show, whose musical numbers, sketches, and monologues ventured into the then comic terra incognita of sexual harassment, auto-cannibalism, madness, and droit du seigneur, edited together with no laugh track and no narration. *Thompson*, which was one of the first independent productions on the BBC, aired in prime time, opening in the wake of Thompson's extraordinary double BAFTA win. There was a lot of heat around the show, which, as Barclay said, was expected by some to 'change the face of light entertainment.' Instead, it changed Thompson. The show was a flop. She called it 'one of the most seminal experiences of my life.' She had expected controversy but not savagery. 'In the world of broadcast comedy, there's nothing angrier than an audience which doesn't think you're funny,' Barclay said. 'That will teach you Thompson,' 'curtains for Thompson,' and 'comedy of errors from Thompson' were some of the headlines that greeted her. 'It's like having your skin pulled off,' she said, citing the 'intense misogyny' that the show seemed to elicit in its critics. 'Some male reviewers referred to it as 'man-hating,' I guess because so many of the sketches were from a female P.O.V. and not always flattering about male behavior,' she said. 'It felt like a monumental failure, but, of course, it was just what it was – something by a young writer that was good in parts and largely experimental. I learned to shut up and get on with the next thing.' Nonetheless, she never wrote another comedy sketch or monologue. 'It's not really her forte,' the director Richard Eyre said. 'She's not a sprinter. She's a long-distance runner.'

I never thought ahead about work as a career – how can you do that?' Thompson said. 'It's just one job after another, and luck.' Kenneth Branagh, with whom she co-starred in *Fortunes of War*, turned out to be her luck. Thompson remembers the moment on the set of *Fortunes* when she first fell for him. On a break between takes during a night shoot, Branagh tried to amuse her by singing in his slightly falsetto voice. 'I burst into tears because he sounded exactly like my father singing on *The Magic Roundabout*,' she said. Branagh was reminiscent of Eric Thompson in other ways, too. He created the same seclusive climate around himself, wore a carapace of privacy, which Thompson compared to a walnut: 'hard to pry open.' His work-driven absences were also a reiteration of her father's comings and goings. Branagh had to be fetched – a frustration and an excitement that were familiar to Thompson. 'He was incandescent with ambition and performance energy,' she said. His dynamism made him both alluring and hard to wrangle. 'Like two mating lobsters, we clashed claws,' Thompson said of their volatile three-year courtship. In *Thompson*, they tapped and sang 'Have a Little Faith in Me,' but, offscreen, Branagh's infidelities made it difficult for Thompson to keep the faith. 'The Ken stuff put her through the wringer,' Barclay recalled. 'She had a three-hour cry on my shoulder about what a brute Ken was. And then, six weeks later, she said, "And we're getting married. Isn't it lovely?"'

In the race for fame, no British theatrical since Noël Coward had got off the blocks as fast as Branagh. At twenty-one, he was a hit in the West End; at twenty-four, he was the youngest actor ever to play Henry V with the Royal Shakespeare Company, drawing comparisons to Laurence Olivier; at twenty-six, he co-founded the star-studded Renaissance Theatre Company with David Parfitt; at twenty-eight, he published his autobiography. In 1989, the year he and Thompson married, Branagh was nominated for Academy Awards as both actor and director for his screen version of *Henry V*. The marriage elevated the couple to the pinnacle of the British talentocracy. 'I was embarrassed largely by the press version of our marriage,' Thompson said. 'We didn't present as glamorous in any way. I don't think we wanted to be some power couple, and we certainly didn't feel like it. We were lampooned and ridiculed, too – fair enough if you're famous and overpaid – but it's no fun.' In one particularly hurtful low blow, *Spitting Image*, the satirical British TV puppet show, had Thompson calling out, 'Where are you, darling?' 'I'm in the kitchen,' Branagh said. 'Oh, can I be in it, too?' Thompson replied.

Their first Hollywood movie together, the neo-noir *Dead Again* (1991), fades out with a shot of them embracing – a nod to the legendary forties romantic film partnerships and to their own. Lindsay Doran, who produced *Dead Again*, said that when she approached Branagh about directing the film, he agreed only on the condition that he and Thompson, who was then an unknown commodity in Hollywood, would co-star. At the end of the *Dead Again* shoot, Doran met with Branagh to discuss the possibility of his directing what had been her pet project for more than a decade: a film of Jane Austen's *Sense and Sensibility*. She was also looking for a writer for the screenplay, someone 'equally strong in the areas of satire and romance.' 'Not an easy combination, I admit since satirists are often too bitter to be romantic, and romantics are often too sentimental to be satiric,' she said. Doran felt that Thompson had both those qualities, and would bring to the enterprise another unexpected ingredient: 'She believes in virtue,' Doran said.

Prior to her discussions with Branagh, Doran had watched *Thompson*. 'I was sort of prepared not to like it,' she said. 'Instead, I loved it.' In the high-pitched innocence of a sketch in which a Victorian newlywed mistakes her husband's penis for a mouse – 'What an interesting little object it was! I bent over to examine it. Whereupon, on my life, Mama, it shrank into itself like a telescope before my very eyes. I confess I shrieked aloud' – Doran recognized someone who could be funny in period language and who could also '*think* in that language almost as easily as in the language of the twentieth century.' Branagh ultimately bowed out of *Sense and Sensibility*, which was brilliantly directed by Ang Lee, but Thompson accepted the challenge. 'I have one little movie I have to do first, and then I'll get to work,' Doran recalled Thompson saying. She added, 'And that was *Howards End*.'

In February, 1991, Thompson had learned that James Ivory was planning to film E. M. Forster's novel *Howards End*. For the first and only time in her life, she wrote to a director to ask for a part – that of Margaret Schlegel, the well-intentioned intellectual and moral core of the turn-of-the-century tragedy about inherited wealth among the Edwardian middle class. 'I just knew who she was – absolutely knew,' Thompson said. 'I knew her because I sort of *was* her. A bluestocking in Cambridge, just discovering the massive chasm between what men were allowed and what women were permitted, furious. Schlegel was so clear to me – an idealist turned realist, the older sister with what she perceives as vulnerable siblings, her outsized sense of personal responsibility. No character has ever made as much sense to me or felt as near.' Thompson's letter crossed with one that Ivory had already written, offering her the part.

It was Thompson's first major role in a serious film. She gave Margaret Schlegel a remarkable, palpable immediacy. 'Her previous work has been marked chiefly by a wicked adeptness at caricature, but here her acting is unmannered, daringly straightforward,' Terrence Rafferty wrote in this magazine. 'She seems to be making up her character with every breath,' Stuart Klawans wrote in *The Nation*. 'She's so smooth you can't get your grips into what she's doing: you just accept her and marvel.' Thompson's performance earned her her first Academy Award, for Best Actress.

Except for a six-week course with the gruff French clown Philippe Gautier when she was twenty-four – 'a good sort of entry into silliness' – Thompson never took an acting class. Her gift resides in her empathy, or what she calls a 'strange and continual porous state,' which allows her to imagine the other. Since childhood, Thompson said, she has been 'a gibbering empath, which is not always helpful.' 'It happened in primary school, everywhere,' she said. 'If someone was hurt, I couldn't bear it. I would have to help, have to try and put it right.' She added, 'My father once said to me – I was sixteen or something – 'Em, you're a taker like me. Your mother's a giver. We're takers.' I never forgot that. I made it my life's work to become someone who gave all the time. I just thought, Well, I'm gonna disprove that, baby.'

Thompson calls her method of inhabiting her characters

'incredibly releasing.' 'For a moment, the "I" that I recognize doesn't really exist. I'm taking a holiday from myself.' Richard Eyre, who directed her in *The Children Act* (2017), noted, 'I thought she was extraordinary in being able to be hugely intelligent but, at the same time, not do that thing that often very intelligent actors do, showing in parallel what they think about the character. Emma was just subsumed in the character,' he said. Thompson agreed: 'When I do those scenes, I am only feeling what the person is feeling. I know that sounds simplistic, but it's the only way I can do it, and the only way I can describe it. Being there completely – without any parts of you left out – makes the body do what it does. It's entirely somatic.' That immersion, she explained, is all-consuming: 'You're like a piece of blotting paper that has been put into a bowl of water. You cannot absorb anything else. If you're really having to create a different person, you're tricking your subconscious. It's a big fat magic trick. The hat you're pulling the rabbit out of is your own psyche. That's extremely demanding and weird, because you are in a sense no longer yourself.'

If it's true that the show of emotion is the greatest show on earth, then Thompson is a Barnum & Bailey of both pain and joy. Her portrayal of grief in *Love, Actually* (2003), for instance, has become iconic in British popular culture. In the scene, Thompson, as Karen, a dutiful mother of two, sits with her family around a Christmas tree, expecting as a present the necklace she found in her husband's pocket, only to receive from him a similar-looking box containing a Joni Mitchell tape. As Mitchell's bittersweet song 'Both Sides Now' plays in the background, Karen struggles in vain to stave off the anguish of knowing that her husband, played by Alan Rickman, has been unfaithful. 'She's still trying to say bright things and tidy up and keep on top of it,' Caitlin

Moran said. 'And then when she finally cries, for the British, that's the equivalent of a cum shot in a porn film. That's, like, Oh, my God, we finally got there.'

For an exhibition of Thompson's emotional derring-do, nothing surpasses the finale of *Sense and Sensibility*, where, as the buttoned-up, responsible, and lovelorn Elinor, the eldest of the Dashwood sisters, Thompson comes face to face with the secret object of her desire, Edward Ferrars (Hugh Grant), who is engaged to someone else. Elinor sits downcast as Edward arrives, but the news he brings is that his fiancée has experienced 'the transfer of her affections to my brother.' 'Then you're not married,' Elinor says, the idea flooding her like a tidal surge. Gasping and choking back sobs, she turns away from Edward in a hyperventilating collapse. She can't stop herself. 'She was not aware of what was inside her, and it suddenly emerges,' Thompson explained. Edward haltingly admits that 'my heart is and always will be yours.' She holds up her hand, stopping him in mid-romantic flow. Words can wait; in the moment, she is crying tears of anger and joy. Thompson's emotional explosion is at once a great piece of acting and a great piece of comedy. ('I was trying to make it as involuntary as possible. A case of the diaphragm taking over,' she wrote in her diary.) 'Hugh Grant was so cross,' Thompson recalled. 'He said, "You're gonna cry all the way through my speech?" I said, "Hugh, I've got to. That's the gag. It's funny." And he says, "Yeah, but I'm speaking." I said, "I know."'

Of the many liberties that Thompson's adaptation took with the book, the most significant was to change the trajectory of Elinor and Edward's romance. Whereas the novel announces their attraction at the beginning, the film allows them to fall in love in the course of the story, with Elinor claiming her heart's desire in that final bravura burst of weepy elation. For the comic payoff to work, Elinor has to be a master of repression, bottling up all emotion until that point. (Thompson won her second Academy Award for the screenplay of *Sense and Sensibility*.)

Offscreen, in 1995, while the film was being shot, Thompson had to exert a steely control over her own pain. Her marriage to Branagh had collapsed, but they had not gone public with the news. Branagh had started a relationship with one of the stars of his film *Mary Shelley's Frankenstein*, Helena Bonham Carter. Thompson was humiliated, in part by her own stupidity. 'I was utterly, utterly blind to the fact that he had relationships with other women on set,' she said. 'What I learned was how easy it is to be blinded by your own desire to deceive yourself.'

Thompson compared her emotional mess to shattered dishes. 'I was half alive. Any sense of being a lovable or worthy person had gone completely,' she said. The person 'who picked up the pieces and put them back together' was the actor Greg Wise, who played John Willoughby, the doe-eyed heartthrob who sweeps Marianne Dashwood (Kate Winslet) off her feet in *Sense and Sensibility*. ('Full of beans and looking gorgeous. Ruffled our feathers a bit,' Thompson noted of Wise in her production diary.) Thompson has now been with Wise for twenty-seven years, married for nineteen. 'I've learned more from my second marriage just by being married,' she said. 'As my mother says, "The first twenty years are the hardest."'

Early in her marriage to Branagh, before her critical successes in *Howards End* and *The Remains of the Day* (1993), Thompson was often perceived as an extra in Branagh's epic. In 1990, she started a women's group 'to shore up feelings of low self-esteem.' The group was composed of about fifteen actors and writers, plus occasional guests like Germaine Greer and Glenda Jackson. Thompson's original question to the members was: 'Who is the female hero and what does she do?' She was, she said, 'looking for the hero. How could I be heroic? I felt viciously angry, viscerally enraged by the belittling of women.' Even George Eliot, one of her literary heroes, she'd argued in her Cambridge dissertation, was 'unable to commit herself to a heroic heroine or even a realistic mature one. She creates 'deep-souled womanhood' only to deny the test of its worth.'

At first, comedy had offered Thompson a sword and a shield; now, with an actor's bona fides, she turned her attention to screen storytelling. She was looking for ways to dramatize female heroes as more than just a support team for men. 'It's not enough that my little acts of heroism are going to count,' she said. 'It's always the woman saying, 'No, don't go out and be the hero. Stay here.' I want to go and be the hero.'

Thompson embodies the poet May Sarton's observation that 'one must think like a hero to behave like a merely decent human being.' Part of female heroism, Thompson says, is decency and taking care of others: 'Women will look around and often be aware of what others need. They have to be like that because no one else will fucking do it. Women look after everyone endlessly – and without them there'd be nothing.' Her urge to take care of others has led her from the soundstage to the world stage. For Action Aid, she has travelled to South Africa, Uganda, Liberia, Ethiopia, Mozambique, and Myanmar. She has also toured the Canadian and the Norwegian Arctic for Greenpeace and chipped in to help the charity buy land around Heathrow Airport to prevent a proposed third runway and limit London's carbon emissions. Her environmental videos have promoted the work of Greenpeace and the Extinction Rebellion, at whose anti-fracking demonstration in 2016 Thompson took even more shit (from a local farmer, who, outraged that the protesters were on his land, sprayed her with liquid manure) than she gets in the tabloid press, where she has been slagged off as 'an eco-luvvie' and 'the grandmother of woke.' When Thompson flew from L.A. to London in 2019 to attend an Extinction Rebellion rally, the tabloids found a new way to hate her. She has a framed miniature of a *Private Eye* spoof of the *Mail on Sunday*'s front page, with the headline 'YES, IT'S DAME EMMA HYPOCRITE' propped up in her guest bathroom, a totem of her struggle and her resolve. Thompson calls the tabloid brouhaha a 'downright lie' – 'I was publicising *Late Night* in LA. My visit was paid for and booked by the distribution company and when I had finished my duties I went, as is the usual process, home,' she said.

About twenty years ago, she began throwing an annual Christmas party at the Refugee Council, a charity to support refugees and asylum seekers for which she is a patron. In 2003, Thompson was dishing out food, when she was approached by a slight young man with a warm smile who wanted to thank her. His name was Tindyebwa Agaba, and he was a sixteen-year-old Rwandan refugee. He had a few words of English and French; they spoke mostly in semaphore. 'His spirit was there to be seen – so clearly – in his eyes. He was alive to everything, though at the same time silent,' Thompson recalled, adding, 'He saw something in me he wanted to talk to.'

Agaba's story was one of devastating loss. When he was nine, his father died of AIDS; when he was twelve, rebel soldiers stormed his village and kidnapped him and his three sisters. (His mother and his sisters were listed as presumed dead in 1999, following the 1994 Rwandan genocide.) He was trained in the bush as a child soldier. At sixteen, with the help of a Care International worker, he escaped to England. Because of a bureaucratic glitch – he didn't claim asylum within twenty-four hours of arrival – he received no governmental provision and spent his first five nights sleeping rough around Trafalgar Square. 'I didn't have any friendships. I didn't know how to navigate the city. It was cold. Every white person looked the same to me,' he said. He'd gone to the Refugee Council for a hot meal and stayed on for the Christmas party.

'He was very traumatized, clearly, and very lonely,' Thompson said. She offered him a ride back to North London, where he was staying with a Nigerian family, and invited him to her home for Christmas Eve dinner. 'I was quite suspicious of someone giving me courtesy and good will,' he said. Nonetheless, he took up the offer and found himself in the hubbub of Thompson's family and friends. To Agaba, everything seemed strange: the high spirits, the drinking, the sight of Greg Wise handing around platters of food ('I couldn't understand a man doing it'). 'I was scared to ask for things,' he told me. 'I didn't know what would make people laugh. My village time and my bush time had made me not really expect anything.'

In the next six months, he and Thompson took frequent long walks on Hampstead Heath, where she learned his story and worked with him on his pronunciation and vocabulary. Soon, Agaba became part of the family, referring to Thompson and Wise as 'Mum' and 'Dad,' travelling to Scotland with them, and spending weekends at Law's house in a flat he called 'the Palace.' Thompson also paid for him to take speech lessons with the acclaimed dialect coach Joan Washington. 'For someone who had been in the country eight months, those lessons were a game changer, a godsend, really,' Agaba said. In the spring of 2004, in a Shakespeare class at Chelsea and Islington College, where he was studying for his G.C.S.E.s, his teacher showed the class Kenneth Branagh's film of *Much Ado About Nothing*. Agaba was flabbergasted to watch a movie populated by familiar faces: Law, Imelda Staunton, and Thompson herself. 'I was absolutely shocked,' he said. 'I went to my teacher and said, 'How was this film made? Because I know these people.' She laughed her head off. 'Don't be ridiculous. These are famous actors.' She couldn't believe a word I was saying.' The next week, his teacher brought in the *Daily Mirror* with a photograph of Agaba leaving Thompson's house on his bike. 'Is this you?' she said. 'That was how I got to know that my mother was somehow well known. I had no idea,' he said. Since then, he has earned a master's degree in human-rights law, spent a decade in human-rights activism, and become a detective in London's Criminal Investigation Division.

In 1999, Thompson had given birth to her daughter, Gaia Wise, who is now an actress. 'We tried for another child, but it didn't work,' she told me. 'I often think, if it had worked, there wouldn't have been space. So I'm very grateful the I.V.F. didn't work, because every day I'm grateful for Tindy.' Agaba recalled feeling that he 'didn't have anything to give,' when he met Thompson and Wise. 'What *hasn't* he given!' Thompson said. 'So much joy, so much insight to share in his empathy and his understanding of the world. We laugh – and he helps me to laugh – at the weirdness of people, at the strangeness of life, at its cruelties and absurdities. It's such a comfort.'

Thompson's kindness to others seems to have helped her become kinder to herself. For years, she struggled to see herself in a generous light. 'My capacity for self-punishment is horrible,' she said. 'Being successful, earning money, being famous – guilt, guilt, guilt, guilt.' In 2010, she told the BBC, 'That punitive conscience is part of my psychiatric problem. My mum's Scottish, so the Presbyterian thing is strong within me.' That same year, Thompson presented the American Film Institute's Life Achievement Award to Mike Nichols, whom she referred to as 'my second father.' (Nichols cast her as the Hilary Clinton character in his film adaptation of *Primary Colors* (1998); as the eponymous divine messenger in his HBO production of Tony Kushner's *Angels in America* (2003); and – in one of the most extraordinary of her nuanced characterizations – as the sardonic English professor dying of ovarian cancer in his HBO film *Wit*(2001), for which Thompson and Nichols co-wrote the script, based on Margaret Edson's play.) Addressing Nichols directly, she said, 'You and I share the same kind of conscience that both longs for and deplores approval.' Then, from beside the lectern, she produced a hand-painted wooden box, which she called the 'Post-Tribute Punishment Kit.' On one side, in large black lettering, was written 'Portable Chastisement at Last.' She dug around inside the box, pulled out a flail, and began whipping her back. 'Ow! Ow! That works,' she said. The burlesque was an oblique nod to the big challenge of her own artistic life: to navigate between the desire to be great and the desire to be good.

Thompson's approach to her acclaim has always been to tease it, a way of pre-empting both envy and egotism. In 2018, when she was made a Dame Commander of the Order of the British Empire – she turned up at Buckingham Palace in white Adidas sneakers and a Fawcett Society Equal Pay badge – Thompson referred to the pinning of the large medal and insignia to her teal-blue suit as 'a bit of a nipple moment.' Even Thompson's Academy Awards – she is the only person in the history of the Oscars to win in two different categories – are displayed in her bathroom, above the toilet, with a can of Brasso metal polish between them.

'I think I was a fierce and restless octopus,' she told me. 'But they have three hearts and only live for two years. So now I'm in search of a more peaceful existence where I'm not so angry and my one heart will last a bit longer.' Agaba, she said, 'has been part of the healing.' The musical *Nanny McPhee* will, she hopes, also be 'part of that metamorphosis from boiling to a nice simmer.' 'Whatever I do now,' she told me, 'it has to serve the happiness of people. It has to uplift. I think that's my job.'

On a bright July morning, nearly a year and a half after she'd first played me the song 'Is It Wrong to Eat a Baby,' Thompson clambered out of a black cab in front of the stately offices of Working Title – the production company that was funding the musical's first table read. She was followed by the director Katy Rudd (Thompson had, in the end, decided against directing it herself), Rudd's four-month-old baby, and her mother, whose job it was to keep the infant occupied while eleven actors worked through the script during the next four days. Thompson, in sky-blue overalls and a red gingham shirt, spotted me and rushed over. 'I'm so excited,' she said, then whispered, 'I'm so scared.'

The unusually capacious rehearsal room, on the third floor, had a large patio looking out on plane trees, whose lustrous green leaves lent a sense of exuberance to the minimalist space. Thompson and Rudd took their seats at the end of a long table, flanked by members of the cast, who sat like attentive students, with their blue script binders open in front of them. 'What we're really looking to explore is the emotional journey,' Thompson told them. 'So I'm expecting you to go, "No, that doesn't work," or "It doesn't matter." Be really honest and bold.'

After their first pass at the material, the cast ate lunch on the patio. Thompson sat away from the glare in a corner of the room and considered the morning's work. 'I'm just thinking about making the stakes very much realer,' she said. She spoke about Nanny McPhee's mission to bring order, by unorthodox means, to a grief-stricken household full of anarchic children acting out their fury at losing their mother and, in a way, losing their father, who seems preoccupied and unable to cope. There were clear parallels with her own childhood. 'That happened to us when our dad died,' she said. 'Our mum couldn't – absolutely couldn't – cope with our grief, couldn't cope with us, couldn't cope at all. Nanny McPhee is a great heroic presence. She knows exactly what to do, loves without reservation, then must go. So she sacrifices. She always has to leave those that she loves. She's about non-attachment. Perhaps that's why she's such a powerful figure to me, because I'm far too attached to pretty much everything.'

In the afternoon session, Thompson and the cast got down to the meat and potatoes of interrogating the script and the songs. She filled up her notepad with ideas for the opening, line adjustments, ways to expand the characters and differentiate the personalities of the children. Then, toward the end of the session, as she and the cast were discussing the number 'Evil Breed,' a rowdy rant against stepmothers, Samuel Blenkin, who was playing the most *terrible* of the *enfants*, observed that none of the songs made mention of the mother. It was a eureka moment. 'From the point of view of that lyric, what would you add?' Thompson asked him, worrying that a reference to the mother 'might be too painful.' 'Stepmothers can't do this,' Blenkin suggested, as a strategy for defining the absent maternal presence. Thompson riffed on the notion. 'They can't wipe away your tears / They can't cuddle you when you fear . . .'

'It's moving toward that but not quite,' he said.

'Maybe I'll try and add what step-mothers can't do. Yeah, it could be a little sort of moment, each one has a little line. That would certainly work better. It changes it completely,' she said.

By the last day of the reading, to which the creative team was invited, the actors had thoroughly massaged the script. As they went over it for a final time, Thompson leaned forward at the table, mouthing Nanny McPhee's lines and laughing at her sister, Sophie, who was reading Mrs Quickly, the foolish widow with eyes for Mr Brown, and whose fluting hysteria got applause from the table. 'It's just so clear where it works and where it doesn't work. All the little bald patches that you can't see when you're looking at the words on the page,' Thompson said afterward.

The next day, she and the creative team reconnoitred in a plush library adjacent to the rehearsal room to trade 'headlines' about what they felt needed to be woven into the script before the next workshop, in October. The designer Rob Howell talked to Thompson about the artist Louise Bourgeois and a recent London exhibition of her sewn sculptures. 'Bourgeois came from a family of tapestry menders. She's a repairer,' Howell said. He saw Bourgeois's notion of stitching as emotional reparation as akin to Nanny McPhee's attempts 'to keep things together and make things whole.' And he showed Thompson some related preliminary ideas in his sketchbook. She took to them like a bass to a top-water lure.

As Thompson sat barefoot in the middle of the group, it became clear from the team's talk – 'the fabric of a scene,' a 'tear,' 'stitched into the family DNA' – that the meeting itself was a kind of sewing circle. They were repairing a musical about repair. Thompson seemed to enjoy the give-and-take, explaining the adjustments she was already planning for the next draft and collating new ones that came out of the conversation: Mr Brown needed more romantic complication; the children needed more shading; the virago, Great Aunt Adelaide, the show's comic tyrant, needed a backstory so that her cruelty could be understood and somehow redeemed at the finale. And what about Nanny McPhee herself? 'If we're moving toward this sense of her stitching up these torn lives, each one has to have a moment with her, some sort of magic, healing touch. Little threads that draw them in,' Thompson said. By the end of the afternoon, she knew she had her work cut out for her. Could she do it? 'It remains to be seen, doesn't it?' she said.

On my way out, I ran into Greg Wise, who was there to take Thompson to dinner for their wedding anniversary. I asked him how the week had gone at home. 'She came in, three days into the workshop, clutched me, and said, "Thank fuck I'm not directing it,"' he said.

I didn't see Thompson again, but I heard from her. She e-mailed me Nanny McPhee's envoi, which she had rewritten, with this explanation: 'Sometimes when I am travelling I write well – a feeling of being free to think of only one thing, perhaps. I wrote the whole new end in a kind of frenzy on the plane – longhand

– paper everywhere, the attendants were most amused.' The lyric was now more specific, more poignant, and, perhaps, even more personal:

> When the cloth
> In life's patchwork
> Starts to fray and tear
> Then I shall be there
> To sew
> And when I finish
> With mending
> Every tattered shred
> Then I have to go
> But I will always
> Leave you
> With needle and thread.

Caught in the Act

What drives Al Pacino?

Nearly fifty years ago, when Al Pacino was at the start of his career, Marlon Brando gave him two pieces of advice: don't go to court and don't move to Los Angeles. At seventy-four, Pacino has managed to avoid the courts but not Beverly Hills, where he has taken up reluctant residence, for more than a decade, in order to share custody of his now thirteen-year-old twins, Anton and Olivia, with their mother, the actress Beverly D'Angelo. (Pacino, who has never married, also has a twenty-four-year-old daughter, Julie Marie, an aspiring writer and filmmaker.) Every half hour or so, an open-topped tour bus crawls its way along the wide, manicured boulevard where Pacino holes up for most of the year, with a cargo of rubbernecking out-of-towners, cameras at the ready. Inevitably, they stop in front of his rented house, which, like the actor, is elegantly dishevelled. Green canvas has been woven through the bars of the long iron fence to hide the place from street level; low-hanging Indian laurel trees seal off any visible signs of life from above. Nonetheless, the buses stop, the guides burble, and the tourists crane for a sign of the actor or his children. On my second day with Pacino, I happened to be parked in front of his house as a tour bus rolled up. The guide leaned down. 'You were here yesterday,' he said. 'You know Al?' I nodded. Above me, camera shutters clattered.

At that moment, Pacino was reclining in a deck chair at the far end of a wide lawn behind the house, doing business on a cell phone. Beyond him was a fenced-off swimming pool, and beyond that was what he calls 'the bunker' (as in 'I hunker in the bunker'), a drab beige outbuilding, where he sometimes goes to incubate his roles. Pacino was dressed for the bright day in his usual sombre getup: black jacket, shirt, slacks, and shoes, with a long gray cravat loosely knotted at the chest. He keeps a well-pressed assortment of these dark camouflage outfits on a wardrobe rack in the alcove off his living room, alongside his infrequently used barbells and a folded-up running machine. His comfortable house, with its absence of texture, is remarkable for its indifference to externals: no paintings, no designer furniture or fripperies. Pacino's focus, the house makes clear, is resolutely inward.

As an actor, Pacino has always been unafraid to do what he needs to in order to be in the moment; he trusts his instincts and explodes with whatever feelings come up. Performing, for him, is not so much a profession as a destiny. 'This is what I'm meant to do,' he told me. 'It's the cog in my life. With this, everything suddenly coheres. And I understand myself in that way.' Pacino has given complex shape to some of his era's most memorable creations: Michael Corleone, the college boy turned Mafioso, in *The Godfather* trilogy (1972–90); Frank Serpico, the police whistle-blower, in *Serpico* (1973); Tony Montana, the Cuban drug lord, in *Scarface* (1983); the hapless thief Teach, in *American Buffalo*

(1983); Sonny Wortzik, the would-be bank robber, in *Dog Day Afternoon* (1975); the gangster Big Boy Caprice, in *Dick Tracy* (1990); Ricky Roma, the smooth-talking salesman, in *Glengarry Glen Ross* (1992); and Roy Cohn, the closeted lawyer, in the HBO version of Tony Kushner's *Angels in America* (2003) – to name just a few of the more than a hundred roles he has taken onscreen and onstage. In recent years, he has painted brilliant, eerie film portraits of such obsessives as the euthanasia activist Jack Kevorkian, in Barry Levinson's HBO movie *You Don't Know Jack*, and the eponymous swami of rock and roll, in David Mamet's HBO film *Phil Spector*. Pacino regrets that many of his Hollywood movies of the past decade (*Righteous Kill*, *The Son of No One*, *88 Minutes*, *Jack and Jill*) have been business chores, taken on for primarily financial reasons. 'If you don't have that alacrity of spirit, then you have to check yourself – because where's the pony in all this horseshit?' he said. 'I worked for United Parcels once, and I don't want to have that feeling with my own craft – that it's just a job.'

Because of the protean nature of his attack, Pacino has often been compared to Brando, another truth-seeking force of nature. When Pacino was thirteen and performing in a school play, an adaptation of *Home Sweet Homicide*, he already identified so strongly with his role that when his character was supposed to get sick onstage he became nauseated. ('Somebody came up and said to my mother, "Here's the next Brando." I said, "Who's Brando?"' Pacino recalled.) But between Brando and Pacino there is this crucial difference: Brando, who, over time, became reclusive and indifferent to acting, disappeared into his gift; Pacino has survived his – and is still working to refine it. 'I believe I have not reached my stride, which is why I persist,' he told me in an e-mail. 'The day I turn to you and say, "John, what I just did in this role was a real winner," I hope you'll have the courage and decency to throw a wreath around my head, and then so very quietly and compassionately shoot me.'

Pacino has three films awaiting release in the next year: Barry Levinson's *The Humbling*, in which he plays an aging actor who has lost his magic; David Gordon Green's *Manglehorn*, a film about an eccentric small-town locksmith; and Dan Fogelman's *Danny Collins*, an amiable redemptive fable about a slick pop star who wants to turn his art and his lush life around. At seventy-four, Pacino sometimes asks himself, 'When am I just gonna sit back and smell the golf balls?' But, with two new movies waiting in the wings (Martin Scorsese's *The Irishman*, about the man who supposedly killed Jimmy Hoffa, and a Brian De Palma bio-pic about Joe Paterno), and a David Mamet play, *China Doll*, in the works for Broadway in 2015, the answer is not soon.

Most of Pacino's house has been ceded to his kids. The den is a sort of Camp Pacino, overflowing with toys: a pinball machine, a drum kit, electric guitars, dolls, a mound of games, balls, rackets, and swimming gear crammed into baskets against the back wall. A low table holds a sprawling Lego construction in progress. Outside, a punching bag hangs incongruously beside the patio barbecue. (It's there for Pacino's son; when I asked Pacino if he used it, he said, 'Like Oscar Wilde, whenever I get the urge to exercise I lie down until it passes.') Pacino usually spends weekends with the twins, because 'their mother knows I'm a slacker at the homework.'

At one point, Olivia came in to ask a favor:

OLIVIA: Daddy, I really want to see the boy next door. He usually comes over by the weekend.

PACINO: Does he really? But I don't even know what his name is. What's his name?

OLIVIA: I forgot. It's been so long since I've seen him.

PACINO: Do you want to go over and say – What do you want me to do? Me? I'm the – What am I, the go-between?

OLIVIA: No. Just see if Jared [Pacino's weekend assistant] can call.

PACINO: But Jared's not here. He could do it tomorrow, when he comes in. Do you want Mike [Pacino's regular assistant] to do it now? Mike will do it.

OLIVIA: I don't think Mike knows anybody there.

PACINO: Jared knows someone there? Ask Mike if he could just find out.

Pacino's father left him and his mother when he was two, and he carries the shadow of that abandonment with him. 'It's the missing link, so to speak,' he said. 'Having children has helped a lot. I consciously knew that I didn't want to be like my dad. I wanted to be there. I have three children. I'm responsible to them. I'm a part of their life. When I'm not, it's upsetting to me and to them. So that's part of the gestalt. And I get a lot from it. It takes you out of yourself. When I do a movie, and I come back, I'm stunned for the first twenty minutes. These people are asking me to do things for *them*? Huh? I'm not being waited on? Wait a minute. Uh-oh, it's about them! That action satisfies. I like it.'

He pointed out a watercolor beside the fireplace. 'My son painted this when he was four. 'New York in the Fall," he said, then steered me back into the living room and deposited me on a sofa to watch *Wilde Salomé*, a docudrama he directed, starred in, and largely bankrolled, which premières this month. The film represents Pacino's eight-year attempt to 'inhale' Oscar Wilde by chronicling the mounting of a 2006 Los Angeles production of Wilde's 1891 tragedy, in which he was Herod to Jessica Chastain's Salomé. (*Wilde Salomé* will be released in tandem with a film of the play itself.) Pacino first encountered *Salomé* in London in 1989, without realizing that it was written by Wilde. 'Who wrote this? I'd like to know this person,' he recalled thinking. 'I just felt a connection. A kindred spirit. I think it was a mischievousness, a subversiveness.' Pacino relates to Wilde as an outsider. 'I feel like an outsider who got on the inside, so I'm inside out, if you know what I mean. Or outside in,' he said.

Like *Looking for Richard*, Pacino's 1996 movie about Shakespeare's *Richard III*, *Wilde Salomé* is a dramatic mosaic that jumps from historical facts to performance to interview to enactment. Pacino is the director yelling at the crew to hurry up; he's the lubricious Herod eyeing his gorgeous daughter; he's the interviewer prodding Tom Stoppard, Tony Kushner, Gore Vidal, and Bono to talk about Wilde; he's the professor offering tidbits of Wildeana; and he's the anthropologist trudging through the desert with kaffiyeh and camel. At one point, Pacino, with a carnation and a floppy handkerchief in his jacket pocket, even pops up as Wilde himself. Part of Pacino's fervor for Wilde comes from a desire to claim the writer's intelligence and eloquence. 'I'm quite timid when it comes to challenging the status quo,' he said. 'Oscar had the brains to back it up.' Pacino, whose formal education ended in tenth grade, grappled for years with a sense of intellectual inadequacy. Early in his career, after a breakthrough performance in Israel Horovitz's 1968 play *The Indian Wants the Bronx*, Pacino appeared on *The Merv Griffin Show*, and, in front of a television audience of millions, he froze. 'He just couldn't do it,' Horovitz recalled. 'He felt he had nothing to say. He was humiliated by his own presence. He wasn't the character he was playing – he was Al.' Pacino's devotion to acting is, in a way, a defense against that self-doubt. Having a script to work from gives him, he said, a kind of license. 'I can *talk*, I can *speak*, I have something to *say*,' he explained. 'You don't need a college education. All the things that you were inhibited to talk about and understand – they can come out in the play. The language of great writing frees you of yourself.'

Most actors of Pacino's stature – Brando, Jack Lemmon, Dustin Hoffman, Robert De Niro – began in theatre and rarely returned. Pacino, however, craves the derring-do of working in front of a live audience, an activity he compares to tightrope walking. Stage acting, he likes to say, quoting the aerialist Karl Wallenda, is life 'on the wire – the rest is just waiting.' Onstage, in the zone, he told me, 'you're up in the sky with the theatre gods – love it, love it, love it.' As a list of some of Pacino's more esoteric stage work demonstrates – Eugene O'Neill's *Hughie*, Bertolt Brecht's *The Resistible Rise of Arturo Ui*, Shakespeare's *Richard III* and *The Merchant of Venice* – the theatre is where he goes to challenge himself and to think. 'There are more demands put on you when it is on the stage,' he said.

To Pacino, there is no such thing as a fourth wall. 'The audience is another character in the play,' he said. 'They become part of the event. If they sneeze or talk back to the stage, you make it part of what you're doing.' Once, when he was performing *The Basic Training of Pavlo Hummel*, the first play in David Rabe's *Vietnam* trilogy, in Boston, in 1972, Pacino made a strong connection with a pair of penetrating eyes in the audience. 'I remember feeling a focus I never experienced before – intense, so riveting that I directed my performance to that space,' he said. 'I found at curtain call for the first time that I needed to find out who belonged to those eyes. So, as we were bowing, I looked over to the space where I believed the look was coming from and there it was, two seeing-eye dogs still looking at me. They must have found the curtain call as engaging as the performance.'

Acting, according to Pacino, is about 'getting into a state that brings about freedom and expression and the unconscious.' Mamet compares Pacino's excavations of his characters to the way Louis Armstrong played jazz: 'He's incapable of doing it the same way twice.' While Pacino was shooting his last scene for the movie *Devil's Advocate* (1997), in which he played Satan, for instance, he suddenly broke off from the script to launch into a rendition of 'It Happened in Monterey.' 'It's just absolutely out there, surreal and brilliant,' the actress Helen Mirren, whose husband, Taylor Hackford, directed the film, said. In the final movie, Pacino lipsynchs to Frank Sinatra's version of the song; according to Mirren, the studio had to pay 'a huge sum for the rights, but it was worth it.'

Pacino sometimes develops his characters by observing others. When he was working on his performance in *The Indian Wants the Bronx*, he would walk for hours with Horovitz. 'What he was doing was finding a character in life,' Horovitz told me. 'He'd spot a guy on the street and go, "Wait, wait, wait!" We'd follow the person for hours, just to observe the walk, the posture. And the costume was important, too. He had to find the costume, rehearse in the costume, live in the costume.'

'Some actors *play* characters. Al Pacino *becomes* them,' Lee Strasberg, the longtime director of the Actors Studio said. 'He assumes their identity so completely that he continues to live a role long after a play or movie is over.' Once, when Pacino was playing Richard III in Boston, Jacqueline Kennedy came backstage to greet him. 'I didn't even get up,' he said. 'I was so into it that night that I continued to be the King. I can almost not forgive myself for that.'

When preparing for a role, Pacino has a tendency to circle the airport before arriving at his destination. 'I'm a slow learner,' he said. 'I don't believe in memorizing lines. That's not how I come upon a role. My thing is eventually coming to the words, making the words part of you, so that they're an extension of your emotional state.' Pacino's 'nibbling away at a character,' according to Barry Levinson, is a subtle process. After the first few readings of the script for *You Don't Know Jack*, Levinson recalls wondering 'when Kevorkian will show up.' 'I remember we were in wardrobe. Al had his hair done, and his suit. We were talking and, all of a sudden, I could sense that Kevorkian was coming alive,' he said, adding, 'Once he latches on, then he's off to the races.' At the finale of *You Don't Know Jack*, after Kevorkian has unsuccessfully defended himself in court, the judge looks at him and asks if he wants to take the stand. Pacino doesn't answer at first. 'It takes literally a minute,' Levinson said. 'He's trying to decide if the defense rests. It's a brilliant moment. No words – it's a look, a glance, small things that really inform the character.'

Over the years, there have been rumblings about Pacino's overacting. He can certainly roar; he can pound the furniture; he can go big with the facial expressions; he has made some dud movies. But the drama, for Pacino, is almost always inherent in the character he's hoping to convey. His portrayal of the blind Lieutenant Colonel Frank Slade in *Scent of a Woman* (1992), for instance, was considered hammy by some, but, in Pacino's thinking, the character was a lunatic – a suicidal, narcissistic man who drew attention to himself through his affectation of swagger – and he played him that way. 'I paint the way I see it, and some of the colors are a little broader and a little bolder than others,' he said, adding, 'Sometimes you take it to the limit, sometimes you may go a little overboard, but that's all part of a vision. I say, go with the glow. If an effort is being made to produce something that has appetite and passion and isn't done just to get the golden cup, it isn't a fucking waste. Yes, there are flaws, but in them are things you'll remember.'

Pacino protects his talent by leaving it alone, which accounts for his vaunted moodiness. 'There are various superstitions connected with reaching his center, and he doesn't want to discuss them ever,' Mike Nichols, who directed Pacino in *Angels in America*, said. 'He's consulting somewhere else. And the somewhere else does not have to do with words.' Pacino almost never talks shop. When he was at the Actors Studio, in the late sixties, whenever Strasberg gave him notes, he said, 'I would actually count numbers in my head not to hear what he was saying. I didn't want to know. I thought it would fuck up what I was doing, where I was going with my own ideas.'

Even Pacino's speech patterns, which forge a kind of evasive switchback trail up a mountain of thought, serve as a defense against too much parsing of his interior. 'Al is dedicated, passionately, to inarticulateness,' Nichols said, pointing out that in conversation Pacino has no 'chitchat.' Playing dead in social situations is his instinctive strategy. 'He was so sensitive that he was insensitive to his surroundings,' Diane Keaton, with whom Pacino had an on-again-off-again relationship in the seventies and eighties, wrote in her memoir *Then Again*. 'Sometimes I swear Al must have been raised by wolves. There were normal things he had no acquaintance with, like the whole idea of enjoying a meal in the company of others. He was more at home eating alone standing up. He did not relate to tables or the conversations people had at them.'

Pacino refers to acting as 'close to magic.' To invoke that spell, he observes many rituals, which sometimes include shaking hands with everyone on a film set before shooting a scene, and heading off for a walk before going onstage. 'The calm before the storm – only sometimes the calm becomes the storm,' he explained. In 2012, when he was appearing in Mamet's *Glengarry Glen Ross* on Broadway, Pacino was skulking around midtown in a hooded coat when a parking attendant accosted him. 'You! Get out! What are you doing here?' Pacino recalled him shouting. He added, 'Oh, it felt so good.'

While working on his first production of *Richard III*, in 1973, at the Church of the Covenant, in Boston, Pacino and his assistant developed a pre-show routine for launching him into the role of the anarchic, manipulative 'lump of foul deformity' who would be king. Pacino's dressing room was the church rectory. 'She'd peek through the door and say, "Half hour," then, "Fifteen minutes." She'd come back again and say, "Five minutes." I would say, "Fuck off," each time,' Pacino told me. 'She'd say, "The audience is out there waiting for you." And I'd say, "Fuck off !" She'd say, "I'm coming to get you." She'd grab at me, and she'd throw me out of the dressing room. I guess it was the right spirit, because it worked. They called me out six times after I bowed.' After the show, he added, 'I would bawl my eyes out. I roused so many things in myself.'

Pacino's allegiance to the stage, his compulsion to connect with a live audience, is due, perhaps, to a need to re-create his relationship with the person he calls his first and 'indeed my best audience,' his mother, Rose. To be seen and to be accepted was the promise behind his early performances. The theatrical interaction gives him, he said, 'a sense of being at home, together again.'

Pacino's father, Salvatore, was eighteen when Alfredo was born, in East Harlem, in 1940, and twenty when he left. He paid a few memorable visits, twice going to see his son perform in high-school plays, but Pacino saw very little of him, even after he had become a star. By then, Salvatore, who married five times and for decades worked as an insurance salesman for Metropolitan Life, owned Pacino's Lounge, a restaurant and bar in Covina, California, where he frequently joined the band to sing, play the maracas, and shake his booty. 'When a friend met my dad, he looked at him and said, "There it is with you, Al. I see it. The survivor,"' Pacino said. 'I got that from my dad.'

Rose, according to Pacino, was a reader who had 'a sensitivity and a connection to the theatre.' She took Pacino to see Tennessee Williams's *Cat on a Hot Tin Roof* on Broadway. She was playful, with a good sense of humor, but also volatile and reclusive. She often refused to leave her room when company came over. 'She reminded me of a Tennessee Williams character. She would have been a really good Laura, also a good Amanda. She had both,' Pacino said, referring to Williams's play *The Glass Menagerie*. In other words, she was a troubled, fragile, controlling, somewhat hysterical soul, who fought a losing battle against her own desperation. Despite the family's meagre income, Rose scraped together enough to pay for visits to a psychiatrist. To treat her chronic depression, she resorted to electric-shock therapy. Eventually, she became addicted to barbiturates, which may have been the cause of her death, at forty-three, in 1962. The stain of her possible suicide hangs over Pacino's memory of Rose. 'Poverty took her down,' he said. Not long before she died, Pacino recalls rushing to a casting session for Elia Kazan's *America America*. 'I had one of the few fantasies I've ever had in my life,' he said. 'I would do well, my mother would be O.K. with it all, and I could say, "Mom, we got it. We're gonna make some money. It's gonna be O.K."' As it happened, Pacino arrived late and missed the audition.

After Salvatore left, Rose and Sonny (as Pacino was known throughout his childhood) moved in with her parents, James Gerardi, a plasterer who was an illegal immigrant from Corleone, Sicily, and his wife, Kate. In their cramped three-room apartment in the South Bronx, which sometimes housed as many as seven people, Pacino never had a space of his own. ('I remember years of sleeping between my grandmother and grandfather,' he said.) At the same time, he was an only child, often left to his own devices. 'I was always sort of building stories, creating stories,' he said. 'It was a way of filling up the loneliness.'

Storytelling ran in the family. In warm weather, Pacino's grandfather, with whom Pacino had what he calls 'one of the great relationships of my life,' would sit with him on the tar roof of their tenement and spin tales about his rough Dickensian youth in turn-of-the-century New York. 'He got the shit kicked out of him by cops with helmets and big clubs – "You little wop! Get over here, you stinking Guinea!"' Pacino said. 'He'd talk about running away from home, living off the farms, how he would steal milk. He just loved talking to me, like we were on some little rowboat.' The roof, Pacino added, 'was our terrace. There was this cacophony of sound – the Poles, the Jews, the Irish, the German, the Spanish. This definitive melting pot is what I came from. In some Eugene O'Neill plays, you hear the same thing.'

Among many odd jobs, Rose worked as a cinema usherette, and when Pacino was three or four she began to take him to the movies. 'The next day, I would act out all the parts,' he said. 'I think that's how it started.' Pacino was often coaxed into performing scenes for his extended family, which included a deaf aunt. His party piece was an imitation of Ray Milland in *The Lost Weekend*, playing an alcoholic writer desperate for a drink. Pacino would open cupboards and doors, pretending to search for a hidden stash of booze. 'I never understood why they were laughing, because I didn't think it was funny,' he said. 'But I knew it produced laughs.'

On Bryant Avenue in the forties and fifties, people escaped their small, hot apartments to sit on stoops or hang out under street lamps to roll dice or play poker. To disarm bullies and find friends, Pacino used the same strategy on the street that he'd used at home: he performed and enlisted others to perform with him, earning the nickname 'the Actor.' 'We'd act out parts from joke books and comic books,' he told me. 'Kids make videos today, but it was kind of an unusual thing then to get street urchins to join you in acting out comics. Of course, it never got off the ground; there's a comedy in there somewhere.' 'He was always full of drama,' said his neighbor Ken Lipper, who would later become the deputy mayor of New York and a producer and screenwriter of *City Hall* (1996), in which Pacino starred. 'He loved to take on different personae. He used to go to 174th Street and pretend he was a blind child.' Pacino's bravado and good looks got him noticed. 'The girls in the neighborhood would say, "Sonny Pacino, the lover bambino." The boys would say, "Sonny Pacino, the bastard bambino,"' Pacino told me. 'It started early.'

Pacino was smoking at nine, chewing tobacco at ten, and drinking hard liquor at thirteen. He walked the edges of rooftops and jumped between tenement buildings. His favorite place was 'the Dutchies,' a swampy labyrinth on the Bronx River, where truant kids hid in high marsh grasses. Pacino played third base for the Police Athletic League team, the Red Wings, which became a 'quasi street gang,' with Al as its de-facto leader. In black wool jackets with a red stripe down the sleeve, the Red Wings patrolled their turf and protected it from roaming invaders, like the Young Sinners and the Fordham Baldies. Once, when they were twelve and sitting on the steps of a tenement after finishing a game of stickball, Lipper said, 'some guy came over who was thirtyish and started menacing us. Al got up and whacked him with the stick.' Pacino's wild crew, 'tough kids with high I.Q.s and tragic endings,' became a template on which he modelled many of his memorable characters. 'These people were a springboard for my profession,' he said. 'They were part of what I consider the best time in my life.'

Pacino was less popular with the authority figures around him. 'I wasn't out of control, but I was close,' he said. 'My mother had to come to school to talk to the teachers. Their conclusion? That I needed a dad.' When Pacino's junior high-school drama teacher, Blanche Rothstein, climbed the five flights of stairs to talk to his grandmother about his acting skills, it was, he said, 'the first time I ever had encouragement.' He went on, 'The world we came from, the encouragement just wasn't there. We weren't seen. Or we weren't regarded. Do you think ever, once in my life, my mother or any adult ever said, 'How was school today?' Never! It was unheard of.' Nonetheless, Ms Rothstein spotted a spark when Pacino read Bible passages in school assembly – 'I didn't know what I was talking about, but I felt it,' he said – and she cast him in school plays. Thanks to his talent, at the end of junior high Pacino was voted 'most likely to succeed.'

Pacino was accepted into Manhattan's High School of Performing Arts, which meant that his South Bronx street life was more or less a thing of the past. 'All that remained was acting,' he said. His stay at the school, however, was a short one. 'You gotta be kidding,' he told his Spanish teacher, when he discovered that the class was conducted entirely in Spanish. And he found the Stanislavsky method boring. 'What does a kid who was thirteen, fourteen know about Stanislavsky?' he said. 'All I knew was you sing, you dance, you have fun, you imitate. Now I was looking at my navel twenty-four-seven. It took me I don't know how many years to get over that.' By his own admission, Pacino was a 'dunderhead' at academic work, and by the time he dropped out of school, at sixteen, to support his mother, he was ready to go. Rose, who had at first approved of his ambition, now saw it as foolhardy. 'Acting isn't for our kind of people,' she told him. 'Poor people don't go into this.' Pacino said, 'I didn't know what she was talking about. On an unconscious level I did, but it didn't mean anything to me. I'm a survivor. Survivors only hear what they want to hear.'

Between odd jobs, Pacino attended auditions, where he soon learned that, as an Italian-American of a certain class and demeanor, he didn't 'look right' for most parts. His instinct was to bide his time. 'I knew, when the opportunity came, all I'd have to do is be there,' he said. But his mother's death, when he was twenty-one, sent him into a tailspin. Within a year, his grandfather, too, was dead. Pacino had buried the two people to whom he was closest. 'And I had no father,' he said. 'I think that was my darkest period. I felt lost.'

On Pacino's living-room mantelpiece is a small moody photograph of him in profile in his early twenties, in an Off-Off Broadway production of August Strindberg's play *Creditors*. The image marks the seminal moment, he said, 'when I knew that nothing mattered except that I became at one with the play.' *Creditors*, a tragicomedy about a credulous young artist whose mind is poisoned against his wife by her bilious ex-husband, was directed by Charlie Laughton, an actor turned acting teacher at the Herbert Berghof Studio, whom Pacino first met in a Village bar when he was seventeen. Laughton, who'd also had a hardscrabble early life, recognized both Pacino's talent and his difficult circumstances. Over time, he became Pacino's mentor, his sidekick, his drinking buddy, his dramaturge, and, ultimately, his business partner. Laughton also introduced the teenage Pacino to the works of Joyce and Rimbaud. 'He would read them, and then I would read them myself,' Pacino told me. In those knockabout years, he added, 'I dealt with whatever was bothering me through reading. You could not find me without a book.'

Still, in the early days of rehearsing *Creditors* Pacino, surrounded by classically trained actors, panicked and wanted to quit the show. Laughton sat him down and went through the script with him until he fully understood what was going on. Pacino had been spooked in that way before, in his Off-Off Broadway début, in a production of William Saroyan's *Hello Out There*, which grew out of Laughton's classes. Pacino's first line got a laugh, but he didn't understand the joke. In the alley, during intermission, he burst into tears and didn't want to continue. Laughton talked him through it. 'It was a very important moment for me,' Pacino recalled. 'I went back in there and finished the run.'

Laughton, who was for years wheelchair-bound with multiple sclerosis and who died in 2013, at the age of eighty-four, remained an emotional bulwark for Pacino until the end. Pacino visited him in his last days, at a hospital in Laughton's class at the Berghof Studio and performed a scene from Reginald Rose's *Crime in the Streets* in front of Berghof and the rest of the school. After he finished, he said, 'Berghof got up there and started to put me down. He started screaming at me, "How dare you!" He was absolutely flipping out.' Pacino asked Laughton, 'What was going on?' 'A new era,' Laughton said. 'He saw a new era.'

On January 17, 1967, for his first scene at the Actors Studio, Pacino presented a monologue from Eugene O'Neill's *The Iceman Cometh*, which morphed into a soliloquy from *Hamlet*. It was risky, but, as Pacino said, 'It's a risk *not* to take risks.' Breaking a long-standing Studio tradition, the audience of actors applauded his performance. Lee Strasberg then asked Pacino to play O'Neill's character, Hickey, as Hamlet, and Hamlet as Hickey. Afterward, he addressed Pacino. 'The courage you have shown today is rarer than talent,' he said. Pacino had broken through. 'I was now an actor,' he said. 'I had an identity.'

He spent much of the next year in Boston doing plays (Clifford Odets's *Awake and Sing!*, Jean-Claude van Itallie's *America, Hurrah*), in which, he said, 'I played notes that fell flat and I didn't connect.' But when Israel Horovitz delivered his one-act *The Indian Wants the Bronx* to Pacino, in a messy basement room in a building on West Sixty-eighth Street, where he was earning fourteen dollars a week as a superintendent, Pacino found the perfect vehicle – a script about two taunting teenage louts in the Bronx who take out their frustrations on an Indian man at a bus stop.

Over the next months, Pacino and Horovitz performed the play in and out of town to raise interest in a production. But when a producer was eventually found she had her own ideas about casting. 'On audition day, she brought in the actor she wanted: blond, blue-eyed, tall, untalented,' Horovitz wrote in a memoir. 'I said no, absolutely no. She said, fine, O.K., she wouldn't produce the play. I said, "Let both actors audition."' Pacino was furious with Horovitz for putting him in this position; since he didn't belong to Actors' Equity, he was forced to attend an open call. 'It seemed like every young, non-union actor in New York City showed up that day,' Horovitz recalled. When it was Pacino's turn, he came out singing, then crossed to downstage center and looked directly at the producer: 'Hey, Pussyface, can you hear us? Can you hear your babies singin' to ya?' 'Startled and terrified,' according to Horovitz, she agreed to cast Pacino.

The Indian Wants the Bronx opened at the Astor Place Theatre, on January 17, 1968. Of all the débuts I attended in more than fifty years as a theatre critic, Pacino's was the most sensational: immediate, arresting, and inexplicable. 'I saw an actor up there with a shaking jaw, who was on the verge of tears,' Horovitz recalled. 'The circumstance of the play was bringing him to a deep place of pain. And the audience connected to this terrible sense of humiliation, of unworthiness.' Pacino won an Obie for Best Actor, and a Tony the following year, for his performance in Don Petersen's *Does a Tiger Wear a Necktie?*

'All I could see was Al Pacino's face in that camera. I couldn't get him out of my head,' said Francis Ford Coppola, who nearly got fired from *The Godfather* (1972) for insisting that Pacino play Michael Corleone, the educated youngest son of Don Corleone, the Mafia kingpin. The studio lobbied for such bright box-office names as Robert Redford, Warren Beatty, Jack Nicholson, and Ryan O'Neal. But Mario Puzo, who wrote *The Godfather* and adapted it for the screen, came to Coppola's defense and gave him a letter to be used at his discretion. 'Above all, Pacino had to be in the film,' he said.

On the day of his first screen test, however, Pacino was hung over: he didn't know his lines, and he ad-libbed the scene. Puzo felt that Pacino 'was terrible. Jimmy Caan had done it ten times better.' Puzo went over to Coppola. 'Give me my letter back,' he said. 'Wait a while,' Coppola said. Pacino tested three times for the role. The back-and-forth agitated him to such a degree that he finally refused to take Coppola's calls and made the actress Jill Clayburgh, his girlfriend at the time, speak for him. '"Francis, you're making him crazy. He doesn't want to be where he's not wanted,"' Pacino recalls her saying.

When Pacino was finally offered the part, he almost couldn't take it. A few months earlier, he'd signed on for an adaptation of the Jimmy Breslin book *The Gang That Couldn't Shoot Straight*, and M-G-M and the producer, Irwin Winkler, refused to release him. Winkler and Horovitz were sharing a house on Fire Island, and Pacino begged the playwright to intercede on his behalf. 'This was the door opening, and they wouldn't let him out of his contract,' Horovitz recalled. 'I went crazy with Irwin, and he said, 'You find me a young Italian actor that's as good as Pacino, and I'll let him out.' Horovitz took Winkler to see a performance by a young unknown named Robert De Niro. 'He took De Niro, and he got two options on Pacino and two on De Niro,' Horovitz said.

After Pacino got the *Godfather* role (for which he was paid a flat fee of thirty-five thousand dollars), he walked from his apartment, on Ninetieth Street and Broadway, to the Village and back, thinking about how he'd play it. 'I didn't see Michael as a gangster,' he said. 'I saw his struggle as something that was connected to his intelligence, that innate sense of what's around and being able to adjust to things.' He added, 'The power of the character was in his enigmatic quality. And I thought, Well, how do you get to that? I think you wear it inside yourself, and you find a way to avoid, as much as you can, the obvious.' However, after his first week of avoiding the obvious, according to Pacino, 'they wanted me fired – they didn't see what I was doing. Luckily for me, the Sollozzo scene' – in which Michael earns his Mafia spurs by executing two men in a Bronx restaurant – 'was the next day. When they saw that scene, they kept me.'

Pacino's performance in *The Godfather* put him at the center of one of the great cinematic sagas of the century and on a first-name basis with the world. He was showered with accolades and offers. (Coppola asked him to star in *Apocalypse Now*, but he declined. 'You know, sometimes you look into the abyss?' Pacino said. 'I'm, like, this is the abyss. I'm not gonna go there.' He also turned down *Star Wars*, *Die Hard*, and *Pretty Woman*.) But perhaps the most satisfying response came from Puzo, who wrote, 'It was, in my eyes, a perfect performance, a work of art. I was so happy . . . I ate crow like it was my favorite Chinese food.'

Pacino's other great early successes – *Serpico*, *The Godfather, Part II*, and *Dog Day Afternoon* – only added to his momentum. But, of all his performances in those years, the sleeper was his embodiment of the garish, vulgar, sensationally violent Tony Montana, an impoverished Cuban refugee who becomes the most powerful drug trafficker in Miami, in *Scarface*. The role was dismissed as 'macho primitivism' at the time, but, over the years, it has emerged as a challenger to Michael Corleone as Pacino's most popular creation. The director, Brian De Palma, designed *Scarface* as a kind of hyperbolic pageant. 'The picture had a fire to it,' Pacino said, in 'Al Pacino: In Conversation with Lawrence Grobel.' 'The violence blown up, the language blown up. The spirit of it was Brechtian, operatic.' To play Montana, Pacino drew inspiration from the swagger of the Panamanian boxer Roberto Duran and from Meryl Streep's committed rendering of the traumatized Polish immigrant Sophie, in *Sophie's Choice*. As an actor, Pacino said, 'you're always looking for that thing that's going on besides the words.' In *Scarface*, he connected with Montana's raging ambition and the rebelliousness in his epigrammatic lines: 'All I have in the world is my balls and my word, and I don't break them for no one'; 'You know what capitalism is? Getting fucked!'; 'You wanna play rough? O.K. Say hello to my little friend!'

In the twenty years following the release of *The Godfather*, Pacino made seventeen films and was nominated for an Academy Award six times. (He finally received one, in 1993, for his performance in *Scent of a Woman*.) But he was discombobulated by the distractions of his success. 'I felt like the fighter that was in Round 8, exhausted in the corner, they're pouring water over my head and rubbing Vaseline on my face, then *ding* went the bell, and I was back out there in another film,' he recalled. 'It was a whirlwind.' Pacino disappeared into work, and, after hours, into a bottle. 'I don't remember much of the seventies,' he said. 'All that stuff – the explosiveness of my life change. It would be almost fair to say I wasn't really there. It was too much for anyone to handle.' Eventually, Laughton called Pacino on his alcohol abuse, which had been a constant since he was a teenager. He stopped drinking in 1977.

During his first year of sobriety, a time of great stress, Pacino made *Bobby Deerfield*, a plodding Sydney Pollack melodrama, in which he played a celebrity race-car driver, who hides his vulnerability behind sunglasses and a carapace of toughness. His next movie, *Cruising* (1980), William Friedkin's thriller about a serial killer who targets gay men – which sparked protests in the gay community – was 'a terrible experience' for Pacino as well as for the critics. *Author! Author!* (1982), which was written by Horovitz, was also a bust. *Scarface* came out to mixed reviews, and was followed by *Revolution* (1985), in which Pacino played a Scottish fur trapper with a Bronx accent, who gets embroiled in the Revolutionary War. *Revolution* was proof, if more was needed, that on the Hollywood merry-go-round Pacino had lost track of who he was. The movie cost twenty-eight million dollars to make and grossed less than $360,000. It was one disaster too many.

In a radical move, at the height of his celebrity, Pacino called a halt to moviemaking and moved to Snedens Landing, in Palisades, New York, with Diane Keaton. There he settled, he said, 'into something that was wonderful with Diane and my life. I didn't feel rushed or that I had to put out. I felt relatively content.' The stoppage was a crucial emotional recalibration. 'It is the very nature of fame that the light is on you a lot,' he said. 'I sort of wanted to turn the light out of my face, so I could see.'

Pacino's return to New York was also a return to theatre. He appeared in Dennis McIntyre's *National Anthem* at the Long Wharf Theatre, in New Haven. He played Mark Antony, in a disastrous *Julius Caesar* at the Public, a role he could never find his way into. But his main creative focus was on *The Local Stigmatic*, a little-known 1969 one-act by Heathcote Williams, about two British ne'er-do-wells who grievously harm a famous actor whose success enrages them. Pacino produced and starred in a fascinating film version of the play. 'I took almost a year to edit this fifty-two-minute play,' he said. 'I had no one wanting it to work or not work. It was under my control. I was free.' (The film was never released theatrically but was included in the DVD boxed set *Pacino: An Actor's Vision*.)

Although Pacino remembers this time as 'probably the best period' of his adult life – 'It was as close to egoless as I've ever been' – four years into his self-imposed exile from Hollywood he was running out of money and Keaton was running out of patience. One day, according to Pacino, she read him the riot act. 'What do you think you're doing?' he remembers her saying. 'Do you think you're gonna go back and live in a rooming house again? You've been rich too long, buddy. You can't go back. You think you're on the A-list, but you're not. You're out because you put yourself out. You've got to go back to work.' Keaton added, 'This script. This is your thing. This is what you've got to do.' She handed him Richard Price's screenplay for *Sea of Love*. 'It was so sweet of her,' Pacino said. 'It was so giving, so caring. I have to say, she was right.' *Sea of Love* (1989), the story of a cop in a midlife crisis who falls for a woman who may be the killer he's pursuing, made a star of Ellen Barkin and restored Pacino's box-office clout. In the next five years, he made *Dick Tracy*, *The Godfather, Part*

III, *Frankie and Johnny*, *Glengarry Glen Ross*, *Scent of a Woman*, *Carlito's Way*, and *Heat*.

As Pacino paced his living room, a tall, striking woman with long auburn hair swept in, draped an arm over his shoulders, and pulled him to her, like a swan taking a cygnet under its wing. Lucila Sola, a thirty-five-year-old Argentinean actress, spoke in Latin-inflected English. 'I am his longest relationship – seven years,' she said, by way of introduction. Sola, who studied law and sociology before switching to acting, is the latest in a long line of strong, smart actresses with whom Pacino has been involved – Tuesday Weld, Kathleen Quinlan, and Marthe Keller, among them. The two met at a dinner party in 2005, when his twins were four and her daughter, Camila, was seven. They were both dating other people, but their kids got along and they found themselves going to movies together, swimming in Pacino's pool, taking trips to San Diego, the beach. 'We were friends. For two years – *two years* – nothing,' Sola said. 'When people ask, "How long have you been together?," I say, "Forty-nine years."' A year with Al is like a dog year because it's so intense.' She explained, 'He's a medium. He's channelling something. When he's doing a part, it's hard to be around him because he's very different. Al has left the building.'

The conversation turned to Diane Keaton's bittersweet second memoir, *Let's Just Say It Wasn't Pretty*, which had been published the week before and in which she discussed 'the lure of Al.' 'His face, his nose, and what about those eyes?' Keaton wrote. 'I kept trying to figure out what I could do to make them mine. They never were.... For the next twenty years I kept losing a man I never had.' Sola expounded on the astuteness of Keaton's observation. 'Al has this ephemeral, childlike quality about him,' she told me. 'His friend Charlie used to say he's like smoke. He's there, but he's not there. That's maybe what drove the women crazy. You want to catch him, but you can't because Al is –'

'Leave John alone,' Pacino cut in, bringing the conversation effectively to an end.

Sola had persuaded Pacino to accompany her to a friend's birthday bowling party the next day. That evening, complaining about the 'fucking bowling shoes' – 'I can't stand putting on my shoes every day. Imagine putting on bowling shoes,' he said – Pacino got behind the wheel of his white Range Rover and headed for Lucky Strike, in Hollywood, which turned out to be more of a bowling den than an alley.

A bookshelf extended from the entrance into the large underlit space; jokey signage – a poster advertising '10 Rules for Sleeping Around' – hung from the walls; from a distance, beyond the bar, came the echo of ricocheting pins. The birthday girl, Kam, in blue satin shorts and a diamanté tiara, waved Pacino and Sola over to the leather banquette where her posse of svelte girlfriends and their men were huddled. While Sola plunged into the crowd of chatty celebrants, Pacino took a barstool at a table behind them and ordered a plate of barbecued chicken. As he ate, the standup comedian Billy Bellamy, who is credited with coining the phrase 'booty call,' appeared. 'We're blessed, man,' Bellamy said. 'I'm blessed. You killed in that Liberace shit, man.'

'That was Michael Douglas,' Pacino said, wiping barbecue sauce off his fingers.

As Pacino was putting on his bowling shoes, a Lucky Strike staffer approached. 'Sorry to disturb you,' he said, holding up his cell phone to indicate a promotional photo op. 'But would you mind?'

'I don't do that,' Pacino said.

Sola pulled him away toward the party. 'Once that starts, it's over,' she said.

Pacino guttered his first ball. His second swerved left and picked off five pins. By the next frame, his score was fifteen. He sat down on the sofa.

'I usually get myself into a Zen place and am just very quiet,' he told me later. 'People give you room when you get real quiet with your disposition.' At the bowling party, however, the tactic wasn't working. The phones came out, and Pacino was swarmed with requests for selfies. Having done his duty, he slumped back down on the couch. From his body language, Sola could tell that the night was over. Thirty minutes after they arrived, she was leading Pacino toward the exit.

In the garage, he fumbled for his parking ticket and couldn't find it. 'You know me, I'm in pictures,' he said to the attendant. At the exit, he struggled again, this time to fit his new ticket correctly into the machine. The barricade finally lifted. 'I'm a natural, baby,' he said, as he accelerated into the balmy night. 'I just pick things up.'

In mid-2010, Pacino learned that his business manager, Kenneth I. Starr, had been arrested for embezzling his clients' money in a Ponzi scheme. (Starr is currently serving seven and a half years in prison.) There had been warnings. Early on, Mike Nichols, who had taken his money out of Starr's company, had raised suspicions. 'I'll get to it,' Pacino told Nichols. 'Then I never got to it,'

he said. 'Millions of dollars were gone,' Sola said. 'Gone.'

Pacino took the loss in stride. 'I thought, Hey, this is the world. It's real,' he said. 'Not one day I saw him down or depressed,' Sola said. 'He was, like, "O.K., now what do we do? Roll up our sleeves and go to work."'

Pacino's agent, John Burnham, told me, 'In his halcyon days he made around fourteen million a picture, but the industry's changed. Nowadays, he gets five million. With a gun – seven million.' It has taken Pacino four years to work himself back to a position where, he says, 'compared to a normal person, I have a significant amount.' He sold a Snedens Landing property, did commercials, took out a loan, and signed on for Adam Sandler's dismal but profitable *Jack and Jill* (2011) – a 'kids' movie,' according to Pacino, in which he sent up both his legend and his financial predicament. In the film's best moment, a hip-hop ad for Dunkin' Donuts, Pacino can be seen dancing and pitching the 'Dunkaccino': 'You want creamy goodness / I'm your friend / Say hello to my chocolate blend.'

'I've recently come to terms with the fact that I can only do something I am creatively connected to,' Pacino told me. *The Humbling*, based on the 2009 Philip Roth novel, which Pacino optioned, is part of that mission. The novel tells the story of a depressed, aging actor whose talent is slipping away and who tries to rejuvenate himself through an affair with a younger woman (who in the movie is played by Greta Gerwig). 'I liked the idea that an actor is losing it and wants to revive not so much his career as his life, and finds that there's no life there,' Pacino said. 'He's trying to be a real person, and discovering that he doesn't have the appropriate tools to do this. I felt that these things were sad and almost farcical.'

Barry Levinson, the director, who enlisted Buck Henry to write the screenplay, was also taken with the novel. 'It was a great character study,' he said. 'We wanted to flesh that out a little bit more, to apply some of the things that Al's gone through in his life, and, hopefully, not in a super-serious fashion. There's a dark comedic trail to the piece.' The film was undertaken with a freewheeling spirit. 'We did a lot of improvisation,' Levinson said.' *The Humbling* is about as homemade a movie as you can make. We made it for two million dollars in twenty days. We shot part of it in my house, because we didn't have enough money to go somewhere else.'

Pacino's legend is based on the films of his youth, for which he drew on his anger, his sexuality, his energy. The films he's interested in now tend to dwell, like *The Humbling*, *Manglehorn*, and *Danny Collins*, on old age and the issues of decline. They are of a different amperage and a different spiritual mind-set. They are not, so to speak, the rock-'em-sock-'em Pacino of old but a new Pacino: a man who is consolidating his family, regretting some of his life choices, and living under the strictures of his fame.

In late June, I met up with Pacino in Boston, one of the twenty-three cities in which he would be performing 'Pacino: One Night Only,' a business junket disguised as a lap of honor. The promoters referred to this form of entertainment as 'talk theatre.' In essence, Pacino was taking himself on the road. He had flown in late the previous night from Ottawa, where he'd sold out a twenty-six-hundred-seat theatre at the National Arts Centre. In Boston, he was at the Wang Theatre, a fun palace built to hold thirty-seven hundred customers, who were shelling out up to a hundred and seventy-nine dollars a seat – plus an extra three hundred if they wanted to attend a meet-and-greet after the show. A slick eight-minute montage of clips from Pacino's movies opened the evening. He told Sonny Corleone, 'It's not personal, Sonny. It's strictly business'; he shouted, 'Attica! Attica!'; he jumped Ellen Barkin's bones. When Tony Montana drunkenly turned on the scowling patrons of a swank restaurant ('Say good night to the bad guy!'), the audience roared. The lights came up, and Pacino entered to a standing ovation. He let the volley of sound wrap around him, then, with his hands clasped together in front of him, he bowed low.

After a few reverent questions from Ty Burr, the Boston Globe's film critic, who was his interlocutor for the evening, Pacino picked up his legend and ran with it: performing as a kid for the deaf aunt ('started my overacting, I guess'); the high-school teacher who called him a prodigy ('How do you spell that?'); when he knew he had 'it' as an actor ('I hope I never do'). Pacino played off the hoots of approval – 'riding the bull,' he calls it – taking the audience into his confidence, and, when he went off course, letting it guide him back to his story. 'Where was I? Oh, yeah – I was a superintendent. I put an eight-by-ten picture of me on the door – kind of looking handsome. Underneath, I wrote "Super." And there wasn't a girl that went into that apartment that I didn't go after!'

Afterward, at the meet-and-greet, Pacino sat on a stool in front of a camera for forty-five minutes while premium ticket holders lined up for a photograph. The night before, he had obliged a blind woman who handed off her cane and asked him to dance. Tonight, the fans approached him solemnly, like communicants, uncertain how to arrange themselves beside their icon. Some leaned in, some stood apart, some asked if it was O.K. to put an arm around his shoulder. (It was.) One woman planted a kiss on Pacino's cheek, then placed a lily and a rose in his lap. Another woman, in formal evening gloves and a gray dress, who positioned herself in front of Pacino to speak to him, told me later that she had devoted her life to theatre after seeing Pacino act in *The Resistible Rise of Arturo Ui*, on her twenty-first birthday, thirty-nine years before. 'He gave me a passion for the theatre,' she said. 'It was a great gift.'

At Logan International, a private jet was waiting to take Pacino and his crew to New York. 'There'll be a crowd at the airport,' Pacino warned me, as the bags were loaded into his two-car convoy. As predicted, a group of autograph hunters were waiting like spectres outside the reception area. 'It's their job,' Pacino said. 'At first, I didn't know. I just thought they were strange people who kind of looked alike, but they do it for a living.' As he got out of the car, the scrum of about twenty pushed forward. 'Al! Al! Over here, Al!' they called, flourishing photographs and memorabilia. Head down, Pacino walked straight through the glass doors and into the bright silence of the lounge.

At takeoff and landing, Pacino crossed himself and kissed his fingers. During the flight, he talked about another kind of blessing he'd felt that day. In the late afternoon, with his bodyguard a hundred feet away, Pacino had spent an hour on Boston Common, sitting unnoticed on a bench and watching the passers-by. 'It felt like I was back on the block, back home,' he said. 'I felt lonely, but I always feel that way. I could feel connected to myself, just like when I sat there fifty years ago. I started there, in that park and that town. I didn't feel I had changed. I was still me. The park was still the park. I'll remember that moment.' The temporary anonymity had brought 'a kind of peace,' which, he said, 'is pretty much a luxury.' Later, he told me, 'I haven't been in a grocery store or ridden the subway in fifty years. My kids have a difficult time going out with me publicly. We have yet to go on a camping trip. But one day I want to rent a small house on a lake. It's my dream – I don't know how to get to it yet, but I'll give it another year.' Still, he said, 'I'm fine not having anonymity. I've learned how to live with the other thing, and the sort of enjoyment that comes with that. It ain't bad.' He added, 'Not that I recommend it, but, like they say, you should try it sometime.'

Epilogue: Petrified

The Horrors of Stagefright

The legends in this collection are masters of their craft and inevitably also masters of their fear. Performance is about the show of command. It's a flow, an eloquence, a rehearsed ease and concentration whose subliminal charm is to appear never at a loss. The actor's specific glamour is an encounter with perfect personality, 'one who is not wounded or maimed or worried or in danger,' as Oscar Wilde said of his particular astonishing performance of self.

Terror is the crucible in which performance is forged. 'Lose yourself and you lose your audience,' Noël Coward said. To lose poise is to lose the illusion of invincibility. For the performer, it's a catastrophic collapse, a kind of living death whose humiliation haunts the enterprise of performing before the judgemental eyes of others. 'I died out there', 'I corpsed' – the actors' lingo hints at the lurking anxiety of annihilation which is always the dark side of brilliance.

This essay on stage fright was chosen among The Best American Essays *of 2007.*

In February, 1995, the thirty-seven-year-old British actor and comedian Stephen Fry was starring with another popular British comic, Rik Mayall, in the West End production of Simon Gray's *Cell Mates*. Fry had the role of George Blake, a spy and traitor who is sprung from Wormwood Scrubs, where he is serving a forty-two-year sentence, by a prison friend, Sean Bourke, and who then, through a series of stratagems, keeps Bourke living with him in Moscow for two years. Fry, a multifaceted performer (he was Oscar Wilde in the 1997 film *Wilde*, and a featured player on Rowan Atkinson's TV comedy *Blackadder*), had 'the manners of a convivial prelate,' as Gray subsequently wrote in *Fat Chance*, his account of the production. On the Sunday after the show's opening, when the weekend reviews hit the stands, however, Fry woke up feeling a 'sort of clammy horror.' He told me, 'I had something to do, something annoying – I had agreed I would do narration for *Peter and the Wolf* in a church somewhere. I woke up. I looked at the ceiling. I thought, I can't let this person down on *Peter and the Wolf*. But I can't go back to the theatre. I cannot.' He added, 'It was just a feeling of impossibility. It's inexplicable. I'd never, ever, had stagefright and I'd done things like appear in front of close to eighty thousand people at Wembley for Nelson Mandela's birthday.'

Fry fulfilled his *Peter and the Wolf* obligation at midday, returned to his apartment, wrote a series of letters to his cohorts, and then went into the garage to kill himself. 'My finger was on the ignition key,' he said. 'But then pictures of your mother appear in front of your eyes. You cannot do that to your parents. At least I couldn't. I had tried when I was seventeen.' Instead, Fry fled. 'I drove to Bruges and struck east through to Germany. I had it in my head that the tip of Jutland would somehow suit me. I would buy a small wooden, quite well-heated hut. I just somehow imagined that British people didn't go there. I would learn Danish. I kind of liked the idea of going around in a big white pullover and a pipe and teaching English in some school in Denmark, meanwhile writing peculiar novels.' He added, 'I thought I had burned every bridge.' Fry's disappearance was a subject of scandal and concern in England, where it dominated the headlines. A substitute was found for *Cell Mates*, but the production never recovered, and it closed prematurely three weeks later, with a loss of some three hundred thousand pounds. 'I really believed I would never come back to England,' Fry said in his documentary *The Secret Life of the Manic Depressive*. 'I couldn't meet the gaze of anyone I knew.'

In a sense, the term 'stagefright' is a misnomer – fright being a shock for which one is unprepared. For professional performers, the unmooring terror hits as they prepare to do the very thing they're trained to do. According to one British medical study, actors' stress levels on opening night are equivalent 'to that of a car-accident victim.' When Sir Laurence Olivier was in his sixties, he considered retiring from the stage because of stage-fright. It 'is always waiting outside the door,' he wrote in *Confessions of an Actor*. 'You either battle or walk away.' The Canadian piano virtuoso Glenn Gould, who suffered from disabling stage-fright, did walk away, abandoning the public platform for the privacy of the recording studio. 'To me the ideal artist to-audience relationship is one to zero,' he said.

Stagefright is a traumatic, insidious attack on the performer's expressive instrument: the body. According to the psychoanalyst Donald Kaplan, who studied this morbid form of anxiety, the trajectory of stagefright begins with manic agitation and moodiness, proceeds to delusional thinking and obsessional fantasies, and then to 'blocking' – the 'complete loss of perception and rehearsed function.' The actor stiffens, trembles, and grows numb and uncoordinated. His mental and aural processes seize up. His throat tightens, his mouth goes dry, and he has difficulty speaking. The experience, with the metabolic changes it sets off – sweating, confusion, the loss of language – is a simulacrum of dying. 'I died out there' or 'I corpsed,' actors say. In defense against the immobilizing terror, sufferers often split off. They disassociate. They report out-of-body experiences, a sense of watching themselves go by. ('It's a negative ecstasy,' Fry says. 'Remember that "ecstasy" means "to stand outside." You stand outside yourself.') The actor's feeling of physical as well as mental coherence disintegrates. Instead of being protected, as usual, by the character he is playing, he suddenly stands helpless before the audience as himself; he loses the illusion of invisibility. His authority collapses and he feels naked, as if he were exposing to the judgmental spectators 'an image of the man behind the mask,' as the anthropologist Erving Goffman puts it. Actors sometimes refer to this momentary collapse as 'drying': nothing flows from them to the audience or from the audience to them. 'There is this catastrophic loss of confidence,' the American psychoanalyst Christopher Bollas, who has treated many stage and screen actors, says. 'You lose your radar – like a surfer. You can ride a ten-foot wave with real confidence, not thinking about it, just doing it. Then, all of a sudden, you become too self-aware. You think too much. You get wiped out.' The paradox of acting is that, like surfing, it requires both relaxation and concentration. If there is concentration without relaxation, or relaxation without concentration, the performance doesn't work.

'Composure is repose,' the playwright Clifford Odets observed in his diary. What the public wants, and what the performer sells, is the illusion capturing the blissful state of the infant, who develops strategies to insure his mother's collaboration and to prevent the agitation that would lead to his being 'put down' or 'dropped.' Poise is an expression of the desire to be wanted and loved – a form of social security, which is never at play in solitude, when, Rangell writes, 'there is no danger from without, no fear of ridicule: one is not at the moment being observed and judged.' Actors, of course, watch themselves like hawks. Some, like Noël Coward, turn poise into a philosophy of life: their careers are a perpetual performance of charm. 'I have taken a lot of trouble with my public face,' Coward said. 'Lose yourself and you lose your audience.' The psychoanalyst Harvey Corman, speaking of his friend Barbra Streisand, who suffers from chronic stagefright, says, 'Her greatest talent isn't acting or singing; it's her ability to hide her fear.' ('Break a leg' and 'Merde' – the backstage mantras for good luck – are acknowledgments of the actor's terror of losing control of his body and of making a mess.)

'Performers don't talk much about stagefright,' Ian McKellen wrote in a defense of Fry that was published in the London *Times* in 1996. 'The spectre of a tongue turned to stone and vomit where the lines should be is all too frightening to be evoked.' One of the few to describe the trauma in detail is the British actor Ian Holm, who abandoned theatre for nearly fifteen years because of it. In 1976, before the final preview of the Royal Shakespeare Company production of *The Iceman Cometh*, in which he played the central role of Hickey, Holm, as many sufferers do, had a presentiment of disaster. 'I knew – I knew – that something was going to happen,' he writes in *Acting My Life*: 'Somehow I got through the first part of the play, though I do remember sweating in the wings while I was waiting to go on, suddenly feeling cold and clammy, and people asking me if I was all right. Although I did not realize it, I had started to seize up. Then the moment arrived when I knew I would not be able to continue. I was giving a monologue from a chair at the front of the stage. The rest of the cast was behind me and, despite their previous efforts, now unable directly to intervene or assist me. I kept drying, even at one point addressing the audience with something like, "Here I am, supposed to be talking to you there are you, expecting me to talk." Getting off the stage was quite complicated and involved a choreographed manoeuvre through and past the other actors, who were frozen in a kind of tableau. I had only been off stage for a few moments before I knew some kind of buffer had been reached, that the game was up. I walked briskly past the stage manager, who waved a flimsy arm at me and uttered something polite like, "But you're due back on almost immediately, Mr. Holm."

"I'm off," I replied. "And I'm not coming back.". . .

'By the time I got back to the dressing room area, I had even lost the ability to walk. The black curtain which slowly cowled my brain had become a complete hood. I experienced complete meltdown. I was unable to speak or to focus on anything. My eyes were wild and staring.'

Holm ended up being comforted by a fellow-actor backstage. 'We were both on the floor, my head in his lap,' he writes. 'He was caressing me like a child.'

The poster for Alfred Hitchcock's 1950 film *Stage Fright* reads, 'Hands that applaud can also kill.' In fact, it's not the hands of the audience but their observing eyes that are lethal. The pianist and critic Charles Rosen writes, in his mischievous essay 'The

Aesthetic of Stage Fright,' 'The silence of the audience is not that of a public that listens but one that watches, like the dead hush that accompanies the unsteady movement of the tightrope walker poised over his perilous space.' Without an audience, or the fantasy of one, there is no stagefright. The actor's success depends on his ability to conquer the audience, which is why the encounter is so often fraught with excitement and danger. 'The relationship is undoubtedly sexual,' the British character actress Anna Massey says. 'You get to know an audience very, very quickly. Within the first five minutes. They become your friends or they become difficult to woo. Sometimes they're never won.' Fry, before his first professional engagement – in Alan Bennett's *Forty Years On* – was found by Paul Eddington, one of the show's seasoned stars, peeping through a hole in the curtain at the sea of strangers. 'Never look at the enemy,' Eddington told him. Performance is, for the actor, a form of battle – as the idioms of theatrical success make clear: 'I killed 'em,' 'I slaughtered 'em,' 'I knocked 'em dead.'

In the 1989 show *Back with a Vengeance!*, Barry Humphries, as the 'housewife / superstar' Dame Edna Everage, perfectly parsed the role of the audience and the effect that its cruel gaze can have on frightened actors; he also made the audience itself feel the fear. At one point in the show, Dame Edna patrolled the edge of the stage in her high heels and diamanté harlequin glasses, looking for someone from the first six rows 'to do nude cartwheels onstage.' 'And now the mood has completely changed, hasn't it?' she said. 'I don't know what you'd call it. Blind terror, I think, don't you . . . But don't be nervous. Please . . . Supposing I chose, for argument's sake . . . you! In the third row. Yes. Yes. What is your name?'

'Emma.'

'Hello, Emma. Have you done much cartwheel work? We've

found audiences prefer an amateur nude cartwheelist, they do. They have a way of falling over which is vulnerable ... and, well ... strangely appealing. Don't scratch your eczema, Emma. Because you will not know you're doing these cartwheels, Emma. Do you know why? You'll be in deep shock, Emma. You will. Because whenever we women are very, very frightened, our bodies do a funny thing. . . . Did you know, Emma, that we women have a little wee gland about half the size of a little fingernail tucked in an intimate nook? ... This gland of ours, Emma, has a duct jointed on to it ... And whenever we women have to do something a little, oh, unacceptable or even a little bit yucky, Emma, you know what this funny little gland of ours does? Do you? It squirts. It squirts. And it oozes. And drips. And we black out, Emma ... And that'll be you. You will literally not know that you've been tonight's nude-cartwheel girl until you're leaving the theatre and you notice people pointing and laughing at you. And saying things like "She wasn't a natural blonde, was she?"'

All the central traumas of childhood – being alone, abandoned, unsupported, emotionally abused – are revived for an actor when he appears before the paying customers, who have the power to either starve him of affection or reward him with approval. What the child gets from his mother – rapt focus, adoration, a sense of self – is what the actor needs from the audience. When things are going well, the stage and the house merge and a sort of imaginative union is achieved. The intimacy is palpable on both sides of the footlights; the audience seems to breathe with the actors. 'There is brilliant intellectual clarity, a sense of boundless, inexhaustible energy as the chambers of the brain open up,' Holm says of a successful performance. 'Your whole existence is lit up by a dazzling sense of potential.' Fry, explaining why he put himself through the stress of acting, says, 'You're trying to recapture the "first fine, careless rapture." The first time you felt king of time and space, the first spinning joy of it all.'

When the actor cannot make contact and the audience withholds its affection, however, the experience brings back a primal anxiety. 'Every time I went onstage, there was that heavy feeling,' Fry says. 'I felt the audience was not on my side almost from the get-go.... It was a sweaty sense of not being in control ... constantly behind rather than ahead.' He adds, 'Everybody else had some transformative magic power that was completely denied me. I had no business being there.' Fry blames his attack of stagefright partly on a scene that he had to perform in his underwear. 'I was putting on a lot of weight,' he says. 'I was clearly a middle-aged man with a big gut.' The audience, he adds, 'sees the shrivelled penis in your head.' For Olivier, whose much loved mother died when he was twelve, the audience was, to some degree, his parsimonious father. 'My father couldn't see the slightest purpose in my existence,' Olivier wrote. 'Everything about me irritated him. I was an entirely unnecessary extra burden on the exchequer.' In what seemed to be a gesture of pre-emptive defiance, before a show Olivier used to stand behind the curtain muttering at the audience over and over, 'You bastards.' Shirley MacLaine, contemplating the unfathomable energy and fierce focus of Frank Sinatra, with whom she worked for a time, came to the conclusion that 'it has more to do with remaining a perpetual performing child who wants to please the mother audience.' She continued, 'He desperately needed her to love him, appreciate him, acknowledge him, and never betray his trust. So he would cajole, manipulate, caress, admonish, scold, and love her unconditionally until there was no difference between him and her.'

The parent in the audience who needs to be won over is also, in some cases, a theatre critic. In *Fat Chance*, Simon Gray makes it clear that a bad review played a large role in Fry's stagefright. Gray remembers reading Fry's 'ambiguous suicide letter' to one of the producer's associates, Peter Wilkins. 'Wherever he was going, whether to his untimely end, or into a hospital, or a monastery, or just into hiding,' Gray writes, 'the letter made it unequivocally clear that (a) he wasn't going to appear in *Cell Mates* again, indeed was never going to act again, and (b) the reason for this was he believed that he was letting Rik, me and the whole production down.' Gray added, 'He followed this with a kind of spiteful lampoon on himself – "the lumpen, superior 'act' which I inflict on a bored audience every time I open my mouth."' Gray recalls hearing Wilkins let out 'something that sounded like a gasp':

WILKINS: But that's the *Financial Times* review.
ME: What?
WILKINS: Almost word for word. The *Financial Times* review.

Fry, who claimed not to read reviews, had gone out and bought the Sunday papers; if the actor couldn't actually see the judgmental eye of the audience from the stage, the words of the critic were in cold type and impossible to miss. 'Fry is the all-time façade: so damnably English on the one hand, and so perplexingly inexpressive on the other,' Alastair Macaulay had written in the *Financial Times*. The impact of the review was, Fry says, 'phenomenal.' He describes the sense of acute self-consciousness and loss of confidence that followed as 'stage dread,' a sort of 'paradigm shift.' He says, 'It's not "Look at me – I'm flying." It's "Look at me – I might fall." It would be like playing a game of chess where you're constantly regretting the moves you've already played rather than looking at the ones you're going to play.' Fry could not mobilize his defenses; unable to shore himself up, he took himself away. E-mails from his father and from Hugh Laurie, his friend and comedy partner, eventually found Fry in Hamburg and coaxed him to return briefly. By then, he'd seen his name in headlines and pictures of the police clamoring around his family's home in Norfolk. After a stint in America, staying first at John Cleese's Santa Barbara beach house and then at an apartment he'd bought in New York, Fry went back to his London flat in the fall of 1995. Around that time, he was asked to star in the Oscar Wilde bio-pic. 'The idea that so much faith was put in me was a big thing,' he says. 'The film was one of the happiest experiences of my life.' Since 'the Debacle,' as he calls it, Fry has written six books, appeared in several films, including the Academy Award-winning *Gosford Park*, and made a handful of documentaries. He has not, however, returned to the stage.

Stagefright, with its ties to both terror and shame, inspires a powerful desire to hide. 'I was always looking for exits, literally looking for ways to escape,' the singer and songwriter Carly Simon, who suffers from chronic stage-fright, told me. 'It felt claustrophobic being in the spotlight and being expected to finish a song. So I left myself the leeway of being able to leave the stage at the end of every song. What I tell myself now is "If I just get through the song, I'll be able to leave."' Olivier wrote of his famous performance in *Othello*, 'I had to beg my Iago, Frank Finlay, not to leave the stage when I had to be left alone for a soliloquy, but to stay in the wings downstage where I could see him, since I feared I might not be able to stay there in front of the audience by myself.'

The entertainer's journey through fear is the burden and the blessing of performance; it's what invests the enterprise with bravery, even a kind of nobility. 'There was no other treatment than the well-worn practice of wearing it – the terror – out,' Olivier wrote. The battle takes many strange and creative forms. Some performers drink to give themselves courage; some pop beta-blockers; some meditate or practice various other tension-reducing exercises; some play inspirational videos in their dressing rooms; some, like Charles Rosen, simply see stagefright as an inevitable and appropriate result of a virtuoso's perfectionism. 'Stagefright is not merely symbolically but functionally necessary, like the dread of a candidate before an examination or a job interview, both designed essentially as a test of courage,' Rosen writes. 'Stagefright, like epilepsy, is a divine ailment, a sacred madness . . . It is a grace that is sufficient in the old Jesuit sense – that is, insufficient by itself but a necessary condition for success.'

One of Olivier's ways of coping with stagefright was to ask his fellow-actors not to look him in the eye. 'They generously agreed, and managed to look attentively to either side of my face,' he wrote, of his performance as Shylock in the National Theatre production of *The Merchant of Venice*, in 1970. 'For some reason this made me feel that there was not quite so much loaded against me.' Fry had the opposite experience. 'If you're going well, the one thing you hate is being onstage with an actor who won't look you in the eye,' he says. 'If they're not going to meet your eye, there's something wrong with them, or they think there's something wrong with you.'

Sviatoslav Richter, whom Prokofiev thought 'the best pianist . . . in the whole world,' coped with his stagefright by turning the lights on the audience and – except for a reading light on his sheet music – off himself. The illusion of invisibility freed Richter and allowed the listener, he said, 'to concentrate on the music rather than on the performer.' Some performers, like Carly Simon, on the other hand, choose to have the lights on the audience 'because of the empathic reaction.' She says, 'When I feel I don't have the audience, when they're not warm, I'll pick out one person, usually in the first four rows, and sing a song directly to that person. He or she will get embarrassed and turn to people on his right or left. Therefore the embarrassment, or the focus I'm putting on him, takes it away from me.'

On tour in 1995, Simon discovered that another way to handle her stagefright was to lie down onstage. 'Rock and roll is so good because it accepts so much,' she said. 'I had a couch onstage so that I could be languorous ... I could ease my way up to the mike. I do it in stages. I'm lying down on the couch, then I put my knees around and I sit up, and then I stand up at the end of the first song.' These days, Simon says, eighty per cent of the time she has beaten her stage-fright before she's vertical. As part of her arsenal of attack, she keeps a hairbrush under the couch cushions so that she can brush her hair during the set, a gesture that helps to calm her palpitations. Simon has found that physical pain often trumps psychological terror. 'If you have something that's hurting you physically, the pain is the hierarchy,' she said. To that end, she has been known to take the stage in tight boots, to jab her hand with clutched safety pins, and even, just before going on, to ask band members to spank her. At a celebration for President Bill Clinton's fiftieth birthday, at Radio City Music Hall, in 1996, Simon, terrified of following Smokey Robinson, invited the entire horn section to let her have it. 'They all took turns spanking me,' she says. 'During the last spank the curtain went up. The audience saw the aftermath, the sting on my face. I bet Olivier didn't do that.'

The acting coach Susan Batson, whose clients include Juliette Binoche, Jennifer Lopez, and Nicole Kidman, advises her students to try to displace the fear onto the role they're playing, to make it part of the performance, part of what she calls the 'previous circumstances' of the character. When one of her actors has stagefright, she says, her response is 'Can we use this?' Batson considers stagefright a 'civilian issue,' not an artistic one. 'If you are a people pleaser' – worried about whether the audience is going to like you – 'you're bound to have stagefright,' she told me. 'If you have an issue of not feeling like you're good enough, you're bound to have stagefright. The people who survive it are the ones who can take control of the situation and override it.'

Kidman falls into Batson's 'people pleaser' category. 'My job with her is to scare her, really terrify her, tell her that she'll do awful work if she continues that kind of shit,' Batson says. 'Then she gets the courage, and she's O.K.' In the early nineties, Kidman wanted to audition for the part of the icy Las Vegas hustler Ginger McKenna, opposite Robert De Niro, in Martin Scorsese's *Casino*, a role for which all the Hollywood swamis said she was wrong. 'She worked like a dog to prove that she could do it,' Batson recalled. On the day Kidman went for her audition, according to Batson, 'she felt awkward' and 'lost it.' Scorsese took her in to meet De Niro, Batson recalled. 'She could feel everything just falling apart.' Her legs got wobbly and she felt hives coming on, but she pushed ahead and went straight into a scene that required her to strike her co-star. 'All she could think of was "Stay in the character's circumstances." She reared back, and she slapped the shit out of De Niro.' Batson added, 'They didn't give her the part'

– it went to Sharon Stone – 'but they were impressed. That's literally the artist overcoming the terror. She had no choice. She said, "I was gone. The only thing to do was to do the slapping. To get through."' Courage generates more courage. 'Once you go through it and lift it, you feel very, very courageous. It's a high that you pray everybody has,' Batson said. 'I'm always terrified of the person who doesn't have it, because it means that the commitment is not fully there.'